D1156629

Indexed in
Essay and General
Literature Index

Pruning
the Genealogical Tree

Pruning
the Genealogical Tree

Procreation and Lineage
in Literature, Law, and Religion

Gian Balsamo

Lewisburg
Bucknell University Press
London: Associated University Presses

Associated University Presses
440 Forsgate Drive
Cranbury, NJ 08512

Associated University Presses
16 Barter Street
London WC1A 2AH, England

Associated University Presses
P.O. Box 338, Port Credit
Mississauga, Ontario
Canada L5G 4L8

The paper used in this publication meets the requirements
of the American National Standard for Permanence of Paper
for Printed Library Materials Z39.48-1984.

Library of Congress Cataloging-in-Publication Data

Balsamo, Gian, 1949–
    Pruning the genealogical tree : procreation and lineage in
literature, law, and religion / Gian Balsamo.
        p.   cm.
    Includes bibliographical references and index.
    ISBN 0-8387-5409-0 (alk. paper)
    1. Genealogy in literature.   2. Literature—History and criticism.
I. Title.
PN56.G46B35   1999
809′.93355—dc21   99-13997
                                                                              CIP

PRINTED IN THE UNITED STATES OF AMERICA

To Armanda and Tito

Contents

CONTENTS

Preface

LAW AND RELIGION, AN ODD ALLIANCE? CAN ONE TALK OF GOD WITH the prudence of the jurist? Can one argue the law with the rationality of a god? We have a conventional term to indicate the way one contends about the nature of the divine: *theology*—the rational discourse, rational insofar as *lógos* was the aim of reason among the Greeks, about the crux of human irrationality. And we have a conventional term about the way one administers the law, the way one adjudicates, arbitrates the competing assertions of a plaintiff and a defendant: *jurisprudence,* the prudence *(prudĕntia)* of the jurist, which, as Vico points out, shares with the reason of the ancients a stance of caution toward the value of human judgment. Law and Religion: Justice and Truth. True jurisprudence, Vico says, is knowledge of divine things.

No pair of disciplines is better attuned, more homogeneous with each other than the administration of the law and the conversation on the sacred. There is Law, though, and there are prescribed laws, just as there is Religion and there are revealed religions. There is Truth (granted that we learned from Derrida to write the copula *is* under ontological erasure), and there is blind faith, just as there is Justice and there is distortion of human rights. This book situates itself between the two extreme poles of the absolutely sacred, just, true, legitimate, and the absolutely arbitrary, contingent, opinable, profane. It is a work of literary criticism, in other words, a work that studies the manifold configurations of procreation and lineage in classical and modern literature, in philosophy, and in Scripture as well, from the perspective of religious and legal culture. This explains the wording of the subtitle: *Procreation and Lineage in Literature, Law, and Religion.* It explains also the need for this premise, written, as Hegel would have it, as an afterword, long after the completion of the book—a premise to the introduction proper, which follows as chapter 1, under the title, "Pruning the Genealogical Tree: An Overview of the Critique of Genealogy and Procreation."

I got rather far into the present work before I began to realize that it constantly broaches two disciplines of inquiry, theology and jurisprudence, that are customarily engaged separately by the scholar. And I had to puzzle over the curious fate of two fields of investigation whose intimate affinity Vico stressed in all of his writings. Why are theology and jurisprudence kept separate from each other? Why is the domain of thought circumscribed by these two disciplines broken systematically into two independent spheres of discourse? Is it because the notion itself of academic discipline does not tolerate their reciprocal contamination, which amounts, at least in our secular eyes, to a contamination of the sacred and the profane? Or is it because religious and legal authorities favor and welcome a separation of competence that leaves the cure of the soul to the former and the administration of the body to the latter? Spiritual proselytism on one side of the equation, material domination on the other?

Be that as it may, this book breaks the convention and violates the complicity. I write this premise to reconstruct briefly the circumstances and accidents, and especially the array of personal influences (the latter far from accidental) that led me to this theoretical move. The names of two scholars, John Sallis and Thomas Altizer, come to mind when I try to envision the unity of my project. John Sallis's lectures on continental philosophy at Vanderbilt determined me to explore the difference between philosophical and physiological re-production, in the specific configuration, for instance, of the separation between the theory of mimesis and the *fait accompli* of human conception and procreation. I intended this study as a ramification of Derrida's early deconstructions of the concept of origin, which he first undertook from the abstract viewpoint of pure geometry, and later from the concrete viewpoint of the structure of the primitive Hebrew and Christian family.[1] In time, Derrida's frequent visits to the United States, and especially his participation in the Colloquium on "Deconstruction and the Possibility of Justice" (Cardozo Law School, October 1989)[2] brought to my attention that a deconstruction of the notion of human procreation would require a study of the matter's legal aspects, which study, in turn, could disclose a virtual middle ground separating reproduction as philosophical concept from reproduction as social, historical, or natural event. Finally, it was my encounter with Thomas Altizer, at a rather advanced stage of elaboration of this book, that made me aware that the nature of my inquiry is intimately theological. I won't deny that in the process of writing this book, my first in English, I had published a book in my mother tongue, *Rachele accucciata sugli dèi: il Fallo e la Legge,* devoted to procreation and genealogy in the family of the Old Testament.[3] Yet, even in that case, and in spite of a subtitle addressing the reciprocal encroachment of the phallus (of God) and the law, I resisted the idea that I had written a book of theological hermeneutics. I called it a book of feminist deconstruction; it is, of course, a feminist deconstruction of the Bible, with the caveat that any such deconstruction must pass through the *forche caudine* of hermeneutics. Hence, it took the authority of Thomas Altizer to lift the veil that thirty years of apostasy (I'm a bona fide Joycean, after all) had settled in front of my eyes. I took a fresh look at my interpretation of procreation and genealogy, and understood that I was writing a theological book, a book, precisely, that would broach the affinity of legal and theological discourse.

In writing this book I became personally indebted to a number of scholars and friends, especially Roy Gottfried, who initiated me into James Joyce's heresies and apostasies, and Brook Thomas, who introduced me to the critical legal studies movement. I am also grateful to Paul Mariani for reviving my appreciation of Italian poetry, Dante's especially, a heritage I had foolishly vowed to repudiate at the time of my emigration to the United States; to John Plummer for inspiring my Lacanian studies of medieval sexuality; and to Mary Kinzie for sheltering my intellectual quest within the program she directs at Northwestern University. William Franke at Vanderbilt and Regina Schwartz at Northwestern have been two ideal colleagues, constant sources of inspiration and emulation. Michael Kreyling helped me relate Joyce's oeuvre to the landscape of American Modernism. The participants of my two *Finnegans Wake* reading groups, meeting respectively at Northwestern and at the Great Expectations bookstore in Evanston, have supplied me with abundant food for thought; Andrew Blom in particular has been a source of tremendous insights. Sean Erwin has constantly animated the Derrida reading group that sustained my probing of the possibilities and limits of deconstruction. And Lawrence Lipking has contributed with exceptional acumen to my Faculty Colloquia at Northwestern. My understanding of law and the social sciences benefited long ago from the teachings of Claudio Napoleoni and Carlo Marletti at the University of Turin, Italy. In Turin I also wrote, under the guide of Bruno Contini, my dissertation on the economics of gender discrimination. It was a solitary endeavor at the time, but the purpose that moved me has since found a fertile soil in my new country.

Chicago
November, 1997

Partial drafts of chapter 4, "The Reluctant Son," chapter 7, "The Law of the Outlaw," and chapter 10, "Son, Knight, and Lover" appeared previously in *Exemplaria* 5, no. 2 (October, 1993), *Language and Literature* 23 (1998), and *Qui Parle* 10, no. 1 (Fall/Winter 1996), respectively. I thank the editors for the permission to reprint.

Part I
Genealogy and Procreation

1

Pruning the Genealogical Tree: An Overview of the Critique of Genealogy and Procreation

J'espère que [. . .] votre famille immediàte (puisque vos parents semblent être comme les feuilles de la forêt) se trouve, saine et sauve, autour de l'arbre maître et . . . utilisable.
—James Joyce to E. Branchbar, 30 July 1940

(I hope that [. . .] your immediate family (since your relatives seem to be like leaves in the forest) are clustered, safe and sound, around the paternal and . . . utilisable tree.)

I WISH I COULD CLAIM THAT AS THE SUBJECT OF THIS BOOK RAMIFIES it bursts into a spontaneous germination of discourse, but such a statement, however attuned with the trope of the genealogical tree, would contradict the nature of a critique of genealogy. Only the time-honored metaphor of the Book of Nature, in its presumption to capture, from their germinal seed and in their entirety, both Nature's and Discourse's order of reproduction, could claim for its subject the predicate of a spontaneous germination.[1] But this is not the case with the "unnatural" dimension of genealogy. Genealogy is endemically exposed to those "genetic crossovers and hazardous disseminations" that, in Jacques Derrida's words, reveal the delusion intrinsic to "all the genealogical chances that set adrift the notion of legitimate filiation." One must engage genealogy as a *construct,* whose contrived architecture is best exemplified in the trope of the genealogical tree: a modular assemblage of legitimate filiations, a treelike structure, whose ramifications, apparently all-inclusive, hide the intricacy of exclusion, discrimination, and abusive graftings. The present work espouses Derrida's thesis that genealogical legitimacy is

17

structurally exposed to collateral ramifications; it is more often than not the outcome of an imposition, a deliberation, or a prescription, rather than the spontaneous flow of the bloodline. This thesis, developed by Derrida especially in *Ulysse gramophone: Deux mots pour Joyce,* a study devoted to Joyce's two major works, *Ulysses* and *Finnegans Wake,* has contributed to the orientation of my book toward an inquiry into "the concern . . . about familial legitimation (that) makes both *Ulysses* and *Finnegans Wake* vibrate."[2]

It is well known that *Ulysses* presents Leopold Bloom as a middle-aged man tormented by the errantry of his patronymic, Virag—the Hungarian word for "flower." Leopold is unable to perpetuate in a legitimate line of transmission a family name that his father's unilateral decision turned into an English "pseudonym," Bloom. Leopold goes as far, in his nostalgia for his "real" family name, as to sign the letters of his anonymous correspondence with Martha Clifford with the thinly counterfeited name of Henry Flower. At the end of *Ulysses,* this lifelong concern finds a few hours of transitory suspension in Bloom's chance encounter with Stephen Dedalus, a young man who might become (but does not, as chance determines) a virtual substitute for the son and heir Bloom lost long before.

Stephen Dedalus, in turn, is responsible for the famous pronouncement in *Ulysses:* "Paternity may be a legal fiction" (*U* 9.842–43), an indication, echoed symptomatically in one of Joyce's letters to his brother Stanislaus,[3] of the Irish writer's perplexity with regard to the patrilineal connotations that inform the trope of the genealogical tree. I will anticipate a conclusion whose premises will be substantiated later in the book: in *Ulysses* the affirmation of the ancestral line is often made an object of comedy, satire, and parody. Pathetically comic, for instance, is the predicament of the "mariner" who, in the "Eumaeus" episode, returns home from his wanderings only to find "(n)o chair for father" in the kitchen, where his spouse holds "(h)er brandnew arrival on her knee, *postmortem* child" (*U* 16.437–38).[4] As in the case of the supposed blue blood of Lord John Corley, the second squalid personage met by Stephen in "Eumaeus," the possibility that genealogy is "a complete *fabrication* from start to finish" (*U* 16.153, my emphasis) is always left open in *Ulysses.*

Genealogical legitimacy becomes a fiction of chance ramifications and collateral graftings when it is "assigned," as Derrida puts it in *Mémoires d'aveugle,* "to the blind man's buff of the proper names."[5] More specifically, homonymic transmission is bound to failure when it attempts to impose the collusion of the physiologic order of nature and the cultural order of discourse— when it attempts, in other words, to certify the identity of one's own imposed name with one's consanguineous descent. It is not so much that the telling of the physiologic, literal facts of one's line of descent sets immediately at play the trope of the genealogical tree, as a metaphor of consanguineous continuity; it is rather that the genre of discourse that establishes an order of genealogy, be it biographical or juridical, tends to be systematically inadequate in its attempt to verify ascendancy and descendancy, to certify parentage and succession through an organic construct of ascent and descent. In a sense, one might say that the order of genealogy prohibits the full coalescence of the semantics of one's patronymic and the physiology of one's consanguinity. The inscription of a proper name upon a birth certificate stands for a spectrum of normative customs and legal codes that diverge from the natural event of procreation.

Questioned on his paternity by Athena in book 1 of the *Odyssey*, Telemachus declares that "never yet did any man know, on his own, who gave him life";[6] mothers are the only authoritative source (but how reliable?) about the act of love that gives man life. Later on, Telemachus will realize that the nature of Athena's question goes beyond the boundaries of paternal consanguinity. The question as to his father's identity is raised a second time by Athena herself, on the beach of Ithaca, then is raised by Nestor, in his *oikos* at Pylos, and finally at Sparta, by Helen and Menelaos. Telemachus will need to prove that his royal condition, as the son and legitimate successor of Odysseus, satisfies criteria much broader than mere consanguinity. Nobility, equanimity, responsibility, solidarity, courage—these are the attributes that will provide Telemachus, in the twenty-four books of the Homeric *epos,* with an authoritative answer to Athena's question.

The fundamental gap between consanguinity and genealogical legitimacy seems to be one of the reasons why both Joyce and Derrida have devoted great effort to turning their own biographies not so much into a matter of, respectively, literary or philosophical discourse, as into a matter of generic bifurcation. Singularly preoccupied with their respective lines of consanguineous descent, Joyce and Derrida have pursued the goal of a subversion of the discourse of lineage and descent with such determination that in several of their major works they trespass systematically, and with devastating consequences for their respective genres of discourse, upon the threshold that separates the *sense* of the textual, in its supposed semantic universality, from the *fact* of the physiological, in its natural and historical contingency.

JOYCE'S PRUNING OF HIS GENEALOGICAL TREE

The "concern about familial legitimation . . . that makes *Ulysses* and *Finnegans Wake* vibrate,"[7] reflects the intensity of Joyce's dedication to the history of his family. Throughout his indefatigable European wanderings, Joyce was determined not to leave behind his family portraits. It was, with the notable exception of his mother's portrait,[8] a veritable gallery of patrilineal genealogy, one which, so many times in his childhood, he had seen float away—literally, on a float[9]—toward the pawnbroker's shop.[9] James Joyce must have been about eight years old when Alfred Bergan reported seeing his father, John S. Joyce, nod dejectedly at these portraits, as they were brought out of his house. "There goes the whole seed, breed and generation of the Joyce family," John Joyce commented, unaware that he would manage to rescue them once again;[10] unaware, also, that this same "seed, breed and generation" would follow, paradoxically, his firstborn son in his self-imposed exile from—to use the words of Stephen Dedalus—"home, fatherland, and church" (*Portrait* 247).

The irony is evident. On the one hand, one cannot fail to appreciate Joyce's attachment to the portraits of his paternal ancestors. On the other hand, one can hardly contain one's surprise when in *Ulysses* the genealogy of humankind is turned into this very "seed, breed and generation," which Eve, of all women, sells "for a penny pippin" (*U* 14.301)—to whom, the so-called story of the Fall of Man in Genesis makes it easy to guess.

Furthermore, it was in order to guarantee to his grandson Stephen James the right to sign with his own name, and to claim the copyrights of his literary works, that James Joyce consented to marry Nora Barnacle under English law, after they had lived together as man and wife for twenty-six years. Quite significantly, as Richard Ellmann remarks, "Joyce chose his father's birthday, July 4, as the wedding day." In a letter to Harriet Weaver, his lifelong patron, Joyce wrote: "(T)wenty-six years ago I didn't want a cleric with a pen behind his ear or a priest in his nightshirt to interfere in my matrimonium." But at the registry office in

London he declared that he and Nora were married in Trieste in 1904, at which the clerk objected that he could not marry them a second time, unless they were first divorced. Joyce's solicitor, Lionel Munro, managed to appease the clerk with some persuasive rhetoric; Nora and James Joyce had decided to marry, in Mr. Munro's unintentionally ironic phrase, "for testamentary reasons."[11]

We could draw the following conclusion from this anecdote: Joyce's legal signature stands at a bifurcation in his genealogical tree where the legal affirmation of paternal consanguinity is escorted by an act of derision toward the ceremonial apparatus of the law. It is a bifurcation where legal discourse flows into an apparently incompatible order of discourse, whose genre may be variously classified as farcical, satiric, comic, parodic, subversive, oppositional, etc. As Derrida would put it, in order to *dire oui,* to say *yes* to the legality of his patronymic, he who signs the name of Joyce *rit,* laughs in the face of the law.[12]

DERRIDA'S GENEALOGY: PRUNING AND AMPUTATION

Analogously, the concern about familial legitimation that Derrida sees at work in *Ulysses* and *Finnegans Wake* is the same concern that transposes Derrida's frequent engagements with his own name into a family history involved "in all the genealogical chances that," as he points out, "set adrift the notion of legitimate filiation ..."[13] In his *Circonfession,* Derrida establishes a convergence between theoretical discourse and personal biography; a kind of convergence that only a few decades ago would have been unthinkable in a philosophical text:

(T)he fact that (my) forename [the name of the prophet Elijah, ... who carries the newborn on his knees before the ... unnameable sacrifice] was not inscribed (on my birth certificate, as were the Hebrew names of my family ...) signified ... that they wanted to hide me like a prince whose parentage is provisionally concealed to keep him alive ... until the day that his royalty could ... be openly exercised, without risk for the precious semen.[14]

Derrida's legal signature is obscured behind the screen of his birth certificate. In declaring that Derrida came to life in El-Biar, near Algiers, on 15 July 1930, this legal document omits mentioning the forename he acquired at the excision of his foreskin, after the "unnameable" ritual of circumcision to which he was subjected when eight days old. This act of "domestication" of the *nom propre* is reflected in the idiomatic custom, diffused among Algerian Jews in the thirties, to substitute for the noun *milah,* circumcision, the Christian word communion.[15]

The above passage from *Circonfession* tells the story of the virtual unreadability of a part of Derrida's name, that part—Élie in French, Elijah in English—he inherited at the *milah* from his paternal uncle, Eugène Eliahou Derrida. The noninscription, the invisibility of Élie vis-à-vis the law signals a resistance and a family solidarity; it entails the amputation of a significant branch of the genealogical tree, aimed at keeping the newborn boy from being incorporated in legal discourse and subjugated therefore to the dark forces of political history. In a narrative that reminds one of *The Thousand and One Nights,* Derrida tells of his family's attempt to slip the newborn into a protective crevice of relative anonymity, wherein his physiological ability to procreate a legitimate Jewish dynasty could survive the impending wave of anti-Semitism. As the ritual noun *milah* could be idiomatically distorted into a Christian noun, *communion,* that appeared to "naturalize" its racial implications, so an attempt could be made at pruning away from his ascendancy a branch that proclaimed the Semitic nature of his bloodline.

But in spite of such virtual invisibility, the trace of the name is inevitably contextualized by history and by culture. Around the age of ten Jacques Derrida, the best student in his class at the elementary school of El-Biar, has to yield his place of honor *devant le drapeau,* in front of the flag, at the morning hoisting of the French tricolor, to the second-best student, who is not a Jew.[16] This touching scene corresponds to a radical shift of position for young Derrida: from one side of the "curtain" to the other, from discreet, tactical invisibility behind the silence of a legal text to full, shameful visibility in second place before the national flag. In substance, one's own name cannot be left unwritten. As long as holocaust does not consume the genealogical tree and its prunings, the amputated branches can root and eventually blossom, again and again.

In Derrida's case, as he suggests, the omitted part of his name is found in the annular scar around his prepuce. This scar, this ring is a name per se, an idiom of identification stronger than any textual omission, and a bud, also, that cannot be excised from the genealogical tree. It is, to echo Derrida's fabulistic tone, a narrative emblem, a heraldic device that guarantees consanguinity against all threats of usurpation from spurious, collateral descent. This scar contextualizes the natural call of the blood, the bodily idiom of family and race identification; it turns consanguinity, as the order of natural descent, into a text, an order of discourse whose paradigms are embedded in the collective idioms of political history.

NAME AND IDIOM

Joyce's and Derrida's distinct way of translating their own biographies into hybrid, bifurcated forms of narrative and philosophical discourse blends the textual and the domestic; more specifically, it contextualizes private affections as it transposes their domestic history into public discourse.

If genre may be taken to be a formal encoding designed to assign distinct conventions of intelligibility to all instances of discursive communication, as claimed by various structuralist theories of genre,[17] then the question now to be raised is which genre would be proper to define the transgressive engagements of Joyce's and Derrida's "autobiographies." One must determine whether or not these two distinct treatments are made irremediably impure to the extent of being unintelligible, by the simultaneous presence in their hybrid texts of two heterogeneous *generic dominants*:[18] the textual idiom of intellective veracity and the domestic idiom of sentimental affection. Such generic duplicity is a crucial factor to be considered when one studies the significance of genealogical legitimacy on the order of human existence. The discourse aimed at the legitimation of lineage is always deceitful, always torn between evidence and appearance, fact and sense, physiology and legality, intimacy and politics. The riddle of genealogical legitimacy must be solved in the textuality of a discourse, after all, but textual discursiveness is not immune from the problems of resolving the riddle. The generation of discursive meaning and, more specifically here, the generation of the normative paradigms of genealogical legitimacy, constitute only one aspect for resolving the riddle. The other aspect is physiological, the act of procreation with its unresolved dialectic between paternal insemination and maternal conception.

If I may take a final step into the circle of duplicities intrinsic to the thematics of genealogical legitimacy, I will submit that the dialectical irresolution between the paternal and maternal contribution to procreation helps explain why the correlation between the signature of the patronymic and the legitimacy of lineage tends spontaneously to turn the domestic idiom of family affections into a public and manifest text, a text, paradoxically, *at home* in the marketplace and in the public square, in the court of law and in the battlefield; hence, a text eccentric with respect to the maternal intimacy of the domestic abode, where family affections are sheltered from the gaze of unfamiliar eyes.

DESCRIPTION OF INDIVIDUAL CHAPTERS

In the next few pages I provide the reader with a brief map of this book. Not that I think that there is an ideal route to follow in exploring my arguments. If, as I said above, the mirrorlike metaphor of the Book of Nature does not apply to my subject, the model of its spontaneous germination is even less appropriate when it comes to retracing my patterns of thought. I believe, on the contrary, that only a reader who is competent to determine his or her autonomous progression through the different chapters of the book may profit from it. Accordingly, I have designed each chapter to be self-contained and self-explanatory (aside from the customary cross-references), so that it may be read in isolation from the rest of the book.

Besides the present overview, part 1, *Genealogy and Procreation,* includes chapter 2, "The Gift of Life: The Theme of Genealogical Legitimacy in Borges's 'The Circular Ruins.'" I conceived this chapter as an introductory case study, which exemplifies the interpretive opportunities and range proper to a legal and theological investigation of procreation and genealogy. "The Gift of Life" illustrates the adumbration of the archaic paradigms of genealogical legitimacy to be found in the simple plot of one of Borges's best known short stories. This story seems to be characterized by a devious, intriguing silence as to the traditional agencies of androlineal, ritual, legal family descent. Using a Neoplatonic interpretation of the role played by fire as one of the primordial elements in the cabalistic tradition, I maintain that Borges's short story is devoted, to a significant extent, to those very emblematic agencies of legitimation that appear to be completely absent from the surface of the plot—an absence, in my opinion, that cries out to be thematized, a silence on Borges's part that calls attention to a hidden intentionality.

Part 2, *Genealogy and Joyce,* includes four chapters. They are all centered on the thesis that Joyce revokes the interdependence of genealogical legitimacy and paternal primacy. His major works, particularly *Ulysses,* dislodge procreation from gender opposition; as we will see, they do so insofar as and to the extent that they outwit the rules and conventions of literary genre. Joyce's epicene treatment of the parental role goes hand in hand, in sum, with his parodic treatment of conventional poetics.

Chapter 3, "Poetic Creativity and Maternal Fecundity: Mallarmé, Dante, and Blake in Stephen Dedalus's Vampire Poem," shows that by conjoining the mother in Mallarmé, the virgin in Dante, and the devil in Blake, Stephen Dedalus inaugurates in *Ulysses* a poetry of heretic self-resurrection, a blasphemous homage to his own artistic Passion among "crucified shirts" and "sails brailed up on the crosstrees" (*U* 3.156, 3.504). Stephen's vampire poem is concerned with evil *logos,* the dark, sinister *logos* spoken by the manipulators of information and cheapeners of patriotic sentiments. The muse of poetic inspiration is Stephen's ally, a maternal principle of good *poiésis* and pagan fecundity that earns him derision and artistic isolation in Dublin. His vampire poem celebrates an apotheosis of maternal (pro)creativity that is antithetic to Catholic orthodox doctrine; it finds in the virgin womb that delivers the Son of God to his mortal body and, ultimately, to his death, the redemptive antidote against the repugnant, self-destructive fecundity of Stephen's own mother.

In chapter 4, "The Reluctant Son: Satire of the Epics and Tragedies of Lineage in 'Scylla and Charybdis,'" I argue that in *Ulysses* Joyce undertakes a satire of the epic and tragic narratives of genealogical legitimacy. "Scylla and Charybdis" is a highly parodic episode. In it, Stephen Dedalus ridicules the concern with primogeniture and consanguinity that prevails in the stories of Homer's Telemachus, of Aeschylus's Orestes, of Noah's son, Ham, from Genesis (as well as in the tragedy of Hamlet, Shakespeare's irresolute incarnation of Ham, the father-hater, and of Orestes, the mother-killer). However, parody and its ancillary comic connotations are orchestrated by Stephen; they are the competence of the character's agency, so to speak. The satiric thrust of sociopolitical critique pertains instead to Joyce's authorial intentions. The dominant impulse behind this chapter is derived from the consideration that most ancient genealogical chronicles are indistinguishable from etiological tales: in providing a fundamental contribution to the shaping of the epic and

tragic genres—which I call, in a broad sense, the classic *epos*—
they tell the extraliterary story of the origins of communal laws,
norms, and civilized customs. "Scylla and Charybdis" may be
said to accomplish an analogous service for the benefit of our
modern notions of family and procreation. Joyce's epicene treatment of the pairs: gender/genre and procreation/genealogy, turns
the opposition of maternity and paternity, endemic to the classic
epos of lineage, into the target of his satire.

Chapter 5, "Parliament of Flatulence: The Genre of the Parable
and the Riddle of Lineage in *Ulysses*," relates the unfolding of
the theme of lineage to the emergence of the parable as privileged genre in the "Aeolus" episode of *Ulysses*. First, it shows
how the riddle of genealogy that Stephen Dedalus asks of his
students in the "Nestor" episode betrays Stephen's perplexity as
to whether in matters of lineage preeminence must be attributed to paternity or to maternity. Then it shows that Stephen's
riddle presents connotations that are homogeneous with the
Evangelical genre of the parable. Finally, it brings these two arguments together by arguing that the Evangelical allegories of
fertility and reproduction implicit in Stephen's riddle of genealogy are befouled in "Aeolus" by his lascivious Parable of the
Plums.

In chapter 6, "Aengus of the Birds: Stephen Dedalus and Vico's
Legal Fiction of Paternity," I submit that Vico's studies of the
norms regulating legitimate paternity in ancient Roman jurisprudence play a central role in Joyce's characterization of Stephen Dedalus, not only in *Ulysses,* but already in *A Portrait of
the Artist as a Young Man.* This chapter challenges the usual
view that textual evidence of Vico's influence over Joyce's work
can be found only in Joyce's latest writings. It refers to Donald
Verene's application of Vico's *universale fantastico* to the thun-
derclap in *Finnegans Wake* to draw a relevant set of inferences
on the interplay of biographical, autobiographical, and fictional-
biographical constructs in *Ulysses* (I am referring, specifically,
to Joyce's, Vico's, and Stephen Dedalus's respective thunder-
phobias). But, above all, this chapter demonstrates that Stephen's anxiety with regard to the roles played in his sentimental
and artistic life by his father and mother translates into an urge
to reassess and reconsider the Roman juridical tradition inherent in the figure of the *paterfamilias* and in the legal fiction of
homonymic transmission—a tradition, investigated in its sub-
tlest details by Vico, which subordinates the maternal contribu-

tion to procreation to the legal and religious norms that inform androlineal genealogy.

Part 3, *Genealogy, Law, and Religion,* includes four chapters. They are centered on the thesis that in the Judeo-Christian tradition androlineal descent comes before the law. More specifically, they show, from different perspectives, that the prehistory of modern civil right is grounded on the religious primacy of the father, the patriarch, or the *paterfamilias.* A consequence of this argument is that the legal arbitration of legitimate kinship and of family succession is based on the absurdity of a legal system attempting to regulate the religious principle that informs the most intimate nature of its norms.

Chapter 7, "The Law of the Outlaw: Family Succession and Family Secession in Hegel and in Genesis 31," undertakes a critique of Hegel's views regarding legitimate filiation. According to Hegel's *Philosophy of Right,* the Roman notion of *paterfamilias* provides a fundamental contribution, via its evolution in the Christian era, to the formulation of the modern code of private right and, particularly, to the formulation of the law of legitimate family succession. In this chapter, I contrast the Roman customs of succession and lineage with those of Torah pertinent to the Hebrew family. Most of the chapter is devoted to a consideration of Rachel's rebellion against paternal authority, with particular attention being devoted to the episode of her theft of Laban's idols in Genesis 31. Although Rachel's theft can hardly be qualified as "legal," its contribution to the Semitic norms of tribal lineage is unmistakable. Rachel's deception of her father amounts to a symbolic patricide, but one with devastating juridical as well as cultural consequences, because it warrants a family without household gods, a family in which the head of the household is not a *paterfamilias,* narrowly defined, nor the personification of the law. It is only after Rachel's desecration of the law of her father that Jacob's sons will be able to take the law in their own hands and plot, independent of their father's intentions, the massacre of the Shechemites (Genesis 34). In foreclosing all ulterior possibilities of symbolic patricide, Rachel's patricide neutralizes the proverbial identity of the phallus and the law; it befouls it, as we will see, with the blood of her fictitious menses.

Chapter 8, "Right of *Paterfamilias:* The Roman Law of Family Inheritance in Hegel, Montesquieu, and Vico," gives further articulation to my critique of Hegel's speculative derivation of the concept of legitimate family succession from ancient Roman jurisprudence. Hegel's position is flawed by a logico-historical fallacy, to the extent that it subordinates the affirmation of legitimate kinship to the authority of legal arbitration, when it is arguably legal arbitration that, within the axiomatics of his speculative system, derives normative authority from the structure of kinship inherent in the Roman family. The deconstruction of Hegel's fallacy requires that I concern myself with Vico's and Montesquieu's studies of the Roman juridical construct of the *paterfamilias*. Since Hegel excavates the foundations of modern civil right from classical Roman jurisprudence, and particularly from the legal configuration of the *paterfamilias*, this line of inquiry entails a denunciation of Hegel's failure to properly engage the religious tradition of androlineal primacy intrinsic to the right of *paterfamilias*.

Chapter 9, "Etiology and Genealogy: Totems and Moral Taboos in Derrida and Kant," contends that genealogical chronicles often perform the functions of etiological tales, in the sense that they tell us of the primordial cause of customs and usages that still affect our modern world. More specifically, this chapter shows the extent to which certain emblematic myths and legends of genealogical dissipation, such as the cycle of Oedipus and the cycle of Orestes, exhibit a sort of imperative authority, capable of playing a central role in the unfolding of the moral standards of different ages and cultures. This authority germinates at the crossroad where the ethic of the moral law and the aesthetic of the genealogical chronicle get substantially entangled with each other. In archaic literature, this crossroad is encountered when the commemoration of the origin of a moral norm and the intimation of its binding nature dovetail into a myth, legend, tale, or chronicle. As I show, with the help of Derrida's writings on jurisprudence, this is the *locus* where the rational ground of Kant's categorical imperative is made infirm by the infiltration of the faculty of imagination. More specifically, I maintain that the coincidence of etiology and genealogy entails an instance of collusion between the theoretical faculties attributed by Kant to the subject of free will and this subject's aptitude for remembrance and forgetfulness. The cognitive comprehension of the ethical cause of a moral prohibition goes hand in hand with the aesthetic recollection of its archetypal transgression. The ancient tales of the crimes and aberrations perpetrated in the name of consanguinity provide this chapter with several emblematic case studies. A warning is in order as regards this chapter: aside from the premise and the conclusion, where I describe the nature of the inquiry and its implications vis-à-vis the critical interpretation of genealogy, the central body of my argumentation is strictly philosophical, and the reader untrained in continental philosophy may find its specialized terminology impenetrable. This is the only chapter for which such a warning is called for.

Chapter 10, "Son, Knight, and Lover: The Legal in Jacques Lacan and the Maternal in Chrétien de Troyes," illustrates a remarkable congruence between the sexual dynamics at play in Chrétien's *Perceval* and the Lacanian opposition of maternity and legality. Given that Lacan derives the hierarchical order subordinating the structure of the unconscious to the dictates of the so-called "Law of the Father" from the fundamental principles of Freudian psychoanalysis, I argue that at bottom Chrétien's poem of martialism and seduction exhibits a significant attunement with the logic of gender opposition that grounds Freudian psychoanalysis. This logic, in turn based upon an autarchic and "barricaded" sexuality, seems to find the exemplary *locus* of its affirmation in the sterile and self-inclosed configuration of civil community depicted by Chrétien. Designed as an interpretive application of Lacan's paradigmatic approach to linguistic analysis, this chapter leads to the conclusion that the analytic paradigm of the maternal "lack," what Freud calls "envy of the penis," is the fundamental bias at the heart of Lacan's legal discourse.

Part 4, *Genealogy and Consanguinity,* includes two chapters. The trope of blood, as the literal and figural sap of the genealogical tree, is the unifying factor of this section. Chapters 11 and 12 share the thesis that the drive toward consanguinity and dynastic integrity is the cross-cultural impulse behind the forces of national identity and nationalist expansionism.

In chapter 11, "The Covenant of Dynasty in the Old Testament: Consanguinity and the Nationalist War Syndrome (A Neo-Viconian Interpretation)," I argue the thesis that in our archaic past nationalistic war and international expansionism were the continuation of dynastic strife by different means. This is not a purely "academic" speculation. The basic motivation of this chapter derives from the terrifying political scenarios found in Western and Eastern Europe after the so-called end of the Cold War. This chapter is based upon the following three positions: (1) My problematization of the thesis (developed by Regina Schwartz in *The Curse of Cain*)[19] that monotheistic covenant and nationalistic expansionism are homogeneous with each other; (2) My conviction that the correlation between (mono-

and polytheistic) religion and nationalistic expansionism must be viewed as a corollary to the correlation between religious cult and dynastic supremacy *within* a given community. The preeminence of the latter correlation requires that civil faction-alism be considered as a basic determinant of external aggres-sion and nationalistic hostility; (3) My purpose to attend to the *vera narratio* conveyed by the myths, legends, and chronicles from the remotest past of humankind. The neo-Viconian thrust of this inquiry is to be identified in the presumption that a close study of archaic religious fabulations may help unveil the fundamental lines of transformation within the cluster of tradi-tions, institutions, languages, and laws that constitute the fertile soil of national identity.

In chapter 12, "Procreation and Degeneration: War and Civil War, Gender and Genre, Begetting and Memory in Plato's *Repub-lic*," I submit that Plato's *Republic* is informed by a degenerate *lógos,* a *lógos* whose genre may only be described as polymor-phous. This thesis puts me in position to reverse the conven-tional view that the Socratic city of the *Republic* is a "barricaded," sterile *locus* of gender segregation and reproduc-tive sterility. I maintain, instead, that by properly attending to a discourse radically unmoored from generic orthodoxy one may come to appreciate the political actuality of Plato's treatment of the communal policy of human reproduction. On a broader plane, this chapter is attuned to one of the tragedies of our politi-cal reality, namely, the devastations brought about by the forced coexistence of distinct national, ethnic, and religious groups under the banner of a single state. The increasing dimensions of this tragedy derive from a legacy of intolerance and antago-nism that dates from the most ancient attempts to establish firm criteria for national, racial, and religious identity. I believe that in Plato's *Republic* one may find the basic paradigms for chal-lenging the principles of consanguinity and patrilineality that served to distinguish the archaic communities from one another.

A LEGAL AND THEOLOGICAL INTERPRETATION OF GENEALOGY

As my last remarks pertinent to the nature and contents of this book, I should add that the studies presented in chapters 7, 8, 9, 10 from part 3 and chapter 6 from part 2 are intended as contributions and, at once, amplifications to the debate begun by the critical legal studies movement as regards the interpretation of literary and legal texts. A basic tenet of the critical legal studies movement is that literary and legal texts may be interpreted by means of the same poststructuralist devices. In the last two decades or so we have seen a proliferation of studies devoted to antiformalist readings of law and literature, together with innumerable attempts to extend to the praxis of legal adjudication the interpretive modalities inherent in the deconstructive, new historical, reader response, and interpretive community approaches. A criticism sometimes made of the poststructuralist interpretation of the law is that the intentionalist criterion still represents a valid approach to the understanding of the letter of the law.[20] A further, much less conciliatory criticism contends that the praxis of legal adjudication is incompatible with most, if not all, modes of literary interpretation; because of its coercive character, legal adjudication would only be susceptible to a hermeneutic objectivity aimed at unveiling the true meaning of the letter of the law.[21]

In this book I use several literary, religious, and philosophical texts as legislative texts at large; more precisely, I work under the assumption that certain eminent literary, religious, and philosophical texts may be treated as texts that "make the law" by means of legal fictions. In the case of *Ulysses,* for instance, it is my conviction that Joyce's masterpiece provides a substantial contribution to modern notions of genealogical legitimacy and paternity. Such a contribution has arguably had a sensible impact, albeit hardly quantifiable and obviously diachronic, on the modern ethico-juridical views as to family succession, foster parentage, adoption, and reproductive rights.

The concept of legal fiction, whose classical definition we owe to Henry S. Maine, is grounded upon the dissolution of the conventional separation between legislation and adjudication. By "conceal(ing), or affect(ing) to conceal, the fact that a rule of law has undergone alteration, its letter remaining unchanged, its operation being modified,"[22] a legal fiction attributes to the adjudicational act the competence of a legislative event. Also, in turning the plaintiff's and the defendant's competing assertions into the unified storyline produced by his or her adjudication, the judge in the court of law assimilates the terms of a legal injunction to such a unified storyline, hence conceiving and expounding a rhetorical transposition of the letter of the law into the fiction, the plot that he or she has derived from the legal case at hand. This narrative transposition, this emplotment of the legal dispute corresponds to the event of a legal fiction in a twofold sense, i.e., in the sense that two antagonistic claims are "thematized" into a single narrative "through the appeal to (a) legal principle,"[23] and second, as we saw above in regard to Maine, in the sense that the judge acts either under the pretense or under the assumption that the spirit of the legal principle, whose letter has been interpretively enforced, has undergone no substantial alteration.[24]

I am convinced that, as Vico intuited in his early juridical writings (and as Joyce seems to have inferred from his readings in Vico), the concept of legal fiction finds its most effective domain in the religious problematics relating to genealogical legitimacy. The questioning of genealogical legitimacy goes back to the origins of the Western humanistic tradition. In the *Odyssey,* Telemachus journeys through an imaginary landscape wherein consanguinity and identity enact the full extent of their symbolic conflict. In the *Oresteia,* Orestes is caught in the dilemma of patrilineal or matrilineal filiation; did his own life spring out of Agamemnon's insemination of the maternal womb, as Apollo argues, or was it conceived primarily through Clytemnestra's gestation of the paternal seed, as the Furies contend? At the end of book 2 of the *Aeneid,* "Father Aeneas" describes the prototype of what I call the "human machine of androlineal filiation": sitting on his shoulders, his father Anchises carries the statuettes of the family gods; his son Ascanius holds his right hand; his left hand holds the sword and the shield; his wife, Creusa, is left behind, to fall under the murderous rage of the Greeks. And then, of course, comes Joyce's Stephen Dedalus, the Modernist culmination of all these ancient archetypes, and particularly of the archetypal figures of genealogical errantry engaged in this book.

By his own admission, Stephen is the son of "a legal fiction" (*U* 9.844). He wants to appropriate to himself the phallocentric order of genealogical legitimacy that pertains to his father Simon. Stephen's disfigurement of the symbols of paternal authority occurs gradually, from *A Portrait of the Artist as a Young Man* to *Ulysses.* It starts with his juvenile polemic against his father, whom he reduces to "a drinker, . . . something in a distillery, . . . a praiser of his own past" (*Portrait* 241), and it peaks with his reluctant celebration of motherhood in the indecent fragment of the vampire poem: On swift sail flaming / From storm and south / He comes, pale vampire, / Mouth to my mouth (*U* 7.522–25). In *Ulysses,* Stephen's phallocentrism results sub-

jugated to the natural cycle of maternal fertility, represented by
the periodic visitations of the blood-sucking incubus, "his bat
sails bloodying the sea" (*U* 3.397–98). Stephen's composition of
the vampire poem reflects his obsession with the double fantasy
of woman as "bird of day," the "luminous envoy of the fair courts
of life," and woman as nocturnal creature, the "batlike soul waking to the consciousness of itself in darkness and secrecy" (*Portrait* 172, 183, 221)—the bat of the menses, the symbol of the
physiological function by which the womb counters and possibly
undermines the "necessary evil" of paternity (*U* 9.828). Stephen
is the victim of the classical opposition between night and day,
fact and sense, evidence and appearance, physiology and legality,
flesh and spirit—ultimately, the opposition between freedom
and necessity. The *necessity* of nature belongs to the selenitic
world of night, carnality, and the womb, while the *freedom* of
spirit belongs to the solar world of day, spirituality, and the phallus. The former is the precultural realm of *fact,* of the mother's
certainty as to the physiological provenance and lineage of her
child, while the latter is the cultural realm of *sense,* of the normative succession by which the father identifies and elects the
child as his own.

In the episode of "Scylla and Charybdis" from *Ulysses,* Joyce
describes Stephen's attempt to find a way out of the existential
conundrum determined by this opposition. Stephen's strategy
of escape exhibits distinct Viconian traits, especially at the juncture where he elaborates the formidable intuition that the contamination of day and night, of sense and fact, of paternity and
maternity, boils down to the reciprocal contamination of language and religion. According to Vico, human language found
its primal root in a frightening thunderbolt. The brutal and
speechless progenitors of the human race identified this noise
with the wrath of Jupiter, the father of gods and men. Their
primitive interjection of fear at the power of thunder was the
cry "*Pa!*," which later evolved into "*Pape!*," the root of Jupiter's
definition as the gods' and men's παπα, Papà (Italian for the
English "father") (*SNS1* § 448).[25] And their immediate response
to the fright caused by the thunder was a flight away from the
light of day and into the protective darkness of womblike caves.
Human language, the principal vehicle of expression for the
thoughts, ideas, and concepts of civilized humankind, was then
born out of a terror of primitive imagination, a terror at the
same time filial and mystical. In all the above pairs—day and
night, sense and fact, paternity and maternity—one side of the

opposition cannot subsist without the other, cannot even be named or conceived without the implicit naming or conceiving of the other, yet the solution to the friction between the two opposing elements does not seem to lie, according to Joyce, in a dialectical subordination or conciliation of opposites.

A third factor, genre (the kind or type of discourse engaged in the constitution of lineage), is always at play in the yoking together of these pairs. Genealogical legitimacy imposes a normative and androcentric sense over the maternal moment of procreation through a "legal fiction," as Stephen tentatively concludes in "Scylla and Charybdis"—"[f]atherhood [being] a mystical estate, an apostolic succession," occasioned and asserted in full daylight through the ritual of legal speech (U 9.838–39, 9.844). Yet, maternal procreation undermines androlineal genealogy with the fictional construct of a begetting that takes place in storytelling, in a maternal report of carnal origins and nocturnal deeds that no father can substantiate with the unchallengeable evidence of fact. A "legal" fiction plays against a "carnal" fiction, an assertion in full daylight plays against a nocturnal riddle, a normative "sense-making" of genealogy plays against the unescapable factuality of consanguinity. Stephen Dedalus comes eventually to the realization that the carnal language of maternal procreation and the legal language of paternal recognition dovetail respectively into the Catholic dogmas of the Immaculate Conception and the Holy Trinity, two theological mysteries inseparable, as we will see, from the unfolding of the full historical power and secular actuality of *Ulysses*.

2

The Gift of Life: The Theme of Genealogical Legitimacy in Borges's "The Circular Ruins"

All are washed in the blood of the lamb. God wants blood
victim. Birth, hymen, martyr, war, foundation of a building,
sacrifice, kidney burntoffering, druids' altar.
                                        —Joyce, *Ulysses* 8.10–13

THE WESTERN NORMATIVE OF GENEALOGICAL LEGITIMACY IS DOMI-
nated by a code of war: war of genders, war of genres. "Give me
children or I shall die," goes the epic lament that Rachel addresses to her master, Jacob, in Genesis 30:1.[1] One knows too
well the dialectic of gender segregation that informs androlineal,
homonymic descent, the patronymic coming to signify the subordination of genetic origin to the legal discourse that makes
lineage legitimate. Under the headings of gender and genre are
conventionally grouped two different lexicons of genealogy; one
applying to physiology, i.e., the power of gender to generate a
consanguineous offspring, and the other applying to discourse,
i.e., the power of genre—the power, especially, of legal discourse—to verify ascendancy and descendancy, to legalize parentage and succession through a narrative construct of
(patri)lineal descent.

In this chapter, I discuss how the archaic paradigms of genealogical legitimacy, with their salient connotations, are adum-
brated in the simple plot of "The Circular Ruins." My
engagement with Borges's short story will be devoted primarily
to those emblematic agencies of patronymic, genealogical, ritual,
legal, and sexual legitimacy that appear, at first sight, to be completely absent from it. As I said above, this is an absence that
cries out to be thematized, a silence, on Borges's part, that calls
attention to its hidden intentionality. In addition, an exemplary
passage from *Finnegans Wake,* wherein Joyce makes a connec-

35

tion between the modern acceptance of lineage and the archaic patterns of sociosexual legitimacy, will help me stress the peculiarity of Borges's omissions.

"The Circular Ruins" is the story of a man who dreams into existence his own son, only to find out that he is himself the creature of another man's dreams. No woman is involved in this episode of conception, nor is there a social arena wherein the son may be identified and recognized as the offspring of so-and-so. How can filiation possibly occur, as it does in this story, without being triggered by an act of fecundation, and without being regulated by a normative of legitimacy? How can the pro-creation of a man's descent escape at once the social and seminal prerequisites that, in different yet impressively compatible disguises, have informed procreation for millennia, long before the time of Rachel's imploring to be "given" children (or better, say, to be enabled to give to her master the children he will have been giving to her)? Is filiation unencumbered by a normative of legitimacy in "The Circular Ruins" because it is parthenogenetic, asexual, while postlapsarian filiation is, by definition, transgressively, sinfully bigendered? And lastly, on a more programmatic note: may a thematization of the issue of genealogical legitimacy help weave into "The Circular Ruins" a parodic intent, hinged upon the strategy of reticence and omission by which Borges appears to disrupt the myth of Creation found in the Book of Genesis? These are the questions I will deal with in this chapter.

THE RUINS OF GENEALOGY

As a parody of the Book of Genesis, "The Circular Ruins" satirizes the "cloning thrust" inherent in those layers of the biblical story that turn God's creation of man—*in [His] image, after [His] likeness* (Genesis 1:26)—into a model for what Gena Corea has belligerently called "the patriarchal urge to self-generate."[2] In contrast to the most ancient accounts of postlapsarian genealogy, which "include named women who conceive and bear children," the later genealogical accounts that the documentary hypothesis[3] attributes to the priestly scribes are "perfectly patrilineal." "No women are named," Nancy Jay remarks. "Wives are not even mentioned as existing."[4] An emblematic instance of strict patrilineality occurs, for example, at the very origin of Adam's lineage: "Adam begot a son in his likeness after his image, and he named him Seth" (Genesis 5:3). As it satirizes this patriarchal "cloning thrust," Borges's fiction hampers its mimetic impulse by depriving it of the element of gender opposition. In "The Circular Ruins" a child is begotten by his own father without the contribution of a female companion. And it is only a matter of narrative convenience, I submit, that keeps Borges from narrating the matrilineal story of a nameless woman dreaming into existence her nameless daughter. The age-old contention between Apollo and the Furies in Aeschylus's *Eumenides*—whether or not, in matters of procreation, the semen has priority over the menses—becomes futile when gender opposition is not involved in procreation.

A further connotation of Borges's parody of the Book of Genesis lies in the namelessness of the protagonist and of his son. In the second version of the biblical story of Creation (Genesis 2), God and Adam are simultaneously engaged in naming all the creatures around them; God keeping to himself the privilege of naming Man and his female companion, Woman. In this case, again, God's hierarchical derivation of Woman's name from Man's will be duplicated, after the Fall, by Adam's derivation of Woman's proper name, Hawwah (Genesis 3:20), from the subordinate role he assigns her, as the womb of all the living, as, in Mieke Bal's words, a "captive of motherhood."[5] In the world of postlapsarian genealogy, proper names, although they are not necessarily imposed by the father, signal genealogical legitimacy. The frequency of maternal naming-speeches in Genesis[6]—from Eve's naming of Cain, the child she "has gained" (*qanithi*) with the help of the Lord, to Rachel's and Leah's naming of eleven of Jacob's twelve sons[7]—does not detract from the close connection between names and patriarchal genealogy. Jacob, for instance, will peremptorily change the name of his last born, from the name chosen by moribund Rachel, Benoni, "son of my sorrow," to Benjamin, "son of the right"—the "right" representing in the Israelite tradition, according to Nancy Jay, "the proper line of paternal descent."[8] And the two patriarchs who did not lose control of their line of descent in Genesis, namely, Abraham and Jacob, shared the divine imposition of a new name—from Abram to Abraham and from Jacob to Israel[9]—that appeared to operate as a warrant against any matrilineal infiltration within their future genealogies.[10] That the women's power of naming is limited, and subordinate, above all, to patrilineal lineage, is also clearly indicated, as Ilana Pardes points out, by "the very fact that Biblical mothers name only their sons and not their daughters (with the exception of Dinah)."[11]

But in "The Circular Ruins" it is never a matter of proper, legitimate lineage. First, as I said before, this story does not involve gender in procreation. Second, the characters are nameless. Third, the mimetic order of patrilineality ("in [His] image, in [His] likeness"), that in Genesis, together with name and gender, is supposed to assign the prerogatives of primogeniture (and especially the rights of succession at the head of the paternal tribe),[12] is not lineal but circularly oneiric. I contend, in fact, that it is more than plausible to extrapolate a substantial convergence in "The Circular Ruins" between the opening scene, in which "the obscure man kissed the mud, came up the bank . . . and dragged himself, nauseous and bloodstained, to the circular enclosure crowned by a stone tiger or horse," and the scene that precedes the arrival of the obscure man's son to "the other broken temple whose debris showed white downstream, through many leagues of inextricable jungle and swamp."[13]

As the creature, the projection, the derivation of his father, a son dwells in a condition of duplicity; insofar as the source of his generation is not left unchanged (genealogically, juridically, affectively, etc.) by his birth, a son is, or becomes, a constituent part of the matrix out of which he sprouts. One might say that the youth created in the dream of Borges's story, having undergone a generation drastically divorced from the world of senses, generates his own father, in turn, as the creature, or the phantom, of another man's imagination. "With relief, with humiliation, with terror, [the father] understood that he too was a mere appearance, dreamt by another."[14] In sum, "The Circular Ruins" is a fiction wherein the thematics of genealogy reach a crystalline degree of abstraction, unimpeded by the slightest agency of patronymic, consanguineous, genetic, and sexual lineality.

GENEALOGICAL LINEAGE

Is this singular state of affairs permissible in Borges's fictional universe simply because there is no human society to speak of, in the story? Well, it is not that Adam wakes up from his uncreated slumber to find a preestablished community waiting for him in the Garden of Eden. And yet, no sooner does Adam come to life than he finds himself bound by a normative of legitimacy expressed in his and his female companion's names. Eventually, their postlapsarian predicament is turned into the discursive legacy of memory, into the handing down to posterity of a personal identity and a family history: "Adam begot a son in his likeness after his image, and he named him Seth." By contrast, the birth of the youth dreamed into existence by his father in Borges's story is accompanied by the immediate effacement of all and any story of origins: "But first [the man] instilled into [his son] a complete oblivion of his years of apprenticeship," so that he would never know he was a phantom.[15]

The tribal society of Genesis requires a process of procreation that legitimizes itself through some sort of discursive (re)fabrication of the past. And the imperative of this historical (re)fabrication is complementary to the institution of a genealogical tree capable of extending its branches into the farthest future.

> Abraham was the father of Isaac, and Isaac the father of Jacob, and Jacob the father of Judah and his brothers, and Judah the father of Perez and Zerah by Tamar, and Perez the father of Hezron, and Hezron the father of Ram, and Ram the father of Ammin'adab, and Ammin'adab the father of Nahshon, and Nahshon the father of Salmon, and Salmon the father of Bo'az by Rahab, and Bo'az the father of Obed by Ruth, and Obed the father of Jesse, and Jesse the father of David the king. (Matthew 1:2-6)

Let us try again. Is the singular state of affairs regarding genealogy in "The Circular Ruins" permissible because procreation, contrary to the postlapsarian dictate, is parthenogenetic in Borges's story? Borges's singular silence as to the absence of sex from this fiction cannot possibly be accidental. To paraphrase one of his narrative axioms, the only prohibited word in a riddle about gender is the word "gender" itself.[16] Borges's silence may be taken to suggest that gender difference is *the* crucial satirical element in "The Circular Ruins." The biblical myth of Creation entails a close convergence between the normatives of genealogical legitimacy and the patriarchal custom of gender segregation; and this convergence hinges on the imperative to engage in a discursive fabrication of a genealogical tree within whose branches runs the unadulterated blood of the master inseminator—who is, in turn, nothing but a clone, or, to say it Platonically, a mimetic image of its divine source. Borges's parody, on the contrary, seems to envision a divergence between procreation and our discursive ability to control it in a historical narrative of legitimacy. The oblivion of origins instilled into his son's mind by the obscure man of Borges's story turns out to signify not so much a predilection for historical forgetfulness as the advocation of a different manner of remembrance—the advocation of a discourse capable of violating the saturation of human procreation and family lineage in terms of genetic and generic primacy.

JOYCE'S VIEW

The lineage from Matthew's Gospel, cited above, is the emblem of emblems of the genealogical tree. It stands like a millennial oak, ineffable, run through by an intricate ramification of veins carrying the sap of consanguinity up to the heavens. Like most majestic trees, it can be climbed up and down with relative ease. One starts from Abraham and, in the space of sixteen branches, or versets, one reaches Mary's conception of Jesus. Abraham, however, is only the visible origin, the trunk, of the lineage, but not its source. If one digs down to the roots of Jesus' genealogical tree, one journeys backward through the twenty generations that separate YHWH's creation of Adam from Terah's begetting of Abram. And it turns out that the consanguinity claimed by these twenty generations, bilineal and endogamous, inherently incestous, differs from the androlineal criterion of patrilineal consanguinity warranted later on by the Abrahamic norm of circumcision. One might say that the genealogy illustrated in Matthew 1:1–16 implies the substitution of the contractual token of *paternal* consanguinity represented by the scar of a man-given wound for the physiological norm of *parental* blood purity. The ritual of circumcision erases, through a legal fiction, all risks of blood adulteration brought about by mixed marriages with idolatrous women; it imposes a gender-exclusive normative of legitimacy upon the discursive (re)fabrication of the history of legitimate procreation, of racial and national unity. Ultimately, in positing androlineality as a direct expression of the covenant with YHWH, circumcision invests the *fact* of the original event of procreation with a (ritual and contractual) *sense* external to, or, by all means, virtually independent from it.

As I suggested before, in *Finnegans Wake* Joyce draws a close connection between the archaic and the modern paradigms of genealogical legitimacy; it is a significant connection in the structure of the present chapter, because it allows me to introduce the still missing piece from the laconic puzzle of Borges's short story, namely, the discussion relating lineage to sacrifice. In the light of the previous observations with regard to the genealogical tree of the Hebrew patriarchs, one might venture that Joyce is *semantically* justified in *Finnegans Wake* when he assimilates the Phoenixlike "perpetuation" of a man's lineage first to the "perpetration" of a "foenix culprit" (the Miltonian *felix culpa*)[17] and then also to the "petrification" (or monumental legitimation) of the male side only of the line of consanguinity.

> ... perpetrified in his offsprung, ... the moaning pipers could tell him to his faceback, the louthly one whose loab we are devorers of, the lipalip one whose libe we drink at, ... our breed and washer giver, there would not be ... a yew nor an eye to play cash cash ... (*FW* 23.30–24.1)

Joyce's point, however jocular, is strikingly well taken. Let me sketch a paraphrase of the above passage from *Finnegans Wake.* The morning papers ("moaning pipers"), Joyce writes, could tell man to his face (and behind his back as well) a certain crucial fact about his offspring ("offsprung"). What fact exactly? That were it not for the High One ("the louthly one")[18] (to whom we sacrifice in return for the gift of our generation ("breed") by devouring his bread/flesh and drinking his wine/blood lip to lip ("lipalip"), there would not be a trace of human society, not a you ("yew") nor an I ("eye") to play the "cash cash" game of sociosexual reproduction. Here the repetition of the term "cash," playfully suggestive of childish secrecy,[19] may be taken to stand for both social and sexual reproduction ("cash" as the signifier of the legal tender of commodity exchange, of course, but also as the inverted anagram of "hsac"—plain "sex," or else, on a philological level more closely attuned with the thematics of lineage developed in *Finnegans Wake,* a contraction of "sahaq," the laughter that names the fruit of Sarah's withered womb in Genesis [17:17–19, 18:12]). In other words, Joyce intimates that human civilization establishes a set of rigorous priorities in the order of genealogical legitimacy: both the events of sexual reproduction and of social reproduction find their condition of possibility, respectively, in the binary logic of gender and subject ("yew" and "eye") separation. And this separation of agencies finds its sense, lastly, in the (il)logic of the experience of the divine, in the absurdity of a "louthly one" who will accept, as worthy sacrifice, only the blood of his own offspring. *Finnegans Wake* indicates a significant evolution in Joyce's concern with family lineage. It is not just, Joyce suggests in the above dense passage, that sense comes before nature in the order of procreation, and the memory of genealogical legitimacy before the physiology of procreation, but that, first of all, the sense of procreation is verified in the mystery of religious rituals. The god of *Finnegans Wake* "clop(s) his rude hand" (23), thunders, and shoots destructive fire-bolts, until man learns to pay him homage by compatible means: noisy rituals of sacrifice, frantic rites of covenant, burnt offerings of lives in return for more life and greater fertility.

THE FIRE OF LIFE

In "The Circular Ruins," the man living in the temple of fire has a purpose that is terrifyingly simple. He is going to dream a man and insert this man into the world of senses. He will, by means of a sort of immaculate conception that takes place during his sleep, give birth parthenogenetically to a man similar to himself. He will clone himself, if you will. Through an extended succession of dreams, the man completes a man, a youth, but he dreams him asleep. Try hard as he can, his dreamed creature "cannot stand alone." "(T)his youth could not rise nor did he speak nor could he open his eyes. Night after night, the man dreamt him asleep." The dreamed creature is a captive of the domain of sleep. It is as though the power of the man's breath, exhausted by the Heraclitean task of keeping the youth, conceived in the arms of sleep, from slipping into the embrace of death, were inadequate to fill his creature's lungs with *pneuma,* with the spirit that animates the form of life. Then, one day, the man throws himself down "at the feet of the effigy [of the god] whose earthly name was Fire."[20]

This episode brings about a curious twist in Borges's tale. By imploring the help of the god in the ruins of whose temple he lives, the man seems to succumb to that very power of divine creation that, together with the imperative of gender separation, was his original intention to usurp. Is the man surrendering to the power of the divine *demiourgòs,* whose fabrication of "man in his image" is mimetically reproduced in the "cloning thrust" of the Hebrew patriarchs? I do not think this is the case. Why would the man, otherwise, choose the ruins of the temple of fire to pursue his purpose, when "he knew that downstream . . . [there was] another propitious temple, whose *gods* were also burned and dead"?[21] Why does the man elect the temple of fire, of all temples of all gods, as the "propitious" abode for the accomplishment of his unimaginable feat of procreation?

I submit that this turn in the story signals the radicalism of Borges's inquiry into the order of genealogical legitimacy. As we saw with regard to the Abrahamic norm of circumcision, which is a ritual and contractual substitute for bilineal consanguinity, genealogical lineage does not find its normative sense exclusively in the natural events from which sprouts what Foucault has called *sanguinité*. In *La volonté de savoir,* Foucault argues that the normativity of the law is rooted as much in the rational paradigms of its intelligibility as in the violence of the instincts that make one's death always imminent, and always precarious the life of one's bloodline. "Easy to shed, subject to drying-up, too ready to mix, very susceptible to corruption,"[22] blood resists the containment of universal codes of legitimacy; it is hard to pour it intact into the vessel of tribal endogamy or of ethnic, national integrity. It is not in blood itself but in the mystery of the experience of the divine, as celebrated, for instance, in the bloody ritual of circumcision, and, in general, in the sacrificial offering of a victim's blood, that genealogical lineage finds its regulatory sense. The nameless man of Borges's story chooses the temple of fire as the place in which to give birth to the son of his dreams. Metaphorically speaking, he chooses, as the shelter for his procreation, a place of religious worship where, traditionally, lives were not given birth by fire, but, rather, as sacrifice, were given death in fire.

In Plato's *Timaeus,* Socrates reminds us that fire is a protean element that can turn itself into water, earth, air.[23] Fire's very name, Socrates maintains, presents a character of epithetic duplicity; since the element of fire, in its protean nature, never appears as such, purely and simply as fire, its name cannot be meaningfully uttered by that rational discourse, that *lógos,* that narrates the myth of genesis (or better, say, the myth of cosmogony) as the divine transposition to the world of senses of a tangible and visible copy (a mimetic image) of the paradigms hidden in the heavens. To a similar extent, in Borges's "The Circular Ruins" the name "fire," which denotes an element capable of turning itself into a bull, a rose, and a tempest,[24] is a name of epithetic duplicity. As one may infer from Jaime Alezraki's *Borges and the Kabbalah,* the metamorphic power of fire reflects the thematic extent to which the Kabbalah's outlook prevails in this fiction by Borges. Fire, whose symbolic figure is the Hebrew letter ש, *shin,* is one of the three primordial elements in the

Kabbalah, together with air *(א, aleph)* and water *(מ, mem).* Alezraki explains that in the Kabbalah "the first emanation off from God was the *ruach* (air) that produced fire, which, in its turn, formed the genesis of water *(Sefer Yetsirah,* III)."[25] These three primordial elements, in turn, are symbolized by the three letters, *aleph, shin,* and *mem,* from which the remaining 19 letters of the Hebrew alphabet are formed. Since for the Kabbalah Creation is the result of the infinite combination of the letters of the Hebrew alphabet,[26] one may say that, in the constitution of the Universe, fire, together with air and water, is an omnipresent metamorphic element.

Borges's inquiry into the order of genealogical legitimacy ought not to be taken, however, as directed simply at the establishment of a principle of genetic primacy. In terms of genetic primacy, one encounters in archaic thought an abundance of theories as to the role played by the elements—fire and water, air and earth—in the constitution of the cosmos. Plato's *Timaeus,* for instance, which is oriented toward a scientific cosmogony, maintains that earth and fire share the original impulse of generation, as the two primordial elements of an endless chain of elemental aggregations and separations.[27] Thales, on the other hand, is oriented toward an imaginative kind of cosmogony that detects in the "watery masses" the fluid prefiguration and poetic mimesis of the entire typology of creation. He attributes to water the role of "womb of all things."[28]

The positions of Plato and Thales are emblematic, in the context of the present discussion, because they exemplify the dichotomy that has traditionally split the discourse of generation into two separate tracks. In the *Timaeus,* Plato is searching for the secret of the physiology (or the physics) of the origin of life, while Thales, on his part, seeks an imaginative discourse capable of appropriating the origin of life to the art of storytelling. The first approach presumes that the origin of life is a subject best left to the investigation of scientific discourse. The second approach, on the contrary, presumes that life can best be explained by trope and metaphor, that is, by the flights of imagination. In "The Circular Ruins," Borges brings together the poles of this dichotomy. Using a ruined temple in the middle of the forest, where the victims of sacrifice were put to death by fire, as the place where a single man gives birth—with the help of fire itself—to the son of his dreams, Borges's inquiry into the order of genealogical legitimacy should not be taken as a mere latecomer in the ancient tradition that investigates the role of the various elements in the genesis of life. Fire is, at once, more and less than one of the primal elements studied by the pre-Socratic and Socratic philosophers. The principal aspect that separates fire from the rest of the elements in Borges's story is its sacrificial purpose. Water and earth were used by our progenitors to return the remains of the dead to the gods of the afterlife, and air was the *pneuma,* the *ruach,* by which the gods breathed life into their inert creations, but it was with fire, upon an altar or a stake, that our progenitors offered sacrifice to the gods, in order to atone for the Promethean theft of the divine spark that gave life to their own progeny.

Genealogy, Fire, and Imagination

The man who, in Borges's story, dreams his son into existence was dreamed into existence by a man who dreamed of a man dreaming his son into existence—and so on *ad infinitum.* In depicting this visionary man "perpetrified," as Joyce would phrase it, "in his offsprung," "The Circular Ruins" appears to be exploring the reciprocal encroachment of procreation and creativity, conception and imagination—the encroachment, on the one hand, of natural fact, of the physiologic process of human life, and, on the other, of cultural sense, of the discursive appropriation and codification of that very inscrutable process through tales, legends, myth, and, of course, the law. As I suggested above, the erasure from the youth's mind of the memory of his own conception may be taken to advocate a different manner of historical remembrance. It is not so much that the facts (far from natural) relating to the youth's procreation are erased so that his mind can feed its own remembrance upon the generic legacy of some code or fable as, rather, that the mystery that ignited the spark of life within the inert matter of his lethargic body cannot be explained as *fact,* nor told, recalled, or legislated, as *(hi)story,* but only celebrated in a sacrifice, only given the *sense* of truth and norm in the formalized pact of a covenant with the divine. As he erases from his son's mind the memory of his own conception, the father makes his son the officiant of the worship of the god of fire, sentencing him, therefore, to a lifelong reenactment of the alliance that gave him life.

Fire has the power to turn whatever it touches into smoke, and, in the process, to turn itself into that same smoke, to become one with it. Fire, then, is that which it burns, the scene of a conflagration where that which is sacrificed to the god undergoes a simultaneous death and rebirth—death to a previous life, to a previous form, and the birth of a resurrection to a new life. In the context of Borges's story, one could say that the nameless man immolates the lethargic life of his unborn, dreamed-up son upon the altar of fire, and fire, having consumed the sacrifice, offers a living son back to the man. Hence, both the god of fire and the officiant of its rituals conceive their own creature as one and the same, as an indispensable agent of the covenantal myth itself. By turning fire into the privileged locus of expiation and justification for the mystery and pride of human fertility, "The Circular Ruins" frames the order of genealogical legitimacy within a bivalent imagery; fire is used, on the one hand, as the ritual that consecrates, that *verifies,* in its paradox, the gift of life given and then taken by sacrifice, the bloody exchange of life for fertility, and, on the other hand, as the metaphor where human imagination, captivated and propelled by that vivid scene of combustion, transfigures fact into feeling, physiology into myth, death into fertility, ritual bloodshed into legitimate kinship.

If one takes a closer look at the genealogical tree from Matthew's Gospel, one can see that its discursive construct is senseless from any anthropological standpoint, grafted as it is upon the ecstatic (il)logic of sacrifice. It is true that the blood of the patriarchs runs like sap through its boughs, from its deepest roots to its highest branches, but its ramification of veins, just as the blood they carry, is a poor metaphorical vehicle for the mystery that it supposes: a sacrificial terror, transcendent of all physiological and/or discursive explanation of human life, lineage, national and racial identity. Matthew seems to reduce the sacred lineage linking Abraham to Christ to a sort of procedural, numerical logic: fourteen generations link Abraham to David, fourteen generations link David to the Babylonian exile, and fourteen generations link the Babylonian exile to Christ (1:17). However, this arithmetic symmetry cannot completely obscure the covenantal symmetry that constitutes the condition of its possibility. The river of the blood of the master inseminator originates in Adam after the covenant of his creation, runs through more than sixty biblical generations, and terminates in Mary's usurpation of the patriarchal role at the eve of the new covenant. No male seed initiates or culminates the flow of Semitic blood, which appears to be running, instead, out of the same covenant onto which it eventually issues. In Matthew's

genealogical tree, blood is turned into an ineffable gift, the substance of Jesus' sacrifice, by which the circular logic of the covenant obscures the lineal logic of genealogical succession.[29]
Paradoxically, this image of the river of blood does not pertain
to the "natural" physio-logic of consanguinity (insemination,
conception, gestation, etc.), nor to the "cultural," or "juridical"
genea-logic of consanguinity (arbitration of primacy, primogeniture, patronymic legitimacy, etc.), but, rather, to the (il)logic of
the experience of the divine. The imagery of the genealogical
river of blood, then, starts and ends neither in human blood
nor in human seed, neither in norm nor in code, but in the
sublime terror of a holy alliance. To engage it in all its devastating significance one needs to transgress, at once, the dictates of
the senses and the dictates of the law—the genetic facts of natural descent, the generic discourse of filial legitimacy, and, ultimately, the entire body of norms that regulates reproductive
rights—so as to open oneself up to a covenantal (il)logic of
reproduction.

BORGES'S VIEW

Borges's inquiry into the order of genealogical legitimacy
catches fire, literally, with the introduction of the cabalistic
power of fire, as a protean element of generation. As I have suggested, the implied contrast between, on the one hand, the partial contribution to procreation given by the elusive divinity
housed in the "circular enclosure [of the] broken temple," and,
on the other hand, the all-powerful generation of life performed
by the Lord of Genesis, may be taken as an intentional parody
of the biblical myth of Creation. Borges's story deprives the myth
of Creation of the gender- and genre-exclusive normative of legitimation upon which is erected the genealogical tree of the
Hebrew patriarchs; which comes down to saying that this story
deprives the myth of Creation of its power of historiographic
memory, based as this power is upon intolerance of genetic and
generic difference.

I want to conclude with a methodological note on the thematic
nature of my approach. "The Circular Ruins" is a timeless tale,
a story devoid of clear-cut temporal or epochal connotations,
unrelated to the certitudes of historically verified and faithfully
re-created events. Just as the myth of Creation found in Genesis,
and the ones found in Plato and Thales, the tale of "The Circular

Ruins" tells of events that occurred neither in a dark, unacces-
sible prehistory nor at a time and in circumstances open to our
efforts at factual reconstruction. One might say that "The Circular Ruins" is a fiction designed to evoke emotional and intellectual responses to its plot and characters that are as volatile as
the smoke of the sacrificial fire. My decision to thematize the
issue of genealogical legitimacy in "The Circular Ruins" was not
based upon an objective correlative statement in the text, indicating Borges's intention to engage such a theme, for the simple
reason that such a passage cannot be found in the story. My
strategy of thematization was aimed, rather, at the articulation
of an interpretive construct derived from the story's undeclared
purpose. Granted the long and tortuous history of the concept
of intention in literary analysis, I have not attempted to retrieve
or reconstruct Borges's original intentions by means of decisive
documents relating to the composition of his tale, nor have I
intended to unearth, through biography and psychoanalysis, a
set of purposes buried in Borges's unconscious. What I have
proposed, instead, is an interpretation whose persuasiveness is
to be measured against the plausibility of its relevance vis-à-vis,
first, the other thematic concerns that Borges makes explicit
in his story and, second, the textual traditions that Borges has
deliberately set out to engage (here it is useful to remember
that we are dealing with an author whose inspiration is always
profoundly intertextual and intercultural)—two factors that, on
closer analysis, may be reduced to a single suggestive piece of
evidence, namely, the cabalistic resonance that the fire imagery
brings to the deceptively simple myth of generation told in "The
Circular Ruins."

If one looks closely at the myths of Creation mentioned
above—the cosmogony of Plato's *Timaeus,* for instance, that
starts out with earth's and fire's original impulse of generation
in order to provide an ultimate justification for the constitution,
genealogy, and political primacy of the *pólis* of Athens, and the
myth of Genesis itself, on which the rest of the Pentateuch hangs
elaborate narratives of lineage and descent—it appears that the
functional presence of the thematics pertaining to genealogical
legitimacy in such myths is strikingly evident. So is the legacy
of intolerance and antagonism that dates from the most ancient
attempts at the establishment of stable criteria for national, racial, and religious identity, and that has traditionally dominated
the norms that regulate reproductive rights.[30] In this chapter I

have meant to show the extent to which Borges's tale may be read as a violation, or better, a "de-generation," of the two fundamental genres of discourse (the juridic and the physiologic, the cultural and the natural, the metaphoric and the literal) inherent in this immemorial tradition.

Part II
Genealogy and Joyce

3

Poetic Creativity and Maternal Fecundity: Mallarmé, Dante, and Blake in Stephen Dedalus's Vampire Poem

Mother of moth! I will to show herword in flesh.
—Joyce, *Finnnegans Wake* 561.27

DESPITE APPEARANCES TO THE CONTRARY, BRAM STOKER'S *DRACULA* is only an indirect influence in the process of composition of Stephen Dedalus's so-called vampire poem. The vampire poem as such is never presented in a conclusive form in *Ulysses,* but only surfaces as a quatrain—more properly, a four-line fragment—from a short-lived moment of mental rumination in the "Aeolus" episode:

> On swift sail flaming
> From storm and south
> He comes, pale vampire,
> Mouth to my mouth. (7.522–25)

However, the fundamental compositional elements of the poem surface about an hour before "Aeolus," in the incoherent form of an interior monologue in the "Proteus" episode, wherein Stephen muses about the "moon-drawn" sea-tide and menstrual cycle, and about the vampire's kiss, "mouth to her moomb. Oomb, allwombing tomb," and on "bat sails bloodying the sea" (*U* 3.393–402). In the course of this meditation, Stephen is shown scribbling a few lines on a scrap of paper while sitting on a rock on the Sandymount Strand (*U* 3.397–402). The vampirish imagery is usually related to the "association of sex and death" that emerges in the "Aeolus" quatrain and, above all, in the interior monologue from "Proteus."[1] While John Gordon, Robert Adams Day, and Vincent J. Cheng agree that Stephen's short composition describes a "vampire kiss" worthy of Stoker's Prince of Darkness,[2] fraught with elements of necrophilia,[3] they also unanimously stipulate that Stephen's poetic ambition reaches beyond the realm of popular culture. For one thing, Stephen's imagination is obviously under the influence of the symbolist movement of the late nineteenth century (in the essay "Leonardo da Vinci," for instance, Walter Pater describes *La Gioconda* as a vampire who "has been dead many times, and learned the secrets of the grave"),[4] an influence whose specific pertinence to the vampire poem, never satisfactorily demonstrated thus far, is illustrated in this chapter. Although what Stephen scribbles on the beach is a mere pastiche[5] from Douglas Hyde's mediocre translation of the song "My Grief on the Sea,"[6] it is a matter of general agreement that influences more noble, if you will, than Hyde's mediocre poetry or Stoker's gothic imagination are at play, the names most often mentioned being those of Yeats, Blake, and Dante. Furthermore, the significance of the influence of Stoker's *Dracula* is radically reduced once the critic gives proper weight to Adams Day's remark that the "Aeolus" quatrain is "not a poem, but rather an early model for a poem-to-be (a good one)."[7] As a matter of fact, the gap between the intellectual thrust of the preparatory stages and basic compositional elements of Stephen's poem and the resulting "Aeolus" quatrain is so striking that no degree of condescension toward Stephen's talent can explain such a miserable result—unless, that is, one follows Adams Day's lead, and takes the quatrain as well as the monologue that precedes Stephen's composition of it as two mere stages within a more comprehensive process of poetic creation. This is precisely the approach adopted in the present chapter.

This is not to say that there is no vampire in the vampire poem. Of course there is a vampire, and a persistent one it is. In the "Aeolus" quatrain we read of a vampire that "comes . . . on swift sail flaming / from storm and south"; in the meditation that triggers the poem's composition in "Proteus" we read of a vampire that "comes . . . through storm his eyes, his bat sails bloodying the sea, (his) mouth to her mouth's kiss" (*U* 3.397–400); and in the considerations that later on, in "Aeolus," Stephen devotes to Dante's *terzarima,* there is to account, if not for a proper vampire, at least for its voracious mouth, the occasion (or the pretext, as argued by Adams Day)[8] for the rhyming pair "mouth, south." As Adams Day points out, "though a vampire need not always be a bat, this one is"[9]—a close relative, I venture, of the "batlike soul" that Stephen attributes to Emma, his teenage love, in the interior monologue pertinent to the composition of his *villanelle* of the temptress in *A Portrait of the Artist as a Young Man* (221). But this bat may be said to evoke Stoker's fantasies only to the extent that one is willing to set aside the ponderous influence of Blake and Dante, two authors deeply acquainted with that "bat" with many pseudonyms that the ancient Romans called *Hesperus,* the Star of Venus, that Blake and Dante called Satan, and Stephen Dedalus calls Lucifer. "Allbright he falls, proud lightning of the intellect. *Lucifer . . .*" (*U* 3.486): words from the close of "Proteus," it will be recalled, by which Stephen, still in the throes of poetic inspiration, and very much in the manner of William Blake's epic of the death of God,[10] alludes to his own artistic Passion, a profane Way of the Cross amid "crucified shirts" and "sails brailed up on the crosstrees" (3.156, 3.504).

As I indicated above, Stephen is at work on a poem whose completion is never presented to the reader of *Ulysses,* and remains very likely unachieved by the end of the "Ithaca" episode, when Stephen refuses Bloom's offer of hospitality and walks away into the night. However, the process of composition, as shown especially in the "Proteus" and "Aeolus" episodes, matters infinitely more than the quatrain scribbled on the Sandymount Strand. It is to this process rather than to its partial and fragmentary result that I propose to pay close attention.

The interior monologue that reveals Stephen's preoccupation with the subject of the poem occurs as he sits by the sea, and reads as follows:

> Across the sands of all the world, followed by the sun's flaming sword, to the west trekking to evening lands. She trudges, schlepps, trains, drags, trascines her load. A tide westering, moondrawn, in her wake. Tides, myriadislanded, within her, blood not mine, *oinopa ponton,* a winedark sea. Behold the handmaid of the moon. In sleep the wet sign calls her hour, bids her rise. Bridebed, childbed, bed of death, ghostcandled. *Omnis caro ad te veniet.* He comes, pale vampire, through storm his eyes, his bat sails bloodying the sea, mouth to her mouth's kiss.
>
> Here. Put a pin in that chap, will you? My tablets. Mouth to her kiss. No. Must be two of em. Glue em well. Mouth to her mouth's kiss.
>
> His lips lipped and mouthed fleshless lips of air: mouth to her moomb. Oomb, allwombing tomb. (*U* 3.393–402)

In his 1930 commentary of *Ulysses,* Stuart Gilbert describes the contents of this interior monologue as "the primal matter of poetry in the very act of metamorphosis from the particular to the general."[11] Although the complex articulation of imagery and lexicon makes it close to impossible to paraphrase Stephen's thoughts, it is worthwhile to stress the interplay of several crucial thematic factors, in this order: (1) the "moondrawn" sea tide, mentioned above; (2) the "winedark sea," an identification, in Homeric diction, of woman's menstrual blood with the maternal attributes of the sea, "our great sweet mother" (*U* 1.80); (3) the maternal destiny of the "handmaid of the moon," a virgin vestal fated to undergo the transition from "bridebed" to "childbed" to the bed of her own death, "ghostcandled," just like the deathbed of Stephen's mother (*U* 1.274); (4) the bloody, sepulchral womb-kiss of the "pale vampire"; (5) and finally, the "allwombing tomb," a Blakean image, as Gilbert pointed out, evocative of the necessary demise of all that is conceived in woman's womb.[12]

The second crucial passage that reveals Stephen's preoccupation with the subject of the vampire poem occurs in the office of a newspaper, the *Freeman's Journal*. It pertains to a meditation on Dante's *terzarima*. Appearing in "Aeolus" under the rubric RHYMES AND REASONS, it reads as follows:

> Would anyone wish that mouth for her kiss? How do you know? Why did you write it then?
> Mouth, south, Is the mouth south someway? Or the south a mouth? Must be some. South, pout, out, shout, drouth. Rhymes: two men dressed the same, looking the same, two by two.
> ....*la tua pace*
> ....*che parlar ti piace*
> *Mentre che il vento, come fa, si tace.*
> He saw them three by three, approaching girls, in green, in rose, in russet, entwining, *per l'aer perso*, in mauve, in purple, *quella pacifica oriafiamma*, gold of oriflamme, *di rimirar fè più ardenti.* But I old men, penitent, leadenfooted, underdarkneath the night: mouth south: tomb womb. (*U* 7.713–24)

In the case of both passages the context deeply affects Stephen's meditation. By the sea, whose sinister maternal attributes emerged from Stephen's conversation with Buck Mulligan on the roof of the Martello Tower, in "Telemachus," Stephen meditates upon the relationship between life, woman, and poetry: the mother's power to procreate versus the poet's power to give life to immortal verses. In the offices of the newspaper, through whose doors blows tirelessly the "harp Eolian" of journalistic flatulence and empty patriotic speech, Stephen meditates upon the relationship between wind, rhymes, and harmony: the rhyme's power to breathe life into the poet, to become, literally, the wind of his (in)spiration, versus the poet's power to utter harmonious and truthful speech. Stephen's meditation appears to operate in a contextual manner also with respect to his literary influences. Although a complete catalogue of the literary references to be found in the two passages under consideration would be overwhelming (as it is always the case, after all, when it comes to Stephen's intellectual and doctrinal concerns), I submit that the principal influence in the passage from "Proteus" comes from a symbolist poem by Stéphane Mallarmé, *Don du poème*, "Gift of the Poem," and the principal influence in the passage from "Aeolus" comes from a miscellanea of quotations, carefully selected, from Dante Alighieri's *Commedia.*

Mallarmé's influence has been neglected even more than Dante's in the apprehension of the vampire poem. One reason for this is that, contrary to Dante's influence, which is manifest in direct quotations from *Inferno, Purgatorio,* and *Paradiso,* Mallarmé's influence is barely perceptible in the "Proteus" episode. The most explicit reference to the French poet (who is Stephen's namesake, incidentally) occurs only when Stephen crams his "scribbled note and pencil into a pocket" and embarks upon a variation on "*L'après-midi d'un faune,*" which ends with the dionysian declaration, "Pain is far" (*U* 3.440–44). However, just as all the verses by Dante that affect Stephen's interior monologue about (and against) flatulence in "Aeolus" relate intimately, as we will see, to the monologue's specific subject, that is, the relationship between wind, inspiration, and poetry, so the verses from Mallarmé's *Don du poème* relate intimately to the subject of Stephen's meditation in "Proteus," that is, the relationship between the creative powers of the mother and of the poet. It is not irrelevant to my thesis that *Don du poème* was included in Verlaine's anthology, *Les poètes maudits* (1884), which Joyce read and of which he owned a copy by the age of seventeen.[13] Nor is it irrelevant that Stephen's creative drives culminate before a hostile maternal sea, just as in Mallarmé's *Un coup de dés,* as Hayman remarks, the child/poem "is given birth out of a gambol *against* the sea, (a) feminine element." [14]

MALLARMÉ IN THE VAMPIRE POEM

Don du poème[15]

Je t'apporte l'enfant d'une nuit d'Idumée!
Noire, à l'aile saignante et pâle, déplumée,

Par le verre brûlé d'aromates et d'or,
Par les carreaux glacés, hélas! mornes encor
L'aurore se jeta sur la lampe angélique,
Palmes! et quand elle a montré cette relique
A ce père essayant un sourire ennemi,
La solitude bleue et stèrile a frémi.
O la berceuse avec ta fille et l'innocence
De vos pieds froids, accueille une horrible naissance
Et, ta voix rappelant viole et clavecin,
Avec le doigt fané presseras-tu le sein
Par qui coule en blancheur sibylline la femme
Pour des lèvres que l'air du vierge azur affame?[16]

Stoker's *Dracula* (1897) was published about thirty years after Mallarmé's poem. It would be preposterous, therefore, to attribute to Mallarmé the intention of evoking Dracula, when he endows the "black" light of dawn with "bleeding wings, featherless and pale," or when he invites the nursing mother (*la berceuse*) from the second half of the poem to set aside her newborn daughter and feed the milk of her breast to the "starved lips" of his aborted (and abysmally self-referential) poem. However, it is plausible that the reception reserved by young Joyce, and by analogy by Stephen Dedalus, to Mallarmé's *Don du poème* would have been partially influenced by the macabre imagery made popular by Stoker's novel. The wing of Mallarmé's dawn is as bloody as Stephen's "bat sails bloodying the sea"; the breast of the *berceuse* is wet with milk, and she nurses at dawn, just as the "handmaid of the moon," from Stephen's meditation in "Proteus," is woken by "the wet sign (that) calls her hour, bids her rise"[17]—both the *berceuse* and the "handmaid" seem to brace themselves for a demonic kiss; the incorporeal lips of Mallarmé's aborted poem (*horrible naissance*) are eager for the woman's nipple, just as in "Proteus" the pale vampire glues "(his) mouth to her mouth's kiss," or just as Stephen's "lips lipped and mouthed fleshless lips of air . . ." The analogies between Stephen's meditation in "Proteus" and Mallarmé's *Don du poème* are too striking to be considered merely accidental, especially when, together with specific diction, and apart from any vampirish consideration, one pays close attention to the thematic thrust of Mallarmé's poem.

The first line of *Don du poème* addresses a subject very familiar to the reader of Joyce, that of artistic parthenogenesis. It is dawn and the poet carries a baby to his wife. The baby is barely alive, a "horrible birth," but also a "relic" from a mystical night spent in the realm of poetic exaltation; this is the realm of Idumaea, the mythical land whose kings "are supposed to reproduce themselves without sex and without women."[18] This is the aesthetic realm of autarchic self-sufficiency, whose boundaries and possibility of actualization will be explored by Stephen in "Scylla and Charybdis"—that heaven of poetic transfiguration, "foretold by Hamlet [where] there are no more marriages, glorified man, an androgynous angel, being a wife unto himself" (U 9.1051–52). From the secrecy of this gender-exclusive realm of uncontaminated creativity the poet brings back a miserable "gift," a poetic creature badly in need of fresh nourishment. Ominously black, "dawn leaps upon the [poet's] angelic lamp" and reveals his poem, a dying "relic" with hungry lips. This "relic" is a mystic "gift," however; "burnished with incense and gold" like a Nativity scene, it is delivered to the nursing mother upon a bed of palm leaves (Palmes!), just as on Palm Sunday the people of Jerusalem "cut branches from the trees and spread them on the road" in front of the Messiah (Matthew 21:8). But it is also a "horrible birth" that only the breast of an (ev)angelical mother may resuscitate, with the "sibylline white" of her milk, in the "virginal azure" light of the morning. White and blue are the colors universally associated with the Virgin Mary,[19] to whom the Catholics assign the power of absolute fecundity. On a different note, though, the "white" of the Sibyl evokes the habit of Virgil's Sibyl of Cuma to write her oracles on fluttering leaves;[20] leaves as elusive and laconic as the "empty sheet(s) defended by whiteness"[21] that cluttered Mallarmé's desk in Tournon, where he wrote the poem.

What a miserable gift, this misbirth, conceived by Mallarmé in March 1865,[22] when one compares it with the gift of the daughter, Geneviève, that his wife Marie gave him on 19 November 1864.[23] The couple lived at Tournon, where Mallarmé taught English at the local lycée. We know from the poet's correspondence that Mallarmé adjusted with extreme difficulty to the experience of paternity. "Geneviève, who eats up her mother, is as rosy as a flower, but my poor Marie, who is eaten up, is pale and endlessly fatigued. I survive like an old man . . ."[24] Mallarmé was twenty-three years old when he wrote this letter to Henri Cazalis, and Geneviève was four months old.

Another poem that reveals Mallarmé's frustration and creative sterility during the first few months of Geneviève's life has a significant title in the context of this discussion. Brise marine, "Sea Breeze," condenses in the two words of its title the two contexts of Stephen Dedalus's reflections on the vampire poem, the seaside in "Proteus" and the winds and draughts of the *Freeman's Journal* in "Aeolus." *Brise marine* is a chant in praise of the freedom of the sailors, who can run away from the "desolation" of paternal responsibility and poetic sterility, toward the tempests of the ocean and their disastrous shipwrecks. It is significant that *Brise marine* was conceived in March-April 1885, simultaneously with *Don du poème*[25]—it describes the sterile white pages upon which Mallarmé spent his troubled nights at Tournon while Marie Mallarmé nursed Geneviève. It is also significant that it was transcribed in its entirety by Joyce in the copybook entitled, "*Quaderno / di / James Joyce / Via della Sanità No. 2 Trieste / Italia*[26]: "*La chair est triste, hélas! et j'ai lu tous les livres. / Fuir! là-bas fuir! Je sens que des oiseaux sont ivres / D'être parmi l'écume inconnue et les cieux!*[27] Paternal responsibility and creative sterility are dramatically intertwined for the twenty-three-year-old Stéphane Mallarmé, whose attitude toward the maternal power to conceive and nurture life oscillates between resentment and admiration, impatience and open adoration.

In 1904 Stephen Dedalus is twenty-two, as dry a poet, apparently, as Mallarmé considers himself in his letters to Henri Cazalis,[28] and as ambivalent as Mallarmé about the reciprocal influence of paternity, maternity, and creativity. On the one hand, Stephen is ferociously obsessed by the depressing, unpropitious effect of the memory of his dead mother upon his creative drives; on the other hand, he is tirelessly probing and questioning the issue of paternity, from the artistic perspective of male creativity and self-creation, from the theological perspective of the Catholic dogmas of the Father-Son consubstantiality, and, last but not least, from the existential and hypothetical perspective of personal responsibility: "Am I a father?" he wonders, recollecting his visits to the red-light district in Paris. "If I were?" (*U* 9.860).

If in "Telemachus" Stephen celebrates the power of inspiration that dwells in what Yeats before him called the "white breast of the sea,"[29] and especially the poetic cadence inherent in the tidal, or should I say cyclic, life of the sea ("The twining stresses, two by two. A hand plucking the harpstrings, merging their twining chords. Wavewhite wedded words shimmering on the dim tide" [*U* 1.245–47]), in "Proteus" Stephen's ambivalent relation to the memory of his dead mother poses an insurmountable obstacle to the convergence of the feminine power to procreate with the artist's power to "pluck[. . .] the harpstrings" of immortal verses. At the beginning of "Proteus" the color of the sea is defined as "snotgreen," a term emphatically related, in the "Telemachus" episode, to the "bowl of . . . green sluggish bile" at the bedside of Stephen's dying mother (*U* 1.78, 1.106–10, 3.3), and later the sea's snotgreen water is turned by Stephen's interior monologue into the waters of his mother's bitter death (3.329–30). Even the sentence that inaugurates Stephen's meditation on the subject of the vampire poem is evocative of a degrading affinity between maternity and death: "Across the sands of all the world, followed by the sun's flaming sword, to the west trekking to evening lands. She trudges, schlepps, trains, drags, trascines her load" (3.391–93). The imagery, derived from the biblical story of the Edenic Fall, shows a mortal Eve condemned to pain and labor, expelled from Eden by the sword of the Cherub. For Stephen, in sum, any "moondrawn" journey toward aesthetic creation is at risk of sinking in the lethal sea of his own mother's death. According to Stephen's conversation with his friend Cranly, in *A Portrait of the Artist as a Young Man,* May Goulding Dedalus gave birth to "nine or ten" children before she died at a relatively young age (241). Fertility was not the result of her free choice; it was rather forced upon her by the prevailing Catholic custom, fervently honored among the Irish, that stigmatizes most forms of birth control as "Protestant." Stephen could not possibly embrace such a feminine principle of self-destructive creativity.

Yet, the point remains that, as shown above, the monologue from "Proteus," which articulates the essential imagery of the "Aeolus" quatrain, is evocative of Mallarmé's surrender (a reluctant one, by all means) to the maternal power—a power so great as to return to life even an aborted poem. This apparent contradiction may be explained by the metaphorical and self-referential tenor of *Don du poème.* The aborted poem of Mallarmé's is a vampire poem *in absentia,* in the sense that even before the rhetorical question that closes *Don du poème* is uttered (even before, that is, the *"enfant d'une nuit d'Idumée"* starts sucking away at the motherly breast), we realize that the poem has already been reborn in front of our eyes, transmogrified into an excellent poem; the piety of the *berceuse,* in other words, functions primarily as a poetic metaphor, rather than a literal agent of salvation; Mallarmé's verses anticipate the offering of the breast and resurrect themselves. Hence, one may wonder: If Stephen's poem-in-progress is a vampire in need of salvation too, and if salvation must come to it as a gift from a feminine emblem of fecundity, isn't it plausible that the motherly figure kissed, or sucked, by the "pale vampire" may be simply a metaphor, a vehicle for the poem's self-referentiality, rather than a reflection of the real mother in the life of the poet? Or else, isn't it plausible that this figure may be a disincarnate, poetically and ideally transposed metaphor of Stephen's concrete experience of the maternal condition?

THE MOTHER IN THE VAMPIRE POEM

Let us take a closer look at the metaphorical and self-referential tenor of Mallarmé's poem. *Don du poème* is a faux-naïf composition, hinged upon several layers of literal and figural meaning. The speaker, a father and a poet, enters his bedroom shortly after dawn and addresses his wife, who is nursing their baby. While he contemplates his wife holding a vibrant life in her arms, he is sadly aware that all he holds in his arms is a stack of sterile papers, the results of the night he spent in the gender-exclusive realm of Idumaea. In turning his miserable poem into an offering to his wife's solicitude, though, the poet/father manages to salvage his poem, or have it miraculously salvaged, so that the verses we read do actually compose an excellent poem. But the verses we read are also a similitude linking the poet's passion, at its lowest moment, that of self-doubt and self-recrimination, with the temporary glory of Jesus at his entrance into Jerusalem over a carpet of palm leaves; the similitude is paradoxical, insofar as it indicates that doubt and even inglorious defeat are the gates to luminous artistry and transcendence. However, this poet is glorified in his misery to the extent that he is saved by a feminine absurdity, that of a virginal mother who offers her breast to a sheaf of bad verses, that of a maternal "gift" that has the power to redeem the shortcomings of his own poetic "gift."

This synopsis shows the gradual figural shifting of the poem. Personal gloom (we have seen how gloomy Mallarmé's life was at the time of the first conception of *Don du poème*) is gradually replaced by the joyfulness of (ev)angelical imagery. On the one hand, the poem, "*horrible naissance,*" is presented as consubstantial with its maker, the poet himself, insofar as on a literal level it is the poet himself, rather than his poem, who is in need of nourishment and revitalization after a night of impotent writing; literally speaking, the lips that take the place of Gene-viève's lips upon Marie's breast are those of Stéphane, rather than the unsubstantial lips of his verses. On the other hand, the poem, the misbirth of the poet's immaculate conception in Idumaea, must undergo a second immaculate conception in the arms of the virginal mother; this poem is, metaphorically speaking, a cosmic corpse, the Son of God entering his week of Passion in Jerusalem; this poem is Christ as Jesus, the man-god who would never have seen the light of day unless a virgin/mother made him mortal, as mortal as she. And the prodigy of this clash of domestic solidarity and Catholic doctrine is that the resulting poem is exceedingly good.

These considerations enable me to unravel the self-referential thrust inherent in Stephen's meditation in "Proteus." Stephen's poem-in-progress is a vampire in danger of remaining undead, or, in our case, unborn, misborn, aborted. Its only hope lies in the adoption of a *poiesis* capable, as with Mallarmé's *poiesis*, of self-revitalization and resurrection. To become a poem at all, and especially to become the "good" poem precognized by Robert Adams Day,[30] Stephen's vampire poem must break free from the sterility of his gender-exclusive, uncontaminated inspiration, so as to be crafted by a *poiesis* that gives (back) life from the womb of a most paradoxical principle of regeneration: " . . . mouth to her moomb. Oomb, allwombing tomb" (*U* 3.401–402).

BLAKE IN THE VAMPIRE POEM

The influence of Mallarmé's (ev)angelical imagery of the white maternal milk, echoed in "Proteus" by Stephen's allusion to Yeats's "white breast of the dim sea" (*U* 1.244–45), must be complemented at this juncture by the influence of Blake's epic of the death of God:

> And thus with wrath he [the God of this World] did subdue
> The Serpent Bulk of Nature's dross,
> Till He had nail'd it to the Cross.
> He took on Sin in the Virgin's *Womb,*
> And put it off on the Cross & *Tomb*
> To be Worship'd by the Church of Rome.
> —The Everlasting Gospel, ll. 52–56b[31]

Literally speaking, the mother of Stephen's vampire poem is perhaps May Goulding Dedalus, his dead entombed mother, in all the oppression of her son's tormented memories. But the fecund mother of the sea's "twining stresses," which, in "Telemachus," march joyfully on "lightshod hurrying feet" ("two by two," like perfect iambs), is the soul of poetry itself (*U* 1.244–45). Or she is perhaps Calliope, the Muse of epic poetry, but also, more importantly, as will transpire from the "Aeolus" episode, the Muse whose very name (Καλλιόπη, or "She of the Beautiful Voice") is the etymological warrant of good harmonious diction. In its first compositional elaboration in "Proteus," the vampire poem may be understood as a classic invocation to the Muse or Soul of poetry. Calliope returns the humbled kiss of the self-deprecating poet, provides a solicitous shelter to his mortal wounds and errors, makes his verses immortal and his shadow "endless till the farthest star" (*U* 3.408–409). She clings to his soul like "a woman to her lover clinging, the more the more" (*U* 3.421–23).

Mouth, south. Tomb, womb. The relevant rhymes appearing in the "Aeolus" quatrain and in the interior monologue from "Proteus" are questioned by Stephen in his "Aeolus" interior monologue (*U* 7.713–24). In the context of our discussion, this monologue, which I cited earlier in its entirety, inaugurates the transition from the influence exercised by Mallarmé upon Stephen's poetic meditation to the influence exercised by Dante (Blake's influence, as we are going to see presently, operates as an essential bridge between Dante and Mallarmé). Both influences, as I suggested above, are contextual to the respective circumstances within which each interior monologue unfolds, but an incident from the tormented history of the publication of *Don du poème* shows that the transition from Mallarmé to Dante does not entail too radical a thematic switch. The incident, well documented by Carl Paul Barbier and Charles Gordon Millan, editors of Mallarmé's *Oeuvres Complètes*, reveals that an early version of *Don du poème*, entitled *Le Poème nocturne* and signed by "Petrus," appeared in 1867 in a parochial journal called *L'Avant-Coureur*. *Le Poème nocturne* was one of two poems collected under the rubric: POESIE—IMPROVISATION—RIMES SANS RAISON [POETRY—IMPROVISATIONS—RHYMES WITHOUT A REASON].[32] Although I could find no evidence that Joyce was aware of this incident, the analogy between this rubric and the rubric RHYMES AND REASONS in "Aeolus" is a very striking coincidence.

However, the essential bridge, in the transition from Mallarmé's figure of the mother of poetic (re)generation, her "voice

soft like a viol and a harpsichord,"[33] to Dante's feminine figures
of harmonious rhyme, is provided by Blake's epic of the death
of God, which assigns a previously unthought-of power of redemption to the Virgin Mary. Aside from the possibility, already
contemplated in Stuart Gilbert's 1930 commentary, that Stephen had lifted the rhyming pair "tomb, womb" directly from
Blake,[34] my argument is based upon Thomas Altizer's claim that
Blake's theology exercised a fundamental influence both on the
entirety of Joyce's work and on the character of Stephen Dedalus. A scrupulous description of the pervasive presence of
Blake's theology in Joyce's work and principal characters is
found in Altizer's *History as Apocalypse*. "Joyce . . . renewed
and resurrected the archaic and primordial Goddess. This resurrection and renewal begins in Blake's epics, and thus begins
with the first modern vision of the death of God. . . . (Molly
Bloom) is the first female presence in the Christian imaginative
tradition of an actual and living center of joy and grace."[35] Earlier, Altizer writes, "(T)here is an evolution of the identity and
power of Satan in Christian epic poetry . . . (T)he Satan of
(Blake's) *Milton* and *Jerusalem* . . . is the almighty Creator and
Lord, and (his) own final metamorphosis is . . . the very center
of resurrection . . . *Ulysses* and *Finnegans Wake* carry forward
this evolution, but now Satan is indistinguishable as Satan, for
he has . . . become the Satan who knows no fall, or whose fall-
enness and darkness is indistinguishable from light and resurrection" (232).

In light of the verses cited above from "The Everlasting Gospel," one might take the pair "tomb, womb" in Stephen's meditations as an effective lexical condensation of the centrality of
Satan and the Madonna in Blake's theology. This pair of words
indicates the extent to which Stephen Dedalus, in espousing
Blake's infernal theology, has gone beyond his youthful aesthetic
exercises in "applied Aquinas" (*Portrait* 209). Let us briefly look
at lines 55 and 56 of "The Everlasting Gospel": "[The God of this
World] took on Sin in the Virgin's *Womb*, / And put it off on the
Cross & *Tomb*." The first observation to be made is that in his
absolute kenosis on the Cross, the Son of God surrenders to sin
and mortality in the Virgin's womb, to such an unconditional
extent that, in becoming inseparable from Satan, he realizes
with Satan a *coincidentia oppositorum*.[36] This theological principle is clearly articulated in Blake's "The Four Zoas":

> We now behold the Ends of Beulah, & we now behold
> Where death Eternal is put off Eternally.

Assume the dark Satanic body in the Virgin's womb,
A Lamb Divine! it cannot thee annoy . . .
—Vala or the Four Zoas, Night the Eighth, ll. 240–42[37]

The second observation is that Christ's tomb becomes the *locus* wherein Satan is sheltered, fully triumphant as Death Incarnate, only in order to be repelled. The judge, Christ, is his own victim, Satan.[38] It is within this tomb—a transposition and prolongation of the Virgin's womb, a necessary sequel to God's incarnation in sin and mortality—that life and resurrection sprout from death. As Altizer writes: "While there is no Mary, no Mother of God, apart from the Son, it is nevertheless the Mother of God who essentially transcends death, and does so in her very body and flesh."[39] And last, it is important to observe that Blake's attribution of an autonomous redemptive power to Christ's mortal and virginal mother parallels closely the metaphor of poetic redemption via maternal piety invoked in *Don du poème* by Mallarmé. The same consideration applies as well to Blake's resolution of Christ's kenosis into a coincidence of the divine and satanic principles—here, too, one may detect an analogy among Stephen's "pale vampire," Mallarmé's Idumaean infant, and Blake's Lucifer.

DANTE IN THE VAMPIRE POEM

But in his "Aeolus" interior monologue Stephen is principally concerned about the rhyme "mouth, south": "Is the mouth south someway? Or the south a mouth? Must be some" (*U* 7.713–14). The "pale vampire" of the "Aeolus" quatrain must have a *mouth* in order to deliver its kiss, but what about *south*? Adams Day remarks that "it is 'south' (pure Hyde) that bothers Stephen." Stephen would have borrowed from the "despise[d]" Hyde, author of the translation parodied in the "Aeolus" quatrain, "(the) metrical pattern, the idea of someone's arrival, the 'south-mouth' rhyme, and the last line . . . but that is all."[40] Perhaps the consideration that the sun is "southing" during Stephen's meditation in "Proteus," at the moment of his Mallarmean surrender to "Pan's hour," is not significant enough to further justify this word choice for a rhyme. But it is relevant that the proliferation of citations from the *Commedia* in the "Aeolus" meditation—three fragments from *Inferno* (5.92, 5.94, 5.96), followed by a pastiche within which, in spite of two citations from

Paradiso and one from *Inferno,* prevail, thematically speaking, the implicit references to *Purgatorio*—evokes Dante's passage from Hell to Purgatory; a passage from the Northern to the Southern hemisphere, from North to South. It is through this passage from North to South that Hell's "dead poetry," *morta poesi,* finds its resurrection in the breeze, "alive and fecund," of Purgatory (*Purgatorio* 1.7, 28.103–17). As I just said, Stephen's "Aeolus" monologue includes a total of six direct quotations from Dante's *Commedia,* in addition to a variety of implicit references. For the sake of clarity I will indicate the sources of the citations and of the main references.

Rhymes: two men dressed the same, looking the same, two by two [*Purgatorio* 29.83].

....*la tua pace* [*Inferno* 5.92]
...............................*che parlar ti piace* [*Inferno* 5.94]
Mentre che il vento, come fa, si tace. [*Inferno* 5.96]

He saw them three by three [*Purgatorio* 29.110], approaching girls, in green, in rose, in russet, entwining, *per l'aer perso* [*Inferno* 5.89], in mauve, in purple, *quella pacifica oriafiamma* [*Paradiso* 31.127], gold of oriflamme, *di rimirar fè più ardenti* [*Paradiso* 31.142]. But I old men [*Purgatorio* 29.134] . . . (*U* 7.717–22).

I maintained above that the context of the episode strongly affects Stephen's meditation. In the "flatulent" offices of the *Freeman's Journal,* Stephen meditates upon the relationship between wind, rhymes, and harmony. His meditation, triggered by the sight of Myles Crawford's mouth "twitch[ing] unspeaking in nervous curls of disdain," evokes pairs of rhymes Stephen has been juggling with presumably since the "Proteus" episode: "mouth, south . . . pout, out, shout, drouth" (*U* 7.713–14). His rhymes, he considers, are like "two men dressed the same, looking the same, two by two" (*U* 7.714–15). This phrase, evocative of the twenty-four old men (*ventiquattro seniori*) who guide, *two by two,* the Mystic Procession in Purgatory that leads Dante to his encounter with Beatrice (*Purgatorio* 29.83), inaugurates Stephen's meditation on Dante's *terzarima* ("He [Dante][41] saw them three by three . . ."); and it does so as it calls attention to the fact that Stephen, like Mallarmé, tends to prefer rhymes in pairs.

In spite of the typographical centrality assigned by the text to a *terzarima* from *Inferno* (5.92, 5.94, 5.96), Stephen's meditation privileges Purgatory over Hell. I mentioned above the reason for this preference. It has to do with the "windy" context of "Aeolus." The wind that carries the words that Matelda addresses to Dante in *Purgatorio,* as a preparation for the celestial appearance of Beatrice, is as sweet and changeless (*sanza mutamento*) as the sirocco blown near Ravenna by Aeolus (*Purgatorio* 28.7–21)— a benevolent Aeolus, to be contrasted with the vain and frivolous Aeolus of *Ulysses.* It is a powerfully "fecund" wind, "impregnated with generative virtues" capable of making the plants on earth fertile without recourse to any *seme palese,* to any "tangible seed" (*Purgatorio* 28.103–17). It is the same wind that Stephen will talk about at night, in his drunk carousing at the National Maternity Hospital, where he will set the generative powers of the "wind of seeds of brightness" side by side with those of the "potency of vampires mouth to mouth" (*U* 14.242–44).[42] But it is, more importantly, the "wild air of seeds of brightness" that, "harping in wild nerves," brings Stephen poetic inspiration in "Proteus" (*U* 3.266–67). The wind that *si tace,* "stands still," during the episode of Paolo and Francesca in *Inferno* (a further contextual analogy between "Aeolus" [*U* 7.721] and its literary references), does not share in these virtues of insemination. It is a "black and purplish wind" (*l'aer perso*) (*U* 7.721, *Inferno* 5.89), a "malignant wind" (*aere maligno*) (*Inferno* 5.86), a "dead wind" (*aura morta*), and it gives birth to a "dead poetry" (*morta poesí*) (*Purgatory* 1.7, 1.17). Only an exceptional truce with it allows the enamored souls of Paolo and Francesca to utter their enlightening words to Dante, "while the wind, for (their) discourse, is still" (*Inferno* 5.96, *U* 7.719).[43] The malignity of this infernal wind must be equated with the journalistic flatulence and empty patriotic speech spoken at the *Freeman's Journal.* While Stephen listens to the vain eloquence of the journalists in the offices of the Dublin newspaper, he engages in a solitary quest for true poetic *lógos.* With the caustic satire of his "Parable of the Plums" he rejects the cheap patriotic arguments debated by his interlocutors. Meanwhile, his interior monologue opposes the graceful breezes that inspired Dante's supreme vision of love to the winds of patriotic bombast.

Stephen contrasts Dante's multicolored "approaching girls" with his "leadenfooted" old men, "dressed the same, looking the same, two by two." William York Tindall has interpreted the passage as an indication that Stephen reads in Dante's verses a "progress from hell to the rose of heaven,"[44] while his tired rhymes are the vehicle of the opposite journey. Adams Day appears to agree with Tindall when he depicts Stephen reflecting that "while . . . Dante's rhymes in-*ace* are gaily-clad girls, his own back-voweled rhymes are (like) 'old men'"; or reflecting that the "sounds (of his rhymes), in consonance with the gloomy subject, must be dark, leaden, slow, unlike Dante's joyous, front-voweled rhymes moving *per l'aer perso.*"[45]

I am of a different opinion, if nothing else because the scriptural source of Stephen's imagery here is paradisiacal rather than infernal. In fact, Stephen borrows the image of his elders, "two by two," from *Purgatorio,* but Dante, in turn, borrows the image of his twenty-four elders, all "dressed the same" (*U* 7.717) and "crowned," from John's *Apocalypse* (4.4). In the apocalyptic logic intrinsic to the tradition of Christian epic, from Dante to Blake and Joyce, the opposition young-old, gay-leaden does not necessarily bespeak the opposition Heaven-Hell.

If we agree that Stephen's vampire poem is a poem-in-progress, then Stephen's contrast between his tentative rhymes, "dark, leaden, slow," and Dante's timeless rhymes, "joyous (and) front-voweled,"[46] may be taken as the poetic arena wherein Stephen attempts to define a personal poetics. Stephen's praise of Dante's *terzarima,* personified by girls "in green, in rose, in russet, . . . in mauve, in purple, . . . (in) oriflamme," is evocative, as I said, of the Mystic Procession escorting Beatrice's "triumphal chariot." The chariot, preceded by the twenty-four elders and the seven lampstands of the *Apocalypse* (1.12, 4.4), is pulled by a gryphon, half lion and half eagle, a symbol of Christ's hypostasis, or double nature (divine and human). Around the chariot dance seven girls, the symbols of the three theological virtues and the four cardinal virtues, dressed in white (Faith), in green (Hope), in red (Charity), and in purple (Justice, Strength, Prudence, Temperance). The appearance of Beatrice, in white, green, and red (the colors of the theological virtues), prepares Dante for his vision of the Virgin Mary in *Paradiso,* whose flaming colors (*Paradiso* 31.127)—*oriafiamma* (*U* 7.722) being the name of the ancient flag of the Kings of France, a red field spread with golden flames—prepare Dante, in turn, for the vision of Christ.

Here is a symptom of Stephen's repudiation of his youthful aesthetic exercises in "applied Aquinas." As Jean-Luc Marion has shown in *God Without Being,* Thomas Aquinas may be considered the theologian who accomplished a full integration of

Aristotle's thought with Catholic theology. Aquinas reversed all previous Christian doctrines by positing *Esse,* Being, as the very essence of God, rather than Goodness, Oneness, etc. It is with Saint Thomas that theology becomes metaphysical, and God becomes a category of human intellect,[47] a concept mastered by the all-inclusive project of Western metaphysics. Thomism has the peculiarity of unhinging the body of Jesus from the divine Godhead, for God's essence, which is Being itself, remains impassible in front of all suffering, even in front of the corporal suffering of his Son.[48]

Nothing could be more alien from the theological universe of Aquinas than the Dantesque apotheosis of Love evoked by Stephen Dedalus in his "Aeolus" interior monologue. It is Love rather than Being, and Love, especially, toward a feminine divinized principle, that elevates Dante to the completion of his journey of salvation. This was Dante's "gravest heresy," as Altizer points out, one that consists in an ultimate "identification of Beatrice as the incarnate Christ."[49] In Aquinas's universe Christ, the Son of God, a Person of the Trinity, ineffably remote from human misery, does not share the suffering of the mortal body of Jesus. In Dante's heretic reversal of this universe, Christ, as Jesus, becomes the ultimate object of Dante's passionate love for Beatrice. In this light, it is far from accidental that the arrival of Beatrice on the chariot of the Mystic Procession, in Dante's *Purgatorio,* is announced by the cry, *Benedictus qui venit* (30.19); this is the welcome reserved to Christ in Jerusalem (Matthew 21:9), and also the formula sung by the assistant before the canon of the Mass, in preparation for the bodily coming of Christ.[50] Dante's ethereal, "uniquely singular Beatrice"[51] remains, even in her heavenly glory, the young girl dressed most often in "sanguine" garments[52]—here, too, an echo of Mallarmé's and Joyce's chromatism of blood—Dante fell passionately in love with in Florence. "[E]ven in heaven," Walter Pater remarks, "Beatrice loses for Dante no tinge of flesh-colour."[53] Carnal and celestial at once, Beatrice's visage discloses to Dante, as Emmanuel Levinas perhaps would put it, the voluptuous "beyond" where Love and Fecundity outplay metaphysics at its own "gazing" game.[54] Altizer suggests that it would be inaccurate to say that in *Paradiso* Dante gazes at Christ. He never actually *sees* Christ. He has "three visions of the eternal Virgin, and in the last vision he sees the *face that most resembles Christ,* and only its radiance can grant Dante the power to look upon Christ (*Paradiso* 32.86)."[55]

Riguarda ormai ne la faccia che a Cristo
più si somiglia, ché la sua chiarezza
sola ti può disporre a veder Cristo.
—Dante, *Paradiso* 32.85–87[56]

Dante finds himself in the presence of Christ—Christ as Trinity, *nota bene*, not as Carnal Jesus—through a succession of amorous raptures, all informed, guided, and oriented by his love for Beatrice and by Beatrice's love for him. "The only deity that even a transfigured and beatified Dante can finally and fully see is the Goddess, first present in . . . Beatrice . . . and then present in the Virgin."[57] Face-to-face with Beatrice, his earthly love, Dante's imagination is empowered to ascend to his multiple visions of the Virgin Mary in Paradise. Face-to-face with Mary, Dante's imagination is smitten by the *fulgore,* the "blinding light"[58] that consumes his desire for God in a flash of instantaneous intuition—a scorching vision that no human eye can tolerate, let alone gaze at (*Paradiso* 33.48, 33.141–42). But even if Dante's gravest heresy remains the identification of Christ with the Mother of God, an existential and individual identification mediated by Mary's actual embodiment in Beatrice,[59] Medieval Christianity did not notice it in its reception of Dante's poem, for the simple reason that, as Altizer writes, "the birth of the Gothic world occurred with a new epiphany of the Mother of God as the immanent source of grace"[60]—Dante's poem, in other words, provided a timely response to the spontaneous, widespread growth of the Marian cult.

CREATION, PROCREATION, AND THE VAMPIRE POEM

"(T)he mystery of the Madonna which the cunning Italian intellect flung to the mob of Europe": these are the sarcastic words by which, in "Scylla and Charybdis," Stephen adds blasphemy to heresy to acknowledge, however sarcastically, that *amor matris,* the double genitive expressing the mother's generative power and, simultaneously, the mother's unique power to love and be loved by her progeny, "may be the only true thing in life" (*U* 9.839–43). It is by conjoining the mother in Mallarmé, the virgin in Dante, and the devil in Blake that the Stephen of the vampire poem celebrates an apotheosis of Christ as Jesus as Love as Woman. It is by pairing up in his rhymes the tomb of Christ and the womb of Mary that Stephen reverses the inertia of his journey to Satan, and invests the darkness of his gloomy subject with the brightest light of a poem-to-come.

I can now give a direct answer to the question introduced above apropos of Stephen's "Proteus" meditation. The question was: How does Stephen's approach to poetic creativity relate to Mallarmé's homage to the maternal power to give (back) life even to an aborted poem? Wasn't the example of his mother's self-destructive fecundity sufficient to deter Stephen from all assimilation of the creative power of the poet to a feminine principle of generation? My answer is that the power of (re)generation that Stephen extracts from Dante's *Purgatorio* pertains to a maternity that has nothing to share with Catholic orthodox doctrine and Catholic custom, or with the person of Stephen's mother. May Goulding Dedalus appears as a repellent bride in "Circe," holding "a wreath of faded orangeblossoms and a torn bridal veil." She remains after death what she has always been in the life of her son, the voice of doctrinal conformism: "Beware! . . . Beware God's hand!" (*U* 15.4157–219).

Stephen's inspiration to create a new poem, the so-called vampire poem, comes to him when "noon slumbers" (*U* 3.216) and he, caught in the "faunal noon" of a pagan ecstasy, dreams of his Parisian days. Shortly later, "this burning scene" (3.442) inspires in Stephen warm, optimistic feelings toward the few scribbled lines that he crammed into his pocket. Reassured, perhaps, about his poetic talent, he considers that "pain is far" (3.444)—far is that "pain" that "fretted his heart" at each visitation of the "mute, reproachful" ghost of his mother (1.102–10). The ghost of May Goulding Dedalus is a force repugnant to her son's creative ambitions. But in "Aeolus" the women of Dante bring Stephen back to the optimism of a poetry that can be resurrected in a willful embrace and acceptance of *poíesis* per se, the vital energy of life itself. Just as in Mallarmé's "*L'après-midi d'un faune*," or even in "*L'Azur*," poetry must "go South" to emancipate itself from its haunting phantasms, so poetry must open itself, in the particular case of the vampire poem, to the fecund breeze of the Southern Hemisphere, of Purgatory. And in Dante's Purgatory even the pagan Muses of the divine arts, "the daughters of memory" (*U* 2.7), are "sanctified"; even Calliope, the Muse of epic chant and serene harmonies, is invoked like a goddess, invited to pluck the chords of her lyre with the same words *(alquanto surga,* "let Calliope rise up somewhat" [*Purgatorio* 1.9])[61] by which the gods of Olympus used to invoke her in the days of her unchallenged rule over epic poetry: . . . *surgit . . . Calliope*

... *atque haec percussis subiungit carmina nervis,* Ovid wrote in the *Metamorphoses* [Calliope ... rose ... then boldly struck the chords, ... setting her theme to music].[62]

What prevails in the vampire poem as poem-in-progress, in spite of Blake's infernal theology, is a doctrine of life and resurrection. No Christ without Satan, no Life without Love, no Creation without Woman, no Tomb without Womb. I do not agree with the critics who identify Stephen's vampire as a mere harbinger of death. Stephen's vampire is not Count Dracula, a nightly visitor sucking life away from the living, but Lucifer "allbright" in the multiplicity of his carnal manifestations. "Allbright he falls, proud lightning of the intellect. *Lucifer, dico, qui nescit occasum*" (*U* 3.486–87). At the close of "Proteus," Stephen cites this Latin phrase from the Catholic service for the Easter vigil. It translates as, "The morning star, I say, who knows no setting," and it is uttered in praise of the paschal candle, 'acclaiming the light of the risen Christ.'" As Don Gifford points out in *Ulysses Annotated,* however, "the morning star sometimes refers to Christ—'I [Jesus] am ... the bright and morning star' (Revelation 22:16)—and sometimes to Satan—'How art thou fallen from heaven, O Lucifer, son of the morning' (Isaiah 14:12)" (65). Furthermore, as one learns from the impersonal narrator's voice in "Oxen of the Sun," in the morning hours at the end of *Ulysses* this symbolically ubiquitous star is the embryolike guest of the House of Virgo: "And lo, wonder of metempsychosis, it is she, the everlasting bride, harbinger of the daystar, the bride, ever virgin" (*U* 14.1099–101). Drowned in sunlight, the star of Christ-Satan is meant to die, at the close of Joyce's novel, in the Virgin's "allwombing tomb."

Just as the ethereal, bi-gendered Christ Triumphant and Pantocrater of the *Divine Comedy* is inconceivable to the modern Christian ethos without the agony of the Cross and the carnality of the Immaculate Conception, so Jesus's incarnation of love supreme, in the celestial personae of Beatrice and Mary, is inconceivable to Stephen without Christ's absolute kenosis, without the unconditional self-effacement of Christ's Passion. God must die in sin and become Satan before love supreme may be fully incarnated in a mortal woman. In Stephen's quest for true poetic *lógos,* no grace is possible without the freedom to fall, no creation is possible without the doubt of despair, yet freedom, grace, and creation are the poet's goal and offering, and not the negation thereof. Stephen's vampire, then, is sin incarnate in Jesus, the condition itself of Christ's absolute kenosis. Stephen's vampire is evil incarnate in em*bodied* grace, grace turned sensual and mortal, the "proud lightning of the intellect" that falls at the climax of Christ's triumph over death. Stephen's vampire is not the dark, opaque, monochromatic Prince of Darkness, but, rather, "Darkinbad the Brightdayler" (*U* 17.2329–30), "a darkness shining in brightness" (*U* 2.160). And this is a difference, in the matter of poetic ethos, that makes all the difference in the world.

4

The Reluctant Son: Satire of the Epics and Tragedies of Lineage in "Scylla and Charybdis"

> I have reached nearly the end of the Wembley dinner party
> [i.e., a gathering of Weaver relatives and family connections].
> The tangential relationships, the spiral progressions, and the
> presence of the absent remind me of something which per-
> haps I wrote or ought to have written.
> —James Joyce to Harriet S. Weaver, 30 July 1924

"SCYLLA AND CHARYBDIS" TURNS *ULYSSES,* MORE EFFECTIVELY THAN
any other episode, into a satire of the Homeric and scriptural
epics and of the Attic tragedies of consanguinity and lineage.
Although an abundance of parodic materials may be identified
in this episode, the Joycean satire does not amount to a mere
parody. Parody is, rather, the competence of the protagonist,
Stephen Dedalus; in his teasing lucubrations in front of an audience composed of real Dublin intellectuals as well as fictional
characters, Stephen engages in a pastiche of "preformed linguistic or artistic materials"—such as, for instance, the Shakespear-
ian device of the play-within-the-play, the critical devices of
biographic exegesis, even the maieutic devices of the Platonic
dialogue—whose parodic intentions are evident.

In *Parody: Ancient, Modern, and Post-modern,* Margaret
Rose identifies in the practice of "imitation, distortion, or quotation" of other literary forms and/or texts the factor that confines
the reach and effectiveness of parody to the literary realm.[1] One
might say, with Tuvia Shlonsky, that it pertains to satire, rather
than to parody, to mock the literary so as to hit the extraliterary
target of the sociopolitical.[2] Or one might say that parody exhibits a literary agenda, satire an extraliterary one. Agency, how-

75

ever, is rarely discussed as an aspect of the difference between parody and satire. In this chapter I will show that one finds a fundamental separation in agency in the distinct style of Stephen's parody of preformed literary devices and of James Joyce's satire of the classic epics and tragedies of consanguinity and lineage.

This is not the place for an exhaustive illustration of the overall theoretical implications of this thesis, but it is important for the present discussion to understand the specific relationship between the agency of literary parody, for which the fictional character, Stephen Dedalus, is used, and the agency of sociopolitical satire, which is pertinent to the text (or to the author, if you will), but not to its protagonist. In "Scylla and Charybdis," in sum, Stephen *parodies* the rhetoric of the playwright, the critic, and the philosopher, so that Joyce, the author, let us not forget, of the parody itself, may *satirize* the classic literary treatments of consanguinity and lineage.

One can find already in *A Portrait of the Artist as a Young Man* a capability for parody, on the part of Stephen Dedalus, that corresponds to a satiric impulse on the part of James Joyce. Stephen's "refunctioning" of the aesthetic of Thomas Aquinas, for instance, consists of a parodic revisitation of the most prominent Christian theology of the thirteenth century. But the text's satiric purpose goes beyond this. It indulges in a sociopolitical satire of the pedagogic appropriation of Aquinas on the part of the Jesuits at the end of the nineteenth century. In this case, Stephen's "applied Aquinas" (*Portrait* 209) functions as a generic constant through time, easily apprehensible as parody by readers of any period. Joyce's satire, instead, exhibits a temporal fluidity; its sociopolitical implications change according to historical variations in the factors that, through a modification of the aesthetics of reception of different times and places, variously affect the readers' response to the text. The apprehension of the motif underlying the satiric impulse is not constant through time; it is determined to a considerable extent by extraliterary considerations. So, as an extreme but fundamental example, one's response to the satirical implications of Stephen's parody of Aquinas cannot help being influenced by the suspicion that the satiric intent was gradually transformed in Joyce's own apprehension of *A Portrait of the Artist as a Young Man*, a transformation commensurate with the growing impatience demonstrated by the author of *Ulysses* toward the immaturity of his young alter ego.[3]

THE CLASSIC THEME OF LINEAGE AND CONSANGUINITY

In constituting genealogy as the essential theme of its satire, "Scylla and Charybdis" engages in an epicene treatment of those timeless subjects—gender, procreation, and lineage—whose narration among the ancients provided a fundamental contribution to the shaping of the epic and tragic genre, as the two privileged media of circulation for genealogical chronicles and etiological tales. It should be noted right away, to distinguish between the literary and extraliterary agendas pertinent, respectively, to the parody and satire of "Scylla and Charybdis," that most ancient etiological tales are indistinguishable from genealogical chronicles—they share, structurally speaking, the same formal encoding and the same conventions of intelligibility.[4] Suffice it to mention the archaic origins of the prohibition of fratricide intimated in the biblical story of Cain and Abel; the archaic origins of the prohibition of incest intimated in the story of the cursed bloodline of Oedipus and his mother Jocasta, as told by Sophocles in *Oedipus the King, Oedipus at Colonus,* and *Antigone;* and the archaic origins of the prohibition of cannibalism, of human sacrifice, and of matricide intimated in the downfall of the House of Atreus, as told by Aeschylus in the trilogy of the *Oresteia.* A majority among the fictions—legends and myths—that fabulate the aberrations of primitive genealogies, in other words, tell the extraliterary story of the origins of communal laws, norms, and civilized customs. "Scylla and Charybdis" may be said to accomplish an analogous service for the benefit of our modern notions of family and procreation.

It is in "Scylla and Charybdis" that Stephen Dedalus's objection, before a rather skeptical audience, to all simplistic identifications of Shakespeare, the artist, with Hamlet, the fictional creature, allows him to imply his own parthenogenetic identity, as an artist, with both the creator, the creature, and the act of creation, with the father, the son, and their inception. It is here, also, in the course of Stephen's quasi-monologue, that the tower of Elsinore, as the emblematic stage of all tales of transmission of an ancestral line—from the downfall of Esau to the triumph of Telemachus and including the tragedies of Oedipus, Orestes, and Hamlet (an imposing collection of firstborn sons whose fate is commemorated by Stephen)—is turned into the scene where the modern homonymy of father and son entails a sinister and, at once, satirical equivocation of identity.

Simon and Stephen Dedalus, King Hamlet and Prince Hamlet
. . . It is symptomatic that the ancestral identification inherent
in the father's and son's sharing of the same patronymic starts
crumbling, in *Ulysses,* from the very first "Hamletic" word of its
first episode, "Telemachus": just as "stately" is the royal comportment of the ghost of Hamlet's father in his first apparition to
Horatio,[5] so it is "(s)tately" that Buck Mulligan, Stephen's nemesis, emerges from the stairhead of the Martello Tower, at the
opening of *Ulysses* (1.1). Arguably, this is a deliberate equivocation on Joyce's part, which raises the curtain upon the least
likely parody of the battle for legitimate succession fought upon
and around the tower of Elsinore. Furthermore, Buck Mulligan,
the "usurper" of the Martello tower, Ireland's "gay betrayer,"
proves eventually to be only the subordinate foil to his British
friend, Haines, the real usurper, Ireland's "conqueror." Carrying,
à la King Henry II, "an emerald set in the ring of the sea," this
young Englishman is the metonymic personification of "the seas'
ruler," the British usurper of Ireland's independence. When, in
the "Proteus" episode, the Homeric epithet "Old Father Ocean"
will float to the surface of Stephen's inner monologue, it will
apply first and foremost to Haines, as Proteus, the divine shepherd of seals.[6] Indeed, in the Homeric archetype the battle for
legitimate succession is fought on the sea, among "(t)he
whitemaned seahorses, . . . the steeds of Mananaan" (*U* 3.56–7).[7]
One *can* overcome those steeds, those foam-crested waves, especially if one, like Telemachus, strives and succeeds in answering
the emblematic question of patriarchal lineage: Are you the son
of your father?[8] But one will more likely than not be drowned
under those waves' fury, in the "salt green death" of their maternal curse (*U* 10.877)—especially if one (as does Stephen, the
reluctant son) resigns oneself to being "not his father's son," as
the little old man from Cork insinuates in *A Portrait of the
Artist as a Young Man* (94), and as Stephen himself implies
in his exchange with the "mariner" in the "Eumaeus" episode
of *Ulysses*:

> —You know Simon Dedalus? (the sailor) asked at length.
> —I've heard of him, Stephen said. (16.378–79)

The equivocation of identity promoted by Stephen's reluctant
filial condition is aggravated by the frequent intrusion in the
book of the ghost of Stephen's mother, May Goulding, whose
visitations—an evident reversal of Hamlet's predicament, and

an evident parallel, too, to Orestes' persecution by the Furies—
never fail to bring Stephen extreme emotional distress. In "Telemachus," May Goulding all but appropriates to her ghost the
paternal attributes of the ocean, by distorting them into a "snotgreen ... scrotumtightening ... green mass of liquid." "*Thalatta! Thalatta!* She is our great sweet mother," proclaims Buck
Mulligan, turned Xenophon (1.78–80, 108).[9] And in "Scylla and
Charybdis," in the middle of his arbitrary superposition of
Shakespeare's and Hamlet's genealogies, Stephen throws in his
own maternal bloodline by confusing Richard, Shakespeare's
brother, with his own "nuncle Richie" (Richard Goulding,
brother of May) and by identifying in the vaguely incestuous
image of the "lump of love," Crissie Goulding, his mother's niece
(3.76, 88), and Lizzie (Elizabeth) Hall, daughter of Susanna
Shakespeare and Shakespeare's first grandchild (9.1039). But it
would be a mistake to translate Stephen's obsession with the
premature death of his mother into the view, maintained by
Christine Froula in "Mothers of Invention/Doaters of Inversion,"
that Stephen aims at modeling his artistic creativity upon maternal creativity.[10] As shown in chapter 3, the Irish-Catholic type
of maternal creativity is intolerable to Stephen. As to the specific
aesthetic aim pursued by Stephen in "Scylla and Charybdis," one
could hardly overstress the fact that in this episode the pursuit
of artistic creativity takes the place of a battle for primogeniture;
patrilineal primacy and self-affirmation are at stake in both.
However reluctant a son to his father Simon, however inadequate an heir to the name (diphthong apart) of the artificer of
Minos's labyrinth, Stephen aims at mastering a creativity that
will enable him to *father* his own artistic self, a new incorporeal
self indifferent to the laws of nature and the constraints of
fertility.

INCEST AND LINEAGE IN SCRIPTURE

In the words of Buck Mulligan—words whose purposive meaning transcends, as I will show, the intentions of the utterer—
Stephen Dedalus, the ghost ("shade") of Simon Dedalus ("Kinch
the elder"), is a "Japhet in search of a father" (*U* 1.560–61). Apart
from the thematic implication that can be attributed to Buck's
insinuation—in *Ulysses* Stephen represents, after all, the modernist incarnation of a hydrophobic Telemachus in search of a
father, and how many glosses have been devoted indeed to en-

dowing Leopold Bloom with Odysseus-like attributes!—what I want to stress here is the ambiguity inherent in Buck's choice of epithet: Japhet, Noah's second-born son, as the biblical parallel for Stephen, Simon's firstborn son. This ambiguity acquires enormous thematic relevance when one contrasts it with Stephen's consideration, in an interior monologue occurring shortly before Buck's insinuation, that he is "a server of a servant" (*U* 1.311–12). The conventional Hamletic interpretation of Stephen's thought establishes Haines as the British master, Buck as his gay attendant, and Stephen as the jester, the docile subject to the whims of both. Another equally conventional reading equates the "servant" served by Stephen with the second of the "two masters, . . . an English and an Italian," that Stephen, toward the end of "Telemachus," declares himself to be the servant of (*U* 1.638): I am referring to the Roman Catholic pontifex, who is notoriously fond of describing himself as a "servant in Christ."

But I want to engage presently in a third, "scriptural" approach, that sets at play an exegetic reverberation between Buck's epithet and Stephen's dismaying view of himself as a double servant. This scriptural approach will show that Stephen and Buck are remarkably attuned in their choice of a derogatory epithet, when it comes to designating Stephen's filial abjection. If Buck sees Stephen as Japhet, Stephen sees himself, rather, as Japhet's younger brother, Ham, the "server of a servant" whose fate of servitude, as we are going to see, incorporates a cluster of secondary connotations that help define Stephen's filial condition in "Scylla and Charybdis."

In Genesis 9:27, Ham is cursed by his father Noah to become a slave both to his brother Shem, blessed by Noah with the privileges of primogeniture, and to his brother Japhet, assigned by Noah the privilege of "dwell(ing) in Shem's tents." An obvious hierarchy is established between the master, Shem, his immediate subordinate, Japhet, and Ham, a server to both. In this light, Buck's insinuation that Stephen is "a Japhet" may be taken to operate retrospectively as an interpretive key vis-à-vis Stephen's cryptic self-identification with "a server of a servant." We are dealing here, as often in *Ulysses,* with a spread of several simultaneous meanings: besides being the jester at the court of the British Monarch and the prelate by the Holy See in Rome, Stephen sees himself also as the intemperate son, the slave by the tent of the Hebrew patriarch. A caustic scriptural pun may be heard to resonate from Stephen's thoughts. I venture that for once Stephen's Hamletic irresolution anticipates Buck's wit: in his interior monologue Stephen is already contemplating his abdication from Shem's primacy (his willing renunciation, that is, to his own right of primogeniture in the Dedalus family), not so much in order to acquire Japhet's intermediate condition as to debase himself to the abject condition of Ham. Self-debasement, let us not forget, is one of Stephen's favorite predispositions in "Scylla and Charybdis"; suffice it to mention his later identification with Osric, the servile and inane courtesan, the "lapwing" despised by Hamlet and his good friend Horatio (*Hamlet* V.ii.170–77; *U* 9.954, 976, 980). But how does Ham's fate of servitude contribute to the definition of Stephen's filial condition in "Scylla and Charybdis"? And what is the part played by Ham's proverbial sin against his father in the articulation of this condition?

Ham's sin against fatherhood goes far beyond the conventional interpretation of an impure gaze at Noah's genitals or the rape of Noah's women. The list of all the possible combinations of incestous partners delivered by Moses in Leviticus 18, 20, and Deuteronomy 23 reveals how any sexual act between consanguineous partners—any "uncovering of the nakedness" of a family member, as the Scripture phrases it—constitutes a symbolic reversal, and a repetition as well, of the primordial incest, perpetrated by the father on his firstborn. Ham's crime, whatever its factual nature (he may have violated one or some of his father's women, be they his mother, his sisters, or Noah's concubines, or as maintained in the treatise Sanhedrin of the Talmud, he may even have raped his own father, for all this cryptic episode allows a reader to infer),[11] involved a symbolic reversal of this primal biblical incest. I have argued elsewhere, in polemic against the Freudian theory of the Oedipus complex, that this originary incest established, through a violent rape, the father's primacy over his male heir.[12] It consisted of the brutal primal scene that affirmed the legitimacy of the firstborn as his father's successor through the filial acquisition of—to paraphrase a felicitous expression applied by Derrida to the Christian dogma of consubstantiality—"familiarity ... with his own semen."[13] Therefore, any of the incestuous acts legislated against in Leviticus and Deuteronomy amounts, ultimately, to a symbolic rebellion against the primacy of the father. Any incest, in other words, constitutes a symbolic *uncovering of the nakedness of the father,* a rape perpetrated, this time, at the expense of the father. One of the most typical examples of this symbolic reversal is found precisely in the tale of Ham's filial "disrespect," in Genesis 9:20–27.

If he cannot be a Shem, Stephen wants to be Shem's little brother, Ham. In *Ulysses,* Stephen gradually renounces to his alternate impersonation of two emblematic firstborn sons: Icarus, the youth exposed to the frightful secrets of the mythical maker of the labyrinth, "whose name he bore out of his captivity on osierwoven wings" (*Portrait* 224–25), and Telemachus, the mythical epitome of genealogical legitimacy, the son whom Odysseus conceived in a bed *rooted* in the ground of his homeland.[14] He slowly but inexorably turns himself into a reluctant son, the cursed, unwelcome guest at the banquet of primogeniture and legitimate descent: Ham, the sexually intemperate son who fights the battle for primogeniture against his own father, with his phallus rather than with his sword, but also, as "Scylla and Charybdis" does not fail to intimate persistently, Ham-let, the procrastinator who fails to claim his rights of blood because his father neglected, or was unable, to brand him with the "mystical estate," the "apostolic succession" of his ancestral line (*U* 9.835). As often as not in *Ulysses,* the stone of intertextuality kills several birds at once.

Incidentally, my semantic and exegetic elaborations on Ham's and Hamlet's names find a textual echo in "Lestrygonians," where Leopold Bloom jocularly reflects that Ham's breeding gives birth to edible "descendants" as "potted meats" (*U* 8.742). It is well known that Joyce's wit had the power to ennoble the basest of puns.

THE LAW OF PATRILINEAL DESCENT

Stephen Dedalus as the reluctant son. Telemachus as the son rooted in the consanguinity of a genealogical tree. Orestes as the son persecuted by his mother's Furies. Ham as the intemperate son, violator of his own father. Hamlet, an apprehensive incarnation of little Ham, the father-hater, and of Orestes, the mother-killer, as the irresolute son who fails to claim what belongs to him by right of blood. With the exception of Odysseus' only son, the victorious Telemachus, this is a magnificent catalogue of discarded links in the incorporeal line of paternal descent. Bear with me some more: "Mystical" and "apostolic" succession, rather than consanguineous descent, as the fundamental event of patrilineal genealogy. Patrilineal genealogy, finally, as the parthenogenetic inbreeding by which the father-author generates infinite duplications of himself.[15] I have here all the elements to demonstrate my proposition: Genealogy in "Scylla and Charybdis" consists of a satire of our archaic traditions of consanguinity and lineage.

Telemachus and Odysseus, Orestes and Agamemnon, Ham and Noah, Hamlet Junior and Senior, as well as Stephen and Simon Dedalus, are (as Stephen himself would put it) ". . . sundered by a bodily shame so steadfast that the criminal annals of the world, stained with all other incests and bestialities, hardly record its breach. Sons with mothers, sires with daughters, lesbic sisters, lovers that dare not speak their name, nephews with grandmothers, jailbirds with keyholes, queens with prize bulls" (U 9.850–54). The above passage from "Scylla and Charybdis" plays a fundamental role in my anti-Oedipal interpretation of the tale of Ham's downfall. In this passage Stephen illustrates in a progressively comic diction the incestuous character of patrilineal genealogy, a denunciation that may be taken as a further confirmation of the cross-reference—external to Buck's intention, yet reflective of Joyce's satiric purpose—that may be established between Buck's insinuation that Stephen was "a Japhet" and Stephen's meditation that he was, rather, Ham, "a server of a servant."

The "bodily shame" that Stephen attaches to ancestral lineage does not pertain, to be sure, to the "common 'transgression' of the mother's sex"—the father-son complicitous experience of a bodily crossing, in and out, in intercourse and in birth, of the mother's womb—that Jean-Michel Rabaté relates to "the Oedipal pattern" of this passage.[16] It pertains, rather, to the anti-Oedipal symbology of the primal incest—that androcentric "avarice of the emotions" (U 9.781) which, just as its ritualistic translation by the Abrahamic norm of circumcision[17] or its legalistic codification into the Western tradition of patronymic transmission, grounds patrilineal genealogy upon the exclusive "imposition" of filial identity with the father, a filial "familiarity with his own semen."

A symbolic murder is at play all right in the primal scene of patrilineal succession, but it is the murder perpetrated by the father upon the son; it consists of the father's *mortification* and submission to his own sexual whim of his firstborn's virility. This symbolic murder is celebrated in the name of God, of course, the perpetuation of whose "offsprung," to use the polysemantic diction of *Finnegans Wake,* goes hand in hand with the perpetration of a Miltonian *felix culpa* and the petrification, or monumentalization, of the male side only of the line of consanguinity (*FW* 23.16, 23.30).

AMOR MATRIS

In his quasi-monologue at the National Library Stephen opposes *amor matris,* as the timeless double genitive that denotes (which "may be," he posits) "the only true thing in life," to paternity, as the status of legitimacy that denotes (which, again, "may be") "a legal fiction," a *fictio* of kinship, in the tradition, as we are going to see shortly, of ancient Roman jurisprudence(*U* 9.842–43).[18] Of course, *amor matris* denotes also the unreliability of a lineage whose seminal integrity only the mother may testify to, as suggested by Telemachus's sarcastic answer to Athena's inquiry about his paternal ascent,[19] while the legal fiction of paternity denotes the diffusion of all genealogical uncertainty through the normative mode of a legal discourse. Stephen's opposition of the truth of mother love, despite its genealogical uncertainty, with the fiction of paternity, founded upon the normative certainty of a legal construct, is pertinent to an age-old debate whose origins, thanks to Joyce's familiarity with and admiration for Giambattista Vico's studies of ancient civilizations, can be traced back to the infancy of jurisprudence. This opposition entails the separation between the physiological fact of maternal conception and the incorporeal (mystical and apostolic, in the diction of "Scylla and Charybdis") legitimacy of patronymic succession.

According to Vico, legal fictions, or *iura imaginaria,* are operative at the very outset of Roman jurisprudence. The early unwritten legal codes of the Romans consisted of a mystical theology (*teologia mistica*), of "rights as fabled by fantasy," in the sense that it pertained to the *patresfamilias* to define communal norms and regulations through oracular interpretation of divine auspices (Vico, *CI2* § 20–21, *SNS2* § 937–941). This mysticism, this theological fabulation of the law, paralleled the mysticism inherent in the transmission of the privileges of lineage. Only the patrician father had the authority to turn his son into a *filius* (a man entitled to the interpretation of the divine auspices) by passing on to him, together with his patronymic and his estate, the rights and duties of the *vir,* the individual whose civil status is dignified by law (*SNS1* § 526–30, 568, *SNS2*

§ 985–86). It is evident that *amor matris* pertains to a different order of discourse, that of the genetic bond of consanguinity. For the patrician head of the family, the authenticity of fatherhood emanates from his juridical right to impose a surname and legal status upon his firstborn son; the patrician *mater* plays no relevant role in this transmission. It is the social figure of the plebeian mother, the *mulier,* rather than that of the patrician *mater,*[20] who defines the authenticity inherent in a manner of reproduction antagonistic to the normative certainty of *teologia mistica.* Legally incapable of giving birth to a juridical person, the plebeian *mulier* is empowered by nature to give life to a *spurius*—a natural living being, a *homo,* whose deliverance is "established with certainty" according to the law of nature (*natura certo pariunt*) (*CI2* § 21, 37). With no name or estate to pass along to the future generations, the maternity of the *genitor* is an end in itself, justified by love only—analogous to that unconditional sort of love that the reader encounters twice in *Ulysses,* first in the devotion of Cyril Sargent's mother and then in the pure faith of the "motherlight" in the eyes of Mina Purefoy (2.142–43, 165–66, 14.1316).

The attribution of truthfulness to the mother's love rather than to the father's law, to the dedication and generosity of the flesh rather then to the normative control of the spirit, betrays a disconsolate if temporary surrender to the bodily power of maternal creativity on the part of Stephen, a youth whose every action, imbued with intellectual ratiocination, imaginative vigor, emotional susceptibility, shows only condescension toward the "lust" and ribaldry of the flesh (*U* 14.227). The emotional strain betrayed by Stephen's words of praise for *amor matris* is especially relevant if one considers the Hamletic misogyny Stephen repeatedly vents in "Scylla and Charybdis."[21] Long since has Stephen given up his adolescent dream of "meet(ing) in the real world the unsubstantial image which his soul so constantly beheld." Long since has Stephen given up his wait for the Eucharistic "moment of supreme tenderness" in which the encounter with the woman of his ideal love would help him shed, in a climax of love-induced transubstantiation, all "(w)eakness and timidity and inexperience" (*Portrait* 65). In "Scylla and Charybdis" Stephen undertakes, instead, the desperate and futile attempt to reconfigure paternity as a fantastic act of self-sufficient, gender-autarchic creation and reconception. "(I)n the economy of heaven, foretold by Hamlet," he remarks, in a daring alliance of Hamlet's uxorophobia and Matthew's depiction of

man's self-sufficient condition after the apocalyptic resurrection
of the flesh (22.30), "there are no more marriages, glorified man,
an androgynous angel, being a wife unto himself" (*U* 9.1051–52).
Yet, as I mentioned, this effort is constantly obstructed by Stephen's inability to reconcile androcentric creativity with the
feminine power to (pro)create.

CONSANGUINITY AND PATRILINEALITY

To the extent that in "Scylla and Charybdis" he opposes the
physiology of maternal conception to the legal imposition of the
patronymic, Stephen hits dead center upon the dialectic of segregation that informs the duality of nature and culture in genealogy; in the tradition of Western jurisprudence—a tradition,
rooted in ancient Roman jurisprudence, which is paradoxically
reflected, as we will see, in the scriptural narration of Jesus'
genealogical tree—the patronymic comes to symbolize the origin
before one's genetic origin, the family history before the history
of one's conception, the societal mark that obscures the marks
and traits of consanguinity one receives in the maternal womb.
Stephen hits the discursive target of this thematic dead center,
only to beat a strategic retreat into the thematic of art as self-
gestation and self-procreation, whose androgynous, parthenogenetic character seems to leave him far more comfortable than
the issue of gender difference in (pro)creation.

At first Stephen engages the issue of genealogy from the theological perspective of the Church dogma of the Father-Son
consubstantiality:[22]

> Fatherhood, in the sense of conscious begetting, is unknown to man.
> It is a mystical estate, an apostolic succession, from only begetter to
> only begotten. On that mystery and not on the madonna which the
> cunning Italian intellect flung to the mob of Europe the church is
> founded and founded ... upon the void. Upon incertitude, upon
> unlikelihood. *Amor matris,* subjective and objective genitive, may
> be the only true thing in life. Paternity may be a legal fiction. ....
> Sabellius, the African, subtlest heresiarch ... held that the Father
> was Himself His Own Son. (*U* 9.836–44, 862)

But the recognition of the "mystical" (indeed, narrative, legal,
and theological at once) construct behind Christ's paternal lineage entails a menace to the primacy of his own gender that

triggers Stephen's sexual anxiety. He promptly confounds the issue, therefore, by magnifying beyond measure the "authorial" connotations inherent in the paternal act of creation:

> When Rutlandbaconsouthamptonshakespeare or another poet of the same name in the comedy of errors wrote *Hamlet* he was not the father of his own son merely but ... he was and felt himself the father of all his race, the father of his own grandfather, the father of his unborn grandson. (U 9.865–69)

Patrilineality is indeed incompatible with a process of procreation that does not legitimize itself through some sort of grandiose gender-exclusive refabulation of the past. And the need for this refabulation (which consists, more often than not, of a mystical mystification) appears as complementary to the institution of a genealogical tree capable of extending its branches into the farthest future. Matthew's recapitulation of Jesus' ascendancy at the *incipit* of his Gospel is an emblematic example of this point:

> Abraham was the father of Isaac, and Isaac the father of Jacob, and Jacob the father of Judah and his brothers, and Judah the father of Perez and Zerah ... and Obed the father of Jesse, and Jesse the father of David the king. And David was the father of Solomon ... And after the deportation to Babylon: Jechoni'ah was the father of She-al'ti-el ... and Matthan the father of Jacob, and Jacob the father of Joseph the husband of Mary, of whom Jesus was born, who is called Christ. (Matthew 1.2–16)

As we saw in chapter 2, the genealogy illustrated in Matthew 1.2–16 implies the substitution of circumcision, i.e., the contractual token of *paternal* consanguinity, for the physiological norm of *parental* blood purity. The ritual of circumcision imposes a gender-exclusive normative of legitimacy upon the discursive (re)fabrication of the history of genealogy; it invests the physiological *fact* of the bodily event of procreation with its ritual and contractual, patriarchal *sense*. And so it is that one must reconcile Matthew's majestic genealogical tree, which touches the heavens at the moment of the advent of the Son of God, with the fact that his vicarious father, Joseph, provides Jesus with the identity of an ancestral lineage that, although rooted in the blood of the patriarchs, depends ultimately upon a chaste event of maternal inception. *The germ of legitimate fatherhood is not the father's semen.* The "mystical estate" of fatherhood is indeed the mystification of an "apostolic succession," from the Father to the Son and his Vicar and Pontifex, "Peter Piscator" (*U* 14.304).

Simon and Stephen Dedalus are, quite ironically, linked in their identity not so much by a bloodline as by what John's Gospel calls "the Word." In fact, Kevin Egan, the Paris exile who, in *Ulysses,* personifies the Fenian Joseph Casey, identifies Stephen from the paternal attribute of his voice. "You're your father's son. I know the voice" (*U* 3.229). This recognition occurs, appropriately enough, in the "Proteus" episode, which corresponds, in the Homeric structure of *Ulysses,* to book 4 of the *Odyssey,* where Helen and Menelaos recognize Telemachus from his paternal attributes (IV.138–54). This explains why Stephen is "tired of (his) voice" (*U* 9.981)—the voice of Esau, the voice that in Genesis 27.22 does not keep Isaac from falling prey to Jacob's deception and blessing him with his older brother's birthright. It explains also why Stephen does not respond too warmly to Bloom's suggestion, in the "Ithaca" episode, that he should cultivate his tenor voice as a means of personal affirmation (17.963–64). On the contrary, at the sound of Bloom's own "profound ancient male" voice Stephen is quick to visualize himself as "the traditional figure of hypostasis" (17.776–84): the figure of the *stasis,* of the unity-in-strife, that lies under (*hypo*) Jesus' two contradictory natures, the divine and the human, and two divergent genealogical trees, the paternal and the maternal, the normative and the physiological.[23]

Incidentally, hypostasis plays such a significant role in Leopold Bloom's genealogical tree that, at the cost of a small digression, it cannot be neglected in this chapter. A Modernist reincarnation of Odysseus, Bloom is the descendant of a farcical river of consanguinity evidently modeled upon the genealogical tree from Matthew's Gospel:

Leopoldi autem generation. Moses begat Noah and Noah begat Eunuch and Eunuch begat O'Halloran and O'Halloran begat Guggenheim and Guggenheim begat Agendath and Agendath begat Netaim and Netaim begat Le Hirsch ... and Aranjuez begat Lewy Lawson and Lewy Lawson begat Ichabudonosor and Ichabudonosor begat O'Donnell Magnus and O'Donnell Magnus begat Christbaum and Christbaum begat ben Maimun and ben Maimun begat Dusty Rhodes ... and Szombathely begat Virag and Virag begat Bloom *et vocabitur nomen eius Emmanuel.* (*U* 15.1851–69)

As it gives shelter to a hilarious variety of races and nationalities, this travesty of Bloom's lineage manages to silence, to cross out, a fundamental moment in the genealogy of the Messiah. I am referring to that moment which the last five (italicized) words of the above passage point expressly at, namely, the maternal usurpation of patriarchal primacy entailed by the immaculate conception. It is not by chance that Leopold Bloom's mother, Ellen Higgins, appears in only one significant scene of *Ulysses;* this is when her ghost emerges out of the hallucinations undergone by her son in the red-light district, a funny-looking lady whose speech is addressed, rather blasphemously, to the "Sacred Heart *of Mary*" (*U* 15.280–90, my emphasis). Contrary to May Goulding's frequent inauspicious apparitions in *Ulysses,* only one apparition is reserved to Ellen Higgins, but it is rendered memorable by the words uttered by this maternal ghost—laconic words that reverse the (Sabellian) identification of Father and Son, a factor crucial to the order of patrilineality, into a disconcerting homonymy between the Son, Jesus, to whom obviously pertains the cult of the Sacred Heart, and his Mother, Mary. Which homonymy may be assimilated also to Dante's *coincidentia* of Christ and Mary in *Paradiso,* one of the fundamental motifs, discussed in chapter 3, that stimulate Stephen's composition of the vampire poem.

Epic and Tragedy, Parody and Satire

Tinged with sacrilegious overtones, Joyce's satire of the epics and tragedies of lineage resonates of a subdued and bitter laughter. Its blasphemy shares only a partial affinity with the sheer comedy of parody. If we take genre, as I suggested earlier in reference to Deborah Madsen's recapitulation of structuralist theories, to be the formal encoding that assigns conventions of intelligibility to a given discourse, then it is important to remark that Joyce's epicene treatment of gender, procreation, consanguinity, and lineage in "Scylla and Charybdis" is intelligible primarily as satire, rather than as parody; it is endowed with a sociopolitical agenda that, in ridiculing the target of its criticism, obscures to a partial extent the comic effects of the parody. Comic is, strictly speaking, Buck's intervention at the *Entr'acte* of Stephen's quasi-monologue, a genuine "intermission," which Stephen's nemesis opens by referring to the ghost of King Hamlet as the "gaseous vertebrate" (9.484–88). Buck's jocular lines offer a caustic counterpoint meant to turn Stephen's multifaceted parody into a triviality. Irresistibly comic, also, is Buck's parody-within-Stephen's-parody: ". . . I am big with child. I have an unborn child in my brain. Pallas Athena! A play! The play's the thing! Let me parturiate!" (9.875–77)—an evident allusion to Hamlet's conception of the play-within-the-play (II.ii.571) by which Buck manages to cover with ridicule Stephen's ambition to father his own artistic self.

Yet, even in the middle of Buck's carefree tirade, and notwithstanding the much-needed comic relief it provides to the mock gravity of the episode, one's attention is insistently drawn back to the text's sociopolitical agenda. A soon as one recognizes the ideological and cross-cultural implications of Buck's analogy between Athena's birth and artistic "parturition," the preeminence of the satirical over the parodic purpose of this episode becomes obvious.

Buck's jocular lines, in fact, all but utter the word that Stephen, in his maieutic, Phaemerate-like effort[24] to tease an understanding out of his reluctant audience, refuses to pronounce throughout his quasi-monologue. Pallas Athena, the promoter, in Aeschylus's *Eumenides,* of Orestes' exculpation in the trial for his mother's murder, was known to the Greeks with the epithet: *parthenos,* "virgin"—the virgin goddess whose delivery is parthenogenetically accomplished from the brain of her father, Zeus. Parthenogenesis, the core concept of Stephen's gender-exclusive theory of artistic creativity, is explicitly addressed in the text thanks to the least respectful among Stephen's skeptical listeners. If one adds to this pagan dimension of divine parthenogenesis the consideration that the colossal statue of Pallas Athena situated at the Parthenon in Athens represented the goddess with a snake at her feet, a motif obsessively reclaimed by the Christian iconology of the Virgin Mary, one comprehends that Buck's joviality, punctuated with an alternation of references to the pagan and Christian worlds, functions as a vehicle for the sociopolitical and cross-cultural criticism indispensable to the satiric aim of the episode. "Jehovah, collector of prepuces, is no more" (9.609). Once again, we detect in Buck's caustic pronouncement the trace of authorial intentions external to the character's awareness. The satire of "Scylla and Charybdis" has reached its mordant climax. The reader is confronted with the possibility that the Catholic tradition of the immaculate conception derives its essential paradigm from the rigorously patriarchal legacy of polytheism.[25] Stephen's sexism is but a feeble foil to this millennial conspiracy.

In conclusion, I will suggest that the revisitation of the classic theme of lineage and consanguinity undertaken in "Scylla and Charybdis" sets the stage for the "tootoolog(y)" of tolerance and gender desegregation that will be inaugurated in *Finnegans Wake.* It is not accidental that the most refined treatment offered in *Ulysses* of the notion of hypostasis is found in "Oxen of the Sun," the episode that may be taken as the closest stylistic and thematic prefiguration of *Finnegans Wake,* for it is in *Finnegans Wake* that one must search for a clue to the sociopolitical agenda behind Joyce's satire. "In woman's womb word is made flesh," Stephen concedes in his drunken stupor at the National Maternity Hospital, where most of "Oxen of the Sun" takes place. But then, typically, he promptly subverts this apparent surrender to the carnal creativity of the Virgin Mary with a subtle doctrinal disclaimer: ". . . but in the spirit of the maker all flesh that passes becomes the word that shall not pass away. This is the postcreation. *Omnis caro ad te veniet*" (14.292–94). This is, one might say, theo-gynecology.

Stephen is referring to the cosmic extinction of procreation that corresponds to the Apocalypse, the end of human history announced in the Old and New Testament, when the "anastomosis of navelcords" (14.300) that feeds maternal blood into the sap of humankind's genealogical tree will be abruptly broken, the Virgin Mother will be given new birth as *figlia di (suo) figlio,* "daughter of (her) son" (14.302), and finally, "all flesh" (*omnis caro*) will come back to its Maker and coalesce into the unity of the Word—a moment of universal significance (and of controversial doctrinal interpretation) that the Stephen of "Proteus," immersed in the stream of consciousness that sets in play the basic compositional elements of his vampire poem, had already set in a relation of correspondence with the "wet sign" of woman's "moondrawn" menses (3.395–96). Stephen does not know how to keep the godlike potency of genuine creativity—the autarchic, gender-exclusive moment of divine parthenogenesis—separate from the spring of female fecundity. Hence, as his only poetic composition in *Ulysses,* as his only artistic offspring, his vampire poem must celebrate the physiology of menstruation as a manifestation of wo/man's poietic powers.[26]

The cross-reference linking the gravely inebriated theo-gynecology of Stephen in "Oxen of the Sun" to his dark poetic inspiration in "Proteus" intimates the presence of an authorial purpose external to the intentions of the protagonist of these two scenes. Stephen's parody of the rhetorics of the playwright, the critic, and the philosopher in "Scylla and Charybdis" is oriented toward a scrutiny of the possibilities and limitations of a sort of creativity indifferent to the physiology of human reproduction. Joyce's satirical purpose, instead, is to turn the opposition of maternity and paternity endemic to the classic epics and tragedies of lineage into an object of ridicule. The ground is ready, both thematically and stylistically, for the "tootoological" reversal of genealogy explored by Joyce in *Finnegans Wake,* a reversal wherein the dissipation of maternal agency brought about by the end of history is turned into a festive Genesis, a tolerant *theology* of gestures, beginnings, and physicalities, the *tautology* indeed of gender assimilation: "In the beginning was the gest. . . , for the end is with woman, flesh-without-word, while the man to be is in a worse case after than before since she on the supine satisfies the verg to him!" (468.5–8).

As we saw in chapter 3, the theology of carnality and maternity unfolding in "Proteus" (3.391–404) and in "Aeolus" (7.713–24) bears an intricate complex of symbolic meaning and emerges through a subtle succession of scenes. In broadest outline, one might say that the apparition of the "handmaid of the moon" in "Proteus," "trekking to evening lands [and dragging] her load," and the apparition of Beatrice, Dante's terrestrial love and celestial image of femininity, in "Aeolus," in the paradisiac wind and colors of her bodily assumption into heaven, complete a pattern of Dantesque references so broad as to achieve their full completion only toward the end of *Finnegans Wake.*

I am referring to the scene from *Finnegans Wake* that starts in the early morning after the night of the winter solstice. HCE and ALP, in their incarnations as Albatrus Nyanzer and Victa Nyanza, may be seen awake "in their bed of trial" (558.26). The scene is the "interior of dwelling on outskirts of city" (558.36–559.1). In the two bedrooms upstairs sleep their three children: Jerry, whose cry woke his parents; Kevin; and Isobel, their little sister. Isobel is young and undeveloped enough ("still in her teens") to be called Saintette (a French pun for "without teats") (556.7), yet is old enough to be called Pia de Purebelle in the days of her periods ("the redminers riots") (27.17–18). Mr. Nyanzer and Mrs. Nyanza, now metamorphosed into Mr. and Mrs. Porter, climb the stairs to check on their children's sleep. It is here that Joyce's narration sheds the most intense and revealing light on the cryptic figure of the "handmaid of the moon" from "Proteus." And it does so by means of a well-known expedient from negative theology, namely, the revelation of all that is revealable of a particular subject by way of an inquiry into its several names and titles.[27]

When the Porters reach Isobel's room, they enter into a vertiginous domain of pseudonimity. Surrounded by a bouquet of colors as magnificent as the one that surrounds Beatrice's triumphal chariot in Dante's *Purgatorio* ["Here's newyearspray, the posquiflor, a windaborne and heliotrope; there miriamsweet and amaranth and marygold to crown" (561.20–21)],[28] Isobel has become Buttercup, and Charis Charissima, and Boccuccia's Enameron, and, fatally, the "Mother of moth."[29]

The name "Buttercup" puns on the "bitter cup" drunk by Jesus on the Cross, after being "forsaken" by His Father (Matthew 27:46): "(W)hat an excessively lovecharming missyname to *forsake,* now that I come to drink of it filtred, a gracecup *fulled of bitterness*" (561.13–15, my emphasis).

The name "Charis" and its superlative "Charissima" pun, at once, on the French *chair* and on the Latin *caro,* both meaning "flesh"; they evoke, together with the phrase, "Mother of moth! I will to show herword in flesh" (561.27), the citation *Omnis caro ad te veniet,* "All flesh will come to thee," that the "Proteus" interior monologue borrows from Psalm 65:2.

The name "Boccuccia's Enameron," attributed to a sensuous, "more intriguant bambolina" (561.23–24), may be translated as "Enamored Little Mouth." Besides providing us with one of the two mouths involved in the vampire's kiss of "Proteus" (while the other mouth drinks from Buttercup's bitter lips), this name is strongly evocative of the kisses of the sensuous *pasturella* (shepherd girl) of young Dante's *dolce stil novo.* It is evocative, furthermore, of "the fairest sin the sunsaw," which the *Wake* relates to Paolo and Francesca, the couple from *Inferno* whose embrace is pregnant with the mysticism of the Cross: "With kiss. Kiss Criss. Cross Criss. Kiss Cross" (11.27–28). In this regard, it is worthwhile to point out that canto 29 of *Purgatorio,* the canto that inaugurates the procession led by Beatrice, begins with the line, "Singing like a lady *enamored*" (Singleton 315, my emphasis)—adding thereby one further Dantesque perspective on Isobel's "enamored little mouth," and on her symbolically ubiquitous persona as well.

Finally, the "handmaid of the moon," an image which the "Proteus" interior monologue borrows from the Angelus ("Behold the handmaid of the Lord"), surfaces as an attribute, or a bodily limb, rather than a proper name. The phrase, "(S)o, therebetween, behold, she had instantt with her handmade as to grasp the myth inmid the air," describes Isobel grabbing a newborn creature in between her legs, and then dragging it—the "load" that the handmaid of "Proteus" "trudges, schlepps, trains, drags, trascines" (*U* 3.392–93)—out of her (h)airy (and virginal) genitals. Her infant is a "myth," or perhaps a "moth." This is how Isobel-Buttercup-Charis-Boccuccia becomes Mary, the "Mother of moth," the androgynous begetter of "herword in flesh." This is how, in Joyce's doctrinal universe, the Word is made Flesh, out of a "winedark sea," out of an "allwombing tomb" (*U* 3.402), ready to be precipitated into the abyss of mortal sin, ready to further incarnate as the supreme, all-too-human will to love.

5

Parliament of Flatulence: The Genre of the Parable and the Riddle of Lineage in *Ulysses*

THIS CHAPTER DEALS SIMULTANEOUSLY WITH THE UNFOLDING OF THE theme of lineage and the emergence of the parable as privileged genre in *Ulysses*. My central thesis is twofold. In the first place, I argue that Stephen Dedalus broaches one of his innermost concerns, namely, the question as to whether in matters of lineage the decisive factor is androlineality or gynolineality, by means of the paradox of a riddle. In the second place, I maintain that Stephen deliberately constructs this riddle to conform to the New Testament genre of the parable. The two distinct sides of my thesis come together when I show that Stephen first asks his riddle by means of allegories—relying especially on that of the good sower found in Matthew 13—and then brings his allegories to their paradoxical culmination with his carnivalesque Parable of the Plums.

NON SEQUITURS AND OMISSIONS

I will begin with a self-evident axiom and a corollary, both essential to the methodology of my analysis. The axiom concerns Stephen Dedalus's inner life and may be formulated as follows: Most of what the reader of *Ulysses* and *A Portrait of the Artist as a Young Man* knows about Stephen's intimate concerns emerges from the passages that Joyce devotes to Stephen's stream of consciousness. The corollary regards the nature of the reciprocal contamination of Stephen's various concerns, and may be formulated as follows: A great deal of what the reader comes to understand about the matrix of Stephen's preoccupations must be inferred either from the *omissions* that interrupt the linguistic flow of Stephen's stream of consciousness or from the *non sequiturs* that punctuate its not-so-logical progression. While the axiom that Stephen's stream of consciousness is the most direct and exhaustive source of information about his inner life and travails will be accepted as self-evident by most Joyce scholars, the corollary as to the revelatory eloquence of Stephen's most laconic and evasive moments needs some qualification.

The example I have chosen to illustrate this point, selected for its simplicity as well as its pertinence to Stephen's concerns about lineage, paternity, and maternity, appears very early in the "Telemachus" episode of *Ulysses,* precisely at line 1.159 of the Gabler edition. Four words slip abruptly out of Stephen's inner thoughts and appear on the page, in a flash of consciousness, if you will, that breaks in two a speech by Buck Mulligan. It comes after "link(ing) his arm in Stephen's" (*U* 1.147). Buck has been talking at length in hypocritical praise of Stephen and in sarcastic support of Matthew Arnold's *mot d'ordre* to "Hellenize" Ireland. The four words that distract Stephen's attention from Buck's speech are: "Cranly's arm. His arm." Now, if ever there was a felicitous occurrence of intertextuality, this is it. This laconic line from Stephen's inner thoughts is preceded by the virtual omission of the entire dense and enchanting episode from *A Portrait of the Artist as a Young Man* that sees Stephen confiding the reasons for his irremediable discontent with home, fatherland, and church to his friend Cranly (*Portrait* 247). This intimate conversation starts when Cranly takes Stephen's arm "in a strong grip," and ends when Cranly, having induced once more his friend Stephen to open his heart to him as if in a confessional, seizes his arm again and gaily mocks him (*Portrait* 238, 247). The decisive contribution brought to the characterization of Buck Mulligan as Stephen's *next* estranged friend by the four words slipping out of Stephens's conscience may be fully apprehended only by a reader who brings to the passage a diligent perusal or a detailed remembrance of these pages from *A Portrait of the Artist as a Young Man.* The conversation between Stephen and Cranly is essential to the appreciation of the early morning controversy with Buck that poisons the rest of Stephen's day in *Ulysses.* Just as in "Telemachus" Buck will reproach Stephen for not being enough of a "white sepulcher," because he refused, at the request of his dying mother, to kneel down and pray to a God he is indifferent to (*U* 1.91–92), so in *A Portrait of the Artist as a Young Man* we already see Cranly insisting that Stephen ought to overcome his theological doubts and humor his mother by making his Easter duty (*Portrait* 239). Or again, in "Scylla and Charybdis" Stephen will suffer Buck to ridicule his contraposition of the Virgin's *amor matris,* "the only true thing in life," to God's paternity of Jesus, "a mystical estate, an apostolic succession from only begetter to only begotten" (*U* 9.837–44): the ridicule comes from Buck's caustic words, "Himself his own father . . . Wait. I am big with child" (*U* 9.875–76). But in *A Portrait of the Artist as a Young Man* Stephen and Cranly are already engaged in a controversy as to whether in matters of lineage androlineality, intended as the paternal normative of legitimate, if not "apostolic," succession, comes before or after gynolineality, intended as the sentiment of "maternal love" dictated by consanguinity. Cranly maintains that "(w)hatever else is unsure in this . . . world a mother's love is not, . . . whatever she feels, it . . . must be real." Stephen argues, in turn, that Jesus "is more like a son of God than a son of Mary" (*Portrait* 241–43).

Not that the text of *Ulysses* leaves the reader in the dark as to the necessity to perceive the Cranly-Mulligan analogy. The non sequitur that inaugurates the analogy between Stephen's two friends in "Telemachus" (*U* 1.159) is repeated in "Scylla and Charybdis" when, in the middle of a recollection of "Cranly's eleven Wicklowmen," Stephen digresses into the sudden thought, another flash of consciousness: "Mulligan has my telegram" (*U* 9.41), thus establishing the contiguous alternation of the names of his two friends as a pattern to indicate the emergence of feelings of resentment toward an estranged friend.[1] But this confirmation that some sort of equivalence is established between Cranly and Mulligan comes exceedingly late in *Ulysses,* in the ninth episode precisely. Only the reader well acquainted with the circumstances of Stephen's disdain toward Cranly at the end of *A Portrait of the Artist as a Young Man* (248) can be fully aware of the ubiquitousness of Stephen's regretful consideration in "Scylla and Charybdis": "My soul's youth I gave him, night by night" (*U* 9.39); in this passage the personal pronoun *him* applies at once both to Cranly, to whom Stephen "had told . . . of all the tumults and unrest and longings in his soul, day after day and night by night" (*Portrait* 178), and, by the effect of an analogy by contiguity, to Buck Mulligan. A more superficial reader is bound to feel that both non sequiturs, in which Stephen abruptly alternates thoughts concerning Buck with thoughts concerning Cranly, are escorted by narrative omissions that impede a full appreciation of the pairing up of the names of Stephen's two close friends. In sum, the narrative of the Tele-machiad has hardly begun, and by line 1.159 the reader is already invited to practice a sort of inferential reading by (intertextual) contiguity: a reading that will enable the reader to fill with connective meaning the logical and narrative gaps that afflict Stephen's stream of consciousness. In spite of the exuberant verbosity of his inner life, in fact, Stephen's stream of consciousness may be legitimately characterized as laconic and secretive, full of non sequiturs and omissions.

In this chapter I intend to engage a variety of Stephen's soliloquies and monologues to argue that certain among Stephen's early experiences at Clongowes Wood College, which he attended until about the age of ten, induce him to broach his preoccupations with androlineality or gynolineality in the guise of a riddle. In the second place, I intend to argue that Stephen deliberately assimilates the formulation of this riddle to the New Testament genre of the parable. First he asks a riddle relating to genealogical primacy by means of allegories, and then pushes his allegories to their limit when he tells, in the "Aeolus" episode, his Parable of the Plums (see *U* 7.921–1075)—an admittedly derisive and cryptic parable, but one that conforms to the manner of delivery of the Gospel's instructive parables, including an exhaustive code of decipherment.

THE RIDDLE OF THE RIDDLE

In his first year at Clongowes Wood College Stephen is twice exposed to the enigmatic nature of the riddle. The first time an older schoolmate, Wells, asks Stephen if he kisses his mother before going to bed. The riddle is not identified as such by Wells; he limits himself to asking a question whose derisory ambivalence, as the perplexed Stephen soon discovers, lends itself to neither a positive nor a negative satisfactory answer. Stephen's second exposure to a riddle occurs in the infirmary of Clongowes, and connotes a far greater linguistic sophistication. Stephen's wardmate, Athy, "a fellow out of the third of grammar" whose name "is the name of a town" in the county Kildare," asks Stephen if he is "good at riddles." Then he asks Stephen the following riddle: "Why is the county Kildare like the leg of a fellow's breeches?" Unable to find the correct answer, Stephen is doubly frustrated when Athy, after telling him the answer ("Because there is a thigh in it"), complicates the word-game with a riddle about the riddle itself: "Do you know the other way to ask [this riddle]?" (*Portrait* 25). There is an obvious answer to Athy's intimidating question, an elemental syntactic inversion of subject and nominal predicate permitting by definition the symmetrical reformulation of any question involving a copulative verb, but Stephen, at this tender age, is still too linguistically naive to concoct the correct reply to Athy's meta-riddle. However, it seems as though the Stephen of *Ulysses,* about fifteen years older, is very much at ease with riddles asked "the other way"; just as with many of the obsessions and preoccupations that he carries along from infancy straight into the broodings that saturate his mind on the morning of 16 June 1904, he appears bent upon coming back with a vengeance at the victimizing trick of asking riddles in a less than obvious way. At the conclusion of this chapter I will focus on Stephen's notorious Parable of the Plums, delivered in front of what I propose to call Dublin's "Parliament of Flatulence." The Parable of the Plums is an enigmatic riddle and also Stephen's sarcastic rebuke to his narrow-minded interlocutors. Of all the instances in which Joyce provides the reader of *Ulysses* with the means to infer the secrets of Stephen's soul concealed behind the silences and inconsistencies of his stream of consciousness, this parable, in my opinion, is emblematic; it not only betrays the presence of an allegorical strain in Stephen's thought processes, but it also reveals Stephen's disillusionment with the political sterility of androlineality.

Before continuing, however, I would like to stress a theoretical implication of what I am about to demonstrate. If it turns out that Stephen's musings are more proficiently attended to in the allegorical rather than in the symbolical mode, then the inner workings of the personality of this most representative among Modernist characters might be taken as a partial confirmation to Paul de Man's defense of the allegorical mode in modern literature. In "The Rhetoric of Temporality" Paul de Man criticizes the theory, sustained, among others, by Hans-Georg Gadamer, of the progressive preeminence of the symbol over the allegory, the decline of the latter coming to a moment of culmination with the aesthetic of Romanticism.[2] This theoretical implication of the present analysis has far-reaching implications. It suggests, for instance, that Joyce incorporated in the characterization of Stephen Dedalus a predisposition and, if you will, a predilection toward allegory that has been underappreciated by a majority of the critics who have undertaken the definition of the funda-

mental paradigms of Modernism. The duel of wits between
Stephen and Buck on the roof of the Martello tower in "Telemachus" thus has significant repercussions. Buck holds out to Stephen a mirror "cleft by a crooked crack," with the injunction:
"Look at yourself . . . you dreadful bard! . . . The rage of Caliban
at not seeing his face in a mirror. If Wilde were only alive to see
you!" Stephen responds with a witticism that liquidates simultaneously the aesthetics of reflection of Realism and of Romanticism: "[This mirror] is a symbol of Irish art. The cracked looking
glass of a servant" (U 1.134–36, 146). Olympic in his dismissal
of Buck's allusion to that which the mirror realistically reflects
and symbolically reveals of his face,[3] Stephen counterattacks
with the memorable aphorism of his condemnation of the subordinate nature of Irish art:[4] the "servant" of many masters,
including the prevailing aesthetic conventions; the "symbol" of
the sterile stage to be reached presently by the aesthetic of sym-
bolism itself.[5]

RIDDLE AND PARABLE

In spite of the medieval phraseology, imagery, thematics, and
conjectures of Stephen's frequent theological musings, a majority of critics seem to underappreciate the singularity of Stephen's propensity toward the allegorical as a modality of
discourse. Much like his favorite theologians and heresiarchs,
among whom figure eminently Thomas Aquinas, Averroes,
Moses Maimonides, Arius, Sabellius (see for instance U
1.659–60, 2.158–60, 3.50–51, 4.657–58, 9.862–64), Stephen
shows a strong predilection for broaching his favorite subjects
in a roundabout, Byzantine way. This may help explain the allegorical bent of his circumspect and hermetic riddles and parables of genealogy. In this section I will draw a network of textual
connections between, on the one hand, the filial or, more
broadly speaking, the genealogical resonances inherent in the
riddle that Stephen asks of his students at Mr. Deasy's private
school in the "Nestor" episode and, on the other hand, the New
Testament parables that Stephen meditates upon before asking
his riddle, parables that exercise a considerable influence upon
his formulation of the riddle itself. As we will see, Stephen's
stream of consciousness delineates the thematic and generic
connections between the riddle and the parables with great clar-

ity, once the pattern of Stephen's typical non sequiturs and omissions is properly accounted for.

In "Nestor," Stephen asks the following riddle of his students at the end of their morning class. I will call it the "Nestor version" of the riddle:

> The cock crew,
> The sky was blue:
> The bells in heaven
> Were striking eleven.
> 'Tis time for this poor soul
> To go to heaven. (U 2.102–07)

Then, in the "Circe" episode Stephen formulates his riddle "the other way":

> The fox crew, the cocks flew,
> The bells in heaven
> Were striking eleven.
> 'Tis time for her poor soul
> To get out of heaven." (*U* 15.3577–81)

Two observations can be made with respect to this riddle and to Stephen's formulation of it. The first deals with the incoherence of the solution proposed by Stephen to his frustrated students. "What is it, sir," surrenders the student named Cochrane. "We give it up" (*U* 2.113). In response to the student's request, Stephen provides the cryptic answer: "The fox burying his grandmother under a hollybush" (*U* 2.115). Don Gifford is convinced that Stephen's solution of the riddle can be taken at face value, or almost at face value, because what Gifford considers the correct solution ("The fox burying his mother under a hollybush") contemplates only one substitution with respect to the answer uttered by Stephen, and this is the substitution of the word "mother" for the word "grandmother."[6] I agree with Gifford only to the extent that his indication of the lexical imprecision of Stephen's solution opens up the possibility that Stephen is indeed not only asking but even *answering* the riddle "the other way." The fact that Stephen has in mind a mother, his mother more precisely, rather than a grandmother, is clearly shown by the passage at lines 2.143–50, where, with a typical non sequitur, he switches his meditation on motherhood from the subject of the mother of the student Cyril Sargent to the subject of the corpse, or ghost, of his dead mother—which ghost, together with the traces of its visitations upon Stephen, is easily identifiable through the recurrent motif of the "odour of rosewood and wetted ashes" (see *U* 1.103–6, 1.270–72). After designating his mother as "[a] poor soul gone to heaven," Stephen associates her image with that of a fox that, "red reek of rapine in his fur, with merciless bright eyes scraped in the earth, listened, scraped up the earth, listened, scraped and scraped" (2.147–50). Given the complex thematic cluster of Stephen's filial obsessions, I claim that it is textually illegitimate to read in the typical depiction of a furtive predator, busy at digging a passage under the fence of the typical henhouse, the image of a mourning creature intent upon burying a dear relative. If Stephen is here impersonating the fox, he clearly has no business in giving the peace of burial to the "poor soul" of his mother, which, as we learned at line 2.147, has already "gone to heaven." Stephen-the-fox is busy, rather, at metaphorically exhuming the maternal remains that by mid-morning have surfaced three times already in his stream of consciousness (see *U* 1.103–6, 1.270–72, 2.144–47) and, called insistently back by his tormented musings, will repeat their increasingly hideous visits several more times in the course of the day.

The second observation I wish to make about Stephen's riddle consists of its generic analogy with the allegorical modality of discourse proper to the parables of the Gospel. The significance of this analogy is twofold. First, it relates to one of the central tenets of this section, namely, the proposition that the allegorical modality of discourse is intrinsic to Stephen's stream of consciousness. Second, as we will see shortly, this analogy exemplifies the sequential logic overarching the omissions and non sequiturs that punctuate Stephen's stream of consciousness.

Let us take a close look at the sequential logic preceding and leading to the enunciation of Stephen's riddle. Stephen is not in the best of professorial moods when he listens to the student named Talbot recite lines from Milton's "Lycidas." The verses of the poem about a friend of Milton's who died by drowning evoke the image "of him who walked the waves," an image prepared, a few hours earlier, by Stephen's recollection of Buck's having recently saved "from drowning"—or, more specifically, having provided with artificial respiration and medical aid—a young man, the son of Reuben J. On the occasion of this recollection, which occurs in "Telemachus" on the roof of the Martello tower, Stephen declares to Buck: "You saved men from drowning. I'm not a hero, however" (*U* 1.62, see also 3.317, 16.292). The Messi-

anic image coupled with the awareness of his cowardice induces
Stephen to equate the "craven hearts" of his students with the
vileness of heart of Pharisaic people—whom he compares to
himself and, contradictorily enough at this juncture, to Buck
"the scoffer"—intent upon asking insidious questions of Jesus.
The image of the Pharisees evokes, in turn, one of the best
known answers given by Jesus to his hypocritical questioners:
"To Caesar what is Caesar's, to God what is God's" (U 2.86).[7]
Finally, the enigmatic modality of Jesus' answer, "a *riddling* sentence to be *woven* and *woven* on the church's looms" (U 2.87,
my emphases), sets Stephen out in a riddling mood. While Talbot
reaches the end of his recitation, Stephen tells himself the first
two lines of a riddle about riddling:

> Riddle me, riddle me, randy ro.
> My *father* gave me *seeds* to sow. (U 2.88–89, my emphasis)

Shortly after, Stephen asks his students the "Nestor version"
of his riddle.

What remains to be established in this section is the transition
from riddle to parable proper. To do so, I will concentrate on
the two lexical pairs I have emphasized in the last two quotations
from "Nestor," namely, the pairs *father-seeds* and *riddling-
woven*. Whatever version of the proverbially prodigal dissipator
of his father's seeds Stephen may be thinking of when he recalls
the first two lines of the riddle about riddling, his theologically
saturated mind—"supersaturated with the religion" in which he
disbelieves, as Cranly puts it in *A Portrait of the Artist as a
Young Man* (240)—is bound to relate this filial prodigality to the
sterile comportment of Onan, the second son of Judah. As is
well known, in Genesis 38 Onan, in defiance of an ancient custom, "let [his seed] go to waste whenever he joined with his
brother's [widow, Tamar]," refusing thereby to procreate offspring by her for his deceased older brother. I am referring, of
course, to "the sin against the Holy Ghost for which there was
no forgiveness" in *A Portrait of the Artist as a Young Man* (159),
whose consequence the "Oxen of the Sun" episode of *Ulysses*
describes, again, as one "against the Holy Ghost," one that
"nightly impossibilise(s) . . . Godpossibled souls" (U 14.225–26).
But Stephen, "the eternal son and ever virgin" of *Ulysses*
(14.342–43), seems to consider the sin of Onan a more than
permissible practice. Aside from his visits to the brothel, which
may signal a rather deep-rooted habit for the Stephen of 1904,

judging from the "Circe" episode as well as from the double reference to the "street of harlots" in the "Nestor" and "Scylla and
Charybdis" episodes (*U* 2.355–56, 9.1207–8), Stephen's sexual
life appears, in fact, suspiciously autarchic in *Ulysses.*

Stephen's recollection of the riddle about riddling is infused
with another scriptural trace, namely, the unmistakable one
from Matthew 13, whose timeless resonance may be detected in
all such folkloric riddles and sayings about seeds, sowing, and
harvesting. Matthew's so-called "parable of the good sower" contemplates sowing as a practice of dissemination very much
analogous, in my opinion, to the human physiology of womb
insemination and impregnation (with the provision that to be
impregnated—with divine grace—by the "well-sown" seed is not
land or womb but, allegorically speaking, the sower's own soul).
That is why the several images of sterility, or "bad sowing," presented in Matthew 13 can be related to the scriptural story of
Onan—the emblematic description of seminal dissipation in
which the flow of androlineality is broken or distorted. In the
parable of the good sower a portion of the seed falls on the
wayside, a portion on rocky ground, a portion among thorns,
etc.; only the portion that falls on fertile soil grows prolifically. To
secure the later connection with the swollen session of Dublin's
Parliament of Flatulence in the "Aeolus" episode, let me remark
that the trace of Matthew 13 resonates much more manifestly
in Stephen's Parable of the Plums than in his riddle. In the
parable, the "plumstones" that fall from the top of Nelson's pillar
land on Dublin's sterile pavement (*U* 7.1026–27). Here the analogy with Matthew's allegory of the "good sower" is obviously deliberate on Stephen's part. And once the logical and narrative
gaps that afflict Stephen's stream of consciousness have been
exhaustively mapped out and filled with connective meaning,
we will see that the resulting matrix of his preoccupations suggests a complementarity between seminal sterility, flatulent
speech, and empty patriotism.

Matthew 13

Matthew 13 is the parable of all parables. It comprises not
only the parable per se (13:1–9) and an extensive code of interpretation of its allegories (13:18–23), enriched by three variations on the basic theme and a systematic set of further
explicative comments (13:24–48), but it also includes Jesus'

remarkable justification of the parable as instructive genre. When his disciples ask Jesus the reason why he speaks to the people in parables, Jesus answers: "To you it has been given to know the secrets of the kingdom of heaven, but to them it has not been given ... This is why I speak to them in parables, because seeing they do not see, and hearing they do not hear, nor do they understand" (13:10–13). Analogously, the recourse to the form of the parable becomes indispensable to Stephen's theologically saturated mind when he realizes that he is surrounded by people such as Cranly and Buck who, like most of Jesus' followers, "seeing they do not see, and hearing they do not hear, nor do they understand." The connection from riddle to parable is drawn by Stephen in relation to his metaphorically blind and deaf friends.

We saw above how subtle is the transition at lines 2.83–85 from Stephen's thoughts about the Pharisees who try to trick Jesus with doctrinally complex questions to the moral cowardice that Stephen attributes, at once, to himself, to his young students, "aware of ... the fees their papas pay," and to Buck "the scoffer" (U 2.29, 84). The rest of the passage prolongs the same duality of meaning:

> To Caesar what is Caesar's, to God what is God's. A long look from dark eyes, a riddling sentence to be woven and woven on the church's looms. (U 2.86–87)

The recollection of Jesus' proverbial answer to his questioners, "a riddling sentence," which in Matthew 22:15–21 is preceded by Jesus' examination of "a coin of the tribute" handed over to him by one of the Pharisees, highlights the connection drawn in Stephen's mind between the word-play of the riddle and the genre of the parable—given the provision that Jesus' examination of the coin turns the episode, structurally speaking, into what might be called "a practical parable," whose delivery is assigned to an emblematic act, the examination of the coin, as much as to plain words. In the second place, as I have anticipated above, I submit that blind and deaf to the various facets of the "riddling sentence to be woven and woven on the church's looms" are not only the Pharisees, in Stephen's mind, but also his friends Cranly and Buck—or, to be more precise, since the present analysis focuses mainly on the Telemachiad and only refers to *A Portrait of the Artist as a Young Man* as prologue and background to the episodes of interest, I should say that to Stephen Buck is the personification of the hypocrisy of the Pharisees. There is an eloquent textual indicator in the passage from "Nestor" cited above that may help make this clear. If, in fact, the "long look from dark eyes" evoked in Stephen's thoughts must be attributed, in the first place, to the look given by Jesus to the Pharisees, it may be attributed, in the second place, to Cranly himself, the defender, like Buck, of a Pharisaic adaptation to the prevailing religious and social customs and practices. Cranly, it will be recalled from *A Portrait of the Artist as a Young Man,* has the "face of a guilty priest," and sports "the gaze of . . . *dark* womanish *eyes*" (178, my emphases). In light of the textual contiguity between *A Portrait of the Artist as a Young Man* and the Telemachiad of *Ulysses,* it would be difficult to deny, or to attribute to coincidence, the convergent diction in the descriptions of Jesus' and Cranly's dark eyes—the obvious significant difference being, of course, that the former, a seer, could weave and weave the subversive implications of the "riddling sentence" ("To Caesar what is Caesar's, to God what is God's"), while the latter, prone to taking the letter of the "riddling sentence" as an advocation of servitude and conformism, is blind to its implications. Finally, the ping-pong play of equivalences established above between Cranly and Buck is the conclusive element that confirms the extension of Cranly's Pharisaic shabbiness to Buck.

THE PARLIAMENT OF FLATULENCE

The Parable of the Plums is delivered by Stephen at the conclusion of the "Aeolus" episode, while he walks toward Mooney's pub in the company of two of the more pompous protagonists of the episode, professor MacHugh[8] and Myles Crawford, a journalist. Stephen's parable comes as the worthy conclusion of an episode devoted to the flatulent verbosity of the journalists, intellectuals, and loafers that congregate after Dignam's funeral in the "draught[y]" office (*U* 7.396, 399–400) of an organ of the Dublin press, the *Freeman's Journal.*

It is worth observing that the motif of flatulent verbosity has been extensively played upon already in episodes and in characterizations that precede the "Aeolus" episode. In "Telemachus," for instance, we hear Stephen censor certain heresiarchs—such as Sabellius, for instance, who refused to take maternity into consideration in matters of divine genealogy—with the peremptory judgment: "The void awaits surely all them that *weave the wind*" (*U* 1.656–62, my emphasis; see also 2.861–63, 9.862). In addition, Stephen does not confine his condemnation of empty verbosity to the theology of remote heresiarchs, but extends it to himself and his nemesis, Buck Mulligan. In "Nestor," he admonishes himself with the words: "Weave, weaver of the wind" (2.53). This self-accusation comes at the end of a meditation on the relationship between historical actuality and fantastical possibility, a meditation that anticipates his own declaration, further on in the same episode, that he is "trying to wake up" from the "nightmare of history" (*U* 2.377; see also 7.678). Within the field of Aristotelian problematics alluded to by Stephen's meditation, history is, in fact, that stringent chain of actualities whose unfolding is the domain of the historian, and from which one may escape by attending to those potentialities that Aristotle's *Poetics* designates as pertinent to the interests of the poet.[9] Hence, Stephen's self-accusation may be taken to entail a somewhat deprecatory judgment, or at least a disenchanted one, of his accomplishments as a poet.[10] Lastly, Stephen also accuses Buck, both explicitly and implicitly, of being a vain weaver of the wind. The explicit accusation comes in conjunction with Stephen's first reference to Sabellius, "who held that the Father was Himself His own Son. Words Mulligan has spoken a moment since in mockery ... *Idle mockery.* The void awaits surely all them that weave the wind" (1.660–62, my emphasis); here, analogously to the several cases of equivalences established between Cranly and Buck, one may talk of the accusation of empty verbosity applying simultaneously to the heresiarch and to Stephen's friend. The implicit accusation may be derived, I submit, from the sentence, "a riddling sentence to be woven and woven on the church's looms" (*U* 2.87), a sentence that was scrutinized in the first section of this chapter; the implication, qualified above, that Buck is not equal to the subtle weaving and weaving of the "church's looms" suggests, by way of lexical contiguity, that Buck is therefore only capable of an empty weaving of "the wind."

Let us follow in its essential stages the unfolding of the interplay between the motif of flatulent verbosity and the allegory of the seeds in "Aeolus." I shall start my analysis with Stephen's entrance into the office of the *Freeman's Journal,* which Leopold Bloom just left on an urgent errand, and where lounge the pompous windbags that Stephen will soon feel the urge to chasten with his Parable of the Plums. It does not seem fortuitous that Stephen's arrival occurs in the section of "Aeolus" entitled "The Grandeur That Was Rome," since it appears that the protagonists of the second part of "Aeolus" (the first being devoted to Bloom's wanderings in the maze of the rooms and offices where the personnel of the newspaper is at work) have all the intentions, at the moment of Stephen's arrival, to begin a spree of grandiose patriotic rhetoric.

It is relevant to notice that Stephen's entrance into Dublin's Parliament of Flatulence is prepared by Bloom's inner monologues, whose diction prefigures the wind-weaving imagery of empty verbosity that is later going to unfold and dovetail into Stephen's seed-sowing allegory. Shortly after Bloom's arrival at the *Freeman's Journal,* one hears Bloom consider that "[i]t's the ads and side features [of which the foreman, Mr Nannetti, is responsible, that] sell a weekly, not the stale news in the official gazette." After which thought Bloom pictures to himself, among other "side features," the section devoted to the mail from the readers, with the words: "Country bumpkin's queries. Dear Mr Editor, what is a good cure for *flatulence?*" (*U* 7.89–90, my emphasis). Later on, considering the beginning of the career of Myles Crawford, the editor of the *Freeman's Journal,* Bloom reflects on how fast a news item of personal interest, for instance the news of a job opening, will propagate among journalists: "Funny the way those newspaper men veer about when they *get wind* of a new opening" (7.308–9, my emphasis). But most important of all is that Bloom's stream of consciousness provides the motif of flatulent verbosity with a table-turning echo from the Old Testament, one that finally draws home the authorial intention behind Stephen's insistent musings, in "Telemachus" and in "Nestor," on the wind-weaving imagery. While considering the unhappy lot of J. J. O'Molloy, a former man of the law fallen into disrepute, and one of the self-indulgent patriots whose "windy" orations will inspire Stephen to elaborate his parable in "Aeolus," Bloom thinks: "Practice dwindling. A mighthavebeen. Losing heart. Gambling. Debts of honour. Reaping the whirlwind" (7.303–4). The last sentence fragment from this quotation explodes on the page, retrospectively, that is, for the reader whose sensitivity to the nuances of diction has been increasingly responsive to Stephen's modulations of the imagery of the "weaver of the wind." This sentence fragment immediately evokes the admonition that the prophet Hosea addresses to Israel:

They *sow wind,*
And they shall reap whirlwind—
Standing stalks devoid of ears
And yielding no flour.
If they do yield any,
Strangers shall devour it. (Hosea 8:7, my emphases)

Although this is certainly not the first occasion in which
Bloom's and Stephen's minds have worked in partial and intriguing unison in developing the themes of *Ulysses*—one can
identify similar sparks of shared consciousness, for instance,
in Bloom's and Stephen's parallel thoughts about the music of
Palestrina (see *U* 1. 653–54 and 5.405) and in their frequent
recollections of lines and fragments from *Hamlet* (see *U*
1.273–74, 3.14, 5.455, 6.349)—the far from accidental collusion
of lexicon and imagery encountered here is striking indeed, because Hosea's prophecy clearly underscores the lexical and figural contiguity between the wind-weaving imagery, hinged upon
the motif of flatulent verbosity that troubles Stephen hours before he reaches the *Freeman's Journal,* and the seed-sowing
allegory inherent in the parable that Stephen uses to ridicule
the empty patriotism of the intellectuals, journalists, and loafers
who lounge in Myles Crawford's office—among whom is briefly
seen also Stephen's father, Simon, "*giving vent* to a hopeless
groan" (*U* 7.329–30, my emphasis).

We are back now to the Parliament of Flatulence, where the
interplay between flatulent verbosity and the allegory of sowing
persists. First, professor MacHugh embarks upon praise of Ireland, "always loyal to lost causes." The Irish, he claims, are "liege
subjects" of the anti-British alliance that "foundered at Tra-
falgar," where in 1805 Admiral Horace Nelson, the "onehandled
adulterer" of the Parable of the Plums (*U* 7.1018), defeated the
Napoleonic and Spanish fleet (7.551–66). Then Myles Crawford
launches into a praise of Irish journalism, centered on a memorable feat by Ignatius Gallaher at the time of the murders of
Phoenix Park. With the help of Lenehan, whose pathetic stroll-
ing along the streets of Dublin the reader of *Dubliners* is bound
to recall from "Two Gallants," and who defines Gallaher as "the
father of scare journalism," Crawford fishes out of the newspaper's archives the documentation of Gallaher's professional
resourcefulness (7.628–91). However, the reader of *Dubliners*
is bound to respond to these grandiose patriotic praises with
mixed feelings, because he or she remembers Gallaher as the

vulgar friend of Thomas Chandler in "A Little Cloud," a story in which, significantly enough, the London-based journalist sports, on the occasion of his visit to Dublin, a tie the color of his political allegiance to the Orange lodges.

Shortly after, Stephen observes Crawford's mouth "twitch(ing) unspeaking in ... disdain" at the present mediocrity of Irish barristers when compared to the great ones of the past. Crawford's ostentatious speechlessness makes Stephen think of his recent attempt at the composition of the vampire poem in the "Proteus" episode: "Mouth. South. Is the mouth south some way?" Wondering about possible additional rhymes for his verses—"South, pout, out, shout, drouth"—Stephen has an idealized vision of Dantesque verses, a miscellanea from *Inferno, Purgatorio,* and *Paradiso* that evokes a pageant of girlish rhymes, "in green, in rose, in russet," petitioning for admittance into the Comedy—"while the *wind,* as it now happens, *shuts up.*" This line from *Inferno* 5.96, which appears in the original and, noticeably, in an apocryphal version in "Aeolus" ("mentre che il *vento,* come fa, *si tace*"),[11] seems meant to intimate that poetic elevation "shuts up," becomes mute and sterile, when aimed at by a "weaver of the wind" (*U* 7.708–21, my emphases, my translation of the line from *Inferno*).[12]

After this interruption, the flow of patriotic rhetoric is started anew by O'Molloy, who, unaware of the negative connotations attached to his words by Bloom's recollection of Hosea's admonition against the "sowers of the wind," launches into a further celebration of illustrious Irish journalists of the past (7.741–75). Then comes professor MacHugh's turn to embark upon the most patriotic celebration of the day for the Parliament of Flatulence, namely, the celebration of John F Taylor's memorable rebuke of Mr Justice Fitzgibbon's criticism of the Gaelic League (7.791–880).[13] In his speech, declaimed with intense participation by MacHugh, Taylor compares the situation of the Irish patriots to that of Moses, reprimanded by an Egyptian high priest for his youthful pride: "[H]ad the youthful ... Moses ... bowed ... before that arrogant admonition he would never have brought the chosen people out of their houses of bondage nor followed the pillar of the cloud by day." (7.862–66). "That is oratory," are the words with which professor MacHugh closes his declamation. At which Stephen, faithful to the last to the motif of flatulence, thinks: "*Gone with the wind*" (7.879–80, my emphasis). Stephen then suggests that they adjourn their debate to the pub, and, on the way to Mooney's, he delivers his not too veiled satire of the epic overtones that prevailed—especially in MacHugh's apologia for John F Taylor—in the grand patriotic rhetoric of his present boozing companions, the weavers and sowers of the wind of empty speech.

THE PARABLE OF THE PLUMS, OR WEAVING AND SOWING THE WIND

The gist of Stephen's Parable of the Plums (*U* 7.923–1075) is reassuringly simple to summarize, when compared to the imposing cluster of echoes, lexical contiguities, and dovetailing figures of speech by which the motif of flatulent verbosity comes to coalesce with the allegory of good and bad sowing.

"Two Dublin vestals," Stephen fabulates, of fifty and fifty-three years of age respectively, "want to see the views of Dublin from the top of Nelson's pillar." At the foot of the pillar they add to the provisions they bought for the excursion twenty-four "ripe plums" that they buy from a girl—the same girl, in all likelihood, whom Bloom heard peddle her goods at "eight plums a penny" as Dignam's funeral procession passed by Nelson's pillar, in the "Hades" episode (6.294). (Since Bloom saw Stephen walking in a direction opposite to that of the funeral procession shortly before he heard the voice of the peddler (6.39), it is more than likely, also, that Stephen, having seen the girl at work, too, is here having recourse to the reality-enhancing strategy of "local colour" and "composition of place" that he will scrupulously apply in "Scylla and Charybdis" [9.158–63].) The two women ascend the "winding staircase" inside the pillar, "grunting, ... panting, ... peeping at the airslits," until they reach the top, where, after eating their provisions, they "pull up their skirts, ... settle down on their striped petticoats, peering up at the statue of the onehandled adulterer." The parody of John F Taylor's patriotic speech is deliberately crass, and its sarcasm is enhanced by the title that, questioned by his listeners, Stephen gives to his tale: *A Pisgah Sight of Palestine or The Parable of the Plums.* In Stephen's parable, the summit of Pisgah, the mountain ridge from where Moses contemplates the forbidden Promised Land (Deuteronomy 3:27, 34:1), is replaced by the top of a pillar from where the simulacrum of a one-armed Admiral, the effigy of British colonialism, looks down on the streets of Dublin. And at the feet of the "usurper" sit in impromptu adoration two local vestals, elderly virgins made giddy by the titillating sight of the "diminished digits" of the "onehandled adulterer" (*U* 7. 1019, 7.1069).

At the close of his parable Stephen insists on imagery and diction evocative of an onanistic sort of sexuality. The neologism "onehandled," in particular, preferred to the lexically appropriate "one-handed," suggests that the two Dublin women indulge in the fantasy of sexual manipulation at the sight of the one-armed statue. That the evocation of onanism, hence, of the sterility of seminal dispersion, is deliberate rather than accidental seems confirmed by one of the names that Stephen, in a scruple of "local colour" and "composition of place" destined to go unnoticed by his listeners, attributes to the two women. "Their names are Anne Kearns and Florence MacCabe." Now, the latter is the same name that Stephen attributed to one of the two women he saw walking along the shore earlier on, in the "Proteus" episode, and that he speculated to be midwives intent upon getting rid of a misbirth (3.29–37), another image of sterility.

Finally, the two women of Stephen's parable, "too tired to look up (at Nelson's statue) or down (at the views of Dublin) or to speak . . . put the bag of plums between them and eat the plums out of it, one after another, wiping off with their handkerchiefs the plumjuice that dribbles out of their mouths and spitting the plumstones slowly out between the railings." One could hardly concoct a more wicked parody of Matthew's allegory of the good sower; save that, to compound the parody with the satire of the Parliament of Flatulence, the two women, soon to be presumably afflicted with the plums' effect on excretion, are shown sitting like devoted "vestals"—like votaries, if you will, of the god of compounded metaphor—at the feet of a most unlikely personification of Ireland's national liberation.

CONCLUSION

The central thesis of this chapter stipulates that Stephen Dedalus assimilates the formulation of the riddle of lineage—centered on the question as to whether in genealogy the decisive factor is androlineality or gynolineality—to the New Testament genre of the parable. The corollary to this thesis is that Stephen asks first the riddle of lineage by means of allegories, especially the allegory of the good sower found in Matthew 13, and later pushes his allegories—which have meanwhile been complemented with the table-turning imagery of the "sower of the wind" from Hosea's prophecy (introduced by Bloom's stream of consciousness)—to culmination in the Parable of the Plums.

In the demonstration of this thesis we saw how Stephen's theologically saturated mind seems bound to relate the filial prodigality that is intimated in his riddle of lineage—to be more specific, in the hermetic lines from the "riddle about riddling," which is found in "Nestor" at lines 2.88–89—to the vice of Onan, a vice that, apparently, Stephen looks at with a rather tolerant eye. It is a vice, nonetheless, that suggests, first, the absence of fecundity intrinsic to those circumstances of seminal dissipation that can be figuratively ascribed to the instances of "bad sowing" presented in Matthew 13, and second, the sterility intrinsic to that aptitude for vacuous, empty speech, that, in light of the thematic cluster under examination, may be related to the instances of "wind-sowing" denounced in Hosea 8:7. In the interplay of the motif of flatulent verbosity and of the allegory of the seeds in "Telemachus," "Nestor," and finally "Aeolus," onanism appears as the thread that holds together the spectrum of the sterile connotations of generation and lineage engaged, through strategically placed non sequiturs and omissions, by Stephen's stream of consciousness. As I tried to indicate with regard to Stephen's self-accusations of empty verbosity, his resentment against Dublin's Parliament of Flatulence (of which he may be considered a honorary member, no less than Buck Mulligan, or than his cynical employer, Mr. Deasy) betrays a disappointment with regard to the aridity of his past artistic accomplishments. Furthermore, the non sequiturs and omissions of Stephen's stream of consciousness lend themselves to be interpreted as symptoms of some sort of compulsive denial. If one were to broach the complex subject of such an interpretation, one might perhaps detect in Stephen's (interior and exterior) verbosity a typical Freudian reversal, i.e., an irrepressible loquacity aimed at silencing Stephen's own disapproval of his partiality to onanism. Which would entail, in turn, that his riddles, parables, disquisitions, and interior monologues may be read also as a distressed condemnation of the disreputable lifestyle Stephen has fallen into since the end of his Parisian exile.

6

Aengus of the Birds: Stephen Dedalus and Vico's Legal Fiction of Paternity

I leave it to you, as the man with the hump said to his son.
—James Joyce to C. P. Curran, 14 July 1937

Giambattista vico's discussion of legitimate paternity and legal fiction in ancient Roman jurisprudence contributes an essential element to Joyce's characterization of Stephen Dedalus, not only in *Ulysses* but already in *A Portrait of the Artist as a Young Man*. In this chapter I examine some of the recent assumptions about the nature and extent of Vico's influence over Joyce's fiction. For the sake of conciseness I will not address Karen Lawrence's and Ellen Carol Jones's pioneer works on the concept of paternity as legal fiction in *Ulysses*,[1] since they do not contribute to my analysis, nor does my analysis critique theirs. Although both Lawrence's and Jones's contributions focus on an episode from *Ulysses* that plays a most essential role in the determination of Stephen Dedalus's character as intentionally Viconian construct, namely, the quasi-monologue in "Scylla and Charybdis" in the course of which Stephen pronounces his memorable words: "Paternity may be a legal fiction" (*U* 9.844), neither explores this statement's Viconian implications.

The question I will *not* ask, in the illustration of Vico's impact upon the early characterization of Stephen Dedalus, is whether or not Joyce structured his first novel, *A Portrait of the Artist as a Young Man,* according to a Viconian pattern. This thesis has been argued, rather unconvincingly, by Margaret Church. In "*A Portrait* and Vico: A Source Study," Church contends "that Joyce used Vico in his work much earlier than has usually been acknowledged, and the examination of *A Portrait of the Artist* in the longer context of a gradually unfolding Viconian pattern traceable in Joyce's entire canon will demonstrate Joyce's sig-

114

nificant debt to Vico."[2] I have two objections to this approach. The first is that it would be a mistake, as A. Walton Litz has pointed out in "Vico and Joyce," "to think of Vico and Joyce in terms of our conventional notions of literary 'influence'."[3] One must rather place one's understanding of Joyce and Vico within the hermeneutic circle of a logic of reciprocity. As Litz maintains, "in the long run Joyce's art may condition our reading of Vico as much as the *New Science* conditions our understanding of *Finnegans Wake*."[4] My second objection to Church's approach is a procedural one. She relates a wide range of episodes and incidents in *A Portrait of the Artist as a Young Man, Dubliners,* and *Ulysses* to a collection of ad hoc metaphorical constructs of her own making, aimed at smuggling into Joyce's fictions the Viconian patterns of historical decline and cyclical recurrence. This is an idiosyncratically reductionist approach, especially in light of the fact that Church's decoding of these episodes and incidents turns out to be both the result and the premise of her whole argument.

What I intend to argue, instead, is that Stephen's effort "to free *paternity as creation* from the power of the mother," as Jean-Michel Rabaté has put it in *James Joyce, Authorized Reader,*[5] manifests itself in *A Portrait of the Artist as a Young Man* as a need to recover the Roman juridical tradition of the legal fiction of paternity that Vico illustrates in several of his works. This recovery, in turn, entails a subordination of the maternal side of procreation, which depends on the order of nature and instinct, to the legal/societal norms that inform androlineal genealogy. In spite of the centrality Rabaté attributes to the issue of paternity in his analysis of Stephen Dedalus, he develops this issue from a Freudian/Lacanian angle that undoubtedly goes counter to Joyce's intentions. It is well known that Joyce was lukewarm as to the relevance of Freud's theories. In the context of the present discussion it is sufficient to recall the Triestine episode in which Joyce is reported to have declared that Freud had been anticipated by Vico.[6] If Rabaté's psychoanalytical approach sheds light on Stephen's unconscious phallocentrism, a subject we cannot overlook, it does not shed sufficient light on the character of Stephen Dedalus when one views it as intentionally Viconian construct. Rabaté is quite correct in pointing out that the relation between father and son constitutes the essence of the law for Stephen, while the rapport of mother and son is one of prohibition and transgression (69), but his subsequent remark that these relations lie at the very core of the Oedipal pattern is inadequate and misleading when it comes, first, to assessing the role played by the gender-biased norms of genealogical legitimacy in Stephen's concerns about paternal and maternal filiation, and, second, to applying the contribution provided by this Viconian theme to Joyce's characterization of Stephen Dedalus.

The study of Stephen's character as Viconian construct calls for an analysis of the episode of divination under the portico of the National Library in *A Portrait of the Artist as a Young Man,* where we see Stephen posture as an ancient augur, attempting to interpret the flight of "dark darting quivering bodies . . . flying clearly . . . round an airy temple" (*Portrait* 224). These birds are swallows that came back from the south, Stephen thinks: migratory birds, a prophecy of exile. Their cries soothe his ears, their swerving bodies soothe his eyes from the lamenting image of his mother, May Goulding Dedalus. Is Stephen aware that from a Viconian standpoint swallows belong to the family of the *degeneres* birds, from whose flight the Roman plebs derived their "minor or private auspices," as opposed to the "major or public auspices" which the patricians, the *patresfamilias* proper, derived from the flight of the *feroces* birds of prey, such as eagles, hawks, etc? (*SNS1* § 568). Is he aware of the opinion of Vico's as to the ignobility of the auguries derived from the flight of inferior birds?

This question is unanswerable on the basis of textual evidence, and it remains so even if one were to draw a direct parallel, albeit illegitimate, between James Joyce's intellectual education and his characterization of the partially autobiographical character of young Stephen Dedalus. From the research of Domenico Pietropaolo on Joyce's early exposure to Vico's thought we learn, in fact, that such exposure is impossible to prove; it may be considered very likely at the most, on account of the intellectual predilections of Joyce's Jesuit teacher of Italian, Charles Ghezzi. Therefore, whatever kind of lineage one chooses to establish between young Joyce and his young alter ego, the question as to Stephen Dedalus's acquaintance with Vico's thought in general and with Vico's opinions about inferior birds in particular is destined to remain unanswered. However, from Pietropaolo's "Vico and Literary History in the Early Joyce" we gain also the crucial insight that the Viconianism of the mature Joyce was probably extracted "from the theosophical doctrines that Joyce perused in his youth."[7] The unanswerable question as to Stephen's familiarity with Vico's opinions about prophecy leads one directly to the discussion of theosophy, and this is a discussion where a parallel may be easily established between the author and his creature. In fact, not only Joyce but also Stephen nurtured in his youth an interest in theosophy—an interest that, if we are to judge from "Scylla and Charybdis," as well as from the tryptic of the "Telemachiad," led Stephen to a remarkable familiarity with theosophical doctrine.

JOYCE, SWEDENBORG, AND VICO

Both Joyce and Stephen were well acquainted with the works of Stephen's Hyperborean namesake, the so-called Daedalus of the North: Emanuel Swedenborg. In his 1912 lecture on William Blake, delivered at the Università Popolare Triestina, Joyce maintained that Swedenborg's theosophical influence turned Blake into a "winged (artist) on the edge of the dark ocean of God" (*Critical Writings* 222). As to Stephen, his familiarity with Swedenborg emerges first in the episode of divination from *A Portrait of the Artist as a Young Man* and then in the "Scylla and Charybdis" episode from *Ulysses*.

Let us first take a brief look at the textual evidence from *A Portrait of the Artist as a Young Man*. Appeased by the "inhuman clamor" and "the dark frail quivering bodies" of the birds under the portico of the National Library, which help him forget for a moment his mother's sobbing and reproachful face, Stephen lets his mind be invaded by a flock of "thoughts from Swedenborg on the correspondence of birds to things of the intellect and of how the creatures of the air have their knowledge and know their times and seasons because they, unlike man, are in the order of their life and have not perverted that order by reason" (*Portrait* 224–25).

Let us now look at the textual evidence from *Ulysses*. In his tirade in "Scylla and Charybdis" on the subject of William Shakespeare's tormented odyssey between the conjugal love for his wife Anne Hathaway and the "foul pleasures" of sexual promiscuity, Stephen cites the reprobation of "scortatory love" (*U* 9.632) that Swedenborg elaborates upon in his two works, *Delights of Wisdom Concerning Conjugal Love: after which follows the pleasures of insanity concerning Scortatory Love*, and *Marriage Love*. In the latter book, published in 1768, twenty-four years after the appearance of Vico's *Scienza nuova seconda*, Swedenborg lays down those very "thoughts . . . on the correspondence of birds to things of the intellect" that, in the episode of divination in *A Portrait of the Artist as a Young Man,* fly "hither and thither" in Stephen's mind (224). It is indeed in the perversion of the order of human life "by reason," as Swedenborg would put it, that William Shakespeare, Stephen's Elizabethan cipher of the "Scylla and Charybdis" episode, finds a moral justification for his love of adultery, that "scortatory love opposed to marriage love" which, according to Swedenborg's caustic definition, ordinarily "is not regarded as a sin, nor as evil, dishonorable . . . but as permissible *by reason.*"[8] It is evident that Stephen's "thoughts from Swedenborg," in *A Portrait of the Artist as a Young Man,* add a fundamental *coloratura* to the tirade on Shakespeare, which he delivers about two years later in the very same place of his former divination.

Now, although Joyce may have extracted his Viconianism from theosophical doctrines, as Pietropaolo suggests,[9] it happens that Swedenborg maintains opposite views with respect to Vico's when it comes to the superiority of birds of prey vis-à-vis vulgar or degenerate birds, such as swallows or doves. With respect to the contribution that the episode of divination in *A Portrait of the Artist as a Young Man* provides to Stephen's characterization, the difference between Vico and Swedenborg allows for a significant separation of the Viconian elements from the theosophical ones.

Vico's and Swedenborg's respective interests, both in birds of prophecy and in marital love, are radically different. With respect to love and marriage, Vico is concerned with the *coniugium,* or solemn conjugal bond, whose contractual obligations descend from Roman jurisprudence. The Roman solemn marriage (*iusta nuptia*) is celebrated under the protection of *Juno-Lucina,* the Roman Hera, who, according to Vico, makes patricians illustrious, luminous, by bringing their offshoots to light (*luce*). In addition to providing the juridical ground for the transmission of the patronymic to the male successor, the *iustae nuptiae* also legitimize the authority of the aristocratic *paterfamilias* as the lawmaker and as the interpreter of the gods' and the family ancestors' will through the flight of birds of prey. (The Roman plebs engaged in strenuous political struggles to obtain the right of solemn marriage from the patriciate. In time, these struggles found juridical expression in a favorable law proposed by the plebs' tribune Canuleius) (Vico, *SNS1* § 513; *CI2* § 21). Swedenborg is interested, instead, in a form of love based on selflessness and dedication to one's companion, a love dissociated from contractual formalities. As to the phenomena that signal the occurrence of this spontaneous love, Swedenborg mentions three pairs of birds: turtledoves, birds of paradise, swans, the very opposite of the *feroces* birds that dominate the Roman divinatory art.[10] Vico, in turn, remarks that inferior birds, such as doves, are attributed by the Romans to the plebeian Venus; this is the goddess who patronizes love without Eros, love, that is, deprived of that *amor nobile* (noble love) which, under the protection of Juno-Lucina-Hera, generates illustrious "heroes," the legitimate and despotic holders of the family *hereditas* (in-*heri*-tance) (*SNS1* § 513).

Swallows as birds of augury, in sum, would fare rather well with Swedenborg, but would be, at best, second-rate carriers of plebeian auspices according to Vico. Let me add, to secure my second point, that Swedenborg mentions bats among the winged creatures whose flight corresponds to human interests and signals their hidden meaning. Bats, though, "confirm falsities so that they are seen as truths."[11] Later on we will look again at the motif of the bat; it occurs with a frequency that cannot be merely accidental, when we compare the texts of *A Portrait of the Artist as a Young Man* and of *Ulysses* as they present the women in the life of Stephen Dedalus.[12]

PATERNITY AND ARTISTIC EMANCIPATION IN JOYCE AND IN VICO

Since biographical research on James Joyce is inadequate to support my thesis that Vico's legal fictions of paternity are crucial to Joyce's characterization of young Stephen, I will opt for a strategy of textual analysis, precisely, a comparative reading of the episode of divination from A *Portrait of the Artist as a Young Man* and of the "Scylla and Charybdis" episode from *Ulysses,* with a look at other relevant passages from the two works, as well as a revealing passage from Joyce's correspondence with Harriet S. Weaver. I will begin with the correspondence.

Vico was at the heart of Joyce's concerns for a long time, as all scholars know. Joyce himself pointed out this aspect of his intellectual history to Harriet S. Weaver in a letter of 21 May 1926. "I would not pay overmuch attention to [Vico's] theories," he wrote, "but they have gradually forced themselves on me through circumstances of my own life."[13] The "circumstances" Joyce is referring to may be taken, at least on a first approximation, to be in the nature of the intellectual interests that will find powerful expression in *Finnegans Wake*. Joyce's letter to Miss Weaver continues, somewhat humorously for somebody as terrified of thunderstorms as Joyce was, with a conspicuous non sequitur: "I wonder where Vico got his fear of thunderstorm." One should not take this digression of Joyce's with regard to a fellow victim of thunder phobia as a gratuitous witticism, especially in light of the fact that the fear of thunder is another of the Viconian elements that Joyce transferred from his personal biography to the character of Stephen Dedalus (*U* 14.408–28). In truth, Vico was afraid of thunder, but, as I will presently show, he managed to graft this fear onto his theory of the origins of human language. In the context of the letter to Miss Weaver, Joyce's apparently whimsical digression seems to reveal a certain appreciation of this curious fact.

Although Vico's fear of thunder is easy to document biographically, it is immediately evident, as we learn from the analysis provided by Donald Verene in his *Vico's Science of Imagination*, that this fear also reveals connotations of a figurative sort that may not have escaped Joyce's scrutiny. According to Vico, the primitive interjection of marvel and fear at the power of thunder was the cry "*Pa!*," which was later doubled into "*Pape!*," the root of Zeus's definition as the gods' and men's *Papà*, or *Padre* (Italian for the Latin *Pater* and the English Father) (Vico, *SNS1* § 448). Verene observes: "Joyce understood [that thunder is the first human thought] when . . . he placed his hundred-letter clap of thunder on the first page of *Finnegans Wake* . . . (as) the sound of Finnegan's fall."[14] This remark is preceded by a biographical passage on Vico that reads, as I will explain, like an insightful exegesis of Joyce's above-mentioned epistolary comment on Vico's fear of thunder:

> On the first page of his *Autobiography* Vico describes the first memorable incident of his life as a fall from the top of a ladder in which his cranium was fractured . . . Vico sees this incident as having shaped his temperament . . . making him . . . quick as lightning in perception (*che per l'ingegno balenino in acutezze*) . . . Vico's powers of *fantasia* begin in a thunderous fall that produced in him a capacity of mental lightning. This incident . . . is full of symbolism for Vico's thought . . . a symbolism that was not lost on Joyce . . .[15]

The hermetic non sequitur by which Joyce skips from the consideration that Vico's theories forced themselves on him "through circumstances of [his] own life" to a witticism on Vico's fear of thunder (which fear was, undoubtedly, as all biographies suggest, a significant "circumstance" in Joyce's life) seems to gain significance from the implications of the above passage by Verene. Vico thought that human language, as a means of intersubjective communication, found its primal root in a frightening noise coming from the sky, and in the immediate identification of this noise, on the part of the mortals, with the wrath of the father of the gods and men. In sum, according to Vico, human language, the vehicle for the splendid creations of man's *fantasia,* was born out of filial terror. And this Viconian principle applied not only to the collective dimension of social macrophenomena, but also to the private experience of the individual, as shown in the first page of Vico's autobiography. In this light, one might venture that the laconic non sequitur of Joyce's letter to Miss Weaver is indeed very eloquent in its implied meaning. It suggests that Vico's and his own fear of thunder is, at one and the same time, a symptom of subjection to and of emancipation from paternal authority. As it bespeaks man's subordination to authority, the fear out of which sprouts human language constitutes the paradoxical manure that makes the creations of artistic genius (Vico's *acutezze dell'ingegno*) blossom. From both a Joycean and a Viconian standpoint, the drive toward linguistic invention is to be stoically regarded as the marvelous offspring of filial terror.

Joyce's attribution of his thunder phobia to Stephen allows for a metaphoric extension to the fictional character—Joyce's quasi alter ego—of Joyce's own lifelong struggle against the patriarchal and phallocentric (as well as colonial and religious) connotations of the language he elected as his artistic medium of expression. Besides, the characterization of Stephen Dedalus in *A Portrait of the Artist as a Young Man* and in *Ulysses* adds a further dimension, that of the maternal, to the above theme. Stephen's preoccupation with *amor matris* is in a relation of conflict with the paternal and androlineal order of genealogy— the order of what Joyce calls, in *Ulysses* as well as in his private correspondence, the "legal fiction" of paternity.[16] In Joyce, a man's exposure to filial terror may be looked at, paradoxically enough, as the *privilege* that makes possible those intellectual and spiritual acts of self-invention or self-creation—Rabaté's "paternity as creation," or at least a Viconian version of it— that sustain his destruction of paternal authority, as well as his substitution of the father in the chain of patriarchal primacy, a process of power acquisition inaccessible to the female or "natural" elements of the genealogical tree.

STEPHEN DEDALUS'S PLEBEIAN FAMILY

In the episode of divination under the portico of the National Library, Stephen strikes the pose of the diviner, and attempts to derive an omen about his future from the flight of a flock of swallows. First of all, in a proprietary attitude the Joyce reader is familiar with, for having observed Stephen so often immersed in accounting and managerial enterprises of a more or less spiritual nature,[17] Stephen takes care to count the number of birds in his vicinity, which turn out to be an inauspicious total of thirteen. Then he tries to identify their family, and they turn out to be swallows. Stephen feels reassured at first by their shrill cries, because the noise covers the continual murmur of his mother's reproaches in his own mind. At this point the reader might legitimately expect some disclaimer of maternal authority on Stephen's part, or else an expression of filial rebellion: twelve to twenty-four hours earlier, on the steps of the Library's portico, Stephen refused to salute Emma, guilty of "looking at (Father Moran) out of dove's eyes" (*Portrait* 216, 220). But now it is the mother's image, rather than the girlfriend's, that haunts him. After the episode with Emma on the steps of the Library, Stephen had wondered: "And if he had judged (Emma) harshly? If her life were . . . simple and strange as a bird's life . . . Her heart simple and wilful as a bird's heart?" (216). The next day, rather inopportunely, it is May Goulding who takes the upper hand. Why? Is this a sign of emotional immaturity on Stephen's part? Or a symptomatic return of his maternal dependence, as, with several insightful qualifications, Alberto Moreiras has maintained?[18]

A possibility we should keep in mind is the following: When all women turn out to be winged creatures of some sort, as seems consistently to be happening around Stephen, the difference between a bird of day like dove-eyed Emma, "restless all day, tired at sundown" (*Portrait* 216), and a nocturnal being like the ghost of May Goulding, may be passed in silence—they are, by Freud's leave, interchangeable. This is confirmed by the fact that in another twenty-four hours Stephen's imagination turns birdlike Emma—who is, after all, a factual and concrete impersonation of the oneiric girl with "legs . . . delicate as a crane's" and a bosom "slight and soft as the breast of some dark-plumaged dove" (171) whom Stephen contemplated on the beach years before—into a "batlike soul," a close relative of the indecent pregnant temptress who had one night lured Davin, one of Stephen's friends (182–83, 221).

Before reading in the swallows' flight the prophecy of his exile, Stephen's brooding turns a bit more solemn than customary and tells us, or tells him, how archaically poetic his stance as an augur is: "And for ages men had gazed upward as he was gazing at birds in flight. The colonnade above him made him think vaguely of an ancient temple and the ashplant on which he leaned wearily of the curved stick of an augur" (225).[19] Stephen has decided to act as an augur—although he is certainly not a "certified" augur. He is not a *paterfamilias,* insofar as he is of plebeian origins, and unmarried at that. He does not expect, figuratively speaking, to inherit his father's name, insofar as he does not see himself, figuratively speaking again, as the true son of Simon Dedalus. In "Scylla and Charybdis," in the middle of his tirade on *Hamlet,* he broods: "I am tired of my voice, the voice of Esau. My kingdom for a drink" (*U* 9.981). As Esau, who trades his rights of primogeniture for a dish of lentil stew and a piece of bread (but also as Shakespeare's Richard III, who is eager to trade his kingdom for a horse), Stephen is now willing to bargain his primogeniture for a drink.

After the failure of his juvenile project to inaugurate "new filial relations" through an agenda of gratuitous gifts to his family, the institution of a "loan bank for his family," etc. (*Portrait* 96–98), Stephen the teenager had already felt himself "hardly of the one blood with [mother and brother and sister] but . . . rather in the mystical kinship of fosterage, fosterchild and fosterbrother" (98). And then, during the trip to Cork, escorting his father on a nostalgic visit to his hometown, Stephen realized the vague certainty of his own father as to Stephen's filial condition. "Then he's not his father's son," asks a little old man to Simon Dedalus, referring to Stephen. "I don't know, I'm sure," Simon Dedalus answers. And then he adds: "Well, I hope he'll be as good a man as his father. That's all I can say" (94–95)—which, it seems to me, is not saying enough, when it comes to the acknowledgment of one's legitimate offspring. The echo of the Homeric episodes where Telemachos sees his genealogical legitimacy questioned by Athena at the beginning of the *Odyssey,* and later on by Nestor, by Menelaos and his wife Helen, and

by Penelope's suitors themselves, is obviously too deliberate, as
noted in chapter 1, to be passed over silently.

According to his school friend Temple, young Stephen comes
from a *"pernobilis et pervetusta familia"* (*Portrait* 230). But
does the evidence of having a father and a mother, two *genitores*
impoverished, made plebeian by Simon Dedalus's string of fail-
ures in life, give Stephen a *familia* worthy of *stemmata,* of family insignia? From Vico's standpoint, the answer would be
negative. *Familia* is, according to Vico, the Latin synonym of
the term *hereditas,* which designates the right to despotic lordship over the estate of the family, a right enjoyed only by the
pater who is entitled to the auspices of hawks and eagles, and by
his firstborn *filius* (*SNS1* § 513, 529; *CI2* § 37). In early Roman
jurisprudence solemn marriages and burials confer certainty to
family succession. But the term *pater* and the faculty to interpret the gods' thunder and the eagles' flight apply only to the
patrician head of the family, the *paterfamilias* proper, the so-
called "certain father" (whose wife is called *mater*), since only
he has the authority to transmit the patronymic. The plebeian
father, on the contrary, is authorized at the most to interpret
the flight of inferior and *degeneres* birds such as doves; he is
called *genitor,* which means generator or giver-of-natural-life, a
term that applies therefore also to his wife. The *genitor* does
not generate in the son a juridical person, a *filius,* but only a
natural living being, a *spurius.* The *genitores* are also called
parentes, since plebeian mothers accomplish a delivery "established with certainty," according to the law of nature [*natura
certo pariunt*]. The monogamous marriage between plebeians
is "an unbreachable bond between a male and a female," while
the patrician marriage is "the communion of all human and
divine rights between a man and a woman" (*CI2* § 20–21, 37;
SNS1 § 568).

In the episode where he is pressed to add his own name to
the "tail of signatures" in the testimonial of solidarity with the
petition for universal love of the tsar of Russia, Nicholas II, Stephen declares in a self-deprecatory yet ironic tone: "'My signature is of no account" (*Portrait* 198). This statement may be
taken as a signal that Stephen has already drawn his own rather
negative conclusions as to the "nobility" of his "ancient" family.
Just as in the case of Telemachus's perplexity in book 1 of the
Odyssey, when Athena/Mentes asks him to identify himself as
Odysseus' son, Stephen's only "certainty" as to his genealogy may
be ascribed to the order of nature, to the "certainty" of his mater-

nal conception and delivery, rather than to the order of law, to the rightful acquisition of the patronymic. And in direct contrast with the case of Hamlet, the rightful and righteous avenger, albeit a dramatically procrastinating one, of Claudius's violation of the legal bond between King Hamlet and Gertrude, Stephen finds nothing to praise or defend in the brutal bond of marriage that led his mother to premature death after delivering "nine or ten" children in the period of about twenty years (*Portrait* 241).[20]

TEOLOGIA MISTICA

From a Viconian standpoint, if a firstborn son's legitimate paternity (or the legal fiction that grounds it) is in doubt, three consequences ensue: (1) he will not have access to the privilege of the auspices; (2) he will not have the right to the acquisition and transmission of the patronymic; (3) he will be a stranger to the priests and oracles who speak the language of auspices. These three points are strictly interrelated in Vico's theories of legitimate succession in the family. The acquisition of the privilege of the auspices goes back to *teologia mistica,* as Vico calls the ancient Roman jurisprudence anterior to the written laws of the fifth century B.C.E. *Teologia mistica* was concerned with the interpretation of thunder, of the flight of the birds of prey, and of the Lares, the souls of the deceased ancestors, as manifestations of the divine will. An indication of the extent to which this "first" or mystical jurisprudence was imbued with fictionality may be found in Vico's consideration that *teologia mistica* introduced the so-called *iura imaginaria* or, as Vico puts it, "(legal) rights as fabled by fantasy" (*SNS2* § 937–41, 1036; *UIPF* § 220). Incidentally, it is noticeable, as illustrated in chapter 8, that Hegel's *Philosophy of Right* refers to certain interpretations of ancient Roman laws of inheritance by the jurists of the imperial age as *fictiones.*[21]

Teologia mistica, furthermore, conferred upon the interpreter of the auspices the *autoritas* (authority) to legislate, and this social authority pertained only to the *patresfamilias,* the heads of the patrician families, who were the only agents in Roman society entitled to the supernatural mandate of divination. Hence, the right of acquisition and transmission of the patronymic, primarily derived from the *iustae nuptiae,* was directly related to the privilege of delivering the auspices. Second, the authority to deliver auspices, which turned a *paterfamilias* into an oracle, a mouthpiece of the gods, engendered the authority of the *paterfamilias* over his own language, which was the language spoken by all those who predicted the future, because only what they declared to be *teologia mistica* held as unquestionably true, and was subject, norm by norm, to a criterion of divine verification. Through the *patria potestas* (the power of the father) the dead ancestors were considered vicariously alive in the authority of the *pater,* who interpreted their mind and enacted their will. As Vico wrote, in a formulation suggestive, again, of the fabulatory, inherently metaphoric character of the early, unwritten Roman jurisprudence: "Ancient jurisprudence ... treated facts as non-facts, non-facts as facts, children-to-come as already born, living men as dead, dead men as alive in their vicarious authorities ..." (*CI2* § 20; *SNS2* § 1036; *SNS1* § 526–30).

So, in Stephen's case the flight of the swallows is bound to lie to him when he attempts to translate it into a prophetic utterance, no less than if it were a flock of bats. In addition, his name is not his own—he is a failed Hamlet, therefore, and a failed Telemachus as well, with no usurpers to kill.

As to language and religion, we must listen carefully to the voice of the priests in *A Portrait of the Artist as a Young Man.* "Yes, yes," says Father Moran to birdlike Emma, "the ladies are coming round to us." In Stephen's memory of her flirting with young Father Moran, Emma is turned into a "batlike soul ... whisper[ing] of innocent transgressions in the latticed ear of a priested peasant." Yes, says the priest, the ladies are "the best helpers the (Gaelic) language has" (220–21). As an ironic confirmation to Father Moran's words, and as a Viconian element of characterization as well, language and religion go hand in hand in Stephen's early education at the Jesuit schools of Clongowes and Belvedere College. And it is hand in hand, too, that language and religion walk out of Stephen's life. Formal training in the English language was offered to Stephen, initially, as a religious experience, in the "legend[s]" read by Father Arnall out of the book at Clongowes, in the "legendary craft" of the Jesuits and their secret books at Belvedere College (26, 186). But then these legends became progressively unreadable to him. During the trip to Cork, because of his "monstrous way of life," Stephen "could scarcely interpret the letters of the signboards of the shops" (92). Later, on his daily walk to University College through the streets of Dublin, the thought of his friend Cranly, to whom he had often confessed his secret plans and desires as if to a true Catholic priest, brought Stephen to glance, "from one casual word to another on his right or left in stolid wonder that they had been so silently emptied of instantaneous sense" (178–79). And finally, Stephen's learned yet ironic disquisition with the dean of studies at University College leads him to the conclusion (hardly an epiphany) that "[t]he language in which we are speaking is his before it is mine . . . His language . . . will always be for me an acquired speech" (189). Again, this is a dutiful conclusion on the part of a pauper, a plebeian, somebody who is, both in a Viconian figure of speech and from an economic and colonial perspective, a disenfranchised citizen.

PATERNITY, EMANCIPATION, AND ARTISTIC SELF-GESTATION

At this point it must be recalled that together with his father Simon's patronymic, Stephen Dedalus is handed down, diphthong apart, the burdensome legacy of *another* name, that of a mythological father, the artificer of Minos's labyrinth. However one chooses to engage the character of Stephen Dedalus, one is bound to envision him, figuratively speaking, as a Daedalid,[22] a winged creature destined either to soar triumphantly, "sunward toward the sea . . . in an air beyond the world" (*Portrait* 169), or to fall miserably, "seabedabbled," as *Ulysses* puts it (*U* 9.954), by the waves of his oceanic wreckage.[23] Yet, Stephen's aptitude for figural flight is made rather volatile by its very affinity with the Daedalus myth, upon which Stephen hinges so much of his youthful delusions of grandeur. As we will see, it is in the unfolding of the Daedalus myth that Stephen finds eventually the elements that bring to completion his counterpoise of *amor matris* and the legal fiction of paternity.

In the episode of divination Stephen has decided, notwithstanding the inadequacy of the birds at hand, to act as the augur of his own future. Yet, in order to practice even this spurious kind of divination, Stephen must assume that he is a Daedalid, that, like a legitimate *filius,* he is entitled to the patronymic of his mythological father. Which is what he does, through another excess of weary sentimentality: "[A]t the name of the fabulous artificer [Stephen] seemed . . . to see a winged form flying above the waves and slowly climbing the air. What did it mean? Was it a hawklike man flying sunward . . . , a prophecy of the end he had been born to serve . . . , a symbol of the artist forging anew in

his workshop . . . a new soaring impalpable imperishable being?"
(169). An impalpable imperishable being: Stephen Dedalus's future art work, his poetic oeuvre to come? From the vantage point
of reader's hindsight, it is very tempting to question the artistic
accomplishments of a poet whose entire known artistic production amounts to the *villanelle* from *A Portrait of the Artist as
a Young Man* and, if one projects forward to Stephen's later
vicissitudes in *Ulysses,* the quatrain from "Aeolus" related to the
composition of his so-called vampire poem.[24] On the other hand,
as argued in chapter 3, it is more than likely that the "Aeolus"
quatrain is only a preparatory stage within a more ambitious
process of poetic creation; the Stephen of *Ulysses* may very well
have the proverbial ace hidden in his sleeve. Be that as it may,
Stephen himself appears to doubt the validity of his artistic
accomplishments when, about two years after the episode of
augury, he draws a direct parallel between his attempts at divination under the porch of the National Library ("Here I watched
the birds for augury," he recalls [*U* 9.1206]) and the sarcastic
implications of the epithet "Aengus of the birds," which Buck
Mulligan attributes to him in two episodes of *Ulysses* (*U* 9.1093,
10.1066–67)—an epithet derived from Yeats's poetry and from
Gaelic folklore, that designates a semi-god perpetually bent upon
a sterile quest for love and beauty, usually "portrayed with the
birds of inspiration hovering about his head."[25]

In my opinion, Stephen's genuinely artistic masterpiece consists of the oral delivery, in "Scylla and Charybdis," of a parthenogenetic theory of paternity as artistic self-gestation and self-
transfiguration, embellished with his digressions about William
Shakespeare's and Anne Hathaway's scortatory and conjugal
loves. However, this brilliant piece of "performance art" turns
out to orbit the core of somebody else's intuition, more precisely,
an insight that his friend Cranly illustrated to Stephen a couple
of years earlier, earning in return only Stephen's contempt. This
episode is worth recalling. Stephen and Cranly are near the conclusion of their last conversation, near the end of *A Portrait of
the Artist as a Young Man,* when Cranly utters in a meditative
mood: "Whatever else is unsure in this stinking dunghill of a
world a mother's love is not" (*Portrait* 241–42). In *Ulysses,* Stephen will reach the climax of his Viconianism through a polemical appropriation of this opinion, more precisely, through his
broaching of the motherly principle in "Scylla and Charybdis."
As we saw, the latter episode takes place, appropriately enough,
within the walls of the National Library, just around the corner

from the portico where a couple of years earlier Stephen performed his augury, gave the cold shoulder to Emma, and started obsessing about the lamenting image of his mother. "*Amor matris,* subjective and objective genitive, may be the only true thing in life," concedes Stephen in "Scylla and Charybdis," as if he were belatedly responding to Cranly's reproach for his lack of filial affection. "Paternity may be a legal fiction," he adds (*U* 9.842–44).[26] Stephen's laconic pronouncement echoes with the Viconian implications that become explicit in his tirade on art as self-gestation.

As we saw, legal fictionality is precisely the attribute that, in the Western juridical tradition, deeply rooted in Roman jurisprudence, endows paternity with its social and historical preeminence vis-à-vis the legitimation of the offspring. "A father," whose love is far from certain, and the certainty of whose seminal contribution to procreation may always be challenged, "is a necessary evil" for the legitimate transmission of the patronymic, of fatherhood itself (*U* 9.828). Hamlet Senior cannot rest comfortably in his tomb, Stephen suggests to his listeners at the National Library, because the name of the king has been usurped by Claudius. But Shakespeare Senior, William's father, rests very well at night, being "disarmed of fatherhood" and of his patronymic: John Shakespeare, in fact, has successfully transmitted the "mystical estate" of his paternity to his son William, from *pater* to *filius* (9.835). Is Simon Dedalus's family name, one may ask, returning for a moment to Stephen's legal rather than mythological genealogy, to be successfully passed on to his firstborn son, Stephen, through the link of their common "one blood," or is Stephen bound to remain forever in a state of collateral lineage—that very condition that, at the age of about fourteen, as we saw, he calls the "mystical kinship of fosterage, fosterchild and fosterbrother" (*Portrait* 98)?

"Fatherhood," remarks Stephen, "in the sense of conscious begetting, is unknown to man" (*U* 9.837–38). The only exception known to Stephen to this law of biological procreation—and a fictional exception, at that—is Calandrino (9.836–37), who, in the eighth day of Boccaccio's *Decameron,* turns his cape into a womb (Italian: *grembo*) and the front of his shirt into a breast (Italian: *seno*). But apart from such a grotesque immaculate conception, legitimate paternity, Stephen seems to maintain, consists of a succession based on a legal fiction of legitimacy, rather than on a process of mere insemination or on an impossible process of masculine gestation. Paternity, Stephen thinks, is a fiction whose legitimacy is of the "mystical" order, the same order of legitimacy that Vico attributes to the patrician law founded on the divination of the mind of the gods—the same "apostolic" and vicarious order of legitimacy, the same *lex eterna,* normative rather than natural or procreational, that in the passage I am glossing determines the consubstantial essence of divine lineage, from Father to Son, and then from Jesus to his Pontifex, upon which rests, "founded . . . upon the void" of Peter's unsubstantial "rock," the authority of the Church of Rome (*U* 9.839–42, 3.48, Matthew 16:13–19).

THE ATROPHIED WINGS OF STEPHEN DEDALUS

In spite of the mythological presuppositions embedded in the episode of divination, Stephen is aware that his name cannot be that of the "old artificer." He is not a Daedalid when he pauses in the portico of the National Library to divine the flight of inferior birds. He is even less of a Daedalid in "Scylla and Charybdis," when there are no birds around to silence, with their shrill cries, his remorse over his mother's death. But he makes a tactical choice, at the time of the episode of divination, to adopt provisionally his mythological father's name, so as to enable himself to become, as an artist, his own father.

Stephen's choice to be, for a time, a Daedalid leads him toward the autopaternity of the artist, the "priest of eternal imagination," pregnant with his own "artistic conception, artistic gestation, and artistic reproduction" (*Portrait* 209, 221). Stephen embarks so boldly on this juvenile project of parthenogenetic self-gestation and self-transfiguration that he does not refrain from going public with it, even before any solid evidence is provided through his poems of his genuine artistic talent. As we saw in Chapter 4, his nemesis, Buck Mulligan, may therefore jocularly outplay him at the same self-parturient fantasy in "Scylla and Charybdis": "Himself his own father . . . Wait. I am big with child. I have an unborn child in my brain. Pallas Athena. A play! The play's the thing! Let me parturiate!" (*U* 9.875–77). With this explicit reference to Hamlet's conception of the play-within-the-play,[27] Buck's exuberant recitation turns Stephen's theories on Shakespeare's creative drives (as well as Stephen's own Hamletism) into a joke. According to Stephen (insofar as, at least, any argument of his in "Scylla and Charybdis" is not tainted by his own ironic disbelief), Shakespeare wrote *Hamlet* not as a reflection of pain at the death of his own father (Stephen: "Who is the father of any son that the son should love him or he any son?" [*U* 9.844–45]), but, rather, as a reflection of the loss of his child, Hamnet, as well as of the infidelity of his wife, Hamnet's mother, Anne Hathaway. Already in the "Telemachus" episode Buck Mulligan ridiculed Stephen's theories in front of Haines: "(Stephen) proves by algebra that Hamlet's grandson is Shakespeare's grandfather and that *he himself* is the ghost of his own father." At which remark, Haines replies, pointing at Stephen: "What? . . . He himself?" (*U* 1.555–61, my emphasis).[28]

Probably Stephen has not dismissed his poetic ambitions when we meet him on the morning of 16 June 1904, on the roof of the Martello Tower, but he appears harshly disillusioned with regard to his own artistic accomplishments later the same day, between 2:00 P.M. and 3:00 P.M., at the National Library, in the course of his tirade on *Hamlet* and artistic conception. Let us not forget that in this episode George William Russell describes his project to edit a collection of "younger poets' verses" (the book, *New Songs,* had already been published by June 1904, and did not include any of Joyce's poems), and mentions, furthermore, a literary gathering to be held at George Moore's house that evening, to which Buck and Haines are invited but Stephen is not (*U* 9.290–96). It is in this episode that Stephen ponders sourly: "Fabulous artificer. The hawklike man. You flew. Whereto? Newhaven-Dieppe, steerage passenger. Paris and back. Lapwing. Icarus. *Pater, ait.* Seabedabbled, fallen, weltering. Lapwing you are. Lapwing be" (*U* 9.952–54). And in the space of a few minutes he addresses himself twice again, in his soliloquy, with the epithet, clearly derogatory, as we are going to see shortly, of "lapwing" (9.976, 9.980).

We have reached the juncture where the Daedalus myth contributes the essential elements for the articulation of Stephen's counterpoise of the maternal and the paternal order of genealogy—a balance of forces, as I have tried to show, fraught with irresolution. It is in the Ovidian presentation of the Daedalus myth that Stephen's self-parturient fantasies find an adequately winged configuration, a configuration antithetical to his earlier, arrogant identification with the "fabulous artificer" of infinite imagination. Stephen turns himself from a hawklike bird of prey into Ovid's lapwing (*perdix*), from a fabulous artificer into Ovid's garrulous chatterbox (*garrula perdix*): he has resigned himself, in other words, to the condition of an inferior bird (and an inferior poet as well, at least in the eyes of the Dublin intelligen-

tsia).[29] The choice of the lapwing to signify Stephen's disillusionment is far from accidental. The lapwing is a bird despised by
Hamlet, who detects the spirit of the lapwing in young Osric,
the courtesan made (in)famous by his volatile hat and his servile
obsequiousness. Horatio comments to Hamlet: "This lapwing
[i.e., Osric] runs away with the shell on his head." To which
words Hamlet replies: "(He) has . . . a kind of yesty collection
which carries [him] through and through . . ." (5.2.170–75).
Since Hamlet's expression "yesty collection," besides indicating
Osric's awkwardness and the lapwing's jerky flight, is usually
taken to signify an agglomerate of terms and turns of phrase
borrowed here and there, one may sense in Stephen's self-
infliction of the condition of the lapwing an almost desperate
surrender to, or acceptance of, mediocrity—the mediocrity of
the courtesan, the jester whose loquacity is mere entertainment
to the literates gathered at the National Library.

But above all, as I said, the figure of the lapwing is related to
the Daedalus myth in Ovid. As though it were not enough for
Stephen to earn for himself the virtual contempt of Hamlet, the
Shakespearean hero to whom he has always felt so intimately
related by a variety of temperamental and spiritual affinities,
Stephen chooses, for his social metamorphosis from poet to
chatterbox, a bird that laughs irreverently at the funeral of
Icarus, Daedalus's brave son. The Latin name of the lapwing is
perdix. In his *Metamorphoses,* Ovid tells that Perdix is the name
of Daedalus's nephew, of whose cleverness and craft Daedalus
was so jealous that he threw him from the Acropolis of Athens.
The goddess Athena saved Perdix and turned him into a bird,
more precisely, into a bird afraid of altitudes whose jerky mo-
tions recall the quickness of wit of the boy. The bird kept the
boy's name, perdix.[30]

William Blake writes that the *perdix* is a quasi-domestic bird
which, being inclined to flutter around the hearth, is bound to
be captured in the net spread beneath the hearth itself by man.[31]
Weldon Thornton informs us that one of the lapwing's character-
istic traits is that it tries to conceal its nest by flying wildly
around, so as to divert anybody from finding it.[32] In sum, Stephen turns himself willingly into a winged creature that is, first,
bound to fall into the net prepared to capture it (what a miserable fate, compared to his earlier intention to fly by the nets
of nationality, language, and religion! [*Portrait* 203]); a winged
creature, second, that only pretends to be homeless but is in
reality *a domestic spirit,* an energetic protector of its own

house, unequipped, figuratively speaking, for the rigors of exile;[33] a winged creature, third, that is afraid of altitudes, hence reluctant, again figuratively, to undertake daring flights of imagination; a winged creature, finally, that dies as a *"puer,"* a boy, to be reborn of the opposite gender, a *"garrula perdix"* (Ovid, *Metamorphoseon* 8.237, 8.243).[34] As regards this latter trait, one may recall that Stephen has always exhibited a strong aptitude for radical transfiguration: his villanelle, for instance, abounds in aesthetic transfigurations of woman into virgin and into whore, of Christ into Lucifer, of sex into religious elevation. One may say that by undergoing a perdixlike gender transfiguration Stephen assimilates his own self—the self of an artist that nobody in Dublin seems to be willing to take seriously, and who is desperately attempting to reinvent or regenerate himself—to a Calandrino-like personification of the "batlike soul" that has oppressed him throughout his sexual maturation. He becomes an incarnation of the "womanhood of (his) country," which was originally represented, in *A Portrait of the Artist as a Young Man,* by adolescent Emma, submissive to the charms of the church, but, above all, by the demoniac woman imprinted upon his imagination by his friend Davin's storytelling—the woman who, in the guise of a reincarnated Jael from the Bible, "answer[s Davin's] plea for water with a mug of milk" and invites him to her bed (*Portrait* 183, 221.).[35]

Let me engage in a close exegesis of Davin's story that will provide a result fundamental to my argument. Stephen's transfiguration from hawk to lapwing, from Icarus to Perdix, sheds light on the relevance that the episode of Davin's nocturnal encounter with the pregnant seductress acquires in Stephen's later recollection. Davin's plea for water is answered with a mug of milk, the way Jael, after lasciviously opening her "tent" to the defeated Sisera, is asked for water but offers milk instead (Judges 4:17–21, 5:24–27). In "Controlling Perspectives," Danna Fewell and David Gunn have pointed out the sexual overtones of this biblical episode from the Book of Judges. In the first place, in biblical literature a man rarely enters a woman's tent for purposes other than that of sexual intercourse, since the very enclosure of the tent is symbolic of the woman's body. Second, Proverbs 5:15–19, 9:13–18 and the Song of Songs 4:15 show that water is symbolic of sexuality, so that when a woman, after sheltering a man within the intimacy of her tent, answers a request of water with an offer of milk, there occurs a disquieting coalescence of both sexual and motherly, hence incestuous, attributes. Third, after turning herself into a reassuring, motherly figure, Jael perpetrates a reverse rape on Sisera, when she hammers a tent peg into the skull of her sleeping victim. After the phallic shape penetrates his brain, Sisera sinks and lies "outstretched" at Jael's feet, "still, . . . destroyed" (Judges 5:27), just like a rape victim.[36] (It is not accidental that the description of Sisera's corpse adopts a verbal signifier, škb, "to lie," which was typically used to denote the inertness of the raped woman.)[37] Stephen's insistent recollection of Davin's story may be explained by the consideration, then, that in this story reverberates a biblical incident whose reversal of sexual roles applies to Stephen's counterpoise of the maternal and paternal orders of genealogy; both in Davin's story and in Judges we read of the apparition of a woman whose menace to man's supremacy lies in her power to procreate and to seduce.

The firstborn son of a man with "a curious idea of genders," Stephen enjoys, or rather endures, his rights of primogeniture in a world whose eminent symbolic configuration pertains to the order of the phallus (*Portrait* 175).[38] The planet earth, which Stephen's poetic inspiration will envelop within a liturgical "smoke of praise . . . up from ocean rim to rim," is, in a devotional figuration quite appropriate to his villanelle, "a ball of incense [inside a] censer"; but the same planet is also at once, quite blasphemously, an "ellipsoidal ball," a testicle enveloping the soul of the Christian worshiper (*Portrait* 218). Any image, word, event from everyday life may induce Stephen, in his college years, to turn his surroundings into an indecent figuration of male genitalia. The "smoke of praise" of his poetic transport, for instance, pervades Stephen's imagination in the middle of his most intense longing, his most mystical rapture toward Emma; nonetheless, he cannot help recalling Moynihan's sarcastic comment, the day before at University College, apropos the mathematical formula for the ellipse: "What price ellipsoidal balls! Chase me, ladies, I'm in the cavalry!" (*Portrait* 192). As Vicky Mahaffey points out in *Reauthorizing Joyce,* puberty has led Stephen to see "his body as serpentine":[39] his own penis has a life of its own, a "bestial part of his body . . . torpid (and) snaky," which feeds "of his own life" (*Portrait* 139). It is little wonder, then, that Stephen Dedalus, tired of listening to his own, Esau-like voice, and faced with the inadequacies of both his phallic obsession and his self-parturient fantasies, volunteers to trade his primogeniture "for a drink" (*U* 9.981). Stephen attempts to drown the memory of the "womanhood of his country" in the fumes of alcohol, but in the course of the long night between 16 and 17 June, 1904, the alcoholic fumes conjure up, instead, the most nightmarish of his meetings with the ghost of his dead mother. The restless, corpselike ghost of the "once beautiful May Goulding" appears in the "Circe" episode "ris(ing) stark through the floor, in leper grey with a wreath of faded orangeblossoms and a torn bridal veil, her face worn and noseless, green with gravemould." And she urges Stephen: "Beware! . . . Beware God's hand!" (*U* 15.4157–219).

At the end of *Ulysses,* one may be led to wonder if the future holds in reserve for Stephen, a young Dublin poet victim of self-doubt and collective disregard, a second and redemptive meeting with the cranelike girl of poetic inspiration—"the angel of mortal youth and beauty [which] open[ed] before him . . . all the way of error and glory" at the time of his radical rebellion against "God's hand" (*Portrait* 172). One may be led to wonder, further, if this unbearably sensuous girl was an "envoy from the fair courts of life," the Dantesque muse sent to free Stephen from social, religious, and family constraints or, rather, in her dark plumage, another crafty masquerade of the irredeemable womanhood of his country (172). The tormented and unresolved stance nurtured by young Stephen toward womanhood, intended, especially at the time of composition of the "villanelle of the temptress," either as an angelic source of poetic inspiration (birdlike Emma) or as a demoniac source of existential abjection (batlike Emma), is reasserted, but also newly problematized, in the final episodes of *Ulysses.* The fundamental question may be phrased in a variety of manners, but its substance does not change. One must ask: Upon leaving Leopold Bloom's house, does Stephen plunge into a perpetual night or into the expansive brilliance of a new dawn? Does he plunge into the abject night of human sterility and poetic despair, or does he emerge into the purposeful light of a new day, a new and expanded horizon for his artistic skills? Does Stephen fall, "seabedabbled," like Icarus, by the waves "of the dark ocean of God," or does he find the willpower to soar triumphantly, "sunward toward the sea?"[40] Or, once again, is the Stephen we last see in "Ithaca" the bat of the menses, the dark incarnation of the blood-sucking incubus from the "Aeolus" quatrain, or the proud "lightning of the intellect," the rebel whose "star . . . knows no setting?" (*U* 3.486–86).

An abject and despairing Stephen is unavoidably a gender hater—or, should I say, a hater of both genders, his father's and his mother's, and his mother's before his father's. But *Ulysses* closes without giving conventional closure to Stephen's conflict. It is almost as though (almost, but not quite, as we will see shortly) the resolution to this conflict were left to the conscience of each individual reader, a reader, however, with reasons to believe that Stephen's muse can still rise, or *surgere,* as his beloved Dante would put it,[41] a muse still able to strike the chords of his heart and set his theme to music.

STEPHEN DEDALUS REBORN

Almost, but not quite . . . I have referred to the "Aeolus" quatrain as the first stage in the composition of Stephen's vampire poem, still unfinished, as argued in chapter 3, by the end of *Ulysses.* And I have referred to the alternative in the interpretation of the "Aeolus" quatrain between a dark vampire and a gloriously fallen angel, between, in other words, the Prince of Darkness of popular culture and the "allbright" Lucifer from the scriptural tradition (*U* 3.486). In the epic of *Finnegans Wake,* Stephen comes back on stage as a "djowl" or, in Irish, a "diabhal," or, if I may indulge in a little name-calling, as Stephen Diabolus, armored in "feet [faith], hoof [hope] and jarrety [charity]"[42]— the typical personification of Satan as satyr, half-goat, half-man (*FW* 222.30–31). The Stephen we encounter in *Finnegans Wake*—Stephen Diabolus, a down-to-earth, wingless satyr solidly anchored to his ham-shaped hocks ("ankered on his hunkers" [*FW* 225.10])—provides a formidable answer to the question(s) every reader wants to ask at the end of *Ulysses.* Is the fate awaiting Stephen one of hope or despair, damnation or redemption? Is Stephen falling into perpetual night, or rising into the expansive vision of a new dawn?

One should never forget the Dantesque luminosity prevailing at the close of *Ulysses.* Lucifer the "Darkinbad," the Evening Star, becomes the "Brightdayler," the Morning Star, and announces the appearance of "a new solar disk" with "a square round Sinbad the Sailor . . ." This passage, immediately followed by Molly Bloom's monologue, is evocative of the completion of Dante's journey, from the encounter with Lucifer in *Inferno* to the glorious vision at the end of *Paradiso:*

> Qual è geomètra che tutto s'affige
> per misurar lo cerchio, e non ritrova,
> pensando, quel principio, ond'elli indige,

tal era io a quella vista nova:
veder volea come si convenne
l'imago al cerchio e come vi s'indova.

[As is the geometer who wholly applies himself to measure the circle,
and finds not, in pondering, the principle of which he is in need,
such was I at that new sight. I wished to see how the image con-
formed to the circle and how it has its place therein.][43]

Bloom's notorious obsession about the squaring of the circle
finds its celestial solution in the vertiginous metamorphosis of
Venus: at dawn Hesperus, the evening Star of Venus, sheds its
Luciferan attributes to become the Maker of Light, the morning
star. The circle of time is squared by the theological doctrine of
hypostasis, but a most blasphemous hypostasis that broaches,
in the ubiquity of night and day, the identity itself of Christ and
Satan. The theological premises and implications of this identity
were illustrated in chapter 3.

Stephen begins the *Via Crucis* of his mock Passion among
the "crucified shirts" of the third episode of *Ulysses* (3.156), and
undergoes a mock resurrection in *Finnegans Wake,* where he
comes back transformed, appropriately enough, into Shem the
Penman, the man of letters of the *Wake,* a personification, or a
fictional type, of Old Nick, the evil one. Stephen comes back,
in a simplified paraphrases of the text, "panting and spitting,
coughing like anything, weeping his eyes out, and gnashing his
teeth over the brevity of existence and the other lies of the book
of life." He comes back ready for "*(a)cts of feet, hoof and jarrety*"
(*FW* 222.26–31, my emphasis). But he comes back, above all,
from the silence, exile, and cunning of *A Portrait of the Artist
as a Young Man* ("the bruce, the coriolano and the ignacio . . .
Mum's for's maxim, ban's for's book . . . and Unkel Silanse coach
in diligence" [*Portrait* 247; *FW* 228.10–17]), as the personification, or fictional type, of the author of the greatest love story of
modernity, that of Leopold and Molly Bloom; he comes back, in
fact, as the apocryphal, slanderous writer of "Ukalepe" (Calypso),
"Loathers' leave" (Lotus Eaters), "Had Days" (Hades), "Skilly and
Carubdish" (Scylla and Charybdis), "A Wondering Wreck" (The
Wandering Rocks), etc. (*FW* 229.13–16). Stephen's representation of Leopold Bloom exhibits "a great big oh in the megafun-
dum" of his anus, while that of Molly Bloom never "cesse[s] at
waking malters," or never stops making waters, from the orifice
of "her microchasm" (229.20–24). The eschatology of carnal
love, from Eneas and Dido to Tristan and Isolde to Dante and

Beatrice, which, as I hinted in chapter 3, holds together the fundamental doctrinal elements in the tradition of Christian epics, finds its culmination in Stephen's scatological homage to Leo and Molly, this most perplexing, most chaste, most sodomitic couple of lovers. What matters here is not so much the vertiginous hypostasis stressed already in chapter 3, wherein and whereby Satan is consubstantial with Christ, Jesus is consubstantial with Beatrice (and also, Leopold is consubstantial with Molly, ALP with HCE, Mick, or Michael, the angel of the Church Militant, with Old Nick), nor that other hypostasis, staged in the transition from *Ulysses* to *Finnegans Wake,* wherein and whereby Stephen undergoes the mockery of a Passion that turns him into the crucified Diabolus of modern letters, the modern Messiah of copro-eschatology. What matters most is that in *Finnegans Wake* Joyce, having acknowledged and blessed Stephen as his artistic alter-ego, assigns him the task of bringing to closure the bimillennial cycle of opposition between Word and Flesh, which, manifest throughout the entire tradition of Christian epics, and intrinsic to the fundamental dichotomy within the order of genealogy, had been inaugurated for the consciousness of the West by the Pauline writings.[44]

How can one still picture Stephen's fate as swaying between damnation and redemption, fall and elevation? The opposition between these Christian connotations of individual destiny is *ipso facto* emptied of meaning by Stephen's alleged literary production of the epic love story of *Ulysses.* Stephen's *Ulysses* (and such a virtual text exists, if only in the universe of *Finnegans Wake*) signals the end of the doctrinal oppositions inaugurated by St. Paul; and it inaugurates this end through a mode of discourse that brings the Word to re-sound in the Flesh and the sacred to resound in the profane. This mode of discourse, which Stephen finds in and derives from vernacular blasphemy, brings about, as Thomas Altizer argues in *History as Apocalypse,* the culmination and consumption of Catholic theology, the modern and terminal language of Catholic liturgy (210, 215). In the end, and it is the end of Christian eschatology itself we are addressing here, Joyce's Stephen Dedalus does not fall, nor does he take off, full of celestial grace, for a flight of paradisiacal imagination. Nor, inspired by his muse, does he intone a chant of pious piety. Rather, he stages his own irreverent, Phoenixlike rebirth, by undertaking, in parody, satire, and apocryphal writing, the first radical exploration of the sacred ground of modern blasphemy. "Make a shine on the curst. Emen."

Part III
Genealogy, Law, and Religion

7

The Law of the Outlaw: Family Succession and Family Secession in Hegel and in Genesis 31

> ... bearing in his arms the tables of the law, graven in the language of the outlaw.
>
> —Joyce, *Ulysses* 7.868–69

AN ANALYSIS OF THE STRUCTURE OF THE HEBREW FAMILY IN THE Old Testament may help set in play a deconstruction of Hegel's views with regard to the contributions given, respectively, by the Roman and the Christian family to the formulation of a private code of law and particularly of the law of legitimate family succession. According to Hegel, family succession earns its legitimacy through the determinant role played by the *paterfamilias,* the head of the family, in the transmission of the family's name and estate. As Jacques Derrida has shown in *Glas,* the principle that a historical and logical progression necessarily leads from the Greek to the Roman and from the Roman to the Christian notion of *paterfamilias* is fundamental to the Hegelian jurisprudence of civil right.[1] Yet, the necessity of this progression is contradicted by the structure achieved by the Hebrew family through the Mosaic law. A gulf separates the Christian family, whose essential manifestations are characterized by the love of one's kin, and ultimately by the love of the Holy Trinity, from the Hebrew family, whose essential manifestations are characterized by tribal norms, and ultimately by the dictates of the Torah.

In order to question the validity of Hegel's views as regards the primacy of the *paterfamilias,* and especially the applicability of these views to the jurisprudence of civil rights, I will undertake a detailed study of Rachel's theft of her father's idols, or *teraphim,* in Genesis 31. Rachel's theft entails a radical subversion

141

of the law of family succession inherent in the customs and traditions of both her father's and her husband's tribes. This study, which answers the ancient question: "Why does Rachel steal Laban's idols?" and answers it through a systematic revision of current biblical scholarship, enables me to demonstrate the fallacy inherent in the postulates that ground Hegel's concept of the family. Moreover, the ascribing of a crucial symbolic role to Rachel's theft in the reconfiguration of her new family's tribal norms substantiates an insight found in Ilana Pardes's *Countertraditions in the Bible,* namely, the observation that the contribution of women to the history of Israel is unmistakable, even though their acts do not usually pertain to the political sphere narrowly defined.[2] As we will see, the private and the public intermingle to such an extent in Rachel's theft of the teraphim that it would be difficult to separate its effects upon her own family from those upon the house of Israel. A transgression of the law of her polytheistic family of origin and a reconfiguration of the law of her new monotheistic family coalesce in Rachel's theft. In the first place, Rachel neutralizes Laban's revenge against her husband, Jacob; in the second place, she undermines her husband's patriarchal ambitions. Rachel contributes to the history of Israel insofar as she embeds the episode of her filial disobedience within the plot of the narrative of the birth of Israel. The people of the God of Law find the premises for their own existence in the act of transgression by which a young woman, having defied her father's wrath, manages to save her husband's life, and, in so doing, subverts the role of absolute marginality assigned to her own gender by the monotheistic norms of legitimate succession for the head of the family.

THE ROMAN *PATERFAMILIAS* AND THE HEBREW PATRIARCH

Hegel's *Philosophy of Right* attributes the character of the "supreme opposition in ethics"[3] to the conflict between man's and woman's legal personae, the conflict, that is, between the masculine "dominating power over public life" and the feminine submission to the domestic "bond of kinship."[4] Two aspects of the Hegelian sense of gender opposition are to be stressed here. The first is that this conflict of genders is reflected in the subordination of civil right to public right, the former being contaminated by the "feeling" for individuals inherent in consanguineous bonds and family life, the latter being aimed at the regulation of what Hegel calls the *"higher* sphere of the state" (*PhilR* 180:[remark] 122, my emphasis). It is as though, in Hegel's view, civil right presented connotations of only partial— only partially *masculine*—actualization, when compared with the full actualization of public right. The second aspect to be stressed is that the "supreme opposition in ethics" is sublated in the organization of the family, where man and woman come to a reconciliation of their essential conflict.[5] Man "has his actual substantive life" in the laws of the state, while in the family he "lives a subjective ethical life on the plane of feeling." Woman, on the other hand, finds her "substantive destiny" in the laws of the family (*PhilR* 166:114).

From a speculative viewpoint, it is in the right of family property, as well as in the norms of family succession presupposed by the right of family property, that civil right finds the essential grounds for the arbitration and adjudication of the controversies of opposing private individuals. Derrida's *Glas* provides a revealing analysis of the modalities by which Hegel's legal thought assigns a determinant importance to the "lower" moment of the legislation of the family. "There cannot be internal public right unless the property of the family goods and the right of inheritance are intangible." Without the "intangible" private laws regarding the property of the family estate and the right to family succession, the public sphere of jurisdiction would be left hovering over a world of civil anarchy, since the private sphere would turn out to be impervious to all forms of legislation (*Glas* 63a). And, remarkably, it is also from civil right, hence, ultimately, from the essential grounds provided to it by the organization of the family, that, according to Hegel, the *paterfamilias* derives the authority exercised both in the private and in the public sphere (*PhilR* 171:116). Let us take a closer look.

In Roman jurisprudence the figure of the *paterfamilias* exercises such a dominant role in terms of family organization that the Valerian law, promulgated five centuries before Christ, considers whatever crime does not fall under the jurisdiction of public right as a symbolic patricide, i.e., as an attempt to undermine and virtually appropriate the authority of the *paterfamilias*. The family is the legal unit or nucleus that acquires objective existence with the generation of the progeny, and the *paterfamilias* is its head. However, it takes a slow historical progression, from the Greek to the Roman configuration of the family unit, before the *paterfamilias* becomes also the custodian of the counselors and protectors of the family personified in the Penates, the Lares, and the other household gods. Hegel maintains that in archaic societies this role originally pertained to the wife, whose "*intuitive* awareness of what is ethical" authorized her privileged "association with the Penates."[6] From Hegel's standpoint, humankind had to wait for the advent of the Christian era before the *paterfamilias* acquired his full legal and ethical determination in the configuration of the Christian family.

A basic prerequisite for the husband to be a *paterfamilias* is that the act of engenderment of the progeny must be a moment of sublation of the individuality of the father under the universality of the idea manifested in the nucleus of the family. The inaccessibility of this prerequisite to Roman civilization does not derive so much from the formal inadequacy of Roman customs and ethics as from their historical inadequacy and their temporal delay, from the partiality, in sum, of their prefiguration of the Christian era to come. Hegel's advocacy of a correspondence between the self-showing of the concept and its philosophical progression—a correspondence, that is, between the concept's historical and logical order of emergence—is reflected in his stipulation that the Roman concept of *paterfamilias* finds unity with itself only in the Christian era, which signals the end of Roman civilization.[7] One might say that, from Hegel's standpoint, the logical progression of the concept of *paterfamilias* is reflected in the fact that the Christian family, whose essence is love, provides at long last the necessary ground for the jurisprudence of civil right, which could reach only a partially historical actualization in Roman jurisprudence. Hegel's syllogism, as qualified by Derrida, is straightforward: (1) with Christianity, love constitutes the essence of the family; (2) the real external existence of the family finds its proper manifestation in property (*PhilR* 169:116); (3) property is presupposed by civil right (*Glas* 63a); (4) therefore, civil right presupposes Christian love. The Roman *paterfamilias,* custodian of the family Penates and private and public legislator, relinquishes eventually his role as holder of the symbols of the divine to the Vicar of Christ, the custodian of the Host held in the Tabernacle. The Christian head of the family becomes eventually the personification of the achieved reconciliation between the public law of the state and the private law of the family, between, that is, intellect and feeling, rationality and love, man and woman. As Derrida puts it, "Christianity will have . . . brought about that sublation [*Aufheb-*

ung] of the ideal of the sensible representation [of the family] into the infinity of love . . ." (*Glas* 59a).

A serious complication emerges, however, from this Hegelian discourse on Christian ethical and juridical primacy. The Hebrews of the Torah lack the Christian scheme of the Trinity of love; they cannot apply to their idea of family the basic presupposition of this scheme, which consists of the role played by the inner motion of love in the manifestations of the world. Without the Christian scheme of the Trinity of love, there cannot be "a true Jewish family" in the Hegelian sense (*Glas* 57a). The head of the Hebrew family obtains and confers legitimacy through the authority of an impersonal law unmediated by the inner motion of love. Yet, the identification of the Hebrew conception of paternity with law, rather than with the self-abnegation of love as in Christianity, has theoretical implications that exceed the conceptual boundaries set by Hegel in his delineation of the evolution of the concept of family from pre-Christian to Christian.

STRUCTURE OF THE TABERNACLE AND STRUCTURE OF THE FAMILY

In *Glas* Derrida points out that when Abram leaves his father Terah, he does not bring his *teraphim,* his household gods, with him. By replacing the household gods with "the domination . . . of a master all-powerful, jealous, violent, . . . [Abram] himself could not love anything, he could only fear and make others fear. He could not even love his son" (50–51a). With Abram we encounter the first figuration of the monotheistic father without teraphim and without love, the head of a family and a race whose unity comes from a law "external" to race and family (*Glas* 63a). The source of this external law, in its infinity, in its divinity, is intangible; it eludes all representation and all sensible form; it manifests itself in a sensible manner only through the palpability of the transcription of its Word. Moses will eventually receive from the living voice of the God of the Torah the instructions for the erection of the tent to be called Tabernacle, or Tent of the Presence. The innermost receptacle of the Tent, called the Holy of Holies, will house a mere emptiness, a mere allusion to the presence of YHWH: an Ark containing the tablets of the law, an imposing and ever-growing set of written commands—a poor substitute, indeed, from the standpoint of mythological consciousness, for the imaginal power inherent in the polytheistic tradition of the teraphim, the ancient Hebrew household gods.[8] Derrida writes: "The locus and [the] figure [of the Hebrew Tabernacle] have a peculiar structure: they enclose their own emptiness, . . . a hole, an empty spacing" (*Glas* 59a). Instead of the simulacrum of the Lord of the Law, they enclose the letter itself of the Law.

The structure of the Hebrew Tabernacle is reflected in the structure of the Hebrew family. The fearful absence that fills the receptacle of the Tent of Presence evokes the fear of the God of the Torah. This fear, in turn, voices and imposes the patriarchal norms and commandments that the Christian family, according to Hegel, will eventually overcome through the laws generated from its own inside (essentially self-generated) by the inner motion of love—the most significant of these love-imbued norms being the unbreachable laws of family property and of family succession, that is, the laws by which the family estate is made to depend exclusively, as Derrida puts it, on "the indelible mark of filiation from given parents" (*Glas* 63a). But the Hebrew family, in the configuration it achieves through the Mosaic law, derives the laws of family property and succession from norms and commandments that are external to and independent from the intrinsic merits of the patriarch. Derrida points out that, according to Leviticus, "[the Israelite] who had to sell his property or his person because of some need, must recover his real rights in the year of the Jubilee and his personal rights in the sabbatical year." Hence, he argues, "the Mosaic law limits the right of inheritance and the right of property by submitting it to an *external* rule" (ibid.).[9] Nothing could be more remote from the fatherly self-abnegation upon which rests the unity of the Christian family than this external rule; the head of the Hebrew family, the primary vehicle and executor of this external rule, is only a passive agent when it comes to its origin. A logical consequence of this principle of externality, as it applies to the Mosaic legislation of private property and personal rights, is that an individual "can always break [a] prescription when the balance of forces allows or imposes" such a move (*Glas* 64a), or else, when circumstances suggest that the paradigms of the external rule have or may be changed. This view collides dramatically with Hegel's contention that "the right of the family is a right against externality and against secession from the family unity" (*PhilR* 159:262 [addition]).

RACHEL AND MESOPOTAMIAN JURISPRUDENCE

A pre-Mosaic example of a breach of the Hegelian proscription against externality and secession from family unity can be seen in Rachel's attitude toward her father, Laban, and his possessions, when the time comes for her to follow her husband Jacob back to the land of his family. "Have we still a share in the inheritance of our father's house?" she wonders, together with her sister Leah. "Surely [Laban] regards us as outsiders, now that he has sold us and has used up our purchase price. Truly, all the wealth that God has taken away from our father [and given to Jacob] belongs to us and to our children . . ."[10] According to E. A. Speiser, implicit in Rachel's and Leah's complaint is the accusation that Laban violated the "family laws of their country." In fact, tablets from the Hurrian centers reveal that "part of the bride payment was normally reserved for the woman [herself] as her inalienable dowry."[11] So Rachel follows Jacob and the wealth he has appropriated in the last six years of his service with Laban. Before leaving her father's camp, she takes from Laban's tent his household gods, the teraphim. The subsequent encounter of Jacob with Laban, who overtakes the fugitives, shows that there is a necessity for this break in the prescription of filial submission to the authority of the father. More precisely, it is a consequence of Rachel's theft that the balance of forces between father and son-in-law undergoes a radical modification in favor of Jacob's secession from Laban's tribe.

But why does Rachel steal Laban's idols? In the context of the present discussion, current biblical scholarship provides no satisfactory answers. Ilana Pardes, for instance, has argued that Rachel's impulse to steal Laban's teraphim is dictated by her unresolved rivalry with Leah. "Although Rachel is both a mother [of Joseph] and [Jacob's] beloved wife at this point, her son isn't Jacob's first son, which is why the teraphim are needed".[12] Pardes quotes the criteria of family succession from Deuteronomy 21:15–16, according to which the right of primogeniture must be acknowledged and respected even when the paternal preference goes to the offspring from the "beloved" wife rather than from the "first" wife. But Pardes's remark about the rivalry between Rachel and Leah does not provide any justification as to the presumed power of Laban's strange gods, which would be "needed" to neutralize the will of YHWH.[13] It is not only that in a monotheistic tribe pagan deities exercise no power at all. It is also that the powers of the teraphim dissolve at the very moment when they are taken from the abode of their family of origin, whose *fulcrum* is represented by the patriarch himself. A pact of reciprocal protection links these figurines to the patriarch. In order to exercise their protection over the household of the patriarch, over his fertility and that of his people,[14] and to warrant the perpetuation of the tribe's customs as well, the teraphim had to be able to rely, first of all, on the patriarch's protection, on a symbolic level at least, of the safety of their shrine. Removed from the protection of the patriarch, the statuettes of the teraphim lose their power, unless, as we learn from Speiser, it is the patriarch himself who assigns them to his heirs (*Speiser/Genesis* 25: note to 23). The teraphim do not transfer their protection and their power to the thief who steals them. And, once stolen, they are unable to continue to protect the patriarch and his household. Furthermore, their absence from the patriarch's abode deprives the patriarch of his legitimacy as the tribal chief. And this is what really matters. Rachel steals the teraphim because her theft turns Laban into an impotent patriarch.[15]

Pardes bases her interpretation on Speiser's juridical glosses. According to Speiser, the legal aspects of Rachel's theft of the teraphim are strikingly consistent with the Mesopotamian jurisprudence revealed by the Nuzi documents. From such a consistency one could infer, he argues, the authenticity of the biblical episode itself, or, at least, its origin in an oral tradition relating to events that actually occurred in Paddan-aram (the area in which Laban's town of Haran was situated) no later than the middle of the second millennium—events that would anticipate by several centuries, therefore, the writings of the first biblical authors, who could not possibly have been aware of the ancient juridical complexities embedded within the diegesis of this episode.

In the first place, Speiser points out that, contrary to the Hebrew rule of chronological primogeniture found in Deuteronomy 21:15–16, the ancient Mesopotamian legal practice (presumably germane to the jurisprudence practiced in Haran by Rachel's tribe) enforced the rule that the testator could attribute the right of inheritance of the *māru rabū*, the elder son, whose emblem consists of the possession of the teraphim, "contrary to the actual order of birth." Also, Speiser remarks that, "(a)ccording to the Nuzi documents . . . possession of the house gods could signify legal title to a given estate, particularly in cases out of the ordinary, involving daughters, sons-in-law, or adopted sons" (*Speiser/Genesis* 31: comment to 1–54). Hence, the episode of Rachel's theft of the teraphim reflects a radical difference between the customs of family succession prevalent, respectively, in Rachel's and in Jacob's tribes. As we know from Jacob's youth, in the monotheistic tribes of Canaan the *māru şehru,* the younger son, could appropriate primogeniture to himself only through deception (Genesis 27:1–37). Secondly, Speiser remarks that Rachel, in her privileged position as the daughter of the patriarch, was likely "to know, or at least to suspect, that in conformance with local law her husband was entitled to a specified share in Laban's estate" (ibid.). But Rachel, being acquainted also with Laban's persistent deceptions at the expense of his son-in-law, knew too well that Laban would never transfer voluntarily to Jacob a share of his estate, nor the possession of the household gods that would signify Jacob's legal title to such a transfer of personal wealth. Hence, Rachel would take the law "into her own hands" and steal her father's teraphim, with three distinct goals in mind: first, to legitimate Jacob's ownership of the goods that he shrewdly appropriated to himself in the course of his last six years of work for Laban; second, to emancipate Jacob from the condition of self-enslavement he voluntarily assumed within Laban's tribe; third (as also argued by Ilana Pardes), to ensure the possession of the most immediate symbols of primogeniture to her own firstborn, Joseph (ibid.).

The attribution of such a plurality of motives is symptomatic of a poor grasp of the nature of Rachel's theft. She would steal the teraphim to entitle Jacob to the ownership of what he subtracted from Laban, to emancipate Jacob from his condition of semislavery, and to turn her son Joseph into Jacob's legal, if not factual, firstborn son—three motives that share one interpretive perspective, namely, the presumption that Rachel is eager to legalize her family's position vis-à-vis Mesopotamian jurisprudence. My interpretation of Rachel's ultimate motive depends on the opposite presumption. Rachel leaves behind the norms and customs of her tribe of origin and embraces—far from passively, however—those of the house of Israel. She neutralizes her father's resistance to Jacob's departure from Paddan-aram by depriving him of the idols that warrant his patriarchal power; in doing so, she does not appease the Mesopotamian legislator, who is in any case virtually absent from the scene of her crime, but rather contributes a radical turn to the legislation of the house of Israel. No less than Speiser's interpretation, mine is a juridical one, even though, as I suggested above, Rachel's acts do not pertain to the juridical sphere narrowly defined. In any case, my interpretation entails a reversal of juridical perspective that calls for a close scrutiny of Speiser's arguments.

Nahum Sarna's comments to this section of Genesis invalidate the first two of the three goals that Speiser's arguments attribute to Rachel's theft. In Sarna's view, Jacob was neither an adopted son nor a son-in-law incorporated in Laban's tribe. The possibility of adoption, suggested by Genesis 29:14, is contradicted by the fact that "adoption usually (took) place when there (were) no natural-born sons," which does not seem to be the case with Laban (*Sarna/Genesis* 31:18). (Furthermore, Sarna remarks that the verses from Genesis 29:15, 30:25–34, 31:13, 31:18 undo the adoption formula uttered by Laban in Genesis 29:14, by implying that Jacob's legal rights are not those of a Canaanite [*Sarna/Genesis* 31:18]). The possibility that Jacob be considered a son-in-law is contradicted by the fact that "a member of the household does not receive payment for his services" (*Sarna/Genesis* 31:15); the verses from Genesis 30:25, 31:13, 31:18 exclude Jacob's assimilation to the uxorial tribe. Hence, possession of Laban's household gods would not "signify (Jacob's) legal title to (Laban's) ... estate." Sarna maintains that Jacob would be able to claim, rather, the rights of a hireling, "a laborer under contract," suggested in Genesis 29:15, 30:25–34, 31:1, which would entail, in his case, the right to the possession of his wives, whose bride-price he had paid for with his work, and of his natural children. Therefore, when it comes to the teraphim as symbols of the legal ownership of "a given estate," Speiser's justification of Rachel's theft would have to depend on the presumption that she had decided to appropriate to herself, and ultimately to her son, the wealth that Jacob had put together in the last six years of his service with Laban. Possession of the teraphim would entitle her, a consanguineous member of Laban's family, to ownership of Laban's estate. Furthermore, a legal as well as moral justification of this appropriation would derive from the premise that at the time of her marriage Rachel had been deprived of that "part of the bride payment [that] was normally reserved for the woman as her inalienable dowry" (*Speiser/Genesis* 31: note to 15).

In my view, even this third element of Speiser's argument is flawed, based as it is upon the presumption that possession of the teraphim would prove the rights of Jacob's wife in front of a Mesopotamian tribunal. Speiser seems to take for granted that

Laban, after stealing his daughters' dowry and shrewdly reducing his son-in-law to the status of a hireling, would suddenly become afraid of the legal repercussions of his misdemeanors of twenty years. But where is the Mesopotamian legislator whose fear, or respect, provokes Laban's passivity? Are there any sociopolitical elements in Genesis 31 indicating that some supratribal agent of juridical arbitration exercises legal authority over Laban's administration of his own people? I do not see how one can possibly attribute Laban's reluctance to retaliate against Jacob to the prospect of a legal trial brought against him by his two daughters and his son-in-law. Speiser has lost sight of the prehistorical perspective required to gloss the text of Genesis 31. There must be a reason other than his fear of legal misconduct to explain Laban's mansuetude. Once deprived of the idols, Laban is plunged into a state of impotence. How to explain, otherwise, that his resolution wanes abruptly at the easy prospect of overcoming Jacob's men in the hill country of Gilead?[16] In the interval of a few hours the patriarch, apparently obsessed, first, and defeated, shortly after, by the disappearance of his teraphim, absolves his son-in-law and concludes a mutual nonaggression pact with him.

Rachel's theft is meant to disempower Laban, but it would be a mistake to infer from this that Rachel emancipates herself from her father in order to place herself in a condition of passive subordination vis-à-vis her husband. This interpretation would reduce the vibrant energy of this episode to a mere confirmation of Western phallocentrism. Biblical phallocentrism, indeed, is the ideological premise behind the three alternative explanations of Rachel's theft offered by Esther Fuchs in "For I Have the Way of Women." Fuchs contends that the biblical author invested Rachel's motivation with feminine ambiguity so as to contrast the untrustworthiness of Rachel's purposes with the good faith of Jacob, the reformed swindler. Fuchs leaves open three alternative explanations for Rachel's theft: greediness, resentment against Laban, idolatry—three ignoble motives which would serve the biblical author to contrast Jacob's masculine integrity with Rachel's feminine duplicity.[17]

I take a diametrically opposite approach. Rachel's motivations, far from ambiguous or duplicitous, reflect her rebellion against the legal fate imposed upon her gender by the legal and religious customs of both her old and her new tribe. Before her marriage, as a young woman from a polytheistic tribe, and during the first twenty years of her marriage, as the wife of a foreign hireling,

Rachel must comply with the legal codes of Paddan-aram. After the escape from Laban's camp, Rachel becomes the wife of the leader of a Hebrew tribe, and as such she must start complying with the norms and customs of monotheism. With her theft of the teraphim, she accomplishes a legal subversion that disrupts *both* Laban's and Jacob's orders of ethical and juridical priorities. In depriving her father of his teraphim, she subverts the law of the household gods, and anticipates the Mosaic law of the tabernacle, in its configuration as the genuine expression of the empty abode of the Hebrew family—a family wherein the father is a tribal chief but not a *paterfamilias* in the Roman and juridical sense of the word, nor a custodian of family idols. In leaving Jacob unaware of her theft of Laban's teraphim, in turn, she induces her husband to pass on her a virtual death sentence: "Anyone with whom you find your gods shall not remain alive!" (Genesis 31.32)—a sentence which, notwithstanding all specious attributions of a divine cause to Rachel's death in childbirth, shall never be enforced.

FAMILY SUCCESSION AND MONOTHEISM

As I suggested in the introduction to this chapter, one may detect in Rachel's theft of the teraphim a subversion of the marginal role assigned to woman by the monotheistic norms of legitimate succession for the head of the family. The Hebrew mother never had any authority in matters of family succession, which in her tribe were orchestrated by the four phallic precepts of consanguinity, primogeniture, circumcision, and paternal blessing. The Abrahamic introduction of the ritual of circumcision, in fact, reduced woman's contribution to her family's genealogical tree to the dimension of a merely physiological function. Circumcision entails a dramatic expansion of the principle of con-sanguinity, which from Adam to Abram presupposes the racial integrity of both parents, but from Abraham onward requires as a necessary and sufficient condition that only the father be a Jew.[18] Leah's and Rachel's slaves, in fact, as well as Asenath, daughter of the Egyptian priest Poti-phera, will give male heirs, respectively, to Jacob and Joseph, sons destined to head six of the twelve tribes into which Jacob, before his death, divides the people of YHWH.[19]

Twenty years after her marriage to Jacob, Rachel embraces the law of monotheistic religion, inclusive of the four precepts of consanguinity, primogeniture,[20] circumcision, and paternal blessing. Her new status requires Rachel to substitute for her allegiance to the paternal teraphim her allegiance to this new juridical apparatus, inherently informed by a strict connection between legal semantics and paternal insemination. The transition from polytheism to monotheism does not entail any advantage for Rachel's condition and legal status. There is a possibility, rather, that this transition implies a significant disadvantage. According to Hegel, as we saw, the people of antiquity anterior to the Roman empire used to assign the custody of the household gods to the woman rather than to the head of the family. The teraphim are the symbols of Rachel's polytheistic condition, a condition assimilable, if not to that of the holy priest, at least to that of the vestal. Rachel's feminine role and status are degraded by her absorption within Jacob's monotheistic tribe.

Nonetheless, Rachel, on the verge of breaking away from polytheism and embracing the religion of YHWH, commits a crime against the religion and the law of her father. Rachel becomes an outlaw of Laban's tribe at the very moment when she takes upon herself to subvert the procedures by which the head of the Hebrew family obtains and preserves his patriarchal legitimacy.

THE PERIOD OF WOMEN

The rest of this chapter is devoted to the complex nature of the transition, inaugurated by Rachel's theft, from the cult of the tolerant pagan deities, protectors of the patriarch's fertility,[21] to the phallic symbology that circumscribes the Hebrew's rigid laws of succession for the head of the family. The transition from Rachel's deliverance from polytheism to her delivery of Jacob's last son, Benjamin, parallels the reversal of exile into exodus which, as master trope, animates the entirety of the Torah— exodus as a return of the people of Israel "into its own," into an expanded national identity that is something other, something more "abundant," than its originary nomadic self. The epics of the rebellion by which the Hebrew people manage to break free from their exile, and reverse it into an event of national unity and prolificacy, find in Rachel's story an exemplary paradigm, a paradigm that contradicts Hegel's identification of woman as the "internal enemy" of national interests.[22]

"Let not my lord take it amiss that I cannot rise before you, for the period of women is upon me" (Genesis 31:35). These are the words by which Rachel, seated on the "camel cushion" within which she hid her father's idols, welcomes Laban's entrance into her tent.[23] Literally squatting above Laban's teraphim, Rachel pretends that she is affected by the "period of women" (Genesis 31:35)—made infirm, that is, by that "impurity"[24] that the Levitical norms of *nidda* attribute to woman's periodic menstruation (Leviticus 15:19–33). In truth, Rachel cannot be menstruating, since she is already pregnant with Jacob's last son, Benjamin. From a narratologic standpoint, in fact, it is very unlikely that Genesis 32:4–35:20, wherein the diegetic duration of the events immediately preceding Benjamin's birth and Rachel's simultaneous death is submitted to an impressive narrative condensation, may last more than the nine months of Rachel's second pregnancy.[25] Speiser confirms that the duration of this succession of episodes must be intended to be relatively short; specifically, he eliminates as a "short stay" the erection of "houses" at Succoth, undoubtedly the most problematic, from the standpoint of diegetic duration, among the episodes of the transfer of Jacob's caravans from Haran to Ephrath (*Speiser/ Genesis* 33:17).

One might say that Rachel defiles the fertile essence of the paternal teraphim with the pretense of her periodic sterility, a move evidently demeaning to the phallic vitality symbolized by those oblong statues in wood or stone. Should one conclude, then, that Rachel steals the erection from her father to make a symbolic gift of it to her husband? The evidence is quite to the contrary. Rachel's transgression entails a devastating suspicion for the new patriarch of Israel: the suspicion that latency is inherent to his own fertility, sterility to his own power of insemination. The night of his struggle with Elohim, Jacob may become Israel because Rachel has already turned him into the archetype of the Semitic patriarch whose legitimacy is grounded upon a law external to race and family, rather than upon the primacy of the paternal seed—rather than upon the phallic saturation of the concept of genealogy grounded upon the four precepts of consanguinity, primogeniture, circumcision, and paternal blessing. In this regard, it must be stressed that the night of the struggle Rachel is already pregnant with Benjamin, Jacob's last child, and therefore Jacob/Israel will never impregnate again any of his wives or concubines.

Here, again, Esther Fuchs's argument is far from the mark when she states that Rachel's appeal to "the way [or 'period'] of women" amounts to a further manifestation of Rachel's duplicity. Fuchs maintains that the text does not tell the reader whether Rachel is sincere or not when she declares she has her period, and thereby it puts "in (Rachel's) mouth a condemnation of her own sex."[26] This approach would be correct, in my opinion, only if Rachel's appeal to the "way" of women did not come escorted, as it does, by mockery of the other sex. Like an inviolable receptacle, Rachel's vulva covers that which Laban is searching for, namely, the symbolic tokens whose possession would justify and make legal, according to custom and tradition, the patriarch's claim that Jacob's children are his children and Jacob's flocks are his flocks (Genesis 31:43). And without his teraphim the chief of the dynasty, virtually castrated, loses his legitimacy. His genealogical tree is irremediably deracinated, uprooted.

Rachel's theft has violated the sanctity of her former family's teraphim, but not, as Hegel would have it, to turn them into "an ornament for [her] Family," as a woman is prone to do when, as Hegel puts it in the *Phenomenology of Spirit,* she "changes by intrigue the universal end of government into a *private* end."[27] Rachel does not steal her father's teraphim, the symbols of his power, simply to make a present of them to the family of her husband. The latter is the reductive conclusion one might draw out of an expeditious confusion between Rachel, who rebels against the law of her old and her new tribe, and the woman Hegel talks about in the *Phenomenology of Spirit,* an "internal enemy" indifferent to the interests of the community, who derides the wisdom of those who care about it (ibid.). One must not forget that in his logical and historical delineation of the coming into its own of family and community, Hegel was paying special attention to the line of evolution mentioned above, from the Greek to the Roman to the Christian civilization. The woman in whose individuality is personified the "internal enemy" to the life of the community is Sophocles' Antigone, to whom "the worth . . . of the brother [lies in his] being one in whom the sister finds man on a level of equality" (ibid.). In order to justify her disobedience against the decree by which King Creon forbids the burial of her brother Polyneices, Antigone maintains that the corpse of a brother deserves a respect by far superior to the respect due to the corpse of a husband or a son:

> Had I had children or their father dead,
> I'd let them moulder. I should not have chosen
> in such a case to cross the state's decree.

> One husband gone, I might have found another,
> or a child from a new man in first child's place,
> but with my parents hid away in death,
> no brother, ever, could spring up for me.[28]

The Hegelian dictate against "secession from the family unity" finds its ideal agent in Antigone. With the sacrifice of her life, Antigone sanctifies the "celestial configurations" of the law of consanguinity,[29] that is, that "indelible mark of filiation from given parents" (in her case, the Oedipal mark) which, according to Hegel, will constitute the premise for the unbreachable law of family succession (Derrida, *Glas* 63a). Antigone is a partisan of the "patrilocal" law, which attributes primacy to the paternal blood over the blood of the husband;[30] this is, ultimately, the primal law of incestuous consanguinity. In "*Les articulations de la pièce*," Jacques Lacan remarks that the legitimacy of Antigone's rebellion against the will of her king rests upon the laws of *Dike (Δίχη)*, the "companion" of the gods of the underworld, the tutelary Justice residing in the realm of the Dead.[31] It is only natural, hence, that Antigone, in spite of her death chant in praise of eros and maternity,[32] is bound to die as sterile as the realm from which she derives her resentment against the authority of the state. It is also significant that, having chosen Antigone as the individual in which the activity of the necessary movement that introduces enmity within the community finds its contingent incarnation, Hegel may only attribute the negative connotation of youthful immaturity to this individual.

We can see that the spurious association Rachel has assumed with her father's teraphim diverges in a radical way from the association with the household gods assumed by Antigone, because Rachel's rebellion pertains to the age-long struggle that humankind has fought against incest. It is her husband's bloodline that Rachel exalts to the detriment of the paternal bloodline. Rachel deliberately submits to symbolic castration a patriarch in search of confirmation to his own legitimacy as the tribal chief and the personification of his people's vitality; in so doing, one might say that she participates in the monumental process oriented toward the discontinuation of the incestuous customs rooted in the most ancient traditions of the Hebrews.

Laban enters Rachel's tent in search of confirmation of his virility and of the symbolic fertility of his leadership of the tribe. As we saw in Chapter 6, the case is rare in biblical literature when a man enters a woman's tent without the aim of sexual intercourse.[33] In Rachel's tent, Laban "feels" all of Rachel's belongings, vainly repeating that blind "feeling" (even in the Hebrew lexical form, *mishesh*)[34] that twenty years before misled the hands (nor provided any help to the sense of smell) of Isaac, a victim in the deception plotted by Rebekah and perpetrated by Jacob. The sought-for confirmation of his virility could come to Laban, forbidden as he is to "feel" the contaminated body of his daughter, through a broad variety of metaphorical surrogates to incest: through the exultation, for instance, of the tribal chief that learns that a new branch will soon be added to his genealogical tree. At the time of this last conversation with Laban, as I said earlier, Rachel is pregnant with Benjamin. If she decides to keep her father in the dark, it is because the revelation of her condition would amount to a vicarious restitution of the symbolic fertility represented by the teraphim; the revelation of her impending maternity would amount to a confirmation of the fecundity of Laban's bloodline. Rachel deliberately denies this exultation to Laban. Face to face with her father, now almost a suppliant, demeaned as a patriarch by Jacob's secession and especially by the loss of his teraphim, she castrates him.

To Rachel, her father's teraphim have become stolen goods and a matter of mockery. Her theft of the idols symbolizes a radical subversion of their function in the legitimation of family succession and in the perpetuation of the family tree. Her vulva has become their obscene, derisory tabernacle. Her fictitious menstrual blood has become the pollutant of the sacrificial blood shed before them in return for the gift of protection and fertility.[35] Rachel's filial misdeed proclaims that no mark of consanguinity, be it the figural one carved in the statues of the teraphim, be it the genetic one transmitted in the bloodline— be it, one might add, the ritual one left by circumcision on the member of the male successor—is indelible or unnegotiable.

Rachel's mockery provides, in truth, a paradoxical confirmation to a crucial postulate of the Hegelian principle of the "supreme opposition in ethics," namely, to the postulate that the legislation of the family is burdened with a "feminine" component, a whimsical component that renders the letter of the law highly susceptible to arbitrary reinterpretation. But Rachel's confirmation comes escorted by its own radical deconstruction. In fact, Rachel's subversion of the law of family succession consists of a substantial contribution to the future determination of the law of Israel. The very theater of her filial rebellion—

her vulva turned into a blasphemous Ark covering impotent deities—reflects symbolically the structure of the Hebrew Tabernacle, within which dwell the scrolls of the Law of YHWH. In the name of this law she commits a symbolic patricide, one with devastating consequences because it warrants a family without household gods, a family in which the head of the household implements rather than dictates the prescriptions of the law. In disrupting the age-long complementarity between legal semantics and paternal insemination, Rachel's patricide subverts the archaic scheme of patriarchal succession that depended upon the continuity of paternal bloodline.

When leaving the house of his father, Abram undermined the distinction between the family gods and the one communal god, YHWH. Rachel's mockery of her father's idols erases completely such a distinction. A people who rejects this distinction is bound to ignore as well the distinction between civil and public right. Such a people has no statutory laws, just divine commandments, and these commandments must be imposed upon external circumstances even when prudence suggests otherwise. Once again, Rachel's example leads the way. It will be shortly after her desecration of the pagan gods that Jacob's sons will dare, for the first time, to take the law in their own hands, against the will of the patriarch, and slaughter the Shechemites (Genesis 34). One cannot fail to recognize in this episode confirmation that the legal and normative apparatus of the Torah is capable of operating as a firm juridical corpus, completely independent—completely *external*—from the authority of the tribe's leader. To this regard it is relevant to remark that the journey of Jacob's convoy from Succoth to Shechem figures, in Genesis 33–34, as the symbolic repetition of the journey that brought Abram from Haran, the land of his father, to Shechem, where YHWH promised the land of the Shechemites to the patriarch's descendants (Genesis 12:4–9). The slaughter of the Shechemites results, hence, in the military appropriation of a land legitimately claimed by the Hebrews—an appropriation whose legitimacy does not sprout from the whims of a band of sanguinary brothers but from the sacred codes that tell of Abraham's secession from his paternal tribe. It is at this stage of Jacob's journey back to the land of his ancestors that we find in the biblical text an intimation that Israel's exile will be turned into a proper exodus. It is this epic reversal that is inaugurated by Rachel's self-deliverance from polytheism.

MYTH AND HISTORY

An unbridgeable gulf separates the legislation of the family, depicted by Hegel as the *locus* wherein man and woman come to a reconciliation of their essential conflict through the inner motion and force of love, from Rachel's subversion and reconfiguration of the Hebrew law of family succession. In Hegel's speculative system, gender opposition is irremediably reflected in the subordination of civil right to public right; family right, as the branch of civil right wherein woman "has her substantive destiny," is made precarious by its contingent concern with concrete individuals and subjective feelings, while public right, wherein man "has his actual substantive life," derives its stability of purpose from its concern with the regulation and administration of the state (*PhilR* 166:114). Rachel's theft of her father's idols reflects instead a jurisprudence that does not discriminate between right of family succession, private right in general, and law and religion *tout court*. This jurisprudence diverges to a striking extent from the jurisprudence Hegel derives from the historical circumstances and the (theo)logical evolution of the Greek-Roman transition from polytheism to Christianity. Rachel's theft of the teraphim finds its own justification in the theological jurisprudence of the Torah, but it also subverts the subordinate role that the traditional, patriarchal version of this jurisprudence assigned to the figures of the mother and the wife in the Hebrew family. One might say that Rachel's subversion of her own filial and wifely duties brings to completion the prescriptions of the Torah relating to family property and succession.

It would be historically incorrect and politically naive, however, to pretend that this triumph of the "law of the outlaw," contingent upon the Biblical tale and the study of the obscure roots of ancient Hebrew customs, entails an irreversible decline for the juridical and symbolic authority of the *paterfamilias*. In truth, the convergence of paternal insemination and family succession is destined to renew itself, Phoenixlike, in the various configurations it will assume in the Christian era. Hegel's speculative philosophy of right, as we well know, endows with a sort of "modern" legitimacy the double function attributed by the Romans to the *paterfamilias,* as, on the one hand, custodian and interpreter of the household gods and, on the other hand, private and public legislator. But one can also trace the reemergence of the primitive traditions of patriarchal supremacy and seminal consanguinity back to the play of equivalences that Freud recognized between the primordial occurrence of the totemic meal and the symbolic power of the Name of the Father, as well as to the Foucauldean identification of the royal semen with a legal power that makes precarious the survival of the subject's bloodline.[36] The assessment of the genuine significance of Rachel's rebellion against patriarchal authority is an act of textual deconstruction whose validity is not earned once and for all by a straightforward questioning of Hegel's axiomatic foundations of family and civil right. There is more at stake than that, and the validity of such a deconstruction is renegotiated every day through a systematic dissent against the gender-segregated character of the modern institution of the family.

8

Right of *Paterfamilias*: The Roman Law of Family Inheritance in Hegel, Montesquieu, and Vico

> And we came to the land of the Cyclops, an insolent and loveless folk . . . Neither assemblies for council have they, nor appointed laws, but . . . each one is lawgiver to his children and his wives, and they have no regard for one another.
> —*Odyssey* 9.105–15

FAMILY RESPONSIBILITY AND CIVIL RIGHT IN HEGEL

In HEGEL'S *PHILOSOPHY OF RIGHT*, THE FAMILY IS CHARACTERIZED by a purposive ethics of responsibility toward one's own kin. Such an ethics of responsibility, based on the fundamental duties of care, nurturing, service, and education, stems from the life "involved (in the) tie of marriage," which corresponds, in turn, to family life as the "actuality of the race and its life process" (*PhilR* 161:111).[1] In the *Encyclopaedia Logic,* Hegel equates this *actuality of the race* with the "power of the species," which in the distinct moments of sexual intercourse and gender differentiation starts off the "process of the *genus.*"[2] When intended as such an "immediate type of ethical relationship" (*PhilR* 161:111), family life presupposes a bond of consanguinity between its members. Furthermore, in stark contrast to the irresponsible autarchy of the cyclopic family described in the Homeric epigraph to this chapter, the ethical obligations that family life imposes on one's self and one's own kin prepare for the aggregation of a multitude of family units into the plurality of families that Hegel calls "civil society" (*PhilR* 181:122).

My discussion will concern Hegel's speculative engagement of the right of family succession and in particular the right of inheritance of the family estate in classical Roman jurisprudence. This is a subject of major importance to Hegel's *Philosophy of Right* for three interconnected reasons. The first is that the study of classical Roman jurisprudence is fundamental to Hegel's legal thought. The second is that, according to Hegel, the legal entity of the family, both in the Roman and modern juridical view, "has its real external existence in *verrnögen* (estate)" (*PhilR* 169:116.) The third reason is that in Hegel, logically speaking, the ethics of civil responsibility, whose juridical manifestations are found in the normative codes of civil right, are dependent upon the ethics of family responsibility, whose juridical manifestations extend into the right of family property and the norms regulating the right of succession and inheritance within the family (*PhilR* 169:116, 180:[remark] 120). Hence, the importance of Hegel's thought on legal matters pertaining to family lineage in classical Roman jurisprudence lies in the consideration that, from Hegel's point of view, the prehistory of modern civil right, which is grounded in the right of family succession and inheritance of the family estate, may be extracted from the classical configuration of the Roman right of *paterfamilias.*

I intend to deconstruct the speculative fallacy inherent in Hegel's position vis-à-vis the subject of family succession and inheritance in classical Roman jurisprudence. The nature of Hegel's fallacy may be summarized as follows: What in Hegel's conception of the Roman jurisprudence of family lineage comes logically second, that is, a condition of androlineal kinship whose legitimacy calls for and submits to the authority of legal arbitration, turns out historically to come first in the very foundations of Roman civil right. More specifically, I will argue that from the speculative standpoint the norms of legitimacy that apply to the legal arbitration of family succession and inheritance in classical Roman jurisprudence presuppose the *juridical construct* of the *paterfamilias,* as the necessary condition for their legal enforcement. In order to convey the intrinsic nature, historical, logical, and especially cultural and linguistic, of this fallacy, I will engage in the comparative reading of a set of pertinent arguments derived from Vico and Montesquieu. These arguments will show that Hegel fails to lay proper emphasis on the evidence that the *paterfamilias,* that most fundamental figure of kinship, is, in its essential juridical connotations, the *gender-exclusive product of a primitive metaphoric.* We will learn from Vico's inquiry into the ancient Roman jurisprudence of succession and lineage that the normative status of the Roman legislator, as private and public lawmaker, derives from his position as *paterfamilias.* As the "lawgiver to his children and his wives," the Roman head of the family is expected to contribute to the legislation of the affairs of the community to which his family belongs; in this convergence of private and public legislation lies the difference that separates the patrician Roman family not only from the cyclopic family described by Homer, but also from the disenfranchised plebeian family. And this convergence is already at play long before Roman jurisprudence reaches its written stage with the promulgation of the Twelve Tables in the fifth century B.C.E. It is from the earliest days of Roman civilization, from the times when legal rights were "fabled by fantasy," as Vico puts it, that both the formulation and the practice of the law depend upon the *patria potestas,* the "power of the father."

In light of the Viconian contribution, I will maintain that in classical Roman jurisprudence it is the juridical construct of the *paterfamilias,* as the legal core of the family unit, that provides the grounds for legitimacy not only to the juridical arbitration of matters pertaining to succession, lineage, etc., but also to juridical arbitration as such, and, most notably, to civil legislation *tout court.* In classical Roman jurisprudence the right of *paterfamilias*—a gender-exclusive product of the age when the fabulations of primitive religious imagination became, certainly with the help of weaponry and armigers, the germs of the future legal codes—comes before the law; it constitutes the essential condition of legitimacy for the administration of justice in its two interdependent aspects of legislation and jurisdiction; and the rigorous formulations of the norms and prescriptions that codify it are fundamentally entangled with the *tropes and metaphors of sexual opposition.*

In the above summary of the connotations of classical Roman jurisprudence lies the significance of this chapter's subject. It is out of the classical configuration of the Roman *paterfamilias* that one may excavate, speculatively speaking, the prehistoric foundations of modern civil right. Hegel's failure to engage, historically, logically, culturally, and linguistically, the tradition of androlineal primacy inherent in the Roman right of family succession and inheritance bespeaks his inability to appreciate, on the one hand, the essence of classical Roman jurisprudence, and on the other hand, the gender-exclusive metaphor that was part of the legacy passed on by this jurisprudence to modern civil right.

CLASSICAL JURISTS AND FAMILY SUCCESSION

In the Introduction to his *Philosophy of Right* Hegel makes an interesting point against Ritter von Hugo's contention that a "distinctive method of concept formation," equal in rigor to that found in Kant's foundations of metaphysics, characterizes the "classical jurists of the period of the 'highest maturity of Roman Law as a science.'" Von Hugo's claim appears in the seventh edition of his *Lehrbuch der Geschichte des Römischen Rechts*.[3] The supposedly rigorous logic of the classical jurists of the imperial age consists, Hegel retorts, of the utmost "*il*logicality." In order to "preserve the letter" but to subvert the spirit of the laws of the Twelve Tables, which were promulgated by the Roman legislators around the year 450 B.C.E.,[4] these later jurists would *callide* [artfully] devise "empty verbal distinctions [and] . . . foolish subterfuges." In one word, they would have recourse, Hegel points out, to "*fictio*,"[5] a legal term that designates, in classical Roman jurisprudence, the interpretive compromise by which a judge adjudicates a case in the court of law by "conceal[ing], or affect[ing] to conceal, the fact that a rule of law has undergone alteration, its letter remaining unchanged, its operation being modified."[6]

Two of the footnotes that T. M. Knox, translator of Hegel's *Philosophy of Right,* devotes to Hegel's polemic against von Hugo help us appreciate, in their linguistic and gender-inclusive character, the "verbal distinctions" and "foolish subterfuges" of which Hegel accuses the Roman jurists. By the formula "verbal distinctions," Hegel refers to a terminological manipulation of the law of inheritance: the Roman praetors renamed as *bonorum possession* (the possession of the estate) that which was to be legally called *hereditas,* that is, the paternal right to despotic lordship over the family estate, from which the children emancipated from the *patria potestas* (the power of the father), notably the daughters, were excluded. By the formula "foolish subterfuges," Hegel refers to a grammatical manipulation of the law of inheritance: "In certain cases," Knox writes, the Roman praetors had recourse to the legal fiction of "treat[ing] a daughter (*filia*) as a son (*filius*) in order to give her the right of inheritance from which in strict law she was excluded."[7]

It is from the edition of Heineccius's *Syntagma*[8] published in 1752 that Hegel derives the argument according to which it was common practice, among the Roman praetors, to disregard a daughter's gender in legal matters pertaining to family inheritance. However, the argument of the *filia-filius* fictio was "withdrawn as a mistake" from all editions of Heineccius's *Syntagma* subsequent to the 1752 edition referred to by Hegel.[9] Montesquieu's *De l'esprit des lois,* whose first edition appears in 1748, four years before the publication of the fallacious version of *Syntagma,* may provide a possible explanation for this correction. "No distinction was made by the laws of the Twelve Tables as to whether the successor was male or female," writes Montesquieu in the twenty-seventh book (2:196), which is devoted to the origin and evolution of the Roman laws of succession, and which figures, incidentally, among Hegel's primary sources of documentation. In short, the theory of an arbitrary distortion of the laws of inheritance stipulated by the Twelve Tables, which distortion Hegel ascribes to the "artful illogicality" of the legal fictions grafted by the Roman jurists of the imperial age upon the law of family inheritance, would have to be ascribed, rather, in light of the above stipulation by Montesquieu, to the inaccuracy of Hegel's own documentation.[10]

But in spite of this scholarly drawback, Hegel's remark stands out because of its argumentative vehemence. "It is ludicrous," he concludes, "to see the classical jurists compared with Kant" as regards their method of "concept development." Hegel is oriented toward making a drastic contrast rather than a benevolent comparison between the Roman jurists and Kant. On the one hand, he sees the Roman jurists as responsible for an "artful" compromise, through fictional distinctions and sly manipulations, between the letter of an "unjust and detestable" law and their notion of justice; on the other hand, he sees Kant as the eluder of any such compromise. Unconditionedness is the eminent attribute of the rational and subjective (however abstract) praxis of "restriction [of] . . . self-will," which characterizes Hegel's view of Kant's contribution to the science of right.[11] In contrast, pragmatic conditionedness, fictional overdetermination, or, in other words, an arbitrary and subjectivistic evasion of the letter of the law through exegetic manipulation, no matter how ethically praiseworthy in the final analysis, characterizes Hegel's opposite view of the legal praxis of the Roman jurists, who invade with their legal fictions the exclusive domain of the legislator (*PhilR* 180:[remark] 121).

RATIONAL LEGISLATION AND LEGAL FICTION

Hegel's denunciation of the classical Roman jurists' "artful" deceptions suggests the dichotomy between the procedural logic that is inherent to the Roman jurist's duty as arbiter and magistrate, and the fictions that are inherent in his "verbal distinctions (and) . . . subterfuges"; what is more important, it points to the separation between the authority to legislate, to inscribe the spirit of justice in the letter of the law, and the authority to administer the law, to translate the letter of the law into legal provisions, acts of arbitration and adjudication, and legal opinion. The theoretical presuppositions of Hegel's polemics against von Hugo consist, on the one hand, of the gap between procedural logic and verbal distinctions or subterfuges that is internal to the sphere of jurisdiction, and, on the other hand, of the separation between the distinct spheres of legislation and jurisdiction.

I next intend to show that Hegel's denunciation of the classical Roman jurists' "artful" deceptions applies the speculative separation between the human faculties of understanding and imagination to the distinct spheres of legislation and jurisdiction, as well as to the gap between the procedural logic and the legal fictions of the jurist. The logical basis for this thesis is that the "artful" practice of the legal fiction, which Hegel attributes to the Roman jurists' aptitude for an arbitrary reconfiguration of the dictates of the law, may be shown to be installed in a speculative relation of affinity with the faculty of imagination. The historical basis for this thesis is that these legal fictions may be shown to have invaded, in specific circumstances, the exclusive domain of the lawmaker.

With regard to the affinity between the practice of the legal fiction and the faculty of imagination, I will begin with a summary of the most important properties inherent in Hegel's speculative concept of imagination.

1. Hegel offers several different enumerations of the forms exhibited by the faculty of imagination. One such enumeration appears in sections 455–59 of the *Philosophy of Spirit,* a second appears in Boumann's 1845 Addition (*Zusatz*) to the first of the above five sections, and a third and a fourth enumeration appear in two lectures of 1822 and 1825, transcribed respectively by Hotho and by Griesheim.

2. All these enumerations include, among the other forms of the faculty which determines images, those of symbolic phantasy *(Phantasie)* and sign-making phantasy.

3. The Addition *(Zusatz)* to section 455 posits a congruence between symbolic phantasy and sign-making phantasy. And Hegel's Remark to section 457 gives preeminence to sign-making phantasy, as the faculty that adds "proper intuitability" to the sensuous and "subjectively intuitable" images produced by phantasy.

4. In turn, it is in the form of symbolic phantasy, where intelligence still pays homage to images' sensuous and "subjectively intuitable" material, that one finds a significant congruence with the image-making activities related to poetry and allegory, that is, with artistic manners of expression whose generic affinity to the practice of fiction is patent.[12]

The logical order of intelligent thought proceeds, for Hegel, through the concatenation of the "circle of circles" of philosophy;[13] it points to the all-pervasive clarity, to the all-penetrating totality of the Idea. The operation of human imagination proceeds instead through a proliferation and dispersion of conflicting images; it points to the nocturnal evasiveness, to the elusive content of the images extracted by human imagination from what the *Philosophy of Spirit* calls "the ego's own inwardness," where a manifold of images is stored within the subject "without being in consciousness," without being *for* the subject.[14] Only in their sublation to the content of intelligent thought will such images come to be related to one another, from a Hegelian standpoint, in a unity capable of participating in the totality of the Idea.

The sublation of the contents of imagination to the contents of intelligent thought proceeds in tandem with the transition from the first form of imagination, i.e., reproductive imagination, which draws the image into determinate existence out of the "nocturnal pit" of the ego's own inwardness, to the last form of imagination, i.e., sign-making phantasy, where imagination replaces the image's sensuous material as well as its allegorical and metaphorical import by means of the inception of a sign.[15] "The sign is a certain immediate intuition presenting a content that is wholly distinct from that which it has for itself—the pyramid in which an alien soul is displaced and preserved."[16] In sign-making phantasy, presentation becomes objectively intuitable within a sign, within a sensible, acoustic (and, secondarily, graphic) material, which is indifferent to the imaginal, sensuous content and the subjective intuitability of symbolic and allegoric presentation. The transition to sign-making phantasy entails the recourse to an objective being—a sign, a sound, a grapheme—that transgresses the conformity of image and universal or of symbol and intelligence that is installed in symbol-making phantasy. Signs, in Hegel, are organized by norms of pure externality, of pure conventionality, which are left to memory to enforce and apply. Sign-making—speech, in sum, and, secondarily, phonetic writing—must take over the operations of imagination if these are to be turned into an objective attestation of their universality.[17] And this sign-making advocated by Hegel involves a delimitation of legitimacy for the space of allegorical and metaphorical discourse, which discursive space is inherent to the procedure of symbolic imagination.

The congruence, posited by Hegel in the Addition to section 455 of the *Philosophy of Spirit,* between symbolic and sign-making phantasy, consists, properly speaking, of a logical hierarchy. Symbolic phantasy, as the faculty from which proceeds allegorical and metaphorical discourse, must abdicate the autonomous significance of its image-making fictions and subordinate them to the unambiguous grammar of linguistic signs. The affinity between the practice of fiction and the faculty of imagination encounters its logical end (as well as its speculative aim) in the moment of appropriation, wherein sign-making fantasy, as the mole of reason infiltrating the ground of imagination, makes all metaphor *rational,* objectively understandable, linguistically unambiguous.

But this hierarchical structure carries within the germs of its own inversion. With specific regard to the practice of legal interpretation, I submit that no linguistic expression, not even the lapidary inscription of the law, is, from a historical perspective, *singular in meaning.* Theoretically, this submission corresponds to the well-known deconstructive position springing from the renewal in the tradition of phenomenological linguistics inaugurated by Derrida in the sixties. In what follows I begin with a couple of separate observations that relate to the speculative apprehension of the figure and role of the jurist.

1. The codification of the law, as a manifestation, however historically circumscribed, of the progressive coming into its own

of intelligent thought,[18] is impervious, from a speculative stand-point, to subjective interpretation. A written code manifests its degree of participation in the universality of the idea of Justice through the unambiguous meaning of its prescription, no matter how exposed it is to pragmatic and circumstantial overdeterminations. In the specific realm of jurisprudence, the jurist's exclusive duty consists of the application of the letter of the law to each and every case of legal dispute and litigation. He must act as the live "mouthpiece" of the absent legislator, and *say* in the court of law what the absent legislator *means*. Hence, the ideal jurist of speculative philosophy is a *grammarian*.

2. According to Hegel, the Roman jurist's predisposition toward legal fictions in matters of family inheritance engages him in a regressive, antispeculative movement, away from the objective luminosity of the sign and into the dark pit of sensuous imagery. As the executive minister of the law, this jurist violates the objective intuitability of its letter, governed by linguistic norms of pure grammatical and syntactic externality, and indulges in the abusive—never mind how well-intentioned—practice of a subjective reinterpretation, an arbitrary reconfiguration of the very spirit of the law. He imposes a duplicitous signification upon the code, the rigor of whose application and protection he must oversee.

It remains to be seen, however, if it is not the case that this antispeculative regression is structurally embedded in the practice itself of the application and enforcement of the law. Granted that the assignment of a duplicitous meaning to any specific norm corresponds to a "reshaping" of the law, and points therefore to a collapse in the separation between legislation and jurisdiction, it remains to be seen if it is not the case that a movement of permanent reshaping of the meaning and intention of the law is structurally embedded in the linguistic formulation, historical in its intimate nature, of codes and regulations.

The issue raised by the above remarks is one that concerns the intelligibility of legal language through time. One may wonder to what extent human memory is equipped to apply consistently to legal codes the same conventional norms that informed the legislator's formulation of the law. As we will presently learn from Vico as regards the specific case of the Roman praetors' legal fictions of family inheritance, it so happens that the modifications that occurred in grammatical usage between the promulgation of the Twelve Tables and the imperial age of the praetors enhanced to a dramatic extent the degree of approximation and ambivalence inherent, deconstructively speaking, in all acts of linguistic interpretation. Specifically, we are going to see that in these historical circumstances a given linguistic convention, bearing centuries of accumulated meaning, yet grammatically unquestionable in the eyes of its users, ends up operating not as a vehicle for the objective and "rational" comprehensibility of legal language, but rather as the vehicle for a metaphor in the interpretation and enforcement of the law. The jurist responsible for this metaphoric "distortion" is turned therefore by history itself (notably, the cumulative history of linguistic usage and legal formulation) into a full-fledged lawmaker.

HEGEL VERSUS VICO

Let me now recall the original matter of contention between Hegel and Ritter von Hugo. Hegel refutes von Hugo's contention that the Roman jurists' method of concept development equaled the rigor of Kant's philosophy. The Roman jurists of the imperial age, he argues, *callide* (artfully) devised "empty verbal distinctions [and] . . . foolish subterfuges" in their implementation of the letter of the law of family inheritance, as inscribed in the Twelve Tables. In other words, these Roman jurists were engaged in a praxis of legal fictions, irrational in that it contaminated, by means of the abusive metaphors of their jurisdiction, the objective universality of the signs into which the Roman laws of inheritance had been encoded by the legislator. The nature of these metaphors is a familiar one, relating to sexual hierarchy, and embedded in the grammar of gender difference that separates a *filius* from a *filia.* The classical Roman jurists disregarded the grammar of gender difference in order to extend the right of legitimate inheritance to the feminine offspring of the Roman *paterfamilias.* We saw above how poorly Hegel substantiated his reading of these abusive metaphors.

According to Giambattista Vico, a metaphor could actually be found at work in the interpretation given to the Twelve Tables' laws of inheritance by the *collegium pontificum,* the college of jurisconsults that, created by emperor Augustus, reached the peak of its juridical influence in the second century C.E., under emperor Hadrian.[19] But this metaphor reverses the order of intentionality embedded in the praxis of legal fictions posited by

Hegel. It is not a matter of certain jurists who, in facing an iniquitous law of gender inequality, deliberately choose to create legal fictions that would impose parity between the genders in matters of inheritance; it is, rather, a matter of certain jurists who, in facing a law of gender inequality, are brought to misapprehend the intentionality buried within its text because of the metaphoric thrust inherent in their exegetic practices, a thrust anachronistic with respect to the scrupulously literal import of the lexicon and syntax adopted by the legislators of the Twelve Tables. Vico writes in *Scienza nuova seconda:*

> The jurisconsults of the last jurisprudence[20] ... believed that the Law of the XII Tables made the daughters participate in the inheritance of their fathers ... with the word *"suus"* [Latin for "his"], on the assumption that the masculine gender contains also the feminine ... But the heroic jurisprudence[21] ... took the words of the laws in their most proper signification; therefore the word *"suus"* indicated just the son in the family. (*SNS2* § 988–90)

The metaphor at work is based, here, on the image of the masculine gender *containing* the feminine gender, the way a whole body contains a minor appendix, or Adam's chest contains, in one of the two biblical stories of creation, the rib that gives form to Eve. Vico's hypothesis contradicts, by the way, Montesquieu's contention, mentioned above, that "no distinction was made by the laws of the Twelve Tables as to whether the successor was male or female" (*De l'esprit des lois,* 2:196). And although it reverses the order of intentionality attributed by Hegel to the Roman jurists' legal fictions, Vico's hypothesis provides a confirmation of sorts to Hegel's claim that the Roman jurists disregarded the intentions of the legislators of the Twelve Tables in matters of family inheritance. This fortuitous confirmation, however, presupposes a radically antispeculative axiom, in the principle that linguistic signs, and in particular the letter of the law, far from suppressing or at least rigorously circumscribing the space of metaphorical discourse, are exposed to a historical sedimentation and accretion of meaning that turns their objective intuitability into a matter of tropic discourse.[22]

ROMAN JURISPRUDENCE, FAMILY SUCCESSION, GENDER DIFFERENCE

While in the Introduction to his *Philosophy of Right* Hegel detects a patent ludicrousness in von Hugo's attribution of the predicate of logicality to the fictions of the Roman jurists of the imperial age, in the section devoted to "Ethical Life" he refers again to the *fictio* of "nicknaming a *filia* a *filius*," but to praise it as a pragmatic way of addressing the "*necessity of smuggling reason* into . . . [the] unethical provision[s] of the law of succession" (*PhilR* 180:[remark] 121, my emphasis). This formulation subtly changes the terms of the question. It is no longer, on the Roman jurists' part, just a matter of devising "empty verbal distinctions . . . and downright foolish subterfuges," that is, of devising fictions, so as to preserve the appearance of the letter of the Twelve Tables' laws of succession while evading its spirit. On the contrary, it is a matter of making the Twelve Tables rational, of "smuggling reason" into the heart of their text. The ludicrous fictions of the Introduction are now turned by Hegel into the vehicles of reason. Hence, the "ludicrous fictions" of the Roman jurists, deprecated by Hegel in his Introduction as illogical, would exhibit, "in the face of bad laws," the property of imposing rational jurisdiction.

To be sure, this contention of Hegel's that certain necessary fictions can *callide* reinscribe reason within the letter of "bad laws" emanates from the same superficial reading of Roman right that affects Hegel's controversy with Ritter von Hugo. This superficial reading may be conjectured to reflect, in turn, Hegel's prejudice with respect to the place occupied by woman in jurisprudence.[23] Why should Hegel, notwithstanding his well-known acquaintance with Montesquieu's work, embrace without adequate verification the thesis, derived from the 1752 edition of Heineccius's *Syntagma,* that the Roman jurists adopted the praxis of the *filia-filius fictio* to counter the exclusion of daughters from the benefits of the Twelve Tables' laws of succession? Why should he come up with such an inaccuracy, unless his presumptions regarding the purposes of these ancient norms were misguided by a fundamental prejudice? Unless, in other words, he found it irresistible to detect in the norms of family inheritance a patent confirmation of the discrimination of the sexes ingrained in the classical jurisprudence of the Romans?

As we saw, Montesquieu writes in *De l'esprit des lois* that "no distinction was made by the laws of the Twelve Tables as to whether the successor was male or female" (2:196). Furthermore, the thesis of the sexual iniquity of the Roman laws of succession in the age of the Twelve Tables was recanted by Heineccius himself, in the versions of his *Syntagma* subsequent to the 1752 edition consulted by Hegel. Nevertheless, Hegel selects the case of the law of domestic succession to exemplify the principle that "a number of provisions in Roman private law . . . [,which] followed quite logically from such institutions as Roman matrimony and Roman *patria potestas,* [were] wrong and irrational in [their] essential character" (*PhilR* 3:[remark] 17–20). Hegel, in sum, seems inclined to detect the presence of a hierarchical differentiation of the sexes even in legal matters where—according to Montesquieu, one of his main sources of documentation, as well as to Heineccius, at least in light of his recantation of his 1752 position regarding the gender-exclusive character of the Roman law of inheritance—Roman jurisprudence exhibited a certain enlightened immunity to gender prejudice.

Hegel's own prejudices regarding the difference between man and woman are too well known to need detailed illustration here. Suffice it to recall the lapidary definition found in Gans's 1833 addition 107 to paragraph 166 of the *Philosophy of Right:* "The difference between men and women is like that between animals and plants. Men correspond to animals, while women correspond to plants . . ." Nor ought these prejudices be hastily engaged as the *passepartout* that gives access to the psychology of Hegel's erroneous thought processes in this circumstance. When it comes, however, to the specifically juridical opposition between man and woman described by Hegel in the *Philosophy of Right* as "the supreme opposition in ethics," which opposition distinguishes man's "dominating power over public life" from woman's passive submission to "the bond of kinship," the issue of Hegel's views as to gender difference in general becomes relevant because of their impact on his legal thought. Hegel delineates the character of the "supreme opposition" of man's and woman's legal personae in the conflict that divides Antigone from Creon in Sophocles's *Antigone,* a conflict that separates the "law of the inward life, a life which has not yet attained its full actualization," from the masculine sphere of "public law" (*PhilR* 166:[remark] 115). As we saw above, man "has his actual substantive life" in the laws of the state, while in the family he "lives a subjective ethical life on the plane of feeling. Woman, on the other hand, has her substantive destiny in the family" (*PhilR* 166:114).

Consequently, it must be far from accidental if Hegel expresses a concerned discontent but at the same time a sort of transgressive satisfaction with regard to the fictions of succession contrived and enforced, according to his *Philosophy of Right,* by

the Roman jurists in order to "smuggle reason" into bad laws
(*PhilR* 180:[remark] 121). Such an ambivalent satisfaction, such
an irresolute craving for a disruption of the law is never (and
would have no motive to be) manifested by Hegel in reference
to the legal connotations of the "right of primogeniture in the
higher sphere of the state." This sphere, whose ethicality is
"higher" than that of "the ethical moment in marriage," arises
"with estates rigidly entailed," that is, with rules of dynastic succession whose rigid formulation is susceptible to no reinterpretation by means of legal fictions. The ethical moment in
marriage, writes Hegel, is prone, instead, to be contaminated by
"a feeling for actual living individuals" (*PhilR* 180:[remark] 122).
One might venture that for Hegel the ethical moment in marriage presents a *feminine* component that at once weakens the
inevitability of the laws that regulate the relationships among
family members and makes these laws susceptible to reinterpretation by means of legal fictions. It is also relevant that, in addressing the juridical connotations of the "lower" moments of
the ethical sphere, Hegel would pay special attention to the arbitration of legitimate succession within the family. In this he
manifests a significant convergence with the analyses of, respectively, Montesquieu and Vico.

Montesquieu places one of the most radical juridical configurations of the moment of succession within the family at the
very center of the Roman private code of law. From book 11 of
Montesquieu's *De l'esprit des lois* we learn that the Roman law
called Valerian (*Lex Valeria Horatia de provocatione*), which
was promulgated by the Roman legislators about five centuries
before the Christian era, labeled as a quaestor of patricide (*ques-
teur du parricide*) the public official charged with the persecution of all offenses against the private code of law.[24] In the light
of this significant fact, one may say that to the Roman legislator
whatever crime did not fall under the "higher" jurisdiction of
the public sphere amounted to a symbolic patricide, that is, to
an attempt to undermine and virtually appropriate the authority
of the *paterfamilias;* or again, one may say that such a crime
amounted to a symbolically violent discontinuation of the legitimate transmission of the privilege to judge and arbitrate, which
had its fulcrum in the figure of the *paterfamilias.*

And Vico, who devoted very large portions of his *Scienza nuova, De universi iuris uno principio et fine uno,* and *De constantia iurisprudentis* to the study of ancient Roman
jurisprudence, tells us that the Latin term *familia* is a synonym

of the term *hereditas,* which designates the right to despotic lordship over the estate of the family, a right enjoyed only by the *pater* and by his firstborn *filius* (*SNS1* § 513, 529; *CI2* § 37). The Roman *paterfamilias* inherits his father's patronymic and transmits it to one of his sons, preferably the firstborn, his *filius,* who will represent in turn the next *filo genealogico* (genealogical thread) of the family (*CI2* § 20; *SNS2* § 1036; *SNS1* § 526–30).

At bottom, then, Hegel's views as to the gender-exclusive spirit of Roman jurisprudence were finely attuned to the intentions of the Roman legislators, even in the case when a superficial and misleading acquaintance with some of their provisions induced Hegel to see sexual inequity embedded within norms that were, perhaps—at least in the views of the authors of two of his direct sources of documentation—extraordinarily immune from it. At bottom, one may say that Hegel was right to the extent that he was, if not wrong, at least inaccurate from a documentary point of view: the Roman code of private law assumes indeed as its privileged aim the defense of the patriarchal family system, whose structure, centered on the function of the *paterfamilias* as "head" of the family, Hegel himself considers indispensable to the legislation of modern civil right (*PhilR* 171:116).

Vico and the Legal Fiction of the *Paterfamilias*

We saw above that Vico's attribution of sexual inequity to the Twelve Tables' norms of family inheritance, together with his attribution of an *unintentional* purgation of such inequity to the jurists of the imperial age, shares an affinity of sorts with Hegel's contention that the imperial jurists deliberately falsified the law by means of an artfully fictional exegesis. Vico and Hegel agree that a violation of the letter of the law is at work, although they disagree as to the purposes of this violation. However, we are going to see now that the distance separating Hegel's paradigmatic opposition of jurisprudence to fiction and imagination from Vico's assessment of the reciprocal encroachment of jurisprudence, interpretive metaphor, and imagination, could not be greater.

In his *Scienza nuova seconda,* Vico writes that Roman jurisprudence, before the written laws of the fifth century B.C.E., was a "mystical theology" (*teologia mistica*), or the art to "interpret the mysteries of divination." This "first" or mystical jurisprudence is grounded upon the logic of the legal fiction, insofar as it introduces the so-called *iura imaginaria,* or "[legal] rights as fabled by fantasy." The Roman lawmakers of this early stage were called by Horace "interpreters of the gods." Regarding the activity of these early lawmakers, Vico underlines a spurious philological affinity between the Latin *interpretari,* "to interpret [the divine signs]" and *interpatrari,* "to enter into the fathers." *Iupiter,* the Latin name for Zeus, Vico argues, signifies the *Iuris Pater,* the Father of Right. The understanding of the divine signs, which present themselves to primitive man through the sound of thunder and the flight of birds of prey, entails, first, the *penetration* into the mind of the gods, or, what amounts to the same thing, into the will of the divine legislators, and second, the *interpretive* act of legislation, which translates the ascertained divine will into a set of codified norms (*SNS2* § 937–41, 1036; *UIPF* § 220). The first interpreters of divine law, the first Roman lawmakers, are called *autores* (Vico's Latin diction for "authors"); their dominion or *autoritas* [authority] over the rest of society is a reflection of a divine mandate. It is important to stress that this divine mandate over society at large is an enlargement and a direct reflection of the divine mandate and absolute authority that the ability to interpret the divine auspices confers onto the *paterfamilias,* the head of the patrician family: the *paterfamilias'* despotic lordship will manifest itself, at the time of the Law of the Twelve Tables, with the legal provision: "*Uti paterfamilias super pecuniae tutelaeve rei suae legassit, ita ius esto,*" by which the head of the family is established as the unchallengeable lawmaker with regard to the allocation, after his death, of his own goods, his own relatives, his own slaves (*SNS1* § 513; *SNS2* § 942–46).

The interpretation of the divine mind lies at the heart of the Roman conjugal bond. The patrician *paterfamilias* is the "prince of all holy things." It is his duty to sacrifice beside the *focus Laris* (Italian: *focolare*), i.e., the hearth consecrated to the Lares, the household gods. Through his sacrifices, the *paterfamilias* receives the auspices from his family gods. But since the Lares represent the souls of the deceased ancestors, the juridical authority of the *paterfamilias* turns him, in the last analysis, into the reader and the oracle of the mind of the family's dead. Through the *patria potestas* (the power of the father), which term in Roman jurisprudence will later be synonymous with the *sacra paterna* (paternal holy estate), the dead are considered vicariously alive in the authority of the *pater,* who interprets their mind and enacts their will. As Vico says, "Ancient jurisprudence ... treated facts as nonfacts, nonfacts as facts, children-to-come as already born, living men as dead, dead men as alive in their vicarious authorities ..." (CI2 § 20; *SNS2* § 1036; *SNS1* § 526–30).

Later on, the written formulation of the law induces the appearance of a special jurist, the praetor, whose task consists of the promulgation of edicts (*edicta*), in which "the dispute between the litigants [is] defined in a formula (*per formulam*)."[25] The praetor's formula applies the letter of the law to the legal case at hand. It is at the stage of the procedure *per formulam* (and the slightly anterior procedure *per legis actionem*) that Pierre Olivier's *Legal Fictions in Practice and Legal Science* identifies the explicit manifestation of legal fictions in Roman jurisprudence. The procedure *per formulam,* particularly through the operations of the so-called *formula fictitia* (fictitious formula), "enabled (the praetor) to create new law by formulating new actions hitherto unknown to the *ius civile.*"[26] Olivier's research demonstrates that the use of legal fictions is inherent in Roman jurisprudence. In a definition given by Henry S. Maine in his classical study, *Ancient Law* (a definition that applies particularly well, incidentally, to the procedure *per formulam* described by Olivier), "*fictio,* in old Roman law, is properly a term of pleading, and signifies a false averment on the part of the plaintiff which the defendant was not allowed to traverse."[27] Emperor Augustus enlarges the *praetores'* authority to correct and amend civil right through their formulas (the formulas in turn allow the judge to reach a decision in case of legal doubt); he also augments the authority that pertains to the *fideicommissa* to execute the last wills of the dead (the dead being the supreme lawgivers in the case of the patrician testament [*CI2* § 20]). Lastly, Augustus transforms the *pontifices* or jurisconsults, i.e., the interpreters of the law who are not endowed with either legislative or juridical power, into his own spokesmen for the expression of specific juridical opinions. Only with the revision of the *Edictuum Perpetuum,* promoted in 130 C.E. by Emperor Hadrian and composed by the jurist Salvius Iulianus, however, do the jurisconsults become the institutional interpreters of the law, in order to check the praetores' invasion of the legislative sphere (which invasion will take the form, after Augustus, of a proliferation of edicts concerning the jurisdiction of the *fideicommissa,* that is, the jurisdiction of testaments). Under Hadrian, the judge must consult the pontifex instead of the praetor as to the meaning of the praetor's edict: the last word goes to the jurisconsult rather than to the promulgator of the edict.

In sum, the enforcement of the Law of the Twelve Tables necessitates, under Augustus, the institution of an authoritative *collegium pontificum* (college of the jurisconsults), composed of the practitioners of the art of civil right interpretation. Later on, under Hadrian, "civil right interpretation prepares its further transformation," Vico observes. "The discussion of the juridical formulas among the *pontifices* laid down the premises for the civil legislation to come," and therefore for the full emergence of the third stage of Roman jurisprudence, where all the authority previously conferred on the opinion of the first *autores,* or interpreters of divine law, is transferred onto the interpretive wisdom of the jurisconsults (*UIPF* § 209–12; *SNS2* § 442–46); this phenomenon signals the invasion of the legislative sphere on the part of the interpreters of the law, and a jurisprudence rooted in the dismantlement of the boundary that separates the legislative and juridical spheres.

Vico's philosophical procedures, oriented toward the assessment of the reciprocal attunement between the *telos* of "*la storia ideale eterna*"[28] and the factual history of philology (the factual history, that is, of the usage of words and the accretion of meanings), diverge radically from Hegel's speculative idealism. In the above illustration of Vico's reconstruction of paternity as the originary principle and dominant motif of classical Roman jurisprudence, it is easy to see how he takes for granted the possibility that Hegel abhors, that is, the possibility that the spirit of Roman jurisprudence is encoded in a formulation that is grafted upon the legacy of *fabulae* and metaphoric significations. Neither Olivier's nor Maine's work stresses in the least the two crucial points I derive from this reading of Vico's *Scienza nuova seconda,* and particularly of his often neglected *De universi iuris uno principio et fine uno* and *De constantia iurisprudentis.* These two points are, in brief, first, that the use of legal fictions is already inherent in the *iura imaginaria* ("rights as fabled by fantasy") of Roman jurisprudence long before any form of codification takes place—long before the praetorian practice of the *fictio* becomes current in the attribution of family inheritance—and, second, that subsequent Roman legal fictions derive from the ur-legal fiction of legitimate succession, the *filo genealogico* (the genealogical thread) that legitimizes the head of the family as *paterfamilias* and as the exclusive bearer of the patronymic.

One might say that, speculatively speaking, this is the logical order that reflects the historical manifestations of the idea of justice in ancient Roman society: First comes the *paterfamilias,* as interpreter of the gods and spokesman for his dead ancestors; then comes the family unit itself, whose existence presupposes the privileged access of its head to ancestral and divine auspices; and finally comes legislation, as the moment when the *paterfamilias* prescribes the norms and regulations governing his family and also, in a successive, communal moment of consultation between patricians, the norms and regulations governing the plurality of families that Hegel calls "civil society."

I observed in the opening to this chapter that Hegel's engagement of legal matters pertaining to family lineage in classical Roman jurisprudence is of fundamental importance to the speculative configuration of modern civil right. More specifically, it is out of the Roman right of *paterfamilias* that Hegel excavates the basic tenets of modern civil right, notable among them the principle that "the family as a legal entity in relation to others must be represented by the husband as its head" (*PhilR* 171:116). My initial thesis was that a close examination of Hegel's specific treatment of the law of family inheritance as prescribed by the Twelve Tables would reveal the logical and historical fallacy at the heart of Hegel's legal thought. The logical fallacy derives from this, that the norms applying to the legal arbitration of family inheritance in classical Roman jurisprudence suppose, as their condition of possibility, that the juridical construct of the *paterfamilias* be already in place before the head of the family engages in private and public legislation. Far from being rooted in an absolute, timeless idea of justice, whose historical progression would exhibit a correspondence with the logical order of self-manifestation of the concept, the idea of justice embedded in classical Roman jurisprudence is contingent upon the particular configuration acquired by the typical patrician family of the *Urbs* at the time of the early, preimperial elaborations of Roman law. One might argue that the legal arbitration of kinship among the Romans is captive of a logical tautology, to the extent that its practice presupposes kinship itself— more specifically, presupposes the fundamental anchor of kinship, i.e., the *paterfamilias*—as the juridical construct anterior not only to the arbitration of family succession but to jurisprudence itself. In brief, Hegel fails to stress that the prehistory of modern civil right hinges upon the presupposition that *androlineal filiation comes before the law.*

Hegel's historical fallacy is of an exquisitely metaphoric nature. Hegel fails to stress that the *paterfamilias* is the gender-exclusive product of primitive religious imagination. Its juridical construct consists, in the final analysis, of a *fabula;* it is the *ante litteram* ancestor of all legal fictions. As such, the grounds it provides for the modern civil right are weakened by the pervasive metaphors inherent in its original conception. A particularly significant extension of this aspect pertains to the linguistic ground from which the classical Roman jurisprudence of family succession sprouts its codes and regulations; this ground is, in its own turn, threatened by the quakes of the lexical and grammatical ambiguities intrinsic to tropes and metaphors of sexual opposition. Buried within dictates whose rationality is systematically exposed to metaphoric contamination, the intentions of the Roman legislator are to a great extent impervious to objective exegesis. What was actually meant by the legislator can only emerge as a compromise between the letter of the law, given once and for all, and the historically determined adjudications of the judge who, in the spirit of the Roman tradition of the legal fiction, acts either under the pretense or under the assumption that the spirit of the legal principle, whose letter he or she is enforcing, has undergone no substantial alteration.

9

Etiology and Genealogy: Totems and Moral Taboos in Derrida and Kant

> I have been for years staring at an old print of the sacrifice of Cain and Abel and it is only a week ago it struck me how tactful it was of Abel to slit the throat of the firstlings (without any divine injunction as yet to kill the Cains of the flock).
> —James Joyce to Harriet S. Weaver, 25 July 1926

I HAVE LONG BEEN PERSUADED THAT ANCIENT GENEALOGICAL CHRONI-cles are more often than not etiological tales. They tells us of our beginnings, of the origin of customs and usages that still affect our modern world. Classical literature provides us with two separate kinds of genealogical chronicles. The more ortho-dox kind pertains to the epic genre. I am thinking of the impos-ing genealogical chronicles that the Old Testament inaugurates with the "Census of Israel" in Numbers, or of the array of royal ancestries that the *Iliad* displays in the "muster of armies" of book 2, or of the immense chronology from book 6 of the *Aeneid,* rooted in the primordial soil of the *anima mundi* and projected forward into an imperial glory still to come, which the Sibyl of Cuma reveals to Aeneas in Hades. The less orthodox kind of genealogical chronicles, on which I will focus exclusively in this chapter, pertain to the tragic genre and depict, usually, aborted, fragmented, dismembered genealogies.

Take, for instance, the myth of Oedipus from Sophocles' so-called Theban trilogy. The sterility of Oedipus's short-lived prog-eny warns us of the consequences to be expected from the thrust toward self-identity—the uncompromising exorcism of the different—which is intrinsic to the incestuous family. Oedi-pus cannot be that which he is supposed to be by right of birth, that is, the king of Thebes, the natural continuation of his father Laius's lineage, without bringing death and desolation upon his city. By the same token, Oedipus's children—Antigone and Ismene, Eteocles and Polyneices—cannot attend to their royal duties in Thebes without triggering, at once, civil and external war. Eteocles and Polyneices take sides with opposite armies and destroy each other. Antigone, in turn, ignores the laws of the state in order to mourn her brother Polyneices, who joined the ranks of the enemies of Thebes. Antigone's behavior brings Oedipus's city to its knees and terminates Oedipus's genealogical tree. Patricide and fratricide, incest and self-destruction, war and civil war turn even the universal custom of paying one's respects to one's dead into a source of social evils.

Or take the myth of Orestes, the son of Agamemnon and Clytaemnestra from Aeschylus's trilogy, the *Oresteia.* Orestes' permanent exile from the House of Atreus in Argos, the impossibility of repairing his rupture with home and family, tell a different sort of cautionary tale, this time about the consequences to be expected from the movement toward self-identity and the exorcism of the different that is intrinsic to the androlineal family. After Clytaemnestra's murder of Agamemnon, it falls upon Orestes to prove the legitimacy of his royal descent. This is a fundamentally self-defeating task, one at which success brings catastrophe. Orestes is in fact the last branch of the genealogical tree that derived from Tantalus, who offered his own children as a holy meal to the gods. Orestes' father, Agamemnon, who repeated his great-grandfather's crime with the sacrifice of his daughter Iphigenia, was the son of Atreus, who, in turn, served the flesh of his brother Thyestes' sons at a banquet in Thyestes' honor. Confusing consanguinity with seminal descent, Orestes is insensible to his mother Clytaemnestra's revulsion toward the killer of her daughter. He returns from his exile to prove his royal legitimacy through matricide, and so becomes a royal outcast, a fugitive cursed by his mother's Furies, the symbolic personification of the misogyny and sterility of his ancestral guilt.

Or take, finally, that primordial act of cannibalism attributed by Freud to a horde of sons at the expense of a tyrannical father. In this fundamental myth of modernity one might be tempted to trace the operation of the whole matrix of etiological factors disseminated in the stories mentioned above. By eating up their father, a literal expression of the ritual of human sacrifice, the sons incorporate, through a sort of Eucharistic transubstantiation, the paternal qualities of power and supremacy; by ravishing their father's wives, an expeditious appropriation of the rights of the paternal hymen, the sons precipitate the incestuous, hence, unquestionable, identification of the tribe's consanguineous lineage; by instituting the festival of a totemic meal, a diffusion of ceremonial cannibalism into its own simulacrum, the sons confer immortality upon the founder of their lineage, hence, upon the totem of their own genealogical tree.

But in what sense can one argue that these genealogical stories are etiological? Is it that they tell us of the legendary causes of a communal prohibition or prescription, or are they the "performative" vehicles to such a communal prohibition or prescription? Do these tales, in attributing spatio-temporal unity to an age-long moral evolution, explain to us in fictionalized terms how it came about that we choose or avoid a certain course of action? Or do they tell us, rather, that we ought or ought not to make such a choice? Are they a matter of posthumous celebration or a matter of timeless imperative? These are the questions raised by the very concept of etiological tale. What comes first, the moral prescription found in a story, or the story of the moral prescription coming into being? Do we appreciate the beauty of the story of Oedipus, or of Antigone, or of Orestes, because it fictionalizes a taboo that we share with our archaic progenitors, or because we perceive in its aesthetic form the authority of a moral imperative, capable of playing a central role in the unfolding of our moral standards? In sum, is the ethical moment intrinsic or extrinsic to the aesthetic?

THE STORY BEFORE THE LAW

In "Before the Law," Derrida establishes a congruence between, on the one hand, the primordial occurrence of Freud's totemic meal and, on the other hand, the type of possible action whose conformity to an order of universality informs the procedure of moral judgment in Kant. He writes:

> Since the father dead is more powerful than he was when alive, since, . . . very logically, he would have been . . . more dead alive than *post mortem,* the murder of the father is not an event in the ordinary sense of the word. Nor is the origin of moral law. Nobody would have encountered it in its proper place of happening, nobody would have faced it in its taking place. . . . However, this pure and purely presumed event nevertheless marks an *invisible rent* in history. It resembles a fiction, a myth, or a fable. . . . The question of the reality of its historical referent is, if not annulled, at least irremediably fissured. Demanding and denying the story, this *quasi-event* bears the mark of fictive narrativity.[1]

Derrida's "Before the Law" may be said to delineate an inquiry into the conundrum of the totem and its taboo. Which comes first, the totem or its own taboo? What comes first, the moral law that finds its simulacrum in the totem of the father—the law that prohibits that which it germinated from, namely, incest, patricide, cannibalism, and civil war—or rather the simulacrum itself—the "fictive narrativity" intrinsic to a moral law that never originated as such, but came rather into being through the genealogical story told and retold by the totem as effigy, as simulacrum of its own taboo?

Let us take a closer look at that slippery "historical referent" found in the totem erected by Freud's primordial horde. Its simple, linear architecture, presumably covered with apotropaic effigies, is the progenitor, after all, of those "column-like structures of stone" that, according to Hegel's *Aesthetics,* were erected in ancient India, and which are, in turn, progenitors to the Egyptian obelisk. Inadequate to express the separation between architectonic purpose and means, between the function of a building as enclosure and its symbolic meaning (as home, as family abode, for instance), the colossal phalluses of ancient India signified, in an easily recognizable, organic shape, that which they *were,* that is, symbols of seminal fertility.[2] They carried their meaning *within* themselves, in the sense that their meaning *was* their function. The same paradigm applies, I venture, to the totem of the primordial horde. A compact structure unable to accommodate or give shelter to anything alien from itself, all it could "house," all it could give shelter to, was a spectacularly gender-exclusive logic of fertility and insemination.

In this light, one can better comprehend the rationale behind Derrida's perplexity as to the "reality of (the) historical referent" vis-à-vis the origin of the moral taboo. The conundrum of the order of precedence to be established between the totem and its taboo calls for an investigation into an archaic past at the threshold of what we call human civilization, a past anterior to the paradigmatic separation between function and symbol, between the order of reality and the order of (re)semblance. And the absence of this separation, or better say, the hardly imaginable contours of the region wherein function and symbol coalesce into the unified signification of one *thing,* posits an impressive obstacle, usually unappreciated in all its implications, to our understanding of the remote past. It is the impossibility of our paradigmatic procedures to accommodate such a region of discursive "disorder" that forces us to designate certain epochal events in the prehistory of humankind as "quasi-events," just as Derrida does in "Before the Law."

An emblematic occurrence of such a "quasi-event," wherein symbol and function coalesce into the unity of a strikingly elusive signifier, may be found in the Book of Esther. As will be recalled, King Ahasuerus has the prerogative of extending or withdrawing his "golden scepter," according to whether he intends that the subject in his presence be welcomed or put to death. Referring to the episode in which Ahasuerus extends his scepter toward Esther, guilty of the crime of appearing uninvited in his presence, and she approaches until she finally "touch(es) the tip of the scepter,"[3] Robert Alter remarks that the scene "certainly confirms the double sense of Ahasuerus as a man with a shaky scepter."[4] Alter's interpretation, however oriented toward a fusion of function and meaning, still suffers from the shortcomings of a paradigmatic reading; it is based upon a methodology that calls for the differentiation between the "literal data" of the episode, represented by Ahasuerus's extension of the royal scepter, and the "figurative reading" of Esther's manipulation of the king's scepter.[5] My reading, instead, is that we are facing here a beautiful example of, literally, an invisible episode—an episode whose principal historical referent, the royal scepter, is deprived of the referential attributes that pertain to what Roland Barthes calls the reality-effect.[6] By coming uninvited to the king, Esther brings the erotic logic of the harem to the politic logic of the throne. The greatest "discursive disorder" ensues from her move. Can one claim that Ahasuerus extends toward Esther a mere effigy of power? Can one claim that the queen's delicate handling of this effigy merely suggests an act of genital manipulation? The paradigms intrinsic to the mimetic transposition of the nonverbal into the verbal have been set adrift. To what extent can one unequivocally describe a scene in which either an inert effigy or a turgid phallus is being exposed, when it is evident that royal clemency and royal lust cannot be distinguished from each other after the separation between throne and harem crumbles? The etiological distinction between the king's body and the king's persona, between the phallic effigy of royal authority and the king's phallus, is precluded by the slipperiness of the scepter as their ubiquitous "historical referent."

THE CROSSROADS OF ETHIC AND AESTHETIC

In this chapter I intend to explore a specialized aspect of the conundrum of totem and taboo. Of the numerous ramifications that emanate from the hypothesis that one can detect a coincidence of purpose between genealogical chronicles and etiological tales, Derrida explores, at times in almost aphoristic terms, the specialized branch of the relationship between the order of the law and the order of fiction. Derrida's thesis, which in this chapter I will substantiate beyond the aphoristic level, is that the origin of the law, and specifically the origin of the moral imperative in Kant, occurs at the figurative crossroads where the operations of reason and fiction get entangled with each other—the crossroads, in other words, where the question as to the intrinsic or extrinsic relationship of aesthetic to ethic, of the story as fictional commemoration of the origin of the law and the story as direct manifestation of the binding nature of the law, acquires a tautological nature, becomes, as it were, a question about the two indispensable faces of the same coin.

Derrida continues his considerations on the totemic meal and the origin of moral law with the following passage:

> Whether or not (the event of the murder of the father) is fantastic, whether or not it has arisen from the imagination, even the transcendental imagination, . . . this in no way diminishes the imperious necessity of what it tells, its law. This law is even more frightening and fantastic, *unheimlich* or uncanny, than if it emanated from pure reason, unless precisely the latter be linked to an unconscious fantastic. ("Before the Law," 190)

It is important to stress the "imperious necessity" that, according to Derrida, characterizes the law emanating from this reciprocal yoking of reason and fiction with respect to the moral law emanating from pure practical reason. The above passage is one of crossbreeding, wherein Derrida manages to conjugate in a unified discursive modality the analysis of the fictional structure of Freud's story of the totemic meal and the analysis of the rational structure of Kant's theory of moral judgment. This explains the inclusion, in the above quotation, of an ambiguous term, namely, the adjective "unconscious," whose Kantian and Freudian associations diverge radically. In order to focus my attention upon the different degrees of "necessity" inherent, on the one hand, in the law that "emanate(s) from pure reason"

and, on the other hand, in the law that emanates from the "fictive" legacy of universal fables and myths, I propose to bracket
this ambiguous adjective. Such a move allows me to sidestep the
hermeneutic implication of the above passage as regards Freud's
theory of the origin of law, and call attention, instead, to the
philosophical implications of Derrida's thesis.

To attend properly to these implications, we must start with
a close appraisal of their theoretical premises. In "Before the
Law" Derrida declares his concern about the status of the expression "as if" in the formulation of Kant's categorical imperative: "Act as if the maxim of your action were by your will to
turn into a universal law of nature." Derrida argues that this "as
if," this hypothetical modality borne by the formulation of the
categorical imperative, "almost introduces narrativity and fiction
into the very core of legal thought" ("Before the Law," 190). There
comes a moment when the moral coercion conveyed by the categorical imperative "begins . . . to question the moral subject": it
asks of the moral subject what moral stance it would take "if the
action you propose were to take place by a law of the system of
nature of which you were yourself a part."[7] This, according to
Derrida, is the moment when the "rationality [of the law] seems
alien to all fiction and imagination." And yet, even at this crucial
moment of exclusion and interrogation, the hypothetical modality inherent in the formulation of the categorical imperative
reminds one that the "authority of the law . . . *seems* a priori to
shelter [that which it] *seems* to exclude," precisely, empirical
narrativity, fiction, and imagination ("Before the Law," 190, my
emphases).

The complexity of Derrida's argument can best be unraveled
by taking a close look at the "Analytic of Pure Practical Reason"
in the *Critique of Practical Reason* (pt. 1, bk. 1), particularly at
the theorems surrounding the formulation of the categorical
imperative in the seventh paragraph of chapter 1, and then at
the section of chapter 2 entitled "On the Typic of the Pure Practical Judgment." It is in this latter section that the treatment of
the rationality of moral law and of the reflective nature of moral
judgment is exposed to Derrida's deconstructive engagement of
the Kantian separation between the rationality of the law and
the procedures of imagination. The procedures of imagination
trigger, in Kant, the operations of fiction and empirical (that is,
factual, experienced as fact) narrativity: this is a deconstructive
principle of fundamental import to the present discussion.

THE TYPICAL AND THE CONTINGENT IN KANT'S MORAL LAW

Let us begin with the formulation of the categorical imperative. Lewis White Beck provides a slightly different translation
of the fundamental law of pure practical reason than the version
found in the English translation of Derrida's "Before the Law":

> So act that the maxim of your will could always hold at the same
> time as a principle establishing universal law.[8]

The fundamental law of pure practical reason hinges upon
Kant's concept of moral judgment, whose definition depends, in
turn, on the procedures of rationality. What is moral judgment
in Kant, and how can its privileging of rationality over the procedures of imagination be deconstructed? A brief excursus into
the above mentioned theorems from the *Critique of Practical
Reason* will answer the first question and prepare for the
second.

Moral judgment is the movement through which the subject
establishes a maxim of moral conduct by measuring a possible
action in the world of sense against his will's inclination to accommodate this action, as a principle contributing to the establishment of universal law. In the context of moral judgment, the
subject's will must be free from all natural conditions belonging
to the world of senses, such as hunger, violent coercion, etc.
Hence, the moral maxim itself must contain as its determining
ground a legislative form, a formal law, distinct from the law
of contingent causality that provides, instead, the determining
ground for the events in nature. This formal law is a law of
causality in its own right, but one that is independent of contingency, one that predicates the necessary relations between sensible objects, and, as such, is a universal law of nature. In turn,
the will of the subject is free when the subject is led to the
determining ground of free will (which entails the knowledge of
freedom) by the moral law as the ground of the moral maxim.

In other words, the knowledge of the unconditionally practical
principle contained in the moral maxim takes its inception from
the moral law, not from freedom, insofar as it is through the
moral law that the subject overcomes his first exposure to freedom as a negative entity, an entity defined by the overwhelming
scope of its opposite both in nature and in the concept. Since
the moral law is "a ground of determination" that "reason exhibits ... as ... completely independent and not to be out-

weighed by any sensuous condition," it leads to a concept of freedom whose form does not have to be borrowed from that "other faculty," imagination,[9] which, in Kant, apprehends empirical occurrences without reference to a concept of reason.[10] Moreover, freedom is the concept by which the subject gains his cognitive insight into the supersensible idea of the morally good (*Critique of Practical Reason*, 29–30.28–29). Finally, moral judgment, as the subsumption of a possible action in the world of senses under a universal law of causality, is reflective and purposive. It is reflective to the extent that the formal law of nature, i.e., the moral law upon which moral judgment bases its procedure, is not previously given but must be found in the movement of judgment itself. It is purposive to the extent that it represents the conformity of a type of possible action to an order of universality, as would be required were that type of action to be legislated by an understanding.

Kant declares that it would be absurd to apply a law of freedom to a concrete, contingent event in the world of senses, with the aim of turning this event into an exhibition *in concreto* of the ideal of the morally good. In other words, the moral judgment of pure practical reason does not escape the analogous difficulty encountered, in the *Critique of Pure Reason*, by pure theoretical reason vis-à-vis the contingent manifestation of a law of empirical causality; pure theoretical reason, however, manages to escape this difficulty by having recourse to the schemata of imagination, which stipulate what conditions must be met by the intuition of imagination, which is imaginal in nature, so that the latter will match a category of intellect. Pure theoretical reason stipulates a conformity between apprehension, as the a priori intuition that imagination brings to the objects of the senses, and apperception, as the movement by which understanding, as cognition, brings the objects of the senses, the manifold of sense experience as apprehended by imagination, under the universality of a formal law of causality.[11]

Pure practical judgment, however, does not contemplate any such exhibition *in concreto* of the ideal of the morally good. Kant shows that pure practical judgment rests its legitimacy upon the derivation of the *typology* for a moral law, hence for a law of freedom, from a law of nature, under the condition that such a law of nature be engaged in its pure form as an object of the faculty of understanding, rather than in its contingent form as an object of the faculty of imagination. Since the faculty of understanding brings the sensible action into the pure apper-

ception of a formal law of causality through a purposive judgment, it is to this subsumption that the moral judgment owes
its purposive character. The typology for such a law of nature,
in other words, is to be grafted onto the occurrence of a hypo-
thetically "as if . . ." *type* of action, which belongs to the conduct
of intelligible beings, rather than onto the concrete occurrence
of an empirical event in the world of senses. The possibility of
the empirical occurrence of an action belonging to this type, the
possibility of an action belonging to this type becoming an *event,*
is left unverified and is, in fact, indifferent to the procedure of
the pure practical judgment, since its verification would require
recourse to a schema. In sum, as Kant points out, the procedure
of the pure practical judgment does not enable the subject of
free will to show, to represent, to incorporate the ideal of the
morally good in the concreteness of a sensible event, of a given
historical event, whose concept could be given objective validity
only by the subject's sensible intuition.

Kant stipulates that we are to subsume under a pure practical
law a *type* of action, a hypothetical and fictitious action, possible
to us in the world of senses, but whose possibility of empirical
occurrence, being subject to sensible intuition, is unverifiable,
unless we entangle the pure practical nature of our judgment
with something extraneous to it, namely, with a procedure, or
schema, of the faculty of imagination. The procedure of imagination invests the objects of sensible intuition with the concepts
determined by the law of contingent causality. But the procedure
of imagination, as we saw, cannot be involved in the purpose of
the application of the concept of the unconditionally good—only
the faculty of understanding, which may translate a type of action into the pure apperception of a formal law of nature, can
be involved in this movement. Moral judgment occurs therefore
at the level of typology rather than at the level of a specific empirical event, or of a specific historical event. The suprasensible
idea of the morally good, whose only reality for the Kantian
subject depends upon the moral law, and which is mediately
cognizable to the Kantian subject only as freedom, may provide
a ground for the pure practical judgment only insofar as reason
uses physical nature in its pure form as an object of the faculty
of understanding, to derive the type itself for the morally good
from it.

At the moment when the hypothetical action that provides
the Kantian subject with the type for the moral law is grasped
as a concrete event in the world of senses, imagination invades

the operations of understanding, and therefore the procedure of the pure practical judgment loses all its legislative power. A judgment of the lawfulness of an empirical, historical event cannot take place before the tribunal presided by reason alone. A judgment is pure and practical under the double provision that the procedure of imagination be excluded from it and that the sensible actions measured against will's disposition to accommodate them as universal laws of nature be types of actions.

RATIONALITY AND IMAGINATION, REMEMBRANCE AND FORGETFULNESS IN MORAL JUDGMENT

One may wonder, as does Derrida, if some degree of contamination between narrativity and its exclusion, between imagination and its exclusion, between fiction and its exclusion, is not at work in the procedure of determining the type. Implicit in Derrida's remark that the hypothetical modality inherent in the formulation of the categorical imperative seems to shelter, in its authority and rationality, empirical narrativity, fiction, and imagination, is the postulate that the typological discourse conveyed by Kant's "as if" is irreducible to the pure operations of the intellect. However rigorously Kant stresses the withdrawal of the procedure of the moral judgment into the theoretical faculties of the subject, it remains that it is not by the contingency of historical accident that certain episodes of ethical dissipation—say, for instance, the story of Oedipus—are customarily given the self-evident attribute of immorality by the "covert judgments" that, according to Heidegger, Kant sees at work in "common reason."[12] It is not by the contingency of historical accident, either, that the narration of such episodes postulates propositions, moral rules—say, for instance, the abhorrence of incest—that are no less evident, no less *ideal,* in their universality, than the postulates of pure geometry (whose exemplary ideality, incidentally, Kant stresses right after the first formulation of the Fundamental Law of Pure Practical Reason [31.30]). In turn, it is also *because* of historical contingency that moral rules are structurally exposed to forgetfulness, as the extrinsic accidents of human history bury, or occult, under the sediment of either unquestioned traditions or factual destruction, those moral idealities whose imperative evidence is, to put it in the jargon of Husserl's phenomenology, "chained" to the world of factuality.[13]

There is a concrete possibility, in sum, that the value and significance of certain moral rules may be the objects not just of the theoretical faculties of the subject, but also of the subject's aptitude for remembrance and forgetfulness. Or, to put it in a slightly different way, it would appear that the past purposiveness of a moral rule may be taken to be purposively recalled, or exhumed, by the Kantian subject of free will, *as long as* the subject's memory is not erased, buried, or occulted under accidental sediments. This is a thesis that, in positing a certain reciprocal contamination of reason and imagination in the process of determination of the moral type, requires a further enquiry into Kant's theory of the morally good, an enquiry oriented, this time, toward the symbolic relation that links, according to Kant's *Critique of Judgment,* the realm of aesthetics and the realm of understanding. This enquiry leads me to venture that the structure of Kant's categorical imperative neglects the full range and, at the same time, the extrinsic and factual limitations of the ability, on the part of the subject of free will, to preserve and purposively recall ancestral memories. This capability appears to be embedded, at least in part, in narrative configurations. Take, again, the myths and legends relating to Oedipus's incestuous relationship with his mother, or to the domestic cannibalism perpetrated by the progeny of Tantalos, or take the story in Genesis of Lot's incestuous intercourse with his daughters, or the story of Judah's mercenary promiscuity with his daughter-in-law—all myths and legends of genealogical dissipation that are entwined with our modern ethical concerns.

THE KANTIAN CONGRUENCE BETWEEN AESTHETIC AND MORAL JUDGMENT

Derrida remarks rather cryptically, in the description of his attempt at "a discourse on moral law and respect for law in Kant's doctrine of practical reason," that Kant "speaks . . . of a *symbolic* presentation of moral good (the beautiful as a symbol of morality [in the] *Critique of Judgment)*" ("Before the Law," 190). The significance of this remark turns out to play a decisive role in the deconstruction of the privilege accorded to reason by Kant's moral judgment. In what follows I will tease this significance out of Kant's aesthetic theory.

In Kant, a judgment of taste is an aesthetic judgment when the apprehension of a particular object is reflected in the faculties of understanding and imagination, and this reflection entails a judgment of beauty that gives a feeling of pleasure to the subject. Although aesthetic judgment is analogous to the faculties' way of operating in cognition, its aim is not oriented toward conceptual knowledge only, as is the case with the reflective movement of moral judgment. In the fifty-ninth section of the *Critique of Judgment,* Kant maintains that in aesthetic judgment the theoretical character of knowledge and the practical character of taste are combined "in an unknown manner . . . and joined into a unity."[14]

> Taste enables us, as it were, to make the transition from sensible charm to a habitual moral interest without making too violent a leap; for taste presents the imagination as admitting, even in its freedom, a determination that is purposive for the understanding, and it teaches us to like even objects of sense freely, even apart from sensible charm.[15]

In his description of the separation between the intuitive and the conceptual procedures—a separation the two *Critiques* went to great lengths to give a firm foundation to—Kant posits as permissible the attribution of the name "cognition" to both. He argues so on the basis of the differentiation of the procedures of imagination into either a schematic or a symbolic presentation. While the former proceeds by demonstration and is eccentric to theoretical knowledge, the latter proceeds by analogy, first applying the concept to the object of a sensible intuition, then reflecting that intuition onto a different object, of which the former object is only the symbol. Symbolic presentation enjoys a closer proximity to theoretical knowledge than schematic presentation, insofar as it provides a kind of cognition that is functional with respect to determining an object practically, "as to what the idea (of it) ought to become for us and for our purposive employment of it."[16]

These axioms allow Kant to maintain that the beautiful is the symbol of the morally good, a presentation of the morally good by way of analogy that provides a certain understanding as to what the idea of the morally good ought to become for us and for our purposive employment of it. "The morally good is the *intelligible* that taste has in view" when aesthetic judgment "include(s) a claim to everyone else's assent."[17]

In light of the above, one might inaugurate an inquiry into the repercussions that the bridge drawn by Kant between intuitive and rational knowledge entails apropos the stability of the separation between imagination's apprehensive power and understanding's apperceptive power. Such an investigation, however, would lead me too far from the topic I have engaged here, i.e., the substantiation of Derrida's hypothesis that Kant's categorical imperative "seems to" shelter that which it "seems" so crucially to exclude, namely, empirical narrativity, fiction, and imagination. I will limit myself, therefore, to a few closing remarks derived from the archetypal character of the ancestral memories that I mentioned above, as a constituent part of the retentive and protentive capabilities of the subject of moral judgment, and I will ask a few relevant questions as to the implications that the relation of congruence established by Kant between judgment of taste and moral judgment has upon the typological aspect of moral judgment.

MORAL TYPE AND NARRATIVE ARCHETYPE

My questions will presume that both the symbolic procedures inherent in aesthetic judgment and the typological procedures inherent in moral judgment operate by analogy. Analogy, as the key term upon which is hinged the bridge drawn by Kant between the knowledge of imagination and the knowledge of reason, exceeds, at once, both the conventionality of sign-making by which reason expresses its concepts, and the mediation between intuition and conceptual categories by which imagination elaborates its schemata. In the "Analytic of Pure Practical Reason" (*Critique of Practical Reason,* bk. 1), the transition to the section "Of the Typic . . ." marks a transition from the judgment upon a possible action to the judgment upon a type, i.e., the judgment upon a manifold of possible actions that may be taken as analogically affined with one another. Now, in the organization of the subject of this chapter, the coincidence by which literary tradition has attributed to some of these types of possible action the name of *archetype* is, to say the least, intriguing. So, for instance, one wonders how the structure of the categorical imperative could accommodate the disorienting beauty of Sophocles' *Oedipus Rex.* In this tragedy, it is a matter of a beautiful literary artifact that turns into an irresistible symbol of morality on account of its narrative rendition of the primordial, repugnant crime of incest. It is a matter of the generic beauty of the rendition of a human monstrosity, whose factual and originary character—just like the factual and originary character of pure geometry[18]—can never be evidentially established, but only imagined. How can, in other words, the structure of the categorical imperative disregard the immediacy by which Sophocles' fictional realization of one of the remotest memories of ethical dissipation makes itself (as well as the body of its unquestionable norms of negative coercion, of limitation of freedom) known to the subject through the beauty of its artistic rendition? Could there be judgment of the morally good without one's ability to retain, recall, and constructively engage the patrimony of the archaic story's telling of exemplary transgressions of what is good, of exemplary violations of what is right? Could there be moral judgment as a cognitive moment in the experience of the Kantian subject of free will without that spurious cognitive supplement provided by aesthetically driven recollections of the archetypal stories of the origin of morality? It is not by chance that, in facing this paradox, rooted at the heart of Kant's categorical imperative, Derrida digresses into a brief revisit of Freud's meditations on the primordial, olfactory origins of human morality.

> [Freud's hypothesis on] the concept of repression [is that it] is organic in origin and linked with [man's] upright position, that is, to a certain *elevation.* The passage to the upright position raises man, thus distancing his nose from the sexual zones, anal or genital. This distance ennobles his height and leaves its traces by delaying his action. . . . Diversion of the olfactory sense from the sexual stench, repression—here are the origins of morality. [Here Derrida quotes Freud writing to Wilhelm Fliess: 'To put it crudely, the memory actually stinks just as in the present the object stinks; . . . as we turn away our sense organ (the head and nose) in disgust, the preconscious and the sense of consciousness turn away from the memory.'] ("Before the Law," 193)[19]

Freud's meditations on the origins of morality result in a dramatic *stretching,* in the direction of unconscious memory, of the retentive capabilities assigned by Kant to the subject of free will. This leads Derrida to recall Freud's derivation of the cognitive theory of the "totemic meal" from the narrative myth of the "murder of the primordial father" ("Before the Law," 192–98). As I observed earlier, in the primordial act of cannibalism attributed by Freud to a horde of sons at the expense of a tyrannical father, one may be tempted to identify the entire matrix of the etiological factors that lie embedded in the darkness of the Oedipus myth: by eating their father, the sons incorporate his power and supremacy; by ravishing their father's wives, the sons certify the bloodline of the tribe's lineage; by turning the totemic meal into a festival, the sons ritualistically perpetuate their own genealogical tree.

However cognitively improper, however structurally disengaged from the procedures of understanding is the significance of the stories that report such ancestral memories—the stories of the "archetypes," as they are called in the aesthetic jargon of literary tradition, of our primordial violations—still they can be said to belong to the structure of the judgment of the good. More precisely, what belongs to the structure of the judgment of the good, in light of the axioms upon which rests Kant's claim that the beautiful is the symbol of morality, is wo/man's recoiling from an unconditional bracketing, an unconditional relegation to the realm of taste, of the narratives that report his or her ancestral intimacy with crime and sin. In Kant, the categorical authority of the law does indeed appear to shelter the operations of narrativity, of fictionality, of imagination, in spite of the very fact, stressed by Derrida, that practical reason *seems* "alien to all fiction and imagination."[20] This Derridian stipulation is far from innocent, nor is it theoretically harmless. It grafts the operations of narrativity, of fiction, and of the faculty of imagination, upon the authority of a Kantian law which, grounded upon practical reason, ought to be impervious to all fictional, imaginal, narrative contingencies. As to the Kantian subject of free will, whose theoretical faculties shelter the procedures of the moral judgment, this Derridian stipulation has, of course, devastating effects. It determines a reciprocal encroaching between the intellectual faculties of the Kantian subject and the aesthetic experiences of his imagination—an encroachment in which the former faculties can purposively choose to recall or forget the latter experiences.

THE DUALITY OF THE GENEALOGICAL TREE

In this chapter I have investigated a specialized aspect of the hypothesis that ancient genealogical chronicles, and especially the kind of genealogical chronicles that pertain to the tragic genre, often perform the functions of etiological tales. By showing, with the help of Derrida, that the origin of the law, in the Kantian conception of the origin of the moral imperative, occurs at the crossroads where ethic and aesthetic get substantially entwined, I believe I have substantiated my position that certain myths and legends of genealogical dissipation exhibit an authority that is capable of playing a central role in the unfolding of the moral standards of different ages and cultures. These myths and legends, furthermore, evoke virtual events, or what Derrida calls "quasi-events" ("Before the Law," 199); in depicting certain emblematic, heinous crimes, they present the fictive origin of prohibitions whose historical referent disrupts the paradigmatic separation between the order of reality and the order of (re)semblance, the order of the nonverbal and its mimetic rendition. As a corollary to this argument, it remains to be stressed that the law springing from the confluence of genealogy and etiology is one that assumes a single-gender mastery. As I implied above with regard to the primordial totem of the father, the sap running through the genealogical tree is saturated with paternal semen, just as the law of succession inherent in it is saturated with androlineality. Neither the myth of Oedipus nor the myth of Orestes questions the dialectic of gender segregation that informs androlineality—a shortcoming that has virtually been left unchallenged by critics and audiences alike.

It is in the genealogical tree that the thematics of genealogy find their master trope. This trope entails an irradiation of significations interlinked and mutually dependent, from birth to descent, from origin to lineage, from generation to kinship, from race to species, from stock to family, and, to sum it all, *from gender to genre.* In the last several millennia, the semantics of this trope have undergone an imposing process of linguistic saturation, overlayering, or sedimentation, oriented toward the bifurcation of the meaning of this trope into two antagonistic lexicons. As I indicated before, these two lexicons can be effectively grouped under the headings of gender and genre: under gender, we find the lexicon of procreation, hinged upon the power of gender to generate and identify the progeny through a pact with nature called consanguinity; under genre, we find the lexicon of lineage, hinged upon the power of genre persuasively (or coercively) to hierarchize, to verify, to legalize (patri)lineal succession. It is not a matter of a simple duplicity of meaning; rather, it is a matter of the mutually related constellation of forces that have been traditionally ascribed, on the one hand, to nature or, more specifically here, to genital physiology and sexual complementarity, and, on the other hand, to culture or, more specifically here, to the persuasive and/or prescriptive constructs of discourse. It would be naive to expect that a discourse about this bidirectional trope could be fractured into the simultaneity of two separate discourses, the first exclusively interrogating gender as to its physiological, factual relation to procreation and consanguinity, the second exclusively interrogating genre as to its discursive, idiomatic relation to legitimacy and (patri)lineality. It would be either delusional or reactionary, in other words, if one expected to be able to split the bifurcation out of which germinates the figure of the genealogical tree along the neat line that separates one branch from the other, and then proceed to defoliate these two branches in an orderly fashion, impervious to any hint of thematic crossbreeding—the branch of gender revealing the problematics of nature and lineal consanguinity, the branch of genre revealing the problematics of culture and (patri)lineal legitimacy.

The bifurcation of the genealogical tree, in sum, helps one denounce the rhetorical impossibility of a neat separation of the two branches that make up the semantics of genealogy. The way out of this difficulty does not lie in a speculative ascension toward an all-inclusive, self-enclosed concept of genealogy. Such a process would parallel the necessary movement of decantation by which rational speculation systematically jettisons the ballast represented by trope, metaphor, and symbol. The above analysis of the structure of Kant's categorical imperative shows that the operations of imagination, especially in their connection to the textuality of narrative tradition, cannot be excluded from our understanding of the order of genealogy. Rather, this duality of understanding entails that each of the two branches find its proper signification in the other branch: gender bespeaks genre, and vice versa.

10

Son, Knight, and Lover: The Legal in Jacques Lacan and the Maternal in Chrétien de Troyes

These are words the reader will see but not those he will hear.
—James Joyce to Harriet S. Weaver, 27 June 1924

A METHODOLOGICAL PREMISE

IN STRUCTURALIST MODES OF CRITICISM, THE MODEL OF THE SYNTAG-matic and paradigmatic structure of the sentence has been extended to the analysis of literary discourse, on the two presumptions that: (1) the linear arrangement of sentences in a discourse may be viewed as analogous to the syntagmatic combination of units that constitutes a single sentence; and (2) the convergence in a unified signification of all of a discourse's sentences may be viewed as analogous to the paradigmatic convergence in a unified signification of the combination of units that constitutes a single sentence. Lacan's application of the structural model of the sentence to the notion of discourse entails a relevant modification of the structuralist tradition. To the principle that the articulated discourse may be reduced to the syntagmatic (also called contiguous or metonymic) and paradigmatic (also called metaphoric or symbolic) facets that structure the sentence, he adds the postulate that an effect of *rupture,* breakage, analogous to the breakage that is introduced in the sentence by the discontinuity between a signifier's syntagmatic and paradigmatic signifieds, is achieved within the articulated discourse by and through an abrupt interruption of the discourse itself. In psychoanalysis, this interruption, brought about by the manifestation of the neurotic symptom, installs within the discourse its genuine, albeit hidden, signification.[1]

199

Hence, in the Lacanian perspective any discourse can be interpreted according to either a syntagmatic or a paradigmatic reading strategy. It can be read syntagmatically, as the metonymic fiction that depicts "*la lutte combative ou la parade sexuelle*" [the physical struggle or the sexual display] by which the discoursing subject posits himself or herself in terms of "*fonction de maîtrise, jeu de prestance, rivalité constituée*" [function of mastery, play of vigor, constituted rivalry], in terms, to wit, of a strategy of domination directed against other, rival egos. Or it can be read paradigmatically, as the symbolic or metaphoric play of signifiers that structures the unconscious of the discoursing subject in terms of its ontological essence.[2] In the specific case of a paradigmatic reading, the completion of a discourse's signification must not be looked for, therefore, in the literal closure of the discourse itself, but rather in the fundamental *coded message,* which is installed within the paradigmatic, fractured configuration of the discourse's structure.

On the basis of this principle, Roger Dragonetti argues that the true discursive aim of *Le roman de Perceval ou Le conte du graal,* the unfinished work by Chrétien de Troyes, is unveiled by its very lack of closure—its very suspension of the narrative of Perceval's *aventures* upon a fictional void. In a text such as Chrétien's, textual closure would be brought about, traditionally, by the insertion of a ritual conclusion of the sort of "Ci falt le conte du graal." But the insertion of this formula in *Perceval* would be justified only if the text actually delivered the sequel to Perceval's and Gawain's aventures, which it promises to do but does not. Such lack of a conventional close is regarded by Dragonetti as the true triumph of the text, in whose very nature he detects the imposition of a paradigmatic reading performance upon its reader.[3]

In this chapter I intend to perform one such paradigmatic reading of the interrupted discourse that constitutes the text of Chrétien's *Perceval.* In particular, I intend to adhere to the Lacanian precept of the installment of *rupture* within the text. I will therefore endeavor to extract a signification out of the figure of Perceval by concentrating on a small segment of Chrétien's text, namely, on the episode of Perceval's adventure at the castle of Beaurepaire. This episode begins with a newly knighted Perceval eager to return to his widowed mother, and ends, after the adventure at the castle of Beaurepaire in defense of Blanchefleur, with a Perceval dutifully back on his way to his mother's house. In the course of the episode Perceval discovers his (long-since dead) father's inadequacy as the ultimate agent of legitimation for his multiple identity as worthy son, valiant knight, and ebullient lover (of Blanchefleur). Furthermore, he learns that his mother is only a poor symbolic substitute for his father as an agency of legitimacy. So he is left with a lover, Blanchefleur, whom, as a worthy son and a valiant knight, he cannot love, unless vicariously, via the unconditional renunciation to carnal lust implied by his endless quest of the grail.

In the sexual dynamics of this episode I see a most interesting congruence with the Lacanian opposition of the maternal and the legal per se, or, more specifically, of the hierarchical order subordinating the structure of the unconscious to the dictates of the Law of the Father. It is well known that Lacan derived the axiomatics of this hierarchical order from the Freudian analysis of the refractions that the myths of our archaic past undergo in the course of modern family, sexual, and social relations. In this chapter I will show that Chrétien's poem, whose religious overtones cannot be disregarded, exhibits a condition of remarkable attunement with the logic of gender opposition that grounds Freudian psychoanalysis.

LOVE AND WAR

In the course of the episode at the castle of Beaurepaire, Perceval, who:

> *ne savoit nule rien*
> *D'amor ne de nule autre rien,*[4]

[knew nothing / Of love or of anything else,]

is initiated by Blanchefleur into love, and into the *nule autre* that, I will argue, amounts to drive and desire, in the special sense in which Lacan uses these terms. To defend Blanchefleur and her castle of Beaurepaire, Perceval fights against Engygeron and Clamadeus, defeating both. Then he leaves Blanchefleur to go back to the quest of his mother.

I submit that a process of compulsive repetition is at play in the alternation of Perceval's moments of partial intimacy with Blanchefleur:

> *... Et il le basoit*
> *Et en ses bras le tenoit prise ...*   2058–59

[... And he kissed her / And held her tightly in his arms ...]

> *En liu de boire et de mangier*
> *Jüent et baisent et acolent*
> *Et debonairement parolent...*   2360–62

[Instead of eating and drinking / They sported and kissed and embraced / And exchanged courteous words ...]

and of Perceval's fighting episodes against the two knights:

> *Et molt furent li cop estolt,*
> *Tant que Engygerons chaï ...*   2232–33

[And many were the terrible blows / Until at last Engygeron fell ...]

> *En la fin Clamadeu covint*
> *Venir a merci mal gre suen ...*   2682–83

[In the end Clamadeus, against his will, / Had to beg for mercy ...]

This process of compulsive repetition turns Perceval the knight into Perceval the wandering knight. It represents, in my opinion, a turning point in Perceval's experience as a knight; also, it allows one to posit the dynamic factor of the quest as a constitutive component of the figure of the Arthurian knight.

The Maternal and the Legal

The encounter with Blanchefleur deprives Perceval of his original innocence, and prepares him for the next episode, that of the vision of the grail, in which he will find a name and an identity for himself. After the vision of the grail, furthermore, Perceval's quest will be oriented no longer toward the contingency of a maternal relation, but toward the absolute of a symbol of collective order. In such a reversal of priorities, this twelfth-century poem suggests, as I anticipated above, a radical antagonism between the maternal and the legal, or, as we will see further on, a systematic dialectic of opposition between the feminine and the masculine orders of legitimacy.

More particularly, I intend to argue in the following pages that Perceval's remembrance of his mother (*Que de sa mere au cueur li tient* [2918], [which fixed his heart on his mother]) at the end of the episode, and his leaving of Beaurepaire to find her, are installed within a different matrix of motives than the ones that motivated the newly knighted Perceval the day he, having left the castle "*de son oste*," Gorneman de Gorhaut, to continue on his way to his mother's house, happens to ask for hospitality at Beaurepaire:

> *Li noviax chevaliers se part*
> *De son oste, et molt li est tart*
> *Qu'il a sa mere venir puisse.*   1699–1701

[The new knight took leave / Of his host, most anxious / To return to his mother.]

After his partial intimacy with Blanchefleur, he needs to retrieve a memory that has partially dissolved, that of his mother, but, what is most important, he retrieves this memory as a masquerade of another recollection, namely, of the recollection of the vision of womanhood which, up to now, for the entirety of his fatherless youth, has contributed to the articulation of his notions of what is right, what is lawful, what is legitimate.[5] Now he is a man who knows the nature of desire, and especially the delicious torture of its chaste installment within the *appetite* that precedes (and separates one from) the consummation of *jouissance*.[6] Now, thanks to Blanchefleur, he has become a Priapus in red arms. And it is as such a beastly figure that this obscene (and still virgin) knight eventually identifies, in the unreachable icon of the grail, the ultimate symbol of the order of legitimacy that governs the intimate interplay of his lust and his fright of it—in Lacanian terms, of his drive to *jouissance* and his *fear of castration*. The order of legitimacy identified by Perceval is hinged upon the dictates of an order of absence, of withdrawal, of deprivation. It comports a substantial congruence with the specific dissociation of the Oedipus complex, which portrays the figure of the father as distorted, as inadequate to personify the legitimate and legitimizing symbol of the Law in the subject's unconscious—in Perceval's specific case, inadequate to personify the Arthurian order of lawfulness and legitimacy.[7]

Let me take as the focus of my analysis line 1986, *Por che se je sui pres que nue* ... [For although I am almost naked ...].

Blanchefleur has presented herself uninvited in Perceval's bedroom and awakened him with her tears; now she pleads with him not to despise her misery—she is going to kill herself rather than be taken by king Clamadeus, who has sent Engygeron with an army to capture her. Blanchefleur and Perceval spend that night together, *bouche a boche, bras a bras* [lip to lip, arm in arm, 2068]. The syntagmatic structure of the phrase *je sui pres que nue* is of the most sober kind: a triad made up of subject-copula-predicate, plus a modifier. However, its paradigmatic structure seems to support all by itself the logic of love, need and desire that in the course of the episode will subvert the symbolic position of Perceval with respect to the order of legitimacy of the Arthurian universe.

The episode I am interpreting—that of the adventure at Beaurepaire—is composed of a long introduction followed by two war scenes. The introduction culminates in the seduction scene I have just summarized. I call it "seduction," implying the presence of a passive and an active agent, because Blanchefleur is evidently carrying on a plan of her own when she joins Perceval first in his bedroom, then in his bed. The text is explicit about it. After Blanchefleur declares her intention of killing herself before the night is over, we are told:

> *C'onques cele pour autre chose*
> *Ne vint plorer desor sa face,*
> *Que que ele entendant li face,*
> *Fors por que qu'ele li meïst*
> *En corage qu'il empreïst*
> *La bataille . . .*   2040–45

[Since she had come / To shed tears over his face / For no other reason, / In spite of what she gave him to understand, / Than to inspire in him / The desire to undertake / The battle . . .]

And the next morning, after she tries to discourage Perceval from challenging such an invincible knight as Engygeron, the text tells us that:

> *Tel plait li a cele basti*
> *Qu'ele le blasme et si le velt.*   2128–29

[She cleverly pretended to blame / What she wanted him to do.]

The two war scenes are symmetrical to each other. First Perceval defeats Engygeron, the warrior trying to conquer Beaurepaire, then he defeats Clamadeus, the king trying to conquer Blanchefleur's heart. The first time Perceval is talked into the battle by Blanchefleur's seductive arts; the second time he accepts Clamadeus's challenge in spite of Blanchefleur's sincere attempt to dissuade him—her castle, provisioned with food by a providential ship of merchants, is safe now, and her chastity will not have to be sacrificed to the aggressor. The logic of repetition that informs the two war scenes complements the logic of memory as an articulating factor of Perceval's order of legitimacy. On reaching the castle of Beaurepaire and being informed of its stage of siege, Perceval suffers the inner conflict between his duty as a son and his new duty as a knight. This conflict results in a progressive disappearance of his mother's memory from his conscious preoccupations.

In the seduction scene he is still his mother's innocent son, who *ne savoit nule rien / D'amor ne de nule autre rien* (1941–42). His mother had enjoined him before he left her that, if a maid allowed him to kiss her, he was forbidden to ask for more:

> *"Le sorplus je vos en desfent,*
> *Se laissier le volez por moi."*   548–49

["I forbid you to take more; / Give it up for me."]

But in the war scenes Perceval is the valiant knight trained in the martial arts by Gorneman de Gorhaut, the nobleman who, by the way, also instructs him to refrain from ever mentioning the contents of his mother's teachings to his new acquaintances. If the two imperatives received from his mother and from Gorneman de Gorhaut seem congruent in the defense of a *Dame qui d'aïe ai besoig* or of a *pucele desconseillie* [a lady in need of aid or a maiden in distress, 534–35], their inner priorities collide in other circumstances. The alternation of Perceval's passive role in the seduction scene with Blanchefleur and his active role in the war scenes—and the duplication of the war scenes themselves—reveal the dissociation of a subject whose order of universal legitimation is undergoing a severe transformation.

The pivotal figure of the mother surfaces again, as recovered memory, at the end of the Beaurepaire episode, yet its symbolic function within the chain of signifiers that structure Perceval's unconscious has in the meantime drastically changed. Having been emptied of the narrow content of the mother-son relation, it becomes the provisionally metaphoric substitute for the dynamic factor of perennial wandering that the grail will eventually symbolize. Perceval's mother enters in symbolic conflict, first with the demand of Perceval the man for the love of Blanchefleur, and second, with the demand of Perceval the knight for his own supreme legitimation as knight.

Nudity, Weaponry, and Metonymy

Crying and kneeling at Perceval's bedside, Blanchefleur draws his attention, as we have seen, to her own partial nudity, adding, however, that this unusual condition is not meant to suggest any improper attitude on her part, nor to elicit any dishonorable behavior on his. This is the only passage in the whole segment where a character is referred to as a body *in its wholeness*. Perceval's adversaries, Engygeron and Clamadeus, are hardly referred to as bodies at all. In their fight with Perceval it is not a matter, as in most knightly encounters in the poem, of disjointed shoulders, broken arms, bloody wounds, but rather of a *bataille (qui) dura molt* [a battle which lasted a long while, 2231] between Perceval and Engygeron, and of a duel in which Perceval and Clamadeus *se combatent ... as espees ... molt longuement* [fought with their swords for a very long while, 2677].

The almost spiritual unsubstantiality of these warriors' bodies, which in the end are collapsed into two impersonal assemblages of armor, lance, shield, and sword, contrasts with and highlights, within the texture of Chrétien's text, the attribute of wholeness of Blanchefleur's body as it presents itself at Perceval's bedside. Blanchefleur does not point out that her shoulders are naked, or her arms are naked, or her legs are naked. By saying, "*Je sui pres que nue*," she displays the wholeness of her body as the all-pervading substance of the "mental scheme" that, in the next two days, will have to counter, by the only weapon of its frigid *parade sexuelle,* the overpowering kinetic emblems of manly power, of *lutte combative,* that Engygeron and Clamadeus are going to oppose to Perceval.[8] Her body's nakedness displayed at the knight's bedside conveys the silent promise to Perceval that he will soon gain access to the secret of womanhood—that womanhood, that attribute of the maternal body, upon which has been hinged, up to now, the articulation of his order of legitimacy. And such a promise inaugurates, in turn, the strategy of seduction that turns the virgin knight into Blanchefleur's military ally.

Blanchefleur's corporeal wholeness contrasts with the partiality of her nudity. She declares that she is *almost* naked. This condition of partial nudity bespeaks the conditional nature of her body's promise to Perceval. Neither Perceval nor Chrétien's reader may overlook the fact that the role of the legitimate pretender to the secret hidden within Blanchefleur's body still pertains to Clamadeus, the conqueror. The singularity of the attribute of wholeness of Blanchefleur's body acquires a further symbolic valence inasmuch as Chrétien's verses seem to call attention to its figural contrast with the incorporeal dispersion of Engygeron's and Clamadeus's bodies into two soulless assemblages of kinetic weapons. Even before Blanchefleur enters Perceval's bed, the premises are posited for the diversion of Perceval's erotic aggressiveness toward two altered reflections of his own body, those of Engygeron and Clamadeus. In contrast with the symbolically compact wholeness of Blanchefleur's body, resilient, as we will see shortly, even with respect to its subsequent imaginary dismemberment in Perceval's bed, these two hostilely warring bodies will be segmented to the point of unsubstantiality, amounting solely to two imaginary assemblages of pieces of iron, to two collections of cuneiform emblems of war.

But then Blanchefleur enters the bed of her virginal champion, and for two nights in a row. Yet the nudity of Blanchefleur's body cannot be wholly consummated by Perceval, either the first night, before Engygeron's defeat, or the second, before the duel with Clamadeus, because Clamadeus's claim of primacy has first to be successfully contested by Perceval. These two nights in the company of Blanchefleur are spent by Perceval in a tenacious embrace that, in spite of the relief it evidently provides to Blanchefleur, must be somewhat uncomfortable to the knight.

> *Ensi jurent tote la nuit,*
> *Li uns lez autre, bouche a bouche,*
> *Jusqu'al main que li jors aproche.*
> *Tant li fist la nuit de solas*
> *Que bouche a boche, bras a bras,*
> *Dormirent tant qu'il ajorna*   2064–69

[Thus they lay like this all night / Side by side, lip to lip, / Until the morning when day was near. / Night brought her so much comfort / That they slept lip to lip, arm in arm, / Until day broke.]

Perceval lies side by side with Blanchefleur: arm in arm, lip to lip. This scene turns, at long last, Blanchefleur's whole and partially naked body into a fragmentation of contiguous segments: arms, lips, mouth, and, not to be overlooked in its textual elusiveness, the metonymic side by which Perceval lies, which, logistically speaking, can only be the very front of Blanchefleur's body, to wit, her pelvic bone.

Such a delineation of Blanchefleur's erogenous zones—lips, arms, mouth, and pelvis—entails a transposition of bodily functions. Blanchefleur's lips become a contiguous substitute for her vagina, her pelvic bone becomes the convex reflection of Perceval's sexual drive. These anatomical elements operate as contiguous factors, in a manner analogous, if you will, to the syntagmatic logic by which the signifiers of a sentence achieve their literal signification, or what Lacan would call their "*discours effectif.*"[9] But it is only in the poem's transition from this nightly *parade sexuelle* to the *lutte combative,* the battle in full daylight by which Perceval opposes his two rivals—those two eminent assemblages of kinetic, cuneiform emblems of aggression—that Blanchefleur's erogenous zones enter into the state of reciprocal resonance that allots them a paradigmatic, metaphoric meaning. It is in daylight that the wholeness of Blanchefleur's body—its resilience with respect to Perceval's drive to penetration, its echoing of the maternal prohibition of sex—prevails again and again over the fragmentation of her body in Perceval's bed. And conversely, it is only after his final victory over Clamadeus, and the subsequent prospect of his marriage with Blanchefleur, that Perceval will be able to "read" in Blanchefleur's nudity the transparent revelation of her lack of a phallus.[10] The wholeness of Blanchefleur's body is only partial, then—it appears as maimed, now, in the eyes of the legitimate pretender. The genital lack in Blanchefleur's body signifies the symbolic inadequacy of Perceval's own mother, as a woman, to substitute, even provisionally, for his dead father as the supreme agent of universal legitimation. At this point Perceval will have to leave Beaurepaire, and embark on a quest that only to his deluded ego may still appear as the equivalent to the quest that brought him to Beaurepaire, namely, the quest of his mother's house. Indeed, his quest will have reached here a point of no return, the final step in the process destined to turn *li fix a la veve fame* [the son of the widowed lady, 74] into one of the Arthurian wandering knights.

LOVE, NEED, AND DESIRE

Perceval first must submit himself to the logic of love, need, and desire that structures his pugnacious deeds against Engygeron and Clamadeus. The two war scenes repeat each other, in the sense that both amount to configurations of Perceval's quest for his sexual identity, but with a crucial difference. In the first scene Perceval, duped by Blanchefleur, knows that the removal of Engygeron, as a menace to Beaurepaire, will not remove Clamadeus as the "legitimate" pretender to the secret of Blanchefleur's body—he knows, therefore, that after his victory over Engygeron he will remain entitled only to gaze at and caress the physical shell (at once, literal container and metaphoric barrier) of this secret. He enters the battlefield as a tremendously aggressive Priapus, a bi-lanced warrior resigned to mimic the forbidden sexual encounter in a *lutte combative,* a manly fight, resigned, that is, to divert the suspension of his erotic impulses into a deadly struggle with a rival knight. But then Blanchefleur begs him not to fight with Clamadeus because she wants him to stay alive for her:

> *Et tot che ne valoit noient,*
> *Et s'estoit or merveille estrange,*
> *Car il avoit en sa losenge*
> *Grant douçor qu'ele li faisoit,*
> *Car a chascun mot le basoit*
> *Si doucement et si soëf*
> *Que ele li metoit la clef*
> *D'amors en la serre del cueur* 2630–37

[But all her pleadings were in vain, / Which was strange and remarkable indeed, / For there was much sweetness / In her blandishments, / And with each word she kissed him / So sweetly and so softly / That she slid love's key / Into the lock of his heart.]

This time it is Perceval who needs the fight in order to remove one further symbolic barrier (but not the last, as it will turn out) between his sexual appetite and the secret of Blanchefleur's body. Once Clamadeus is gone, defeated by this irresistible, furious Priapus in red, once Perceval has won for himself the heart of Blanchefleur and all obstacles to sexual consummation appear to have been removed, the brave knight is unwilling to enter the last tournament, that in Blanchefleur's bed. Nigel Bryant's otherwise excellent English translation, according to which "The land (of Beaurepaire) would now have been his . . . had his heart not been elsewhere," does not do full symbolic justice to the original, where we learn that Perceval could have had for himself the girl and her land if only his *corage* had not drifted elsewhere.

> *Et si fust soie [la pucele] toute quite,*
> *La terre, se il li pleüst*
> *Que son corage aillors n'eüst*   2914–16

[She and her land would now have been / Completely his, had he kept / His *corage* from drifting elsewhere.]

According to Greimas's *Dictionnaire de l'ancien français,* the word *coragié,* an adjective derived from *corage* for which Chrétien is the cited (presumably earliest) source, means *animé, qui a le désir, l'intention* to do something; Chrétien, we may assume, was interested in the sense of *corage* not just as the "heart" or center of spiritual life, but as the quality of will and desire associated with its secondary meanings.[11]

Why does the *corage* to make love to Blanchefleur desert Perceval? And how are we to interpret the word *corage* in the symbolic context of this episode? The plot-oriented answer to the first question would have to be an obvious one, namely, that as a matter of course Perceval lacks the desire and the intention to make love to Blanchefleur, since the adventure at the castle of Beaurepaire has kept him long enough from returning to his mother—he is anxious to be back on his way. Yet it is in the very formulation of the second question that one sees the inadequacy of this matter-of-fact answer. Perceval's *corage* goes *aillors* when he *de sa mere au cueur li tient* [fixed his heart on his mother, 2918]. His *corage* deserts him when his *cueur* comes back to him—and his heart comes back to him as, indeed, the masquerade of the expression of his original intentions. Indeed, it is not a conscious deliberation to stick with his original plan that deflates Perceval's erotic impulses, but rather an involuntary motion of the faculty of memory. The emergence of the memory of his mother recoils upon his sexual attraction for Blanchefleur and displaces it into an imperative of sexual continence. Here the proper linguistic resonance of the word *corage* figures the event of genital erection, as a most obvious manifestation of sexual drive or lusty appetite.[12]

In Perceval's paradigmatic reading of Blanchefleur's strategically contrived yet innocent declaration of nudity, Blanchefleur reveals also that she is devoid of a phallus. Of course she does not have it—how could she? But she could and maybe will *pres que* have it, or get it, by incorporating Perceval's lust, by embodying Perceval's drive to genital penetration. At the end of this episode the image of Blanchefleur is therefore greatly complicated with respect to her first virginal appearance in Perceval's presence, a maid in whose face:

> *... miex avenoit ...*
> *Li vermeus sor le blanc assis*
> *Que li sinoples sor l'argent* 1823–25

[The red and the white / Made a finer blend / Than vermilion on silver]

This woman God created *Por voir embler les cuers de gent* [To steal people's hearts, 1826]; she is a vessel of love and desire. But the image of Blanchefleur that Perceval brings away with him when he leaves Beaurepaire is imbued with an oppressive sense of bodily reality. We will have to get to the episode in which Perceval first defeats Saigremor and Kay and then is talked into reaching Arthur's camp by Gawain, before the text shows us the full metaphoric import of that first virginal appearance of Blanchefleur. Blanchefleur's image is now duplicated in the image of three drops of blood spilled on the snowy ground by a wounded goose. Unaware of the proximity of king Arthur's camp, Perceval:

> *Si s'apoia desor sa lance*
> *Por esgarder cele samblance* 4197–98

[Leaned upon his lance / To gaze at the sight.]

He becomes so enraptured that he spends hours sitting on his horse, staring at the snow, until the ethereal image begins to melt away. What we have here is a Priapic image of contemplative suspension, the lance pointing at and hovering over the three blood drops like a grotesquely elongated phallus. Perceval thinks he sees his beloved's face in the red and white snow:

> *La fresche color li resamble*
> *Qui ert en la face s'amie* 4200–1

[This fresh color made him feel / That his beloved was facing him.]

I think that his unconscious gaze is enraptured by a rather different vision, though. Be it menstrual blood or a token of defloration, the blood on the snow tells, as I will show now, the untold part of the story of Perceval's retrieved memory of his mother.

THE LANCE AND THE SHIELD

Continence was Perceval's special regimen of initiation to sexual identity. He enters the castle of Beaurepaire as a young man who *ne savoit nule rien / D'amor ne de nule autre rien* (1941–42). The next day he jousts with Engygeron as a warrior made ferocious by his sexual appetite. The night spent arm in arm, lip to lip with Blanchefleur turns him into a Priapus whose previous order of legitimacy fades slowly away, together with the memory of that vision of womanhood, as an attribute of the maternal body, which has contributed so far to the articulation of such order of legitimacy. This same night leaves him with a furious, unfulfilled sexual lust that promptly finds, on the jousting field, its figural reflection in a convex lance to pierce all obstacles and in a concave shield to coat his love's hymen with an unconquerable armor. The third day of his adventure at Beaurepaire, Perceval brings to the battlefield these two complementary emblems of his sexual dexterity (and distress) to challenge Clamadeus, the aggressor, the detainer of power, the local impersonation of the order of legitimacy. All factual obstacles to his love being removed by his victory over Clamadeus, he finds himself swept up into the coils of a signifying vortex: (1) as his sexual drive cannot function from without the order of inhibition imposed by the maternal prohibition of sex, the memory of his mother comes back to him, but it comes back as the memory of the inadequacy of her gender to legitimate the order of his desire; (2) as the convex permanency of his sexual drive perpetuates a visual and tactile parade of the signifier of Blanchefleur's own sexual appetite, his own lust becomes the warrant of her desire for him; (3) as Blanchefleur's genital "lack" reveals the symbolic inadequacy of Perceval's own mother, as a woman, to substitute for his dead father as the ultimate agent of legitimation, the quest for a superior agent of legitimation is imposed upon him.

Turned by his victory over Clamadeus into the cause of Blanchefleur's desire, Perceval is offered a chance at last to penetrate the secret of her body. But Blanchefleur's body has no

secrets to offer at all, insofar as the "thing" that he is looking for
in love, namely, the symbolic legitimacy of the Law of the Father
signified by the phallus, finds in her body only a most remote
approximation, and this not in the form of a bodily attribute
(such as the clitoris, for instance) but in her body's appetite for
his own erection. In order to defend valiantly the fate of the
princess of Beaurepaire, Perceval had to set aside for a time his
original order of universal legitimation, i.e., the maternal order
he was traveling back to at the beginning of the episode. And
for two nights in a row Blanchefleur had seemed to be in the
privileged position of withholding from him, as a gift to be
earned through meritorious deeds, a more basic, more fundamental order of universal legitimation, the key to whose lock
was held in the secret of her body. But now it turns out that all
that Blanchefleur has to offer him is a vulva eager to devour his
erection. Perceval is aware that his phallus might bring to a
coalescence the purity of his beloved's red-and-white face with
the lust of her bleeding, deflowered, cyclically menstruating
vulva. But this coalescence may be attained only at the price of
his abdication from the Priapic condition. And such abdication
would be the equivalent of an act of self-castration. By sacrificing
his erection to Blanchefleur's desire, Perceval would only sanc-
tion and submit to the inadequate nature of his mother's sex,
and accordingly, to the inadequacy of the order of legitimacy that
dominated his youthful, fatherless years. On the contrary, by
preserving indefinitely his formidable erection and embarking
on a search for the superior agency that will legitimize his own
love for Blanchefleur (as well as everything else in his existence)—a quest camouflaged, at first, as his old quest for his
mother's house—he petrifies history, so to speak. The continually renewed parade of the concave and convex emblems of his
sexual dexterity and distress in innumerable knightly endeav-
ors, as well as the obstinate transposition of the *presence* of his
erection and of the *absence* of Blanchefleur's virginal hymen to
the substantiality of the lance and the shield at his side, will
perpetually guarantee the preservation of Blanchefleur's desire
for him. At the same time, the mirage of an absolute legitimation
of his love from the benevolent authority of an unquestionable
agency of universal legitimation will activate the endless repetition of the cycle of the quest itself.

    In Chrétien's poem the quest of Perceval ends at the knight's
hermit uncle's hermitage. Here Perceval is instructed about the
holy nature of the grail. He learns that the king who is served

from the grail the *sole oiste ... [qui] sa vie sostient et conforte* [the single host ... that sustains and brings comfort to his life, 6422–24] is the father of the Fisher King, the father, that is, of the maimed king of the Waste Land. He learns also that the Fisher King and the Fisher King's father are, respectively, his own cousin and his own uncle. The revelation of the consanguinity that links him to the custodians of the grail brings to completion the symbolic articulation of his quest. The ascertainment of his mother's inadequacy to substitute for his dead father as the supreme agent of legitimacy had initially led him to search for an alternative symbol of absolute power. The parallel condition of his dead father and of the Fisher King, both crippled by a castrating wound between the legs—

> "Vostre pere, si nel savez,
> Fu parmi la jambe navrez ..."   435–36

["Your father, though you don't know it, was wounded through the thighs ..."]

> "[le Roi Pescheor] fu ferus d'un gavelot
> Parmi les quisses ambesdeus ..."   3512–13

[The Fisher King "was wounded by a javelin / Through both thighs ..."]

—establishes now that in the economy of Absolute Legitimacy not even his dead father, for whom his mother was but a poor symbolic substitute, represents the ultimate agent of legitimation. The grail, with its mysterious array of beneficial/malefic effects on the people (and lands) exposed to its presence, appears to him as the icon that may provide absolute justification for his love for Blanchefleur. But the revelation of the divine nature of this concave icon requires that Perceval's quest be an impossible one. The example of his hermit uncle implies that the legitimacy with which one's place in the world can be endowed by divine grace is attainable only at the price of renouncing any vindication of such legitimacy in mundane matters. The interplay of concavity and convexity in the body—of limpness and hardness, of abstinence and desire—is turned by the preeminence of the icon of the grail into a hierarchical logic according to which the concave comes before, has precedence over the convex, or, more precisely, according to which desire, as the signifier of presence that one finds signified in the erection of the male, is only an ancillary figure of abstinence, as the true signifier of the order of absence that governs the Oedipus complex. Therefore the imaginary castration that is installed within the moment of *jouissance,* in the form of a temporary loss of sexual potency, can be reconciled with the preservation of Perceval's symbolic integrity only by means of a paradoxical renunciation to the experience of *jouissance* itself.

Here Perceval the knight is assimilated to the two medieval figures of the hermit and the monk. As these two figures function in a peculiar distortion of love and desire, where the longing for an absolute justification for love compensates for the unconditional renunciation of carnal lust, so the figure of the knight is brought in the course of its quest to an analogous distortion, where the longing for the absolute agent of legitimacy is manifested in a repetitive and gratuitous exhibition of sexual emblems. Love for God in the hermit and the monk, conjugated with the absence of carnal lust, complements love for God in the knight, conjugated with the insistent, obsessive presence of the symbolic emblem of lust. The opposition of concavity and convexity, or limpness and hardness, or abstinence and desire, is the criterion of the petrification of history that associates the legendary datum of the quest of the grail with the historical datum of the proliferation of monasteries and hermitages in the mid and late Middle Ages. This criterion, together with its postulate of chastity as a must, may be found at the origin of the cult of the Virgin, as a religious/mundane metaphor of divine grace for the man of faith, of martial prowess for the crusader, and also—a topic I left unexamined in this chapter—of creative power for the poet.

LOVE AND STERILITY

In the adventure of the grail Perceval becomes a fantastic being that parades the emblem of his sexual attributes like a grotesque Priapus. This emblem, that by metonymic contamination becomes an invincible lance, functions in the same register of the exhibition of the body that keeps the potential sexuality of Blanchefleur's nudity away from the moment of actual consummation. Converging onto the figure of Perceval, the opposition of lance-phallus and shield-hymen signifies the petrified condition of a logic of impossibility. Perceval, as the subject of the specific mode of sexual covetousness installed within the dichotomous interplay of concavity and convexity, comes to personify the symbol of a perpetual, unremitting stagnation of desire. "*I am naked too,*" is the silent answer that Perceval gives for three nights in a row to Blanchefleur's admission of nudity. As his erected phallus rests uncomfortably for three nights in a row on the convexity of Blanchefleur's pelvic bone, in a delirious duplication of her own frustrated appetite, his desire for her is slowly turned into the need of the *lutte combative,* the manly fight that he will enact on the stage of the battlefield the next day, and the day after the next. Perceval's sexual drive functions as the prime motive of his martial wrath till all obstacles to penetration are removed, then it recoils upon his longing for the superior agency that will legitimate his love for the object of his desire; as such a displaced drive, his lust is turned upside down, into the dictates of a perennial continence. The sterility of Perceval's portentous instrument of insemination corresponds, in the Arthurian universe, to the sterility of the knight's counterpart, the hermit/monk, in his repudiation of any commerce with the world of human affairs. Both figures, in their autarkic, barricaded sexuality, bring about a self-inclosed configuration of society. The figure of the knight represents a dynamic and mythical configuration of society, which conflates an element from the hero's fictional time, namely, the solipsistic frenzy of the quest, and an element from the writer's historical time, namely, the malaise of a patriarchal society vis-à-vis its feminine, rebellious components. The figure of the hermit/monk represents a static and historical configuration of society, hinged on the somnolent immobility, cultural as well as aesthetic, imposed upon the Middle Ages by the isolation from the world of the laity and the ideological hegemony practiced by the Church Militant.

Part IV
Genealogy and Consanguinity

11

The Covenant of Dynasty in the Old Testament: Consanguinity and the Nationalist War Syndrome (A Neo-Viconian Interpretation)

> But you are either sluggish in the legs
> from battle weariness or hollowhearted
> somehow with fear: you are not, after all,
> the son of Tydéus Oıneïdes.
>
> —*The Iliad* 5.809–13

I CHOSE THE ABOVE HOMERIC EPIGRAPH FOR THIS CHAPTER BECAUSE in its few poignant lines, uttered by Athena to Diomedes, the Greek hero, one finds a conglomeration of the thematic dominants at play in my interpretation of the nationalist war syndrome in the Old Testament. Athena's intimation to Diomedes to go back and fight Hektor under the walls of Troy reminds one, first of all, of the love for war, for *pólemos* and *éris,* that characterizes the anthropomorphic deities installed upon Mount Olympus by the imagination of the ancient Greeks. Second, in her disdain Athena establishes an equivalence between dynastic legitimacy and martial prowess. "If you withdraw from struggle in spite of all my support," she is basically saying to Diomedes, "then you are not worthy of being called the son of your father." In the *Odyssey* Telemachus shares Diomedes' predicament, but the connotations of his situation are more subtle. Athena asks him if he is indeed the son of Odysseus. Telemachus answers: "My mother says that I am his child; but I do not know this, for never yet did any man know, on his own, who gave him life."[1] Having questioned the certainty of consanguinity, as a factor that depends on maternal discretion, Telemachus will discover, in the course of his filial odyssey, that there pertains to dynastic legitimacy a truth that transcends the physiological certainty of consanguinity. It is by giving proof of his courage and wisdom that Telemachus will demonstrate his legitimacy as the successor of Odysseus. Diomedes and Telemachus share a condition of precarious filiation, if you will; their genealogical legitimacy may be challenged as long as they do not prove it in deeds. The third thematic dominant evoked by the Homeric epigraph springs from the above considerations as regards the problematic relationship between consanguinity and dynastic legitimacy established in the *epos* of the *Iliad* and the *Odyssey*. Granted that it is hard to tell whether Homer's art imitated life or vice versa, it remains arguable that, whatever the direction of the mimetic impulse at the moment of the poet's creative inception, Homer's verses exercised a profound influence upon the customs of their readers; Plato's well-known concerns about the social impact of the *logos* spoken by the "mimetic tribes" of the poets indicate that much.[2] The third dominant of this chapter, in sum, must be inferred from the effects that ancient myths, legends, and chronicles exercised upon what Vico called the *sensus communis,* upon the fantasies, that is, by which a primitive people constituted its own customs and traditions. Among the thematic dominants of the present chapter, this is the exquisitely Viconian one.

The entirety of Vico's work may be split up, as to its basic methodology, into two gnoseological vectors that run parallel to each other. On the one hand, one finds the *telos* of *la storia ideale eterna* (eternal ideal history), that is, the providential finality of transcendental history, which leads humankind toward the goal of a return to its own origin, back in the "arms," if you will, of its own Creator. On the other hand, one finds the factual history of human languages, customs, institutions, and laws, whose study provides our only means of access to the certainty of cognition.[3] These two vectors, as I said, run parallel to each other, the crucial difference being that the former is unknowable in its *verum* (truth), while the latter, knowable in its *certum* (certainty), reflects and reveals the truthful substance of the former.

Let me sum up these introductory remarks.

The *polytheistic love for war* is the first dominant of the present chapter; this theme forms the basis for my engagement of the hypothesis, developed by Regina Schwartz in *The Curse of Cain,* that an intimate affinity links the tradition of the monotheistic covenant with that of nationalistic intolerance. The question of *dynastic consanguinity* is the second dominant; it relates to the overarching thesis of the chapter, i.e., the thesis that the causal relationship linking worship and nationalism functions as a subordinate manifestation of the drive, inherent in most religions, mono-and polytheistic, toward the imposition of the primacy of a dynastic line of consanguinity *within* a primitive community.[4] "It was religion," as Vico declares in *De constantia philologiae,* "that invented genealogy."[5] The impact exercised by *stories and chronicles from the remote past* upon the "communal sense" of an entire community is the third dominant; it relates to the comparative study, conducted in these pages, of ancient texts, mostly of a religious nature, such as the Bible, some of the Greek myths dramatized by Homer and Sophocles, and that body of "mystic" legislation described by Vico in his studies of the ancient Roman jurisprudence. My study is grounded upon Vico's presumption that "in their origin the fables were true and severe narrations, whence *mythos* was defined as *vera narratio* [true narration]."[6] In other words, I work under the assumption that ancient myths, legends, and chronicles have exercised a fundamental impact upon *sensus communis,* in the sense, mentioned above, that this impact is reflected in the fantasies by which a primitive people constituted its own customs and traditions, but also in the sense that the age-long ramifications of this "communal sense" still affect significantly the communities we live in.

This aspect needs to be further qualified by an important disclaimer, in whose tenor, by the way, lies the motivation of the prefix "neo" as a signal of the revisionism inherent in my Viconian approach. In strict Viconian terms, a study of the Bible is a contradiction in terms, insomuch as the sacrality of Scripture, to which Vico subscribes, excludes the legitimacy of a theoretical inquiry into it. Although Scripture represents the very genesis of all the matters investigated by Vico in *La scienza nuova,* it cannot be constituted into an "object" of scientific knowledge as such, because the tradition embedded in the Holy Writ, however *vera* (true), does not have the attribute of historical *certezza* (certainty).[7] "[For Vico] sacred history," as Badaloni remarks in *Introduzione a Vico,* "is an incomprehensible datum." The Viconian object of scientific study is "a structured transformation of a complex of traditions, institutions, and human knowledges that sustain one another reciprocally and modify one another conflictually"; hence, it can be analyzed only to the extent that it manifests itself in the recursive phenoma of human institutions, languages, and laws.[8] Frederick Marcus illustrates some of the implications of this aspect of Vico's method in "Vico and the Hebrews." It must not be thought that Vico disregards the sacred history inscribed in Scripture. Sacred history, as a matter of fact, "can function as the philological standard Vico's philosophical criticism needs." According to Marcus, the Hebrews provide Vico's *Scienza nuova* with its moral and scientific paradigms. On the one hand, their history never enters the stages of the *corso* and *ricorso;* hence, it cannot be an object of Vico's study, which is oriented toward the investigation of the providence-driven cycles of [gentile] history. On the other hand, their history, being nonrecursive, "offer(s) a . . . standard of externality"; it "stabilizes the *corso* and *ricorso* [of gentile history]."[9]

In my opinion, the project, typical of a significant portion of the recent biblical scholarship, to engage Scripture as a literary artifact, disproves Vico's prejudices against a cognitive apprehension of the biblical text. Vico's resistance to a positive investigation of Scripture derives fundamentally from his persuasion that all "spontaneous" interventions of divine providence in human circumstances resist positive cognition; therefore, only those stages and components of historical development wherein divine providence manifests itself indirectly through the factual expressions of human freedom may be inquired into by the rational constructions of our intellect.[10] Yet, the recent trends in biblical scholarship entail precisely the delimitation of a broad set of analytical devices suited to the analysis of human freedom, human discretion, even of human censure and arbitrary revision with regard to the transcription of the Word of God, within that "complex of traditions, institutions and human knowledges" described in the Bible—which "complex" circumscribes, in principle, the very object of study privileged by Vico.[11] The primary justification of the modern project to engage Scripture as a literary artifact lies in the aspect, pointed out by Robert Alter, that "the molds of plot, character, dialogue, scene, imagery, word play, sound play," within which are cast the stories of Scripture, are "analogues to the modalities of literary texts" familiar to us;[12] they lend themselves to a sophisticated engagement of the plurality of intentionalities and of intra- and intertextual implications that animate the Bible.

MONOTHEISM AND WAR

Regina Schwartz has argued that nationalism and nationalistic intolerance are rooted within the transposition of the biblical

covenant into secular forms. In her interpretation of the monotheistic covenant as the contract that informs the concept of
nation, and that drives political formations, especially those that
originated as "covenantal communities," toward nationalist intolerance and expansionism, Schwartz denounces the legacy of
monotheism as one of belligerence toward the different. Nationalism and monotheism go hand in hand in her critique. She
writes: "When the biblical text moves more explicitly toward
polytheism, it also endorses a more attractive toleration, even
appreciation of difference."[13] The present section is devoted to
a qualified reassessment of Schwartz's critique of monotheism,
a reassessment, or an appropriation, aimed at making the underlying principles of this critique functional to my representation
of the tradition of dynastic primacy as the primary causal factor
in the triggering off of internal and external, civil and international tensions among archaic communities. My reassessment
is not motivated by a theological urge to defend the virtues of
monotheism, never really deprecated by Schwartz. I subscribe,
in fact, to Schwartz's postulate that monotheism is predicated
upon political polarity, as well as to her view that belligerence
is intrinsic to the ancient and modern concept of nation. However, in the light of the drive toward war and civil war in Europe
and the former Soviet Union that has followed the end of the
Cold War—also in consideration of the complex and contradictory roles played by religion at this specific time—I am of the
opinion that the identification of an exclusive contiguity between monotheism (or "monolatry," as Schwartz aptly specifies)
and nationalist expansionism may distract the analyst from the
deep-seated causes of the contemporary war syndrome. The
present analysis is centered on my conviction that war, which I
intend, with Schwartz, as an act of external aggression compulsive to the nation whose identity is "conceiv[ed] ... in violence,"[14] is the ultimate consequence—the culmination, if you
will—of the steady process of expulsion of diversity endemic
to the primitive community (be it monotheistic or polytheistic)
striving toward the definition of its innermost nature. I am persuaded that political formations have typically found their primary source of erosion and decadence in internal antagonism
and civil factionalism, rather than in external expansionism.

Polytheism is hardly easier to reconcile with political coexistence than monotheism. A partial proof of this point may be
found in that eminent display of polytheistic bellicosity, Homer's
Iliad. The first act of war presented in the *Iliad* is the duel

between Helen's husband, Menelaos, and Helen's lover, Paris, in book 3. This episode clears away all possible objections regarding the love of *pólemos* cultivated on Mount Olympus by the anthropomorphic array of Greek divinities. A large number of gods, each one promoting a separate agenda, are involved in securing a pugnacious development for the duel. A synopsis of this episode will be useful later on, to secure a connection with my thesis that civil war (*stásis,* as Socrates calls it in Plato's *Republic*)[15] is indispensable to the germination of war against an external enemy (*pólemos* and *éris* for the Greeks). The Paris-Menelaos duel results from Agamemnon's attempt to bring to an end the civil strife that ensued from his diatribe with Achilles in book 1.

Achilles asks his divine mother, Thetis, to punish the Greek army for the arrogance of their leader, Agamemnon, who took away his beloved concubine. Thetis flies to Zeus, and, holding his "knee" tightly in her hand, begs him ardently to revenge her son. Obviously aroused, Zeus sends a false dream to Agamemnon, promising victory. Afraid that the army will not follow him after his abuse of Achilles' rights, Agamemnon tests the Achaians by announcing his intention to sail back home. Hera, Zeus's wife, sees the Greeks solicitously preparing to follow Agamemnon's lead and, unaware of her husband's twisted motives, sends Athena to tell Odysseus that the Greeks must continue the war. Odysseus persuades his fellow commanders, and the Greek host line up promptly for a new attack. Meanwhile Zeus sends Iris to alert Priam to the situation. Before the two armies can engage in battle, however, Paris challenges Menelaos to a single combat: the winner will take (or keep) Helen and her gold for himself, and the two armies will part as friends. As soon as the duel begins, Paris is in trouble, overcome by the fury of a man who is as valiant on the battlefield as the vain son of Priam is proficient in the bedroom. At this point Aphrodite lifts up her favorite and transports him directly to his bed, where Helen will shortly reach for him in love. While Menelaos searches furiously (and comically) for his invisible rival, a solitary arrow launched from the Trojan side (the result of Athena's persuasion of an ambitious archer) wounds him under the breastplate. The predictable result of this complication of human and divine motives is a recrudescence of war. Paris's rare moment of generous altruism is rendered ineffectual by the uncoordinated efforts of Thetis, Zeus, Athena, Hera, and Aphrodite, each god solicitous in the protection of his or her favorite and unconcerned about the grander scheme of things. So much for the polytheistic love of peace.

In light of the above evidence—admittedly, an evidence limited to a single text, and an epic saga at that—Schwartz's argument that monotheism is singularly predicated upon intolerance will figure only as a prominent corollary, rather than a decisive thesis, in support of my interpretation of the nationalist war syndrome that has afflicted a majority of peoples throughout the ages. I agree that the primordial covenant, with its tripartite ritual of "severing of animals, . . . severing of . . . participants, . . . and ceremonial meal",[16] plays a decisive role in the constitution of the idea of nation, but with the double caveat, derived from recent theological and anthropological scholarship, that polytheistic religions are no less covenantal than monotheistic ones[17] and, second, that the rituals of the covenant secure not so much a national alliance with one or more deities as, rather, a dynastic line of consanguinity that dictates the structure of power and the distribution of wealth among the ruling families *within* the original community.[18] The covenant is always a "covenant of blood": literally, because it entails ceremonies of bloodshedding, but also, more importantly, figuratively, because it is aimed at the legitimation and perpetuation of the bloodline linking the aristocracy to its divine seed(s). As Walter Burkert puts it in *Homo Necans:*

> Whether in Israel, Greece, or Rome, no agreement, no contract, no alliance can be made without sacrifice. In the language of the oath, the object of aggression that is to be "struck" and "cut" becomes virtually identical with the covenant itself . . . Complicated social structures find expression in the diverse roles the participants assume in the course of the ritual . . . The sacrificial meal is particularly subject to sacred laws that regulate social interaction in distributing, giving, and taking.[19]

What my double caveat entails is that the covenantal institution of the divine alliance may be looked at, first of all, as a ritualistic establishment of hierarchical difference among the dynastic retainers of legislative and executive power within the community, and only secondarily as a setting up of aggressive intolerance toward the infidel nation.

Dynasty and Consanguinity

Having established the above analytical apparatus, I must further stress that *The Curse of Cain* addresses with secure insight the two fundamental factors that must be paired with the covenantal dimension for a more comprehensive interpretation of the nationalistic war syndrome. These two factors, consanguinity and economic scarcity, are both pertinent to the complex interplay of traditions and institutions that pervaded the gradual transposition of the Word of God into the Law of Israel.

Consanguinity may be said to pertain, in Schwartz's agenda, to the moment of the political covenant, the moment hinged upon the "demand of exclusive loyalty to the sovereign"; a Foucauldean moment of coercion in which the biblical writer "adds" to the Word of God, of his own initiative, "warnings to *coerce* singular devotion [to a dynastic lineage] rather than invite *assent* . . ."[20] In *La volonté de savoir,* Michel Foucault designates with the term *sanguinité* an archaic system of power based upon a coercive "menace of death" rather than upon a consensual "administration of life." As we saw in chapter 2, Foucault maintains that dynastic supremacy is rooted in the violence of the instincts that make precarious the survival of one's bloodline. The political discourse of dynastic consanguinity presupposes the carnal discourse of "sanguinity": the violent, often bloody imposition of the supremacy of a bloodline upon all others is an indispensable corollary to the covenantal "demand of exclusive loyalty to the sovereign," into which demand the discretion of the biblical writer translated the Word of God. Yet, "easy to shed . . . *ready to mix . . . susceptible to corruption,*" blood is, at once, the fluid element that determines an endemic adriftness in the constitution of dynastic supremacy.[21] One might say that blood resists the exclusivity upon which is predicated the trope of the dynastic genealogical tree. The covenantal demand of political loyalty to a dynastic lineage depends upon the presumption that distinct lineages are rigorously identifiable and separable, as well as, in the case of "royal" dynasties, rigorously derivable from a divine source. It is this absurd presumption that determines an irresistible drive toward competitive factionalism and antagonism *within* the essential unifying factor of tribal or ethnic consanguinity.

The factor of scarcity pertains to the "economic" dimension of the covenant; its treatment also reflects, in Schwartz's approach, an evident intrusion on the part of the biblical writer within the order of the divine Word: " . . . the Thou-Shalt-Nots that assume a world . . . where lying, cheating, stealing, adultery, and killing are such tempting responses to scarcity that they must be legislated against."[22] Since in the modern perception of

international conflict the factor of economic scarcity plays a crucial role, it is important to make clear that although scarcity is
fundamental, it is not an exclusive aspect of the nationalistic
war syndrome. The scarcity that determines Moses' expansionist
effort in Exodus, for instance, is not an objectively measurable
factor, and should not be considered an independent phenomenon in the determination of the aggression against the peoples of
Palestine. Schwartz's contribution to the discursive and textual,
rather than material and factual, connotations of the scarcity
element is enlightening. The scarcity of resources, she argues,
is hardly an obstacle to the survival of Israel in the wilderness,
nor is it the impulse that motivates the wars of invasion in Palestine. YWHW is a god of "plenitude," quick to "rain down bread
from the heavens"; his Paradise, "the quintessential imagined
plenitude," is irreconcilable with the economic principles of appropriation and accumulation—in the desert the Hebrews learn
that their hoarded manna rots.[23] Like the decalogue of coercion,
the expansionistic strains that pervade the biblical text come, I
venture, as a coercive solution to the containment of "the tempting responses to scarcity" devised by the lower strata of the popu-
lation against the unequal distribution of national wealth. The
Hebrew generations born after Moses' rebellion against the
Egyptian captivity undertake the conquest of Palestine not because of their material need but, rather, because of the legacy
from a *mythos* of their elders—precisely, because of the Divine
command, inscribed upon the rolls held within the ark of the
covenant, that they should do so.

The neo-Viconian thrust of my interpretation depends upon
the thesis that national expansionism, intended as a consequence of the internal factionalism that is determined by dynastic rivalry, is affected, in the case of the Old Testament, by the
unified cluster of four determinants: (1) the biblical covenant;
(2) the infiltration of human discretion within the textuality of
Scripture; (3) the constitution of the aristocracy of kinship; (4)
the influence of economic scarcity.

WAR AND CIVIL WAR

"Israel is threatened from without and [from] within."[24]
Among the threats "from within," upon which I focus exclusively
in this chapter, Schwartz mentions the threat of adultery, with
particular reference to the episode of David and Bathsheba, and

the threats of rape and incest, with particular reference to the episode of Amnon and Tamar. To which I should add, for the sake of completeness, that the House of David is also plagued, in consideration of Absalom's murder of Amnon, by the threat of fratricide. The domestic or endogenous factionalism introduced by Schwartz in her study of the House of David is an endemic consequence of the primacy attributed to dynastic lineage by the primitive community. It is well known to the biblical scholar that the paradigm for consanguineous descent involves a drive toward incest and endogamy. The price for the ostracism of incest and endogamy consists, more often than not, of the affirmation of collateral, "questionable" ramifications within kinship. The price for the perpetuation of incest and endogamy (social crimes that Moses was the first to legislate systematically against) consists, instead, of an unrestrainable process of domestic "self-enclosure": a precipitous movement of self-breeding, an unrelenting convergence of the genealogical tree toward the "germ" of its genuine and primal origin. When the kinship involved in this consanguineous exclusion of exteriority and diversity is the dynastic one, as in the case of the House of David, the outcome may take the immediate form of adultery, rape, incest, fratricide, or a combination of several of these effects, but in the ultimate analysis it amounts to civil war. The nationalist war syndrome figures as an ancillary phenomenon in this scheme, or else, as a *continuation of civil war by other means.*

The paradox of endogamy as the safest foundation for the genealogical tree of the ruling dynasty was tragically familiar to the ancient Greeks too, as indicated by the most universal of Sophocles' plays, *Oedipus Rex.* In the *Republic* Plato attempts, probably more in the spirit of a cautionary tale than with ambition for political reform, to eliminate the primacy of the dynastic bloodline through the curious genopolitics of procreation that Socrates assigns to the Guardians of the luxurious *pólis.* As will be recalled, the Guardians share with each other the community of women and their offspring. In the abolition of privacy entailed by their mating practices, the Guardians succumb to the logic of a social planning inherently incestuous: ignorant of the identities of their parents, their offspring will end up mating incestuously with each other.[25] Ironically, the reversal of dynastic consanguinity into its diametrical opposite, namely, an absolute indifference to the bloodline, falls prey to the very social evil, incest, that it was meant to exorcize. That endogenous factionalism, internal antagonism, or, simply, civil war, was at the heart of the ancient Greeks' political concerns is indicated also, as I suggested above, by the events that precede the Paris-Menelaos duel in the *Iliad*. The drive toward *pólemos* and *éris* that culminates in the bizarre outcome of the duel, in fact, represents for the Achaian army nothing but an expeditious solution to civil war. Inspired by his Muse, Homer personifies the crisis within the Greek camp in the mythic mask of Apollo, who disseminates death among the divided troops. Conventionally, such an instance of death on a massive scale tends to be attributed to the spreading of some contagious disease among the soldiers, just as, for instance, the destruction brought upon Thebes by Oedipus's crimes, in *Oedipus Rex,* is often interpreted as the consequence of a plague.[26] However, I submit that in both the *Iliad* and *Oedipus Rex* the diagnosis of civil war as the principal cause of people's decimation is an equally plausible interpretation. Socrates' ironic remark, in Plato's *Republic,* about the *incipit* of the *Iliad* seems to lend support to my position. In spite of several instances of praise of Homer in Plato's dialogues, in book 8 of the *Republic* Socrates appears to assign Homer's verses to the "vile" category that he eventually censures with severity in book 10 (377e). Socrates' allusion to the inadequacy of Homer's verses is subtle. He asks Glaucon: "Shall we, like Homer, invoke the Muses to tell 'how faction (στάσις) first fell upon [the ruling class]' . . . ?" (545d–e)[27] The rhetorical overtones of the question indicate that Socrates is reluctant to have recourse to mendacious *lógos* to describe the crisis experienced by the Achaian commanders at the beginning of the *Iliad,* a crisis whose proper name is *stásis,* or inner conflict, a crisis that is the civil equivalent of *pólemos* and *éris.* "This is the simple and unvarying rule," he declared a few lines before: "In every form of government revolution takes its start from the ruling class itself, when dissension arises in it . . ." (545d).[28] And in book 5 he explained," "Greece is sick . . . [when] divided by *stásis,* and *stásis* is the name we must give to that enmity . . . When anything of this sort occurs in *stásis* . . . a state is divided against itself . . . such factional strife is thought to be an accursed thing . . ." (470c–d).

Homer's eccentricity lies in that he introduces the epics of the Greek siege of Troy with an episode of civil war. In Socrates' view, his mistake lies in that he misapprehends the Greek *stásis* by personifying it in a furious god, while this *stásis* is the simple outcome of the dispute that opposes Achilles to Agamemnon, which originated in a conflict about the two rivals' right to their respective Trojan concubines. In the adversity of impending defeat, Agamemnon recognizes this much, when he declares to his peers, "it seems the rest of the Akhaians, like Akhilleus, hold a grudge against me!"[29]

The basic factors involved in the establishment of the collective identity of an archaic nation or community—covenant, scarcity, consanguinity, as well as, in the case of the Hebrews, the paradox of a transcendent Word inscribed by humans and at human discretion—can be separated for the sake of analytical discourse, but it must be kept in mind that the complexity in the identification of a nation or a community pertains precisely to the impossibility of separating this cluster of factors into logically distinct categories—although theoretical discourse has attempted exactly such a discursive separation from time immemorial. Religion, be it polytheistic or monotheistic, involves a textual (or imagic, or ideographic) inscription of divine intentions; it regulates the structure of power internal to the community through the institution of a hierarchical separation between kinships; it regulates the distribution of wealth within the community through the social reproduction of the ritualistic distribution of food inherent in the covenantal meal.

Let us take a closer look at this cluster of related phenomena. The closer, the more proximate in terms of consanguineous lineage a family is to the god(s), the more substantial will be its governing role within the community, the more prominent will be its interpretation of the (text of the) divine intentions, the larger will be its liturgical share in the consumption of the sacrificial meal and its effective share in the allocation of the total resources available to and/or produced by the community—the larger, in most cases, will also be its real and/or symbolic contribution of sacrificial victims, as indicated by the parallel cases of Abraham's (aborted) sacrifice of Isaac and Agamemnon's sacrifice of Iphigenia. An analogous set of considerations, incidentally, also applies to the androlineal genealogy that links Adam to Jesus Christ (Matthew 1:2–16), and Jesus Christ, in turn, as the divine matrix transubstantiated in the Eucharist, to the collective body of the Church. The constitution of Christianity into a living Church with a "head" or pontifex and a set of "limbs" or agents operating as vicars of the sacred in the secular world—a living Church as a metaphor of the mortal body of Christ—is mediated by Christ's institution of the Eucharist as sacrificial ritual. In *History as Apocalypse,* Thomas Altizer shows how the sacrament of the Eucharist entails the recuperation of the archaic ground of "an original and primordial sacrifice" to the liturgy of Western Christianity.[30] One might say that it is primarily in the Eucharistic recuperation of the "covenant of blood" that the primitive Christian Church attributes to its members (or "limbs") a rigidly hierarchical separation of potency (spiritual and secular power) within the community.

As regards my stipulation that the basic factors in the establishment of a communal identity—covenant, scarcity, consanguinity, and sacred textuality—function as a unified cluster rather than separate vectors, an emblematic confirmation may be found in Vico's treatment of the "custody" of social orders among the Romans of the preimperial age. In *La scienza nuova,* Vico explains that the private rights of kinship, succession, and acquisition of the family estate pertain to the "custody" of the *certezza delle famiglie,* i.e., to the social imperative that distinct kinships and their identifying family names are to be kept rigorously separate from one another. This *certezza,* this "certainty" of family identification, in which one can already detect the strict interplay of genealogy with the regulation of resource distribution, is legislated for two reasons: first, to neutralize the "pernicious community of women" (to keep incest at bay, that is, while preserving the principle of consanguineous lineage— a concern at the heart of Moses' laws against endogamy in Leviticus), and second, to preserve the possession of wealth within the class of the patricians (*SNS2* § 985–86). At the time of the first written formulation of the Roman law in the Twelve Tables (circa 450 B.C.E.), it is established that the legitimate legislators are those Roman citizens who have access to the sacred auspices, that is, the patrician *patresfamilias.* This form of legislation, private as well as public, aimed at the containment of social unrest and the determination of plebeian consent through the identification of the letter of the law with the divine intentions, is grounded on an exclusive covenant between the noble head of the family and his *deivi parentum,* his deified ancestors. It is because he can *interpatrari,* that is, penetrate the mind of his homonymic fathers, that the patrician may *interpretari,* that is, "interpret" the sacred auspices and transpose them into legal norms *(SNS2* § 937–41). The Roman ceremony of the covenant does not differ significantly from the Hebrew one when it comes to the tripartite ritual of the "severing of animals, . . . [the] severing of . . . participants, . . . and [the] ceremonial meal":[31] the *paterfamilias* derives the auspices for his legislation (of the family and of the community as well) from the sacrifices to the gods in front of the *focolare,* the family fireplace. Vico provides a Latin etymology for the Italian *focolare: focus laris,* "the fire of the family god," an emblematic *locus* of conglomeration for the orders of religion, law, and consanguinity in ancient Roman society (*SNS1* § 526). If "it was religion that invented genealogy," as Vico observes emphatically in *De constantia philologiae* (§ 20), it was genealogy—precisely, the genealogical privilege of the patrician *paterfamilias*—that completed the circle of identification of authority, consanguinity, and religious ritual, with the codification of the body of legal norms that Vico calls *teologia mistica.*

I should stress, also, that the Roman regulation of civil and public right through this strict interplay of religion and dynastic lineage does not appear particularly war-oriented—it has no reason to be so, by all means, since war hardly pertains to the dimension of civil and public legislation. Yet, it is clearly oriented toward the containment of civil war, as demonstrated especially by the disposition: *Auspicia incommunicata plebi sunto* from the Eleventh Table. Presented as an extension to the plebeians of the patriciate's *ragioni civili private,* that is, the right of solemn marriage, of family succession, of inheritance, etc., the Twelve Tables withhold from the heads of plebeian families the access to the divine auspices, that is, the one prerogative without which civil right remains a prescribed coercion rather than a body of privileges and obligations consensually shared among equals.[32]

It is now time to show how the principles so far adduced can lead to insights into the relationship of covenant and dynasty, and also of war and civil war, in the Old Testament. The following section is devoted to the interpretation of the episode of Zipporah's deliverance of her husband Moses in Exodus 4, a proverbially controversial passage, one of the finest renditions, in my opinion, of the apotropaic capacity of consanguineous sacrifice to subdue the divine resentment of mortals.

Covenant and Domestic Strife in Exodus 4

Zipporah's story is a story which, in terms of genre, makes no sense. Here, very briefly, is how the story goes. After forcing Moses to accept his role of national liberator, YHWH changes his mind and seeks to kill him. Instead of reacting and fighting back, as his progenitor Jacob did on the banks of the Jabbok,[33] Moses is strangely passive. But his wife, Zipporah, takes the initiative to save him. And it is a strange initiative, senseless indeed, not just because she, as a woman, will have not been invited, so to speak, to take part in this masculine fight, but above all because she manages to defeat YHWH, in a sense, by doing something whose logic escapes the reader—something, I should venture, whose very meaning exceeds that patriarchal code of struggle which, in the epic sections of the Torah, permits all and any deceitful move as long as the outcome bespeaks the dichotomy victory/defeat. Zipporah grabs a flint, cuts her son's foreskin, sprays the blood of circumcision on "his" (whose?) feet, and utters the apparently irresistible incantation: "You are truly a bridegroom of blood to me."[34] At these words—directed maybe at Moses, maybe at Moses' son, maybe at YWHW himself—YHWH, whose somewhat pagan character in this episode matches and reflects Zipporah's polytheistic origin from the tribe of Midian, subsides as suddenly as inexplicably.

This episode violates the ordered, (chrono-)logical progression of negotiations by which YHWH has forcefully persuaded Moses to undertake the task of liberating Israel; it inaugurates an evident disrupture of the generic dominants established in the collisional conversation between Moses and YHWH in the three preceding chapters of Exodus. Furthermore, with respect to the careful staging of Jacob's struggle with the demon in Genesis 32, in this episode the fundamental detail of the patriarch's separation from his next of kin, in preparation for the fight, is neglected. As a consequence, the virile simplicity of the code of honor that regiments the struggle between Jacob and the demon until dawn, and that compensates the patriarch's stolid resistance with the acquisition of the name of his own community (what a colossal moment of identification between patronymic and posterity!), is substituted in Exodus 4 by a woman's celebration of the circumcision ritual, a celebration strangely instrumental, grotesquely timed, somewhat illicit, imbued with the overtones of a pagan exorcism. One is simply left in the dark as to what the text means, because the text, in truth, refuses to *say* what it *means*. As Ilana Pardes observes, this narrative leaves one with too many unanswerable questions: "Why does Zipporah perform the circumcision (in these distressful circumstances)? Whose feet are touched with (the blood of) the foreskin? What is the meaning of Zipporah's incantation? Who is the 'bridegroom of blood?' Why does YWHW withdraw?"[35] Pardes suggests that Zipporah's deliverance of Moses—who, in the hands of YHWH, seems to have regressed to the passive inertness of the baby in the ark delivered to the waters of the Nile—is an erotic deliverance, a restitution of the phallic vitality, which is the mandatory prerogative of the leader of the nation, as the personified agency of the nation's fertile lineages.

But the eroticism of this episode is fraught with a deceptive background that brings about a subversion of generic dominants. We see this deceptiveness at work in the distortion of the patriarchal code of struggle that hinges upon the dichotomy victory/defeat. And we see this deceptiveness at work as well in the subversion, or de-generation, of the storytelling conventions that submit their epic signification to that very patriarchal code. I should venture, as a partial revision of what Harold Fish writes of biblical poetry in *Poetry with a Purpose,* that we encounter here a swerving into an epic of erotic violence—an episode that substitutes, in the first place, a cryptic "discontinuity" to the "roundedness and closure" of conventional epics,[36] and, in the second place, eroticizes one of the master tropes of patriarchy, namely, the binary opposition of mastery and submission, primacy and subordination, victory and defeat. Interestingly, Zipporah's cryptic and swift, three-line story appears to conflate, together with Fish's notion of poetic discontinuity, the notion of oneiric kaleidoscopic elusiveness that Fish adopts in his approach to the Song of Songs. Zipporah's story is a text with no Aristotelian unity of action, a story that is a dense muddle of different stories.[37] It "makes sense"—to YWHW himself, in the first place, who promptly responds to Zipporah's cryptic incantation—by making, in terms of genre, no sense at all.

And, what is more important in the economy of my discourse, the generically distorted sense of Zipporah's story contributes one further, usually neglected connotation to the character of the Abrahamic dictate of circumcision. One learns from Zipporah's deliverance of Moses that the mandatory ritual of circumcision does not consist only of the apotropaic simulacrum of a ritual of male fertility (as enacted, for instance, in what Eilberg-Schwarts calls the "savage religions"),[38] nor does it simply consist of a token of tribal identification (the token, incidentally, that must have played a crucial role in the identification of the legitimate male participants to the exodus from Egypt). The rite of circumcision, as esoterically performed by Zipporah, orbits a darker and more elusive dimension of primitive tribal customs, an obscure covenantal dimension wherein the eros of consanguineous love breeds the violence of incest, yet, at one and the same time, the violence of consanguineous bloodshed breeds the eros of divine atonement. With respect to genre, Zipporah's feat pertains to the dimension of an unconventional poetics wherein lexical indeterminacy triggers a sort of erotic polyvalence on the part of a woman who appears to trade the favors of her intimacy with three male partners at once, i.e., her husband, her son, and YHWH. Furthermore, it is the woman, and none of the three males involved, who holds a weapon in her hand. And finally, it is the woman, a pagan by origin, that at one and the same time infects the monotheistic deity with pagan attributes and manifests her submission to the monotheistic rite of circumcision by means of a virile act of aggression. The covenantal dimension of Zipporah's deliverance of Moses from the strife of YHWH is imbued, with respect to both genre and gender, with a spiraling logic of reversal and contradiction. The sexual and martial inertness of Moses triggers Zipporah's pugnacious rebellion, a rebellion, however, that contradicts the patriarchal order of struggle, of combat, by directing its aggression first against her own kin. A weapon is grabbed, consanguineous blood is shed: as a result, a divine covenant is stipulated. The order of combat is unrealistic, metaphoric, a sequence of frozen frames that seem to belong to the symbolic logic of the dream.

At the eve of Moses' liberation of his people and constitution of what in time will come to be characterized as the Nation of Israel, this episode introduces an unanticipated complication in the *epos* of war and national emancipation, a complication that the conventions of epic discourse can accommodate to only a partial extent. The complication consists of this, that a paradoxical drive toward internal antagonism appears from the very start to be intrinsic to Moses' task. No sooner does YHWH force upon Moses the role of national liberator than a conflict of self-dissention and self-differentiation emerges rather absurdly from his very persona: the patriarch is inexplicably inert in the hands of his aggressor, who is also his sole ally and the original promoter of his assumption of leadership; the patriarch's wife takes the impolitic initiative of defending him by mutilating her own son; the blood of the patriarch's lineage is shed so as to guarantee, first, the survival of the patriarch himself, and second, on a more symbolic level, the perpetuation and perpetual fertility of the bloodline that will emancipate Israel from the Egyptian captivity. The "absurd" resolution of Moses' conflict with YWHW is achieved when his pagan wife submits to the fundamental monotheistic rite of circumcision through a masculine act of aggression and self-assertion.

Inherent in Moses' attempt to emancipate his own people is that drive toward conflict prevalent in all historical and mythical circumstances wherein stable criteria of national, ethnic, and religious identity are to be defined and put to work. The emancipation from the Egyptian captivity is predicated upon the Hebrews' capacity to antagonize their oppressors, and the instruments of this antagonism are conventionally two, namely, a military capacity of violent aggression and/or resistance, and a cultural capacity for self-differentiation from the oppressor. In Zipporah's story both capacities are metaphorically manifest in their inverse appropriation and activation by a woman, a virtual outsider to the tribe, who at first directs them *against* the blood of the patriarch.

The cultural capacity of a primitive people to give itself an autonomous identity may be defined as the capacity that inaugurates and sustains the expulsion of diversity and the dispensation of foreignness from the "original" community. History has repeatedly taught us that the convergence undertaken by the community toward the "pure" kernel of its innermost nature tends to be, or become, unrelenting and uncompromising. What the unconventional poetics of Zipporah's story intimates, by means of a disruption of the generic dominants of epic discourse—but also, more specifically, by the narration of a three-line conflict that sets all the members of Moses' family at war, at once, with each other and with their divine ally—is that the quest for religious, ethnic, and national purity is bound to nurture factionalism as an endless form of inner conflict. And this internal antagonism may appear to depend on gender-related imbalances of power, influence, and strategic agendas. Moses, in sum, cannot war against the oppressors of his people without being engaged in a simultaneous struggle against his own bloodline. The exorcism of difference brings upon itself the curse of purity and intolerance; it begets disunity of purpose, factionalism, self-dissention. Ultimately, the notion of exile, as that barren and uprooted (*'aqara*)[39] moment fundamental to the Hebrew epic of national liberation (and, in terms of genre, fundamental also to most ancient epics of the Western literary tradition, from the *Odyssey* to the *Aeneid*), acquires sinister connotations when this epic turns out to depend upon an unbroken movement of expulsion, of *exile of diversity,* from the matrix of the "original" community.

CONCLUSION

At the beginning of this chapter I presented its three thematic dominants in the following points: (1) my reassessment of the thesis that a unique kind of intimacy links monotheistic covenant and nationalistic expansionism; (2) my conviction that the correlation between religion and nationalistic expansionism must be viewed as a corollary to the correlation between religious cult and dynastic supremacy *within* a given community. (In the latter correlation I see civil factionalism and economic dispute as the primary causes of external hostility against ethnic and religious diversity. War, in other words, is seen in my analysis as the continuation of civil war by different means.); (3) finally, my purpose to attend to the *vera narratio* conveyed by some of the stories and chronicles from our remotest past. The neo-Viconian thrust of this inquiry is to be identified in the presumption that a close study of archaic fabulations may help unveil the fundamental lines of transformation within the cluster of traditions, institutions, languages, and laws that constitute the crucible of national identity. However disregardful of Vico's reluctance to undertake a "scientific" inquiry into Holy Writ, my revisionist approach pays homage to his method, inasmuch as, granted the full impact of tradition and *sensus communis* upon society, it focuses on the historical phenomenon by which Scripture, with its stratified influence, made an essential contribution to the shaping of the world we live in.

After illustrating the three thematic dominants and the exegetic principles to be derived from their inner logic, I have applied these principles to the Zipporah episode from Exodus 4, an episode whose peculiar textual rendition lends itself especially well to the investigation of linguistic and generic ambiguity. The confirmation of my presumptions as to the thematic reverberation between covenant, consanguinity, dynastic primacy, and, finally, domestic conflict, came escorted by complementary insights into a gender-related antagonism and imbalance of power, which manifest themselves at the very inception of the Hebrew epos of national liberation. This latter aspect of the conflicts attending the birth of Israel opens an important window on the question of civil strife and political dominance. The crux of the matter lies in the inner contradiction of a dynastic primacy that is to be unquestionably consanguineous yet also unequivocally patriarchal. As I already stated with regard to the epigraph to the present chapter, the physiological certainty of consanguinity is more often than not at odds with the historical truth of genealogical descent. The former is a fact of nature, the latter a construct of culture. The former depends on maternal discretion, ultimately on the mother's docile submission to the customs of patriarchy, the latter depends on paternal discretion, ultimately on the father's transmission of his patronymic to his firstborn or favorite son. The former reflects the uncoercible emotions of erotic transport, the latter the coercive impositions of legal discourse. The elucidation of this contradiction points to an angle of approach that Vico's method, in and by itself, is unequipped to cope with. Nonetheless, I have attempted to show that a return to Vico's method is more than worthwhile in the study of our archaic literary traditions. The diction "neo-Viconian" not only accommodates the novelty of revisionism: it calls for it.

12

Procreation and Degeneration: War and Civil War, Gender and Genre, Begetting and Memory in Plato's *Republic*

> just as we have the two terms, πόλεμός and στάσις, so there
> are also two things which these two antagonisms designate,
> namely, the friendly and kindred on the one hand and the
> alien and foreign on the other. Now the term employed for
> the hostility of the friendly is στάσις, and the one employed
> for the hostility of the alien is πόλεμός.
>
> —Plato, *Republic*, 470b

A METHODOLOGICAL PREMISE

In this chapter i undertake a deconstruction of the conventional view according to which the Socratic city of the *Republic*
is a *locus* of gender segregation, of communal and reproductive
sterility, and of aesthetic intolerance. My deconstruction will be
based on the presumption that in the *Republic* Socrates only
pretends to be talking in a "truthful (*alethinòn*) lógos."[1] Socrates' stance of discursive veracity leads one to think that he
means what he says whenever he engages in the building of
cities "in *lógos*" (369a).[2] However, when Critias, in the *Timaeus*,
directs an oblique invitation to Socrates to "degrade" to the fictionality of myth the city which, in the *Republic*, was declared
to be a creature of *lógos*, Socrates willingly complies. Critias
makes this request of Socrates after declaring his own intention
to "transport . . . into the realm of truth" (*talethès* being a crasis
for τὸ ἀληθές)—into the realm, he means, of documentable history—"the city with its citizens which (Socrates) described (to
his guests) the day before, as it were in a *mýtho*."[3] From the
standpoint of textual history, the city Critias is talking about is
not, probably, the luxurious *pólis* described in book 2 of the

Republic, because, as Eva Brann points out in "The Music of the *Republic*," "the year of the *Timaeus* seems to be earlier than that of the *Republic*."[4] However, Socrates' recapitulation of this city in the *incipit* of the *Timaeus* in unmistakable, as Brann concurs, suggesting that probably "Socrates proposed this city on various occasions," so that it came to be regarded as "his (city)." Socrates, in any event, seems eager to recant. "The fact that (Critias's story) is not invented *mŷthon* but truthful *lógos* (*alethinòn lógon*) is all important," he replies (26e), in agreement with Critias's implied presumption that "truthful (*alethinòn*) *lógos*" is not the *lógos* capable of ascending to the intellection of the Good, but, on the contrary, the *lógos* that documents undisputable facts relating to human history. My deconstruction, in sum, will be based upon the presumption that when it comes to negotiating the literal veraciousness of his own words, Socrates exhibits a disconcerting indifference. "Call my speech truthful if you will," he seems to reply to Critias, "or call it mythic if you prefer"; which indicates that his speech does not achieve its intended meaning through generic consistency— the *lógos* of truth pertaining to the genre of philosophical discourse, the *lógos* of myth pertaining to the genre of religious and fictional discourse, roughly speaking—but rather through dialogic context.

An emblematic confirmation, albeit an indirect, inferential one, of my attribution of generic eclecticism to Socrates' words may be found in the *Timaeus,* especially in the "fresh start" of Timaeus's second discourse about the origin of the cosmos (48b). At this juncture in the dialogue—when the dialogue itself degenerates, generically speaking, into a monologue—Timaeus warns his listeners that, in telling of the origin of the universe, he will have to engage in a *lógos* homologous (*omologoyménoys lógoys* [29c]) to that which he will be talking about. The origin of the universe, in turn, Timaeus hinges upon, on the one hand, the interplay of the forces of the primal elements and, on the other hand, the paradigmatic fabrication of the supreme *demiourgós* (29a, 46d–48c)—he subjects the origin of the universe, therefore, to the chaotic disorder of chance and, at once, to the rational, order-making thrust of thought. Hence, Timaeus says, he will have to talk, intermittently, in the true *lógos* (*alethès lógos* [52c]) that is analogous to the rational, order-making thrust of thought; in the likely mythological account (*eikóta mŷthon* [29d])[5] and in the veritable opinion (*dóxa alethén* [51d]) that are analogous to the chaotic disorder of chance; and, finally, in the *bastard logism* (λογισμῷ νόθῳ [52b]) that is analogous to the degenerate character of that which is only subject to "desensitized" sense *(ἀναισθησίας)*, "barely credible" (52b), being neither altogether intelligible via *noesis* nor altogether apprehensible with the senses.

In this chapter I show that the *Republic,* too, is informed by a polymorphously degenerate *lógos*, homologous to that which it talks about. This aspect of the dialogue will allow me to argue the thesis that when it comes to addressing the three social issues of the separation of genders, the communal policy of human reproduction, and the cultivation of poetic craft, the *Republic* advocates a kind of discourse radically unmoored from generic orthodoxy, a *political* discourse whose relevance vis-à-vis our political actuality ought not to be overlooked.

STASIS AND POLEMICS

It is in a rhetorical mockery of Homeric style that Socrates, in book 8 of the *Republic,* utters his invocation to the Muses. "Shall we, like Homer, invoke the Muses to tell 'how faction (στάσις) first fell upon (the ruling class)' ... ?" (545d–e)[6] Socrates is hinting at the curious fact that the *incipit* of the *Iliad,* the epic poem of the defeat and sack of Troy by the Greeks, is not devoted to *pólemos,* to the fight against the Trojans, but to *stásis* (στάσις), to the inner faction, or dispute, among the Achaians.[7] The dispute that opposes Achilles to Agamemnon, which originated in a conflict about the two rivals' right to their respective Trojan concubines, leads to the ruinous withdrawal of Achilles from active fighting. Socrates' invocation is far from epic, though. In addressing his disciple, Glaucon, he wonders about the nature of the *lógos* that would be proper to tell of the *political degeneration* of the luxurious *pólis,* which he illustrated in books 2 through 4 of the *Republic.* Political degeneration appears to occur, Socrates says, when the ruling class, invested by *stásis,* just as the Achaian army at the siege of Troy, loses the freedom from internal dissension (ἀστασίαστος), which is needed to rule *at one with oneself* (545d). Socrates is in search of the right, or just, manner of political discourse, so as to address and ward off the static forces that disintegrate the *pólis* from the inside by bringing about what in the *Sophist* Plato will designate as "the disagreement of the naturally related" (228a).[8]

Three aspects need to be observed as regards the political *stá-sis* of the luxurious *pólis:*

1. *Stásis* is not "of" the Muses. In the case of this particular discussion, it does not pertain to the *musical* madness, or, more specifically, to the epic *lógos* that the Muse Calliope inspires in the epic poet, to explicate political internal dissension.[9]

2. *Stásis* does not denote a state of passivity, of inertness, as the ordinary usage of the word may suggest, but rather a notion of pugnacious self-enclosure within the *pólis.* The political *stá-sis* of the *pólis* consists of a precipitous movement of self-proximity, an unrelenting convergence of the city toward the kernel of its own innermost nature; this convergence, in dispensing of all exteriority, of all diversity, of all foreignness, tends, at the limit, toward the absolute contraction of differentiation and the absolute exclusion of diversity.[10]

3. The political nature of the *stásis* of the self-enclosed *pólis*— the self-identical, a-polemical city at peace, yet fortified, yet capable of πόλεμος, of external war[11]—is one of *internal dissent.* This is a direct consequence of the norm requiring the ruling class to be, so as to rule well, "at one with itself." In fact, dissention is bound to break out among the rulers as to the optimal procedures for the begetting of their successors.[12] Unable to match the norms of good begetting dictated by the "perfect number" of divine begetting, that is, by the celestial cycle of cosmic balance that determines the right season of mating and procreation (*Republic* 546b–d),[13] the ruling class will be progressively peopled by unworthy rulers, and will therefore lose its unity of purpose.[14] *Stásis,* in sum, as the drive toward the absolute contraction of diversity, nurtures *factionalism* as endless inner conflict, as further and further disintegration, self-dissention, self-differentiation.

Before I proceed, let me point out, to secure a later connection, that the soul of the citizen of the static, degenerating *pólis* is only capable of *stásis* and *pólemos.* In "The Music of the *Republic*," Eva Brann treats it as a "temperamental" soul,[15] made up of three *eidē: logistikòn,* or the calculating part; *thymoeidēs,* or the aggressive part, (the *locus,* especially, of indignation against injustice); and *epithymētikon,* or the desiring part (*Republic* 439c–e). Brann remarks that when one compares the

soul of the citizen of the static *pólis* to the soul that enables
humans to ascend to the contemplation of the Good through
intellection (*noesis*), the three *eidē* of the former soul "sink to
mere . . . appetites" (42–43).[16] This tripartite soul is the lurid
soul whose amputated equivalent dwells in the old body of Cephalus, the wealthy, all-headed man Socrates converses with at the
beginning of the *Republic*. Having lost the appetites that subordinate eros to the somatic pleasures in the "service of Aphrodite" (σῶμα ἡδοναί [328d, 329b–c]), Cephalus is left with a
bipartite soul, wherein *logistikòn*, i.e., the ability to calculate
his own interests, and *thymoeidēs*, i.e., his indignation against
the injustices he may have committed in his former life, drive
him to extinguish compulsively all his debts, before the time
comes for him to respond for his just and unjust behavior before
the tribunal of the dead (330d–31b).

The *Lógos* of Degeneration

What, then, is the *lógos* appropriate to address political degeneration so as to heal it, if it is not the poetic *lógos* of Homer?
What is the genre of discourse capable of medicating political
stásis? And, since the concerns of old Cephalus reminded us
that the *Republic* is a dialectical dialogue about the *eidos* of
justice—about the *just* regulation of the *pólis,* which Diotima
defines, in the *Symposium,* as the highest and most beautiful
of virtues[17]—let me also ask: What genre of discourse is capable
of describing a just city?

These are the questions I wish to address in what follows. I
will show that the political degeneration of the luxurious city
described by Socrates can be medicated by a *degenerate lógos,*
unmoored from the factionalism of the logocentric subject.
Then I will argue that the degenerate *lógos* capable of telling of
the just *pólis* addresses the Socratic *pólis* as an *erotic tópos* of
sheltering care for the diverse, for the other: a *pólis* without
walls. It will have to be a degenerate *lógos,* first of all, because,
as argued in the *Timaeus, lógos* is of the same kind (ξυγγενεῖς)
as that which it is about (29b–c); hence, a *lógos* sharing with its
own subject an affinity of static self-dissention—a *lógos* at war
with itself; more specifically, a *lógos* impervious to the "generic
dominants"[18] upon which the genre of theoretical discourse is
grounded. It will have to be a discourse capable of challenging
the generic dominants of theoretical discourse by situating itself

244   PART FOUR: GENEALOGY AND CONSANGUINITY

in an *elsewhere* with respect to the binary logic that regiments those very dominants. Examples of this binary logic that can be found in the works we have so far encountered include the philosophical oppositions static/polemic, same/different, rational/emotional, soul/body, immortal/mortal; the sexual oppositions inherent in mating and procreation: masculine/feminine, semen/menses; and the generic oppositions that differentiate the Muses of poetic chant: tragic/epic, mythic/historic, prosaic/poetic, verisimilar/fantastic. This binary logic informs the generic dominants of theoretical discourse in a matrix of pregiven expectations—literally, a matrix of *prejudices*—that the degenerate *lógos* capable of telling of the just *pólis* will have to carefully circumscribe and keep at bay, so as to release its discourse from the dichotomous strife that the metaphysical tradition attributes to *génos,* as the matrix of *genre,* and also, not to be forgotten, of *gender.* Furthermore, the degenerate *lógos* capable of telling of the just *pólis* will have to be a *lógos* capable of doing, or bringing, justice to its subject by twisting free of the degeneration that turns the self-contraction of *stásis* into a permanent dissension, a permanent motion of exile, of *expulsion of diversity* from the *pólis;* hence, a *lógos* equipped to break free from *stásis* by yoking together, in a regenerative, agonistic *tópos* of nonopposition, the acrimonious forces of friction and confrontation.

In the *Republic,* the internal dissent endemic to political *stásis* is a direct consequence of the controversy among the ruling class as to the optimal procedures for the begetting of their successors. The procreation of the ruling class is mandatorily assigned to mating practices that end up incestuous and "geometric" rather than erotic and necessary (*Republic* 458d). Therefore, the discourse devoted to the degenerations of *Politeía* will have to be told in a *lógos* aimed at doing justice to (at "justifying") *erotic filiation* in the *pólis.* I will maintain that erotic filiation consists of an event that, at play in physiological procreation as well as in philosophical reproduction, reverses the Socratic *stásis* into a centripetal event of hospitable fructification.

EROS AND MUSIC

Besides inspiring the "musical madness" of the epic poet, the Muses inspire, according to Socrates, all kinds of technical *poíesis* (ποίησις), all kinds of fabrication that help things pass "from not being into being" (*Symposium* 205b). Of all these *poíeses,* poetry (the mimetic craft) and statesmanship (the legislative and judicial craft) are two among the highest, as long as they beget an image of the beautiful (as Socrates requires, respectively, of the poet in the *Republic* [399e–401b] and of the ruler in the *Symposium* [209a–e]).[19] Good poetry does not fabricate those mere fantasies—imitations of what never was or will be[20]—that are the art of the *mimetikòn tribes (μιμητικὸν ἴθνος* [*Timaeus* 19d]); instead, good poetry begets in *lógos* the beautiful kind of image that Plato designates as "the most radiant" (*τó νκφανεστατον* [*Phaedrus* 250d–e]), and that consists of a sensible manifestation of the mnemonic trace that the prenatal vision of the Good left inscribed within the human soul.[21] Good statesmanship, in turn, does not fabricate those semblances of just regulation behind which corrupt rulers hide the pursuit of their own advantage;[22] instead, it begets the "best" of constitutions (*Timaeus* 17c) in a body of laws and normative measures conforming to justice,[23] that virtue of the human soul, akin to the beauty of the Good, which, in the *Phaedrus,* Socrates designates as one of the soul's most prized possessions (250b).

The *poíeses,* in short, are the various crafts that human beings apprehend from divine sources. As the Muses, in the *Symposium,* teach humans the various crafts, so the gods, in the *Phaedrus,* inspire in some humans the divine madness that induces them to use their craft to the just end of fabricating beautiful images of the Good. It is thus that humans learned the crafts of weaponry and medicine from Apollo, the god of prophetical madness; the craft of musical harmony and dissonance from Dionysus, the god of mystical madness; the craft of metalwork from Hephaestus, the god of fire, who instills ebullient life within the earth; the craft of patient weaving from Athena, the goddess of discursive veracity; the craft of statesmanship from Zeus, the leader of the gods.[24] A curious degeneration occurs in the correspondences between the several kinds of *poíeses* mentioned in the *Symposium* and the four kinds of divine madness—prophecy, mysticism, music, eros—mentioned in the *Phaedrus;* it consists in the yoking together of, on the one hand, musical madness, the matrix of all crafts, and, on the other hand, of prophecy, mysticism, and eros. The divine madnesses appear to mingle together, music being the rootstock that supports its three dependent branches: prophecy, mysticism, and eros. The way the couplets music/prophecy and music/mysticism pair up is hardly problematic, insofar as we just saw that

Apollo, the god of prophetic inspiration, and Dionysus, the god of mystical rapture, undertake to teach humans the crafts of weaponry, medicine, and music proper. A more complex symmetry intervenes, however, when one considers the pairing in the couplet music/eros. As we will see in a moment, the complicity of music and eros, as two distinct divine madnesses, dominates the pairs music/prophecy and music/mysticism to such an extent that the latter two may be reduced to merely two pairs among the many possible configurations of the complicity of music and eros.

According to the *Symposium,* it is Eros (*"Ερως*), the lover of beautiful Aphrodite, that guides Apollo, Dionysus, the Muses, Hephaestus, Athena, and "even" Zeus, in the invention of their crafts. The preeminence of Eros's guidance of the other gods in matters of *poíesis* sheds light—an erotic sort of light—on the otherwise partially concealed complicity that, as the elemental instance of genetic origin, links the fiery, muscular craft of Hephaestus to fire's masculine impregnation of the earth; or on the complicity that links the patient weaving craft of Athena, the founder of the Areopagus, to the feminine texture of persuasive debate and discursive veracity, dear to poets, jurists, and philosophers, and disliked by warriors and army leaders; or on the complicity that, as an essential condition of stable and durable statesmanship, links the political craft of Zeus to the political concern, which I alluded to earlier, for the sexual secret of proper procreation; or on the complicity that links the firm masculinity of Apollo's archery to the far-reaching implications of oracular vision (I am thinking of the myth of Cassandra in the *Iliad*); or, lastly, on the complicity that links the capricious femininity of Dionysus's revelries to the mystical agonies undergone by the Maenads. At first, the pairing up of music and eros, wherein the winged *daímon* plays the dominant role, may appear to be grounded upon a primordial dictate of gender opposition.

One might say that each of the major crafts related to musical madness, when it is both properly learned, that is, learned from the Muses, and properly practiced, that is, practiced under the same guidance that Eros provides to Apollo, Dionysus, Hephaestus, Athena, and Zeus, in the inception of their "inventions," turns out to be installed in the *tópos* wherein two different divine madnesses, the musical and the erotic, are enabled to fuse with each other. As Socrates declares in the *Republic,* musical matters are bound to end "in erotic matters concerning the beautiful" (403c). And one of the peaks of musical *poíesis,* as we saw, is encountered when the divinely inspired poet, enamored of beautiful imagery, composes a radiant image of the Good. From the carpenter to the poet, from the political ruler to the philosopher, all the musico-erotic artisans are intent upon the task of getting hold of a radiant image of the Good. It is upon this *tópos* of encounter between the two distinct madnesses of music and eros that I will need to keep my attention focused, in the search for the *lógos* appropriate to address the subject of political *stásis,* the subject, that is, of the faction of self-enclosed differentiation that plagues the *pólis.*

EROS, PROPHECY, AND MYSTICISM

There is a further difference, however, between, on the one hand, the *tópoi* where the couplets music/prophecy and music/mysticism undergo their fusion, and, on the other hand, the *tópos* where the couplet music/eroticism undergoes its fusion. Both prophecy and mysticism alternate, as we will see shortly, moments of *stásis* with moments of *pólemos;* and their bellicose character may be shown to prevail in the precarious, treacherous *tópoi* of their respective union with music. Erotic madness, instead, is inherently hospitable and nonconflictual.

Prophecy occurs when Apollo disrupts the trusting blindness, the self-possessed *stásis* of the "man wrapped in his individuality,"[25] by revealing his absorption in what Nietzsche, in *The Birth of Tragedy,* compares to Schopenhauer's *world of torment:* " . . . a stormy sea that, unbounded in all directions, raises and drops mountainous waves, howling . . ."[26] Coming in dreams and visions unhinged from the "incompletely intelligible everyday reality," this revelation extracts a disclosive sort of *pólemos* from *stásis* itself. Ultimately, the relief brought about by the exposure to the "higher truth" of his absorption in torment contributes to a further contraction of the static self of the man wrapped in his individuality; it elevates his inner peace, closer and closer to the divine repose, to the measured self-containment of that which Nietzsche calls the *principium individuationis;*[27] one might say that it turns him into the *Apollinian man* proper.

To the extent that Nietzsche engages the Apollinian kind of visionary or dreamy experience from a male-dominated viewpoint, his approach is only of partial help in defining the erotic—or, by all means, sexual—nature of Apollinian prophecy. When it comes to the gift/curse of the Apollinian visionary experience and its mythical connotations, the tradition of the ancients often contemplates the interplay and, as it were, the reciprocal struggle of both genders. Suffice it to recall, here, the figures of the prophetess Pytho, questioned by Oedipus,[28] of the sibyl of Cuma, questioned by Aeneas, of the double-gendered, androgynous Tiresias, questioned on our side of the Styx by Oedipus and on the opposite side by Odysseus, and lastly, of the supremely cursed Cassandra, the daughter of Troy's king, whom nobody cared to question at all. In the case of these feminine oracles, the *pólemos* of dissention and the *stásis* of self-containment clash harshly with each other; prophecy becomes, first of all, the *pólemos* of the sibyl's dissension against the Olympic, self-contained masculinity of the god. Prophecy leads the sibyl possessed, *invaded,* raped by Apollo, to tear out of the god's inaccessible omniscience the oracular *lógos,* the cryptic modulations by which her speaking-in-tongues *obscuris vera involv(it),* "envelops truth with darkness."[29] Typical, for instance, is the case of Deiphobe, the sibyl of Cuma, "the way Apollo / Pulled her raging, or else whipped her on, / Digging the spurs beneath her breasts."[30] The stubborn, strong-willed Cassandra, who teased the god into *coitus interruptus,* and was turned, therefore, into a dumb oracle, is instead the exception that confirms the norm of bellicose sexuality inherent in the gift of Apollinian prophecy (or should one venture, perhaps, even at the risk of a mild "essentialism," that Cassandra's aversion to love her sexual abuser signals a feminine sort of repugnance for unerotic mating?)

Mysticism, in turn, is defined by the Dionysian motifs of self-separation and musical dissonance.[31] It consists of the *pólemos* of individual fracture that leads the maenadic reveler to be drawn out of himself or herself and, at once, out of the *pólis* (with its deceitful images, with its impoverished *lógos*), so as to receive the frightful vision of his or her mystical union with that abyss that Nietzsche calls "primal ground" (*Birth of Tragedy* 65).

> You could have seen a single woman with bare hands
> Tear a fat calf, still bellowing with fright,
> In two, while others clawed the heifers to pieces.
> . . . And bulls, their raging fury gathered in their horns,
> Lowered their heads, stumbling
> To the earth, pulled down by hordes of women . . .

The Bacchae then returned . . .
By the springs Dionysus had made, and washed their hands
While the snakes licked away the drops of blood
That dabbled their cheeks.[32]

Dionysian mysticism pertains to a kind of Heraclitean human being who shares a certain affinity—partial and distorted, as we will see in a moment, nonetheless somewhat extraordinary—with the rare individual of whom Socrates says that it is "able to approach beauty itself and contemplate it in and by itself" (*Republic* 476b). In ascending to the vision of truth, the Dionysian mystic is drawn out of his or her senses by a musical frenzy, so that he or she sees the frightful truth of the Maenadic frenzy without the mediation of sensuous imagery. When *stásis* overcomes this polemical exceeding of the bodily sensual, when the musical echoes of the Dionysian abyss become inaudible, the mystic returns to the everyday life of the *pólis*, but is unable or unwilling to share in *lógos*—to bring forth in regular, even-tempered diction—the privileged, unsustainable vision (devoid of imagery) that was afforded him or her by the most dissonant music. Agave, the leader of the Bacchae and "fellow-huntswoman" of Dionysus,[33] comes back to her "senses," for example, as soon as she discerns the everyday implications of her visionary experience. And her voice is immediately *silenced;* she is exiled forever from Thebes. "I am in anguish now, / Tormented, who walked in triumph minutes past, / . . . And that prize I carried home, / With such pride was my own curse."[34] This scene is followed by the sentence of exile and Agave's despair: "Farewell, my home! City, farewell. / O bridal bed, banished I go, / In misery, I leave you now" (lines 1369–71).

Erotic Madness

Here is where Apollinian *stásis*, which is mainly informed by the visual/visionary generic attributes of the plastic arts,[35] and Dionysian *pólemos*, which is mainly informed by the musical dissonance pertinent to the tragic genre,[36] draw their lines of separation from erotic madness. It will be the primary task of the philosopher, who ascends to truth (not the same truth of the Apollinian oracle or the Dionysian mystic)[37] by stages, via the yoking together of sensuous imagery and noetic intellection (and who is capable, furthermore, of differentiating the beauty of truth from the beauty of its images),[38] to beget a beautiful creature of *lógos,* in memory of his contemplation of truth.[39] The truth of the Socratic philosopher is of a higher nature than the truth accessible to the prophet and to the mystic,[40] because the soul of the philosopher, the lover of wisdom, is, according to the *Phaedrus,* the most erotic, the one which "saw the most" of the Good, before attaching itself to a mortal body (248d–e).

The Apollinian and Dionysian madnesses are ultimately warlike, either withdrawn in inner strife or projected toward outer confrontation. They both draw the individual out of himself or herself, to become the receptacle of an inscrutable truth beyond the range of his or her intellection. The Apollinian prophecy operates mainly by implosion, the Dionysian mysticism by explosion with individual fragmentation; both are aimed up toward "laying hold" of the vision of truth, the "final secret" hinted at by Diotima in the *Symposium* (211a–b). These two polemical madnesses manage to ascend, mysteriously, to the "secret" revelation—a facet of it, that is—yet they do not convey this secret in political, poetic, or philosophical *lógos,* in the *lógos* of caring for the *pólis*—the *lógos,* in our particular case, that would enable one to address and heal the degeneration of the *pólis.*

Strictly speaking, erotic madness is concerned with the fabrication of all forms of life (life *as* mortal, as Becoming),[41] whereby all creatures are begotten and produced.[42] The craft of procreation is "Eros's own craft"; in the *Symposium,* the erotic being is defined as the begetter who/which loves to beget *upon* the beautiful, *upon,* one might say, the aphrodisiac of that which is lovable, of that which is in the "service of Aphrodite."[43] The erotic human being loves to beget "upon the beautiful by means of both the body and the soul." This definition of the erotic, which Diotima spells out for Socrates in the *Symposium,* presupposes gender separation yet, at once, *applies to both genders:* in the act of mating, both man and woman, driven by the same impulse, look for a beautiful partner to reproduce themselves (206e). Furthermore, I venture that the complementarity of the genders is indispensable in the Socratic discourse of procreation: if man's soul, "piloted" by thought ($\eta o \hat{u} s$) (*Phaedrus* 247c––d), can aim at unveiling, eventually, the celestial cycle of cosmic balance that dictates the right season for mating and procreation, woman's body *embodies,* in the periodic cycle of the menses, a figment of that very secret, namely, the figment, responsive to the "revolutions of the (body's) orbs," which relates to the "cycle of bearing and barrenness" (546a). Socrates' attempt, in the *Republic,* to grasp the secret of the "perfect number" of divine begetting[44] is echoed, in the *Timaeus,* by the analogous, monumental attempt undertaken by Timaeus, in response to Socrates' wish to envision the transition of his luxurious *pólis* from *stásis* into *pólemos* (18b–c). As I anticipated in the methodological premise to this chapter, all of Timaeus's monologue is an attempt at penetrating the celestial cycle of cosmic balance by means of a degenerate *lógos,* intermittently "true" (*alethès lógos,* 52c), "mythological and imaginal" (*eikóta mŷthon,* 29d), and "veritably opinionative" (*dóxa alethén,* 51d).

It is for me now to illustrate the hospitable, nonconflictual character of eros, and contrast it with the dual character—alternately static and polemic—of prophecy and mysticism, as well as with the dual character—again, alternately static and polemic—of the luxurious *pólis,* whose political degeneration, constantly oscillating between civil and outer war, Socrates is attempting to engage in *lógos.* And what better way to illustrate the character of eros than by addressing the very issue of "good" parental procreation, of "good" begetting—whose absence, whose impracticability, constitutes, together with endemic internal dissent, one of the principal causes of the static collapse of the *pólis.* As we saw, good parental procreation is erotic. It is an activity guided by a semi-god, a *daímon* (δαίμον), which stands "between the divine and the mortal," and is neither the former nor the latter. "Being midway between, [Eros] makes [the divine and the human] supplement each other, so that the whole is combined in one."[45] Eros, in sum, has the capacity to overturn the factiousness of the divine against the human— *Symposium* 202e: "God with man does not mingle"—into a yoking together of man and god, of mortal and immortal, of body and soul. However, one ought to refrain from an expeditious identification of the capacity that Diotima attributes to Eros with some kind of idealistic reconciliation or subordination of the opposites.

THE CRADLE OF EROS

In the Socratic discourse, Eros's capacity for yoking together that which metaphysics regiments in terms of opposition allows the transition of things that have no being—things, that, therefore, *are not,* hence, are impossible to conceive in thought or to apprehend in sensuous imagery—into being (*Symposium*

205b). Eros, in short, permits a reproductive behavior based upon an instance of degeneration; it allows two separate kinds, which are not supposed to mingle with each other, to do so—to mate, in sum—as the two begetting agencies of a new mortal being. To sum this up in an aphorism: As a degenerations of distinct *kinds,* erotic mating occurs in the cradle of Eros. In erotic mating, the immedicable opposition *stásis-pólemos* translates into a hospitable yoking together of static self-enclosedness and polemic outer conflict—which yoking together, as I intimated above, consists of neither idealistic reconciliation nor speculative subordination. As Socrates explains to Phaedrus in the *Symposium,* it is the erotic mortal

> who *casts alienation out, draws intimacy in;* . . . leader fairest and best, whom every one should follow, joining tunefully in the burthen of his song, wherewith he enchants the thought of every god and man. (197d, my emphasis)

Erotic behavior is made up of two succeeding impulses: first comes the eagerness to beget, and second comes the eager care of the offspring. In the *Symposium,* Diotima points out to Socrates:

> you must have observed the strange state into which all the animals are thrown . . . when they desire to beget: they are all sick and amorously disposed, first to have union one with another, and next to find food for the new born; in whose behalf they are ready to fight hard battles, even the weakest against the strongest, and to sacrifice their lives; to be racked by starvation themselves if they can but nurture the young . . . What is the cause of this amorous condition in the animals? Can you tell me? (207a–c)

Diotima is asking of Socrates: What does induce the human being to undergo the agonies of procreation and care of the offspring? In the *Symposium,* Diotima explains to Socrates that mortals are erotic begetters because they want to gain immortality. There is an ephemeral but undeniable kind of immortality in giving birth to a new human being; it does not consist of an immortality in being (this would be called "eternity"), but, rather, of an immortality in the becoming measured by cosmic time,[46] which immortality shares a certain affinity with the immortality of the gods created by the eternal *Demiourgòs* (δημιουργὸς [*Timaeus* 28a, 29a]). In Diotima's words, again:

> the mortal nature ever seeks, as best it can, to be immortal. In one way only can it succeed, and that is by generation; since so it can

always leave behind it a new creature in place of the old. It is only for a while that each live thing can be described as alive and the same, as a man is said to be the same person from childhood until he is advanced in years: yet though he is called the same ... he is continually becoming a new person, and there are things also which he loses, as appears by his hair, his flesh, his bones, and his blood and body altogether. ... Every mortal thing is preserved in this way; not by keeping it exactly the same for ever, like the divine, but by replacing what goes off or is antiquated with something fresh, in the semblance of the original. Through this device, Socrates, a mortal thing partakes of immortality ... So do not wonder if everything naturally values its own offshoot; since all are beset by this eagerness and this love with a view to immortality. (*Symposium* 207d–208c)

Hence, humans who beget are not the captives of the temporal horizon that their mortal body cannot escape. They evade this temporality in a paradoxical acquisition of immortality, in a radical, apolemical liquidation of the *stásis* of bodily self-inclusiveness, self-identity. The answer to Diotima's question, as to what factor would induce the human being to undergo the agonies of procreation and care for the offspring, is found in the immortality that procreation confers upon the begetter.

The rest of this discussion will be devoted to illustrating how the immortality acquired by the begetter through the act of procreation is pertinent to a crucial aspect of erotic filiation, that is, the hospitable degeneration of boundaries. The hospitable degeneration of boundaries will be shown to extend, in turn, from the dissolution of bodily self-identity experienced by the biological parent to the dissolution of logocentric subjectivity entailed by the discourse of political justice. In other words, my discussion will concern itself with the thesis that erotic filiation extends "Eros's own craft" beyond the realm of parental procreation, and into the erotic connotations pertaining to the three other *poíeses* that are the subject of my analysis; namely, poetry, statesmanship, and philosophy. To round off the chapter, I will refer to an alternative erotic tradition that originates approximately during the time of Plato, namely, the "Solomonic" Song of Songs, to suggest that the manifold sources of the Western tradition of erotic discourse share a similar convergence toward a political project of eroticization, of erotic dis-closure of the fortifications surrounding the city.

A terminological disclaimer is mandatory at this juncture, in view of the forthcoming discussion of philosophy as the excellent erotic *lógos*. It might appear, in fact, that when Socrates talks about love, he talks mostly about the *philía,* and about the *epithymía* (desire) of intellective affections, rather than about the eroticism of love.[47] The very etymology of the noun "philosopher" points toward love (of wisdom) as *philía,* not as eros. However, the two notions of *philía* and eros enjoy a dialectical coexistence in their Socratic engagement; their mutual hospitality is quite dissimilar to the clear-cut divergence that subsequent philosophical traditions have imposed upon them. In the *Phaedrus,* for instance, the discussion about the best men, into whose birth enters the soul that "has seen the most," enumerates four kinds of human being, two of which invest the object of their love with the *desire* proper of *philía,* namely, the *philosopher* and the *philokáloy* (lover of beauty), while the other two, i.e., the *moysikon* and the *erotikòn,* are, so to speak, erotically at one, in body and soul, with the object of their love (248d). And in the *Republic,* as John Sallis points out in *Being and Logos* (380–81), the discussion of the philosopher as a lover of wisdom repeatedly alternates love as *philía*—as in the examples of the "lovers of wine" (*philoínoys*) and the "lovers of honors" (*philotímoys*)—with love as eros (as in the two successive examples of the lover of boys, designated as *erotikòn* [474d, 475a]). At bottom, only a nebulous demarcation separates eros and *philía;* indeed, they will have to be made coexistent in the Socratic discussion of the erotic philosopher.

EROTIC FILIATION

To Socrates, the divine madness of eros is "the best one" (*Phaedrus* 265b). In fact, beyond the immortality of parental procreation, which partakes of the immortality of the gods, there is the immortality, among others, of poetic, political, and philosophical reproductions. The poet (the "good" poet who is not a member of the *mimetikòn tribes*), the political ruler (the ruler who is not after "his own advantage but that of the ruled ones" [*Republic* 347d]), and the philosopher (the philosopher who does not "roam from city to city" like the *sophistôn génos* [*Timaeus* 19e]) bring forth their "long-felt conception" according to different manners of delivery: the poet in the *poíesis* of the most radiant and beautiful kind of images, whose memory is "immortally renewed in the memory of men" (*Symposium* 209d), the statesman in the justice of his legislation, for which he receives honors such that no other man "ever obtained"

(209e), and the philosopher through a "consorting" with a lovable disciple, a student, among other things, of the "sobriety and justice" of πολιτεία (209a, c). Just as the truth achievable by the philosopher is the excellent one, so is the immortality allotted to the philosopher. I will even venture that the *immortality* allotted to the philosopher partakes, enigmatically—to a partial extent, to be determined—of the *eternity* of the Good. On the part of an embodied soul, to partake, however partially, of the eternity of the Good is a stupendous, exceptional achievement. It is also, of course, an instance of degeneration, of reciprocal contamination between two kinds of temporality so dramatically distinct from each other that one can hardly imagine their analogy, their proximity—one, (im)mortality, being the transient temporality of perpetual becoming, and the other, eternity, being the self-same changelessness of eternal being. How is this exceptional degeneration accomplished? How is it possible for it to be accomplished by an embodied soul, the captive of a mortal body? And, above all, can this degeneration, this dissolution of boundaries be addressed in a philosophical *lógos* true to the ascensional teleology inherent in the metaphorics of the "beautiful summit of the Good," or is it to be addressed, rather, in some other kind of *lógos,* perhaps one discursively engaged in trespassing the very logocentric demarcation between the immortal and the eternal—a *lógos* which, perhaps, at one and the same time abides by the norm of teleological ascension and challenges it? "But tell me," demands Diotima of Socrates:

> "what would happen if one of you had the fortune to look upon essential beauty entire, pure and unalloyed ... ? ... there only will it befall him, as he sees the beautiful through that which makes it visible, to breed not illusions but true examples of virtue ... So when he has begotten a true virtue and has reared it up he is destined to win the friendship of Heaven; he, above all men, is immortal." (*Symposium* 211e–12a)

Besides its power to guide and immortalize parental procreation within the horizon of Becoming, Eros has this ascensional capacity, then, which leads the embodied soul to ascend *by stages*—in contrast to the fulminating visions of prophetic oracle and mystical rapture—and as close as tolerable to its wingless, postlapsarian condition, until it "lay(s) hold of the final secret" of the Good (*Symposium* 211b). Before describing this excellent path to immortality traveled by the philosopher, though, I must further illustrate certain connotations of parental begetting, which Socrates leaves only implicit in his treatment of the subject; notwithstanding the purely physical character of the two parental deeds of begetting and caring for the offshoot, in fact, Socrates seems to intend the evasion from bodily mortality and self-identity authorized by one's erotic parentage as a motion toward one's growing intimacy with the Good—a kind of ascensional power somewhat analogous, obviously to a limited degree, to that of the philosopher's soul, and endowed, as we will see, of a curiously vicarious nature.

This special sort of "ascensional" parentage requires that mating be erotic. Only an erotic mating, in fact, engages in that cosmic harmony, described by Socrates in the *Phaedrus,* by which the begetting of a new body dovetails into the moment when a soul sheds its wings and "sinks down until it can fasten on something solid, and . . . takes to itself an earthly body." The soul is "the organ by which (the newborn will) learn," the source (αρχέ) of the affections, or receptivities (*pathémata*) that will enable his thought (ηοûs)."[48] More precisely, it will be through a *recollection* (ἀνάμνησισ) of what it glimpsed from the summit of the heavens that the soul of the newborn will be enabled to understand what *lógos,* through an act of reckoning *(λογισμῶ),* says (λεγόμενον) in accordance with the *eidē.* This act of reckoning, which collects many sensuous perceptions into the truth of their original *eidos,* is the discursive utterance, the *recollection* in speech, of that very glimpse of the *eidē* that the soul enjoyed briefly before shedding its wings and becoming embodied.[49]

It is through a complex interaction between its reckoning (or [re]collecting) capacities and its dialectical capacities that the soul of the newborn human ascends to the intellection of the truth of *lógos,* via a process of recollection of what it saw in its prelapsarian past. And the requirement that the conception of the newborn human occur in erotic mating appears as a *sine qua non conditio* of his capacity to recognize the truth of *lógos.* Not all souls are equal, in fact. Some have seen more than others before shedding their wings. Some may remember more and better than others. When the soul in search of a body has "seen the most," that is, has, however briefly, sojourned at "the summit of the arch that supports the heavens . . . look(ing) upon what is outside the heavens," the newborn human will be of good stock, either a *philósophos* (lover of wisdom), or a *philókalos* (lover of beauty), or a lover of music, or a lover *tout court* (*èrotikós*).[50] In sum, it is in erotic mating, I contend, that the parents of the newborn human establish a harmonic correspondence between the birth of their offspring and an optimal soul's "sink-ing down to earth." Besides immortalizing his or her own body through an apolemical liquidation of the *stásis* of bodily self-inclusiveness and self-identity, then, the parent of the newborn human of "good stock" enjoys, by the mediation of the ascen-sional power pertinent to the *lógos* of his or her offspring's soul, a certain vicarious intimacy, or, even, a certain genetic complic-ity, with the very spring of goodness and justice.

BEGETTING AND SUBJECTIVITY

As I suggested above, the immortality of the philosopher shares a certain enigmatic affinity with the eternity of the Good. "It is *just* that the mind of the philosopher only has wings," Socrates explains to Phaedrus, "for he is always, so far as he is able, in communion through memory with those things the communion with which causes God to be divine" (*Phaedrus* 249c, my emphasis). The philosopher's immortality is akin not so much to the bodily and mediated immortality of the parent, nor to the parent's vicarious intimacy with the Good, obtained via the ascensional power pertinent to the *lógos* of the offspring's soul, as, rather, to the immortality of his own soul. In the *Sym-posium,* Diotima identifies the progeny begotten by the philoso-pher with the fruit of his teaching of justice:

> what are those things (proper for soul to conceive and bring forth)? Prudence and virtue in general . . . Now by far the highest and fairest part of prudence is that which concerns the regulation of cities and habitations; it is called sobriety and justice. (209a–b)

Later on, the philosopher and the beautiful disciple upon whom this teaching was begotten will nurture and care for their impalpable progeny—in "a far fuller community with each other than that which comes with children, and a far surer friendship, since the children of their union are fairer and less mortal" (209c). One may indeed further qualify Diotima's declaration by designating the progeny of the philosopher as the best of politi-cal *lógoi,* the *lógos* of justice. It is at this point that a twofold dissolution of logocentric subjectivity occurs. Let me illustrate separately its two moments.

First, it occurs that the progeny of the philosopher becomes a part—a hybrid, paradoxical part—of the act of recollection by which the philosopher's disciple—and his disciple's disciple, his disciple's disciple's disciple, and so forth—will have been engaged in a *lógos* directed by thought (*noûs*). As we saw above, this act of recollection (*anámnesis*) is aimed at the memory of a place (*tópos*) visible only to thought, not to the senses; a place whose being—intangible and devoid of images, of the radiance proper to images—concerns human intellection in its highest configuration, that of *epistéme* (*epistēmē*) (*Phaedrus* 247c–d). If one recalls that, of all "existing things," only the soul "has the property of acquiring thought" (*Timaeus* 46d), one must realize that the progeny of the philosopher, as the *lógos* of justice, begotten in the philosopher's dialogue with his disciple, becomes, through the transmission of teaching and tradition, a hybrid, the most enigmatic part of the act of *anámnesis* through which the soul of the lover of learning will have been enabled to understand what *lógos* says about justice, what *lógos* says, or recollects in speech, in accordance with the *eidos* of justice. In short, the progeny of the philosopher is somewhat enigmatically sheltered *outside* the realm of sensible impressions, *beyond* "the summit of the arch that supports the heavens," in that very *tópos* where the soul of the disciple sojourned, however briefly, before shedding its wings. The *lógos* of justice delivered by the mortal philosopher disrupts the generic prerequisite of its separation, its externality, from what it talks about; it trespasses into the ineffable realm of the *lógos* that does not need to be carried by ephemeral sound or evanescent scripture; it undermines the metaphysical opposition between the harmonious conversation of the soul *at one with itself,* the effortless stream, in Gadamer's synopsis of Plato's *Cratylus,* "that flows (from) the dialogue of the soul with itself,"[51] and the laborious ascension accomplished by the erotic dialogue between two mortals. The soul's capacity to see all over again, and to recollect in *lógos,* the beauty of that which is beyond immortality, presupposes the condition that this vision be *double,* shared by the disciple, to whom is afforded by the master's maieutical *lógos,* and by the philosopher himself, who does *not* know, beforehand, what the dialogue with his disciple is going to beget. The double vision of this *lógos* presupposes the dissolution of logocentric subjectivity.

Second, there occurs a reversal of erotic status between the lovable disciple, upon whose beauty the philosopher/lover begets his *lógos* of justice, and the lover himself. I contend that, by making himself similar to the highest things by *homoíosis,*[52] the philosopher/lover becomes, paradoxically, the lovable one in the

eyes of his disciple. For the man who can discern beautiful images from the beautiful itself, love of the beautiful is a progressive climbing, says Diotima, away from the preeminence of the
bodily beautiful and toward the appreciation of the beauty of
the soul;[53] therefore, the turn comes for the erotic philosopher
to undergo a transformation, as his *lógos* makes him lovable,
aphrodisiac. Although in the *Republic* Socrates addresses Glaucon with the appellation of "erotic" (Glaucon, however, accepts
such an appellation only for the sake of conversation [474d,
475a]), it is easy to see how, by the end of their dialogue, it is
Socrates' soul that emerges as the genuinely erotic agency. The
fact is far from accidental, in fact, that Diotima, in the *Symposium,* warns Socrates with these words: "You supposed . . . that
the beloved and not the lover was Eros. This led you . . . to hold
that Eros is all beautiful. The lovable, indeed, is the truly beautiful, tender, perfect, and heaven-blest; but the lover is of a different type . . ." (204c).

The teaching of the philosopher/lover transforms the lovable
disciple into a lover of learning. As such, the disciple, eagerly
attending to his master's *lógos,* is enabled to gaze at the beauty
of the soul of his beloved master, through which shines—if one
can, at this stage of the argument, still pretend to adhere to the
metaphysical separation between image and original—beauty itself. Only one step is left for the disciple to take, so as to trade
places with his master and experience a reversal of erotic status.
This step, which consists of the recollection of that which the
disciple's soul once saw when it traveled in the company of the
gods, is conditional upon the reflection—again, if one may be
allowed, from now on, to "talk metaphysics" under the permanent banner of deconstructive erasure—that the shining beauty
of the master's soul finds in his disciple's own *lógos.* Therefore,
the lovable disciple, turned lover, turned indifferent to the aphrodisiac limitations of his master's body, feels the urge to beget
his own "long-felt conception" of justice upon the beautiful soul
of his master. Philosophy becomes, at last, the reciprocation of
lógoi between the master and the disciple, both of whom are
doubled into a lover and a loved one, into an erotic *daímon*
and a "heaven-blest" beauty. Philosophy becomes as reciprocal
as parental begetting, wherein, as we saw, each parent begets
upon the beauty of his or her complementary gender. Philosophy, in sum, is on its way toward becoming, at long last, *dialeges-
thai.*[54] The immortality of its begotten dialogue, incessantly
renewed in the *anámnesis* of future generations, is, to an ex-

tent, akin to the eternity of the Good; it is the immortality of
erotic filiation, which entails, as I said above, both the dissolution of bodily self-identity and of logocentric subjectivity; it is
the immortality of the dialectical *lógos,* as the hospitably sheltering conversation that brings the measure of eternity to bear
upon the finitude of individual speech.[55]

THE *LÓGOS* OF CIVIL WAR: HOMER VERSUS SOCRATES

The endless human history of *pólemos,* of war against the
diverse, the foreign, the "enemy," nurtures *stásis,* inner faction,
brotherly strife and, ultimately, fratricide, at its innermost core.
Under the majestic, indifferent *stásis* of Troy's walls, the rape
of two of its daughters, namely, Khryseis, daughter of the priest
of Apollo, now concubine of Agamemnon, and Briseis, daughter
of King Priam, now concubine of Achilles, brings about a brotherly diatribe within the camp of the Achaians. Unable or unwilling to designate the crisis with the unambiguous name of "civil
war," and to denounce as well its antierotic nature, Homer, inspired by Calliope, personifies the crisis in the mythic mask of
Apollo, the most skilled of archers, who disseminates death
among the divided, bitter troops. Homer, in sum, is not addressing *stásis* by means of the *lógos* that would help his listeners in warding off future symptoms of civic unrest and dispute.
Instead, he has recourse to the "vile" mimetic *lógos* (*Republic*
377e: κακως [adv.]: vilely)[56] that is drastically censored in book
10 of the *Republic,* and that the *Timaeus* labels as "little better
than children's tales" (23b). Homer is censured by Socrates because he does not seem capable of engaging his verses in the
lógos Socrates is conversing about in *Politeía:* a politico-
philosophical *lógos* of dialogic hospitality, of erotic reciprocity,
which cannot be uttered "within" a *pólis* that does not abdicate,
erotically, the separation from its "outside." Socrates's condemnation of Homer does not convey, hence, an unqualified indict-
ment of poetry *tout court,* but simply the advocation of a poetic
poíesis installed in the *tópos* wherein two different divine madnesses, the musical and the erotic, undergo a complete fusion
with each other—a poetic *poíesis* entrenched at the faultline
where the distinction of separate genres of discourse encounters
its degeneration, and where, furthermore, the roundedness and
closure of the rival idioms of political rhetoric are reversed into
a motion of erotic assimilation to the diverse.

DIALOGIC HOSPITALITY

In the economy of the Socratic quest for the degenerate *lógos* capable of addressing and, at once, warding off the static forces that disintegrate the *pólis* from the inside, philosophy becomes the *lógos* of political justice. It is not a matter of philosophy being intended as a superior form, or model, or genre of discourse, upon which the statesman is expected to formulate his political discourse as some sort of mimetic reproduction. It is not, either, a matter of the *eidos* of justice, intended as a privileged subject of philosophical discourse, taking over the *lógos* proper of political discourse. It is, rather, a matter of a *generic degeneration,* wherein the genre of philosophical dialogue, in its maieutic thrust, impregnates itself with care for the *pólis,* to such an extent that two distinct genres of discourse, the philosophical and the political, as well as their respective themes, or *eidē,* become indistinguishable—to such an extent that their very distinction bespeaks the idiom of injustice.

What we have been contemplating, thus far, is an erotic transformation of philosophy into a doubly hospitable *lógos,* the *lógos* of a conversation wherein the philosopher not only welcomes the intrusion of the disciple's discourse, but cultivates it, in the way one grows and shelters within one's own garden the seeds of exotic plants. The *dialogic* hospitality of this philosophical *lógos* entails, first of all, a stance of adaptation to the disturbance brought about by diversity, by alterity. Second, it entails a degenerate form of discursive self-dissention: faced with that very axiomatic of metaphysical nonopposition that Aristotle ascribed to Platonism, and according to which the master is not the same as the disciple, the listener is not the same as the speaker, and, more to the point, dialogic abortion (of the broad spectrum of political disorders, or "aberrations," discussed in the *Republic* [544b–45c]) is not the same as (or, in a more pertinent formulation, does not engender) begetting (of political justice), this Socratic *lógos* "degenerates" itself by means of a strategy of assimilation to the diverse. I am not talking, here, of the Roman strategy of politico-military assimilation of the diverse by means of polemical subordination, nor of the Hegelian strategy of philosophical assimilation of the opposite by means of logical sublation. I am talking, rather, of a politics of self-identity constituted, as John Sallis would have it, in the self's being different from itself.[57] I am talking of the political *lógos* that is uttered (or that might or ought to be uttered) within the *pólis*-without-walls—within, so to speak, the Babelian *pólis,* the two-headed Jerusalem, Belfast, Sarajevo—of our political actuality.

One cannot set aside, at this point, the logical question as to whether or not one can still talk of a *lógos* spoken "within" the *pólis,* when this *pólis* abdicates its separation from the "outside." One cannot set aside, in other words, the politico-philosophical issue of the tearing down of the walls surrounding the *pólis.*

FORTIFICATION AND FRATRICIDE

In my opinion, the city's wall is by far the best example of that primitive form of architecture which, according to Hegel, bears its meaning within itself. In the *Aesthetics,* Hegel talks of ancient architectures still inadequate to express the crucial separation between architectonic purpose and architectonic means, between the function of a building as enclosure and the significance of a building as symbol. This crucial separation, according to Hegel, will be sublated by the architectonic structure of the Greek temple. In John Sallis's illustration of Hegel's views:

> The (Greek) temple is made to serve the purpose of enclosing the statue of the god, bringing architecture to full realization at the very moment that it is submitted to a religious purpose external to it. (*Stone* 49)

Hegel's examination of the more primitive architectures, inadequate to provide enclosure for the spirit, refers, particularly, to those "monstrous column-like structures of stone" erected in ancient India, colossal phalluses that signified, in an easily recognizable, organic shape, that which they *were,* that is, symbols of fertility.[58] These columns were inseparable from their meaning, to the extent that their meaning *was* their function; they could not *house* anything alien from themselves (unless, of course, they symbolically housed the very absence of their specular opposite, the womb—an absence intolerable to the logic of procreation). One can immediately see that the contrast between the phallic column and the city's wall is radical. The very function of the city's wall, i.e., containment—containment as defensive separation, as differentiation, from an outside—is pertinent to the separation of purpose from means, to the difference between the provision of enclosure and that which enclosure is provided for, namely, the *pólis.* In its being self-enclosed, the *pólis* acquires its identity as a political, cultural, ethnic body, as, in the final analysis, a symbol of communal consanguinities. So, from a speculative viewpoint, the city's wall comes, logically, later than the phallic column. And yet, I venture that, notwithstanding the city wall's pragmatic functionality, its function, just as in the case of the Indian phallic column, is hardly dissociable from its meaning. In a time of peace, for instance, the city's wall *means,* to the citizens it contains and protects, exactly that separation from the diverse that it warrants; at peace, the city's wall is the only reminder, the only tangible symbol, in the eyes of the citizens, of their city's difference from the foreign, the *other* city. One might even contend that, to a certain extent, in the absence of an enemy the city's wall generates the need for one. And at war, as one learns from the opening scenes of the *Iliad,* the wall—or, in the case of the Achaian camp, the fortification—becomes the symbolic *locus* of the precarious balance between war and civil war, between the absolute exclusion of diversity and the absolute contraction of self-identity.

More particularly, one side of the wall, the inner, sheltering side, signifies *and* makes operative the self-constricting sterility of inner *stásis,* of fratricidal strife, of incestuous practices, while the opposite side of the wall, the outer, excluding one, signifies *and* makes operative the formidable opposition of *pólemos,* of the external invasion of or from what is diverse, what is foreign. Contrasted with the gender-segregated eroticism of the giant phallic column (which column, at times, one finds *sheltered,* by the way, within the very city's boundaries), the city's wall suffers from a crucial disadvantage—a dysfunctional disadvantage, I should venture, provided that a metaphorics can accommodate at all a positive or negative notion of functionality—which consists in this, that the city's wall is less conducive of that eros of filiation that is, to a certain, admittedly superficial extent, immanently and intrinsically signified by the very stony, inert stance of the phallic column.

It is perhaps worth recalling here that it is outside of the walls of Athens that Socrates carries on the discourse on eros and recollection of the *Phaedrus* discussed earlier. Also, it must not be regarded as merely accidental that the entirety of the *Republic* presents itself as the Socratic recollection of colloquia occurring in the course of Socrates' promenade "down to Piraeus," the harbor of Athens (327a), and back to the city. As John Sallis points out in *Being and Logos,* there is a deliberate ambiguity in Socrates' walking to and from between Athens and its harbor; Piraeus, which was "about six miles from (Athens) and connected to it by long walls," is not, strictly speaking, *within* the city, yet it "remains most likely within (the city's) walls" (314).

FORTIFICATION AND EROS IN THE BIBLE

As I promised, I will now round off my arguments with a major generic switch, away from the legacy of the Platonic dialogue and into a roughly contemporary tradition, that of the "Solomonic" poetry from the Old Testament, to suggest that a certain convergence may be found between these two distinct ancient traditions, when it comes to the antagonistic logics of Eros and of opposition to the diverse, and especially when the enclosures of the singular body and of the communal body become a reciprocal mirror, the trope of each other. I am referring, specifically, to the Song of Songs, where we read that the Shulamite virgin, with "fingers dripping myrrh," keeps her door open for her lover, and then she wanders through the city, looking for her elusive lover, until her search is obstructed by the merciless "guardians of the walls" (5:2–8).[59] In remaining open yet virginal, liquefied like an overflowing yet untasted "bag of myrrh" (1:13), the erotic "door" of the Shulamite virgin may be taken to figure, in its suspension of erotic fulfillment,[60] a "feminine" refusal of closure, a "feminine" refusal, at once, of the blockage of fortification and of the submission to alien penetration; hence, the "door" of the virgin may be taken to challenge, figuratively speaking, that very spurious, gender-segregated hospitality I briefly alluded to above, offered by the masculine order of fortification of the *pólis* to the masculine symbol of the phallic column.

The Shulamite virgin is proud, it would seem, of her inability to guard the vineyard that her brothers—obsessed, just as the keepers of the walls, about closure and preservation—have made her the keeper of. The question her brothers ask themselves, as to how they may best preserve the purity of their sister, is a question about enclosure that dictates the polemical closure of an answer. "What shall we do for our sister / When she is spoken for?" they wonder. And then, in the idiom of *pólemos,* they find their predictable solution, whose incestuous overtones Ilana Pardes has perceptively stressed in *Countertraditions in the*

Bible (140–41): "If she be a wall, / We will build upon it a silver *battlement;* / If she be a door, / We will panel it in cedar" (my emphasis). To which defensive, asphyxiating (en)closure, the sister, who is all but a wall, as we saw—or is, to say the least, a wall disseminated of erogenous orifices, of unguarded gates—opposes the alternative of a *hardly imaginable* erotic fortification, vulnerable yet impregnable, radically divergent from the *stásis* of isolation: "I *am* a wall," she declares. "My breasts are like towers" (8:8–10, my emphasis). Fragrant "of all the powders of the merchants," she will lie down in Solomon's couch, "encircled by sixty warriors / . . . Each with sword on thigh . . . (3:6–8).

The oneiric elusiveness of this text entails a lack of (chrono)logical progression that fully justifies, in my opinion, the ironic appending of a narrative effect, namely, the virgin's coming to rest in a royal bedroom crowded with robust young men, to a narrative cause, namely, the girl's bellicose vindication of her erotic independence, which follows the effect by several chapters, or stanzas. By the same token, it is a matter of oneiric elusiveness if this much-praised text displays a kaleidoscopic fecundity of meanings transcendent of historical and cultural boundaries:[61] just as Thomas Aquinas reads in the erotic virgin of the Song of Songs the prefiguration of the charitable virgin of the Gospel, the bride who can be married only to her divine son,[62] so one might read in the Shulamite virgin a descendant of Polydore and Polymele, the two virgin mothers who, loved by gods, give birth to two of Achilles' lieutenants in the *Iliad*.[63] The kaleidoscopic fecundity of the Song of Songs goes hand in hand with its harsh poetry of resistance: on the one hand, an adamant resistance against violence, intolerance, segregation, on the other hand, a chaste chant in glorification of eros and desire, two thematic strains remarkably attuned to the order of procreation and degeneration inherent in Plato's *Republic*.

Afterword

THE ORDER OF GENEALOGY IS HARDLY IMAGINABLE OUTSIDE OF MAT-
rimony, a custom, rite, institution, at times a sacrament, whose
very etymology sprouts from a ground of exclusion and discrimination: matrimony as the dowry, endowment, or estate that the
woman brings to the patrimony of her husband. The trope of
the genealogical tree pushes its roots deep into this ground. Yet,
we saw how traces of rebellion against the androlineal paradigms
of genealogical legitimacy may be found in the canonical texts
of the Western tradition, such as the Old and New Testament,
or Plato's dialogues. In a study of the traditional agencies of
lineage, succession, and inheritance from the perspective of religious and legal culture, this book has contended that the Greek-
Judeo-Christian tradition of androlineal descent played a central
role in the definition of the moral standards of human civilization. This thesis was explored in several of its corollaries, and
especially in the four separate presumptions that: (1) the prehistory of modern civil right is an emanation of the religious primacy of the father, the patriarch, or the *paterfamilias;* (2)
genealogical chronicles often perform the function of etiological
tales; (3) dynastic primacy figures as the primary factor in the
understanding of nationalistic expansionism among the ancients; (4) the separation between fact and sense, phenomenon
and text, nature and history, is best understood in the light
of the gap that separates consanguinity from genealogical
legitimacy.

These four presumptions pertain to different orders of discourse, from the legal to the genetic, from the political to the
philosophical, but they are all pertinent to a more profound
comprehension of the dysfunctions and misregulations of our
modern world, be these dysfunctions those of a family unit in
progressive disintegration and redefinition, or those of a Western world increasingly afflicted by war and civil war. And they
are all intended as demonstrations of the efficacy of the alliance
of law and religion, when it comes to that middle ground of
critical discourse that separates the rarefied sphere of philo-

sophical abstraction from the pragmatic sphere of social reform. This is a veritable minefield for both theorists and political operators, the former disinclined, more often than not, to put their ideas to the unmediated test of "reality," the latter unequipped, in most cases, to supply rigorous justifications for their practical interventions on the same "reality." But this minefield may be turned into a gold mine when the right conceptual and analytical apparatus is provided.

As a scholar of literary theory, I carry the bulky luggage of a previous training and professional experience in the empirical field of the social sciences. What started me on the project of this book was a dissatisfaction with theorists and scientists alike. On the one hand, I think that the philosophical reduction of the separation between textual, aesthetic, and physiologic reproduction to a matter of tropical discourse and etymological nuance is socially irresponsible. On the other hand, I consider irrelevant at best the pragmatism of empiric, ad hoc solutions to the immense array of problems affecting the evolution of modern family. I am appalled, furthermore, by those medical establishments that reduce human conception and procreation to a *fait accompli* of brute nature, wherein genetic science, in league with ignorance and superstition, permits all sorts of repugnant experimentations, from lab-cultured human clones to womb-gestated septuplets.

The conceptual and analytical apparatus I have presented in this book is not, however, the predictable one, coming from a literary critic previously engaged in the social sciences. In spite of myself, I had to discard the conventional alliances of law and literature, or literature and economics, in favor of a more eccentric alliance: Law and Religion. My adoption of these two important bedfellows as my privileged fields of study was not aimed, as is mostly the case with the pairs "law and literature" and "literature and economics," at the dual cross-breeding approach, whereby a student of law or economics brings to the field of his expertise certain insights derived from the legal or economic aspects of literary texts. Rather, my "law and religion" approach was aimed at a more complex cluster of cross-breedings. If, conventionally speaking, theology and jurisprudence provide the conceptual apparatus, and procreation and genealogy the thematic subject of my interpretation, the end result is a quadrangular setting of reciprocal deconstructions. Law and Religion, Procreation and Genealogy: a quadrangular matrix wherein each pole of investigation is redefined by its organic correlation with the inner logic of the other three.

As I mentioned in the preface, I was determined to situate the present study in the middle ground between the abstract level of theoretical understanding and the concrete level of social praxis, between, in other words, the idealities of philosophy, theology, jurisprudence, and the contingencies (and gender-related iniquities) of institutional ideologies, religious creeds, and family rights. In the composition of this book, what was primarily at issue and at stake for me was neither the solution to the ontological dilemma as to whether *genos* comes before or after *lógos,* nor the prescription of a legal normative for the arbitration of reproductive rights; a different conceptual and analytical apparatus would be required for either one of these two propositions. Rather, my purpose was to provide, as the indispensable foundation to both sets of problems, a novel comprehension of the convoluted history of procreation and genealogy in Western literature, philosophy, law, and religion— a comprehension that could be warranted only by a radical critique of our traditional views of family and parenthood.

Notes

In citing works in the notes, short titles have occasionally been used. Works frequently cited have been identified by the following abbreviations:

CI2	Giambattista Vico. *De constantia iurisprudentis. Pars posterior: De constantia philologiae.* Italian translation by Sandro Barbera. In Vico, *Opere giuridiche.* Edited by Paolo Cristofolini. Firenze: Sansoni, 1974.
FW	James Joyce. *Finnegans Wake.* New York: Penguin, 1976.
Glas a	Jacques Derrida. *Glas.* Paris: Galilée, 1974 (left column).
PhilR	Hegel. *Philosophy of Right.* Translated by T. M. Knox. Oxford: Oxford University Press, 1967.
Portrait	James Joyce. *A Portrait of the Artist as a Young Man.* New York: Penguin, 1976.
Sarna/Genesis	Nahum M. Sarna. *The JPS Torah Commentary: Genesis.* Philadelphia: Jewish Publication Society, 1989.
SNS1	Giambattista Vico. *La scienza nuova seconda* (1744). Vol. 1. Bari: Laterza, 1942.
SNS2	Giambattista Vico. *La scienza nuova seconda* (1744). Vol. 2. Bari: Laterza, 1942.
Speiser/Genesis	Genesis: The Anchor Bible. Translation and Comments by E. A. Speiser. New York: Doubleday, 1964.
U	James Joyce. *Ulysses.* Edited by Hans Walter Gabler. New York: Vintage, 1986.
UIPF	Giambattista Vico. *De universi iuris uno principio et fine uno. Liber unus.* Italian translation by Carlo Sarchi. In Vico, *Opere giuridiche.*

PREFACE

1. Jacques Derrida, *Introduction,* in Edmund Husserl, *L'origine de la géometrie,* trans. J. Derrida (Paris: Presses Universitaires de France, 1962); Derrida, *Glas* (Paris: Galilée, 1974).

2. Jacques Derrida, "*Force de loi: Le fondement mystique de l'autorité,*" in Cardozo Law Review, 11, no. 5–6: 919–1046.

3. Gian Balsamo, *Rachele accucciata sugli dei: Il Fallo e la Legge* (Roma: Vascello, 1993).

CHAPTER 1: PRUNING THE GENEALOGICAL TREE

1. See Michel Foucault, *Les mots et les choses* (Paris: Gallimard, 1966), chap. 2, especially 40–45.

2. See Jacques Derrida, *Ulysse gramophone: Deux mots pour Joyce* (Paris: Galilée, 1987), 62, 65, 95. The translations from the first and second section are mine, often adapted, respectively, from Derrida, "Two Words for Joyce," trans. Geoff Bennington, in Derek Attridge and Daniel Ferrer, eds., *Poststructuralist Joyce* (Cambridge: Cambridge University Press, 1984): 145–59, and from "Ulysses Gramophone: Hear Say Yes in Joyce," trans. Tina Kendall (with Shari Benstock), in Derrida, *Acts of Literature,* ed. Derek Attridge (New York: Routledge, 1992): 253–309.

3. See James Joyce, *Letters* of James Joyce, vol. 2, ed. Richard Ellmann (New York: Viking Press, 1966), 106.

4. This parody of homecoming, which Mr Bloom pictures to himself in the Cabman's Shelter, echoes Stephen's depiction of Shakespeare's homecoming at the end of his career. See the "Scylla and Charybdis" episode, especially *U* 9.997–1052.

5. See Jacques Derrida, *Mémoires d'aveugle: L'autoportrait et autres ruines* (Paris: Ministère de la Culture) 39, 44. I have adapted the translation from Derrida, *Memoirs of the Blind,* trans. Pascale-Anne Brault and Michael Naas (Chicago: University of Chicago Press, 1993).

6. Homer, *The Odyssey,* trans. A. T. Murray, Loeb Classical Library (Cambridge: Harvard University Press, 1995), 1:214–20. I have borrowed from Robert Fagles's translation to modify Murray's rendering of Telemachus's answer to Athena. See Robert Fagles, ed. *The Odyssey* (New York: Viking, 1996), 1:250–51.

7. Derrida, *Ulysse gramophone,* 95.

8. See Morris Beja, *James Joyce: A Literary Life* (Columbus: Ohio State University Press, 1992), 1.

9. In *My Brother's Keeper,* Stanislaus Joyce explains that at first two floats were needed to carry the family's furniture and belongings, but in time, as the furnishings kept drifting toward the pawnbroker's shop, one float was enough. Cited in Richard Ellmann, *James Joyce* (Oxford: Oxford University Press, 1983), 69.

10. Ibid.

11. Ibid., 637–38; see also Beja, *James Joyce,* 110.

12. See Derrida, *Ulysse gramophone,* 113–15.

13. Ibid., 62.

14. Jacques Derrida, *Circonfession* 86–88, 93, in Geoffrey Bennington et Jacques Derrida, *Jacques Derrida* (Paris: Seuil, 1991), 7–291. The translations are mine, often adapted from *Circumfession,* in G. Bennington and J. Derrida, *Jacques Derrida,* trans. G. Bennington (Chicago: University of Chicago Press, 1993).

15. Ibid., 72.

16. See "Curriculum Vitae," in G. Bennington et J. Derrida, *Jacques Derrida,* 299–300.

17. See Deborah L. Madsen, *Rereading Allegory: A Narrative Approach to Genre* (New York: St. Martin's Press, 1994), 17–22.

18. For the concept of "generic dominant," see Hans Robert Jauss, *Toward an Aesthetic of Reception,* trans. Timothy Bahti (Minneapolis: University of Minnesota Press, 1982), 81.

19. Regina M. Schwartz, *The Curse of Cain: The Violent Legacy of Monotheism* (Chicago: University of Chicago Press, 1997).

20. See Richard A. Posner, *Law and Literature: A Misunderstood Relation* (Cambridge: Harvard University Press, 1988), 229, 240.

21. See H. L. A. Hart, *The Concept of Law* (Oxford, 1962), 93.

22. Henry Sumner Maine, *Ancient Law: Its Connection with the Early History of Society, and Its Relation to Modern Ideas* (New York: Scribner, 1864), 25.

23. See Drucilla Cornell, *The Philosophy of the Limit* (New York: Routledge, 1992), 106–7.

24. See also Lon L. Fuller, *Legal Fictions* (Stanford: Stanford University Press, 1967), 6–7.

25. Parenthetical and endnote references to Giambattista Vico's works are indicated by the abbreviations cited earlier. The English translations from Vico's Latin texts are mine, often adapted from Sarchi's and Barbera's Italian translations.

CHAPTER 2: THE GIFT OF LIFE

1. Genesis, in TANAKH (Philadelphia: Jewish Publication Society, 1985), 3–84.

2. Gena Corea, *The Mother Machine* (London: The Women Press, 1988), 260.

3. The "documentary hypothesis" identifies the scribes who composed the most ancient layers of Torah with the capital letter J, which stands for the unpronounceable name of God adopted by this group of writers. The other groups of scribes responsible for the composition of Torah are identified as E (from their usage of Elohim as the name of God), as P (from the Priestly scribes who wrote most of Leviticus), as D (from Deuteronomy, the title of these scribes' contribution to Torah), and as R (from the Redactors who executed the final revision of Torah after the Babylonian exile).

4. See Nancy Jay, *Throughout Your Generations Forever: Sacrifice, Religion, and Paternity* (Chicago: University of Chicago Press, 1992), 96.

5. See Mieke Bal, *Lethal Love: Feminist Literary Interpretations of Biblical Love Stories* (Bloomington: Indiana University Press, 1987), 128.

6. See the treatment of this subject in Ilana Pardes, *Countertraditions in the Bible: A Feminist Approach* (Cambridge: Harvard University Press, 1992), 40–43, 63–65.

7. See Genesis, 4:1, 29:32, 30:24.

8. Jay, *Throughout Your Generations Forever,* 109.

9. See Genesis, 17:5, 31:29.

10. See Jay, *Throughout Your Generations Forever,* 108.

11. Pardes, *Countertraditions in the Bible,* 41.

12. It is interesting that the norm of primogeniture is perpetually violated by the biblical patriarchs in favor of the younger offspring.

13. Jorge Luis Borges, "The Circular Ruins," trans. James E. Irby, in J. L. Borges, *Labyrinths* (New York: New Directions, 1964): 45–49.

14. Ibid., 50.

15. Ibid., 49.

16. Jorge Luis Borges, "The Garden of Forking Paths," trans. Donald A. Yates, in Borges, *Labyrinths,* 27.

17. *Felix culpa* is to be intended here as the original sin that already posits, in the myth of the Edenic fall, the conflict of the genders.

18. I interpret the word "louthly" as a composite pun on the words "lout" and "Lough." The waters of Lough Neagh were attributed petrifying properties in Ireland. See Roland McHugh, *Annotations to Finnegans Wake* (Baltimore: Johns Hopkins University Press, 1991), 23.

19. *Cache-cache* is hide-and-seek in French. Furthermore, the contiguity of "yew" and "cash cash" is also evocative of the customary Christmas kiss under the yew, mistletoe, or holly.

20. Borges, "The Circular Ruins," 48.

21. Ibid., 45, my emphasis.

22. Michel Foucault, *La volonté de savoir* (Paris: Gallimard, 1976), 193–95.

23. Plato, *Timaeus,* trans. R. G. Bury, Loeb Classical Library, 9 (Cambridge: Harvard University Press, 1989), 49b–d. Translations adapted.

24. Borges, "The Circular Ruins," 48.

25. Jaime Alezraki, *Borges and the Kabbalah* (Cambridge: Cambridge University Press, 1988), 50.

26. Ibid., 49.

27. See Plato, *Timaeus,* 31b.

28. See Friedrich Nietzsche, *Philosophy in the Tragic Age of the Greeks,* trans. Marianne Cowan (Washington: Gateway, 1987), 38, 41.

29. Thomas Altizer remarks that although the motif of the self-sacrifice of God is only "indirectly and ironically present in Christian Scripture, [it is] directly and immediately present in the Eucharistic liturgy, revolving about the breaking of the Host and Victim who is God Himself." See Thomas J. J. Altizer, *History as Apocalypse* (Albany: State University of New York Press, 1985), 240.

30. In this regard, an emblematic example can be derived from the genopolitics of procreation that in the *Republic* Socrates attributes to the Guardians of the luxurious *pólis.*

CHAPTER 3: POETIC CREATIVITY AND MATERNAL FECUNDITY

1. See Robert Adams Day, "How Stephen Wrote His Vampire Poem," *JJQ* 17, no. 2 (winter 1980): 186.

2. See John Gordon, "Notes in Response to Michael Seidel's '*Ulysses*' Black Panther Vampire,'" *JJQ* 15, no. 3 (spring 1978): 230; Robert Adams Day, "How Stephen Wrote His Vampire Poem," 188; Vincent J. Cheng, "Stephen Dedalus and the Black Panther Vampire," *JJQ* 24, no. 2 (winter 1987): 164.

3. Stephen's attraction toward incest and necrophilia has been scrutinized by Ralph Jenkins in "Theosophy in 'Scylla and Charybdis,'" *MFS* 15, no. 1 (spring 1969): 35–48.

4. Walter Pater, *The Renaissance: Studies in Art and Poetry* (London: Macmillan, 1877), 135.

5. See Tibor Wlassics, "Nota su Dante nell'*Ulisse*," *Rivista di letterature moderne e comparate,* 24, f. 2 (Giugno 1971): 152.

6. The last stanza of the song reads: "And my love came behind me— / He came from the South; / His breast to my bosom, / His mouth to my mouth." See Douglas Hyde, ed. and trans., *The Love Songs of Connacht* (Irish University Press, 1971), 21.

7. Robert Adams Day, "How Stephen Wrote His Vampire Poem," 186.

8. Ibid.

9. Ibid., 187.

10. Thomas J. J. Altizer, *Genesis and Apocalypse: A Theological Voyage Toward Authentic Christianity* (Louisville: Westminster/John Knox Press, 1990), 168.

11. Stuart Gilbert, *James Joyce's Ulysses* (New York: Vintage, 1955), 132.

12. Ibid.

13. See David Hayman, *Joyce et Mallarmé*, 2 vols. (Paris: Lettres Modernes, 1956), 1:26.

14. Hayman, *Joyce et Mallarmé*, 2:47 (footnote). My translation and my emphasis.

15. Stéphane Mallarmé, *Oeuvres Complètes*, ed. Carl Paul Barbier and Charles Gordon Millan (Paris: Flammarion, 1983), 192.

16. "I bring you the child of an Idumaean night! / Black, and with bleeding wings, featherless and pale, / Through the windows burnished with incense and gold, / Through the rimed panes mournful, alas, from the cold, / Dawn leaped upon the angelic lamp, / Palms! and when she had offered this relic / To this father trying out a hostile smile, / The sterile and blue solitude shivered. / O mother, cradling your daughter and in the innocence / Of your cold feet, welcome a horrible birth: / And your voice soft like a viol and a harpsichord, / Will you press your faded finger against your breast, / From which in sibylline whiteness woman flows / For lips starved by the air of the virginal azure." See Stéphane Mallarmé, *Collected Poems*, trans. Henry Weinfield (Berkeley: University of California Press, 1994), 24. The present, modified version of Henry Weinfield's translation privileges lexical accuracy at the expense of rhyme and meter.

17. Usually critics relate Stephen's "wet sign" to Horatio's appellation of the moon as the "moist star," in Shakespeare's *Hamlet* (1.1.118), as well as to the "watery star" of Shakespeare's *The Winter's Tale* (1.2.1). See Weldon Thornton, *Allusions in Ulysses* (Chapel Hill: University of North Carolina Press, 1987), 62.

18. Derrida writes that "Idumaea, the land of the Edomites [descendants of Esau], would be the pre-Adamic kingdom: Before Esau was replaced by Jacob, who received his blind father's blessing, the kings of Idumaea were supposed to reproduce themselves without sex and without women." See Jacques Derrida, *Given Time: I. Counterfeit Money*, trans. Peggy Kamuf (Chicago: University of Chicago Press, 1992), 59. I have modified the translation slightly.

19. See, for instance, Pater, *The Renaissance*, 77.

20. Virgil, *Aeneis* (Torino: Einaudi, 1989), 6.74–75.

21. See Mallarmé, *Brise marine, Oeuvres Complètes*, 176, line 7.

22. See Mallarmé, *Oeuvres Complètes*, 193.

23. Ibid., 177.

24. Ibid., 193. My translation.

25. Ibid., 177, 193.

26. See Hayman, *Joyce et Mallarmé*, 36–37.

27. Mallarmé, *Oeuvres Complètes*, 176. "The flesh is sad, alas, and I've read all the books! / To take flight, far off! I sense that somewhere the birds / Are drunk to be amid strange waves and skies!" See Mallarmé, *Collected Poems*, 21. I have modified Weinfield's translation.

28. Ibid., 177.

29. This phrase corresponds to line 11 of Yeats's "Who Goes with Fergus": "And the white breast of the dim sea." See Don Gifford, *Ulysses Annotated* (Berkeley: University of California Press, 1988), 18.

30. Adams Day, "How Stephen Wrote His Vampire Poem," 186.

31. William Blake, *Complete Writings,* ed. Geoffrey Keynes (London: Oxford University Press, 1967), 749, my emphasis.

32. Mallarmé, *Oeuvres Complètes,* 195.

33. Mallarmé, *Don du poème,* line 11.

34. To the rhyming pair from "The Everlasting Gospel," cited above, one must add the pair from "The Gates of Paradise," cited by Stuart Gilbert in *James Joyce's Ulysses:* "Thou'rt my Mother from the Womb, / Wife, Sister, Daughter, to the Tomb" (133). See Blake, *Complete Writings,* 771.

35. Altizer, *History as Apocalypse,* 236–37. A description of the theological implications of Blake's epics of the death of God may be found in the chapter, "Blake and the French Revolution" (175–208). A further articulation of this subject is presented in Altizer's *Genesis and Apocalypse* (161–73).

36. See Altizer, *Genesis and Apocalypse,* 163–64.

37. Blake, *Complete Writings,* 347.

38. See Altizer, *History and Apocalypse,* 240.

39. Ibid., 247.

40. Adams Day, "How Stephen Wrote His Vampire Poem," 184, 186.

41. Tibor Wlassics argues persuasively that the subject of this sentence is Dante. See Tibor Wlassics, "Nota su Dante nell'*Ulisse*," 153–54. To Wlassics's considerations, it may be added that the fragment "three by three" is probably "lifted" from *Purgatorio* 29. Beatrice's triumphal chariot advances along the trace of seven rainbows (not seven strings of distinct colors, as it is often assumed). The wheels of the chariot run above the central rainbow, *tra la mezzana e le tre e tre liste;* three of the rainbows are on the left of the chariot and three on the right. See Carlo Grabher, ed., *Purgatorio* di Dante (Bari: Laterza, 1964), 29.110.

42. Stephen read about the fecundating powers of the westwind in Virgil (see *U* 14.244), but the credence that the westwind, "Zephyros," as well as the northwind, "Boreas," had the ability to impregnate mares, "in the likeness of a black-maned stallion," is already mentioned in Homer's *Iliad.* See Homer, *The Iliad,* trans. Robert Fitzgerald (New York: Anchor, 1975), 16, p. 382, and 20, p. 480 (individual verses are not numbered in Fitzgerald's translation of the *Iliad.*) For individual lines, see M. M. Willcock, ed., *The Iliad of Homer* (New York: St. Martin Press, 1984), 16:150 and 20:225.

43. See Robert Pinsky, trans., *The Inferno by Dante* (New York: Noonday, 1996), 5:86–87. (In the specific context of Stephen's evocation of Dantesque verses in "Aeolus," the diction of Pinsky's translation is too bland, in my opinion. An alternative rendering of *Inferno* 5.96, which I have adopted in chapter 5, could be: "while the *wind,* as it now happens, *shuts up.*") In "Aeolus," line 721, Joyce cites *Inferno* 5.96 in the variant, *"Mentre che il vento, come fa, si tace."* Joyce derived this variant (from the conventional " . . . *ci tace*") from the edition of the *Commedia* he acquired in Trieste, edited by E. Camerini and printed by Sonzogno (Milano). (Apropos, see Mary. T. Reynolds, "Joyce's Editions of Dante," *JJQ* 15, no. 4 [summer 1978]: 380–82.) The variant *si tace* belongs to a "very valid tradition," defended by Antonino Pagliaro in *Il Canto V dell'Inferno.* (See Giorgio Petrocchi, ed., *La Commedia secondo l'antica vulgata* di Dante Alighieri, vol.2, *Inferno* [Milano: Mondadori, 1966], note to canto

5:96.) However, the tradition in favor of the variant *si tace* is contested by a plethora of specialists. A good treatment of the issue is found in two essays by Michele Barbi, in *Problemi di critica dantesca,* Prima serie, 1893–1918 (Firenze, 1934), 263, and in *La nuova filologia e l'edizione dei nostri scrittori da Dante al Manzoni* (Firenze, 1938), 26. See also Charles S. Singleton, *The Divine Comedy of Dante Alighieri, Inferno, Commentary,* 83.

44. See Wlassics, "Nota su Dante nell'*Ulisse*," 153.

45. Robert Adams Day, "How Stephen Wrote His Vampire Poem," 187.

46. Ibid.

47. Jean-Luc Marion, *God Without Being* (Chicago: University of Chicago Press, 1991), 76, 80.

48. Altizer, *Genesis and Apocalypse,* 168.

49. Altizer, *History as Apocalypse,* 125.

50. See Charles S. Singleton, *The Divine Comedy of Dante Alighieri, Purgatorio, Commentary* (Princeton: Princeton University Press, 1973), 734.

51. Altizer, *History as Apocalypse,* 125.

52. Dante Alighieri, *Vita Nuova* (Milano: EDIS, 1995), 2.3, 3.4, 39.1.

53. Pater, *The Renaissance,* 92–93.

54. Emmanuel Levinas, *Le Temps et l'Autre* (Paris: Quadrige, 1979), pt. 4, especially 77–84.

55. Altizer, *History as Apocalypse,* 126, my emphasis.

56. "Look now upon the face which most resembles Christ, for only its brightness can prepare you to see Christ." See the prose translation in Charles S. Singleton, ed. and trans., *The Divine Comedy of Dante Alighieri, Paradiso* (Princeton: Princeton University Press, 1991), 365.

57. Altizer, *History as Apocalypse,* 127.

58. In his prose translation, Singleton renders *fulgore* with "flash." This choice is not completely accurate, insomuch as it suggests that the light striking Dante's mind is as sudden and brief as a *folgore,* a "lightning." The Italian word *fulgore* designates also a steady light, a steady shining. However, the fact that Dante's mind is *percossa,* "shaken," or "smitten," by this light may provide partial confirmation to Singleton's rendering.

59. Altizer, *History as Apocalypse,* 127.

60. Ibid., 125.

61. Singleton, *The Divine Comedy of Dante Alighieri, Purgatorio,* p. 3.

62. Ovid, *Metamorphosen* (Dublin: Weidmann, 1969) 5.338–40. See Ovid, *The Metamorphoses of Ovid,* translated by A. E. Watts (Los Angeles: Los Angeles University Press, 1954), 105.

CHAPTER 4: THE RELUCTANT SON

1. See Margaret A. Rose, *Parody: Ancient, Modern, and Post-modern* (Cambridge: Cambridge University Press, 1993), 52.

2. See Tuvia Shlonsky, "Literary Parody. Remarks on its Method and Function," 797, in *Proceedings of the 4th Congress of the International Comparative Literature Association* 1964, ed. François Jost, vol. 2 (The Hague, 1966): 797–801. Cited in Rose, *Parody,* 82.

3. In a 1919 letter to Frank Budgen, Joyce described the character of Stephen Dedalus as "a shape that can't be changed." In a 1928 letter to Valery

Larbaud he added the detail that Stephen's mind was "full of borrowed words." See Ellmann, *James Joyce*, 459.

4. Formal encoding and conventions of intelligibility are, according to Deborah Madsen, two among the fundamental factors that contribute to the definition of the structuralist theories of genre. See Deborah L. Madsen, *Rereading Allegory*, 17–22.

5. William Shakespeare, *Hamlet* (New York: Norton, 1963), 1.2.202.

6. See Menelaos's adventure with Proteus in Homer, *The Odyssey*, 4.435–61. The earlier image of Mulligan's "sleek brown head, a seal's, far out on the water" serves to confirm, then, the vile submission of Stephen's friend, a *seal* to his shepherd, a "servant" to the imperial *seal* of the British empire. See James Joyce, *Ulysses*, 1.321, 405, 574, 615–16, 744, 2.246, 3.483, 9.102, 14.583.

7. Mananaan MacLir is the protean Irish god of the sea.

8. In a more pathetic mode, one can overcome those steeds if one, like the Lycidas described in jerky recitation by young Talbot in the "Nestor" episode of *Ulysses*, sinks "beneath the watery floor" only to be "mounted high," among the angels who crown him the sea's protecting deity, "Genius of the shore" (*U* 2.60–66). See John Milton, "Lycidas," lines 167, 172, 183., in S. Elledge, ed., *Milton's "Lycidas"* (New York: Harper & Row, 1966), 3–9.

9. Buck's Greek exclamation refers to *Anabasis* by Xenophon (4.7.24).

10. See Christine Froula, "Mothers of Invention/Doaters of Inversion: Narcissan Scenes in *Finnegans Wake*," 289–91, in Susan Stanford Friedman, *Joyce: The Return of the Repressed* (Ithaca: Cornell University Press, 1993), 283–303.

11. In the *Sanhedrin* it is maintained that Ham both sodomized and castrated Noah. See *Sanhedrin*, trans. J. Shachter and H. Freedman (London: The Sorcino Press, 1994), 70a.

12. See Balsamo, *Rachele accucciata sugli dei*, 42–43.

13. See Derrida, *Glas*, 39, left column (my translation).

14. Homer, *The Odyssey*, 23.181–204.

15. As I mentioned in chapter 2, Gena Corea has defined an analogous impulse as "the patriarchal urge to self-generate." Corea, *The Mother Machine*, 260.

16. Jean-Michel Rabaté, *James Joyce, Authorized Reader* (Baltimore: Johns Hopkins University Press, 1991), 69.

17. See Balsamo, *Rachele accucciata sugli dei*, 42–43.

18. For the Roman juridical concept of *fictio*, see Maine, *Ancient Law*, 24.

19. Telemachus declares: "Never yet did any man know his parentage of his own knowledge." Homer, *The Odyssey*, 1.214–20.

20. *Mulier* is a derogatory term reserved for the plebeian woman; the patrician woman is a *foemina*.

21. As to Hamlet's misogyny and uxorophobia, see principally *Hamlet* 3.1.139–42.

22. See also *U* 1.659–60, 17.538–39, 781–85.

23. See also Stephen's meditation on hypostasis as a connotation of the ubiquity of the sacrament of Eucharist, as it is celebrated in all churches of Dublin, "houses of decay" (*U* 3.105–27, 310–19); and Stephen's illustration, in the "Scylla and Charybdis" episode, of the consubstantiality that links Hamlet to the ghost of his father (*U* 9.481).

24. Stephen refers to Socrates' mother, Phaemerate, as a midwife, in "Scylla and Charybdis" (*U* 9.234, 665).

25. Incidentally, two of the earliest figurations of that most emblematic couple, the virgin-mother and the putative father, may be found in book 16 of the *Iliad*, lines 140–206. See Fitzgerald's translation, p. 383.

26. See chapter 3 for a detailed analysis of the vampire poem in *Ulysses*: "On swift sail flaming / From storm and south / He comes, pale vampire, / Mouth to my mouth" (*U* 7.522–25).

27. I am referring especially to the argumentative strategy of *The Divine Names* by Pseudo-Dionysius. See Deirdre Carabine, *The Unknown God* (Louvain: Peeters Press, 1995), 288–289.

28. See Dante, *Purgatorio* 29.73–78: *e vidi le fiammelle andar davante, / lasciando dietro a sé l'aere dipinto, / e di tratti pennelli avean sembiante; / sì che lì sopra rimanea distinto / di sette liste, tutte in quei colori / onde fa l'arco il Sole e Delia cinto.* Singleton translates: "And I saw the flames advance, leaving the air behind them painted, and they looked like moving paint brushes, so that overhead it remained streaked with seven bands in all those colors whereof the sun makes his bow, and Delia her girdle" (*Purgatorio*, p. 319)

29. In this page of the *Wake* Isobel is assigned other names as well, such as Halosobuth, Cunina, Statulina, Edulia, Pussy, but their implications are beside the point of this chapter.

Chapter 5: Parliament of Flatulence

1. In the early afternoon Stephen sent a telegram to Mulligan to let him know that he would not keep his 12:30 P.M. rendezvous at the pub called the Ship (see *U* 1.733, 9.550–51). The spiteful intention of the telegram is indicated by the fact that it was sent shortly after Stephen left Mooney's, another pub, five doors from the Ship.

2. See Paul De Man, "The Rhetoric of Temporality," 187–208, in *Blindness and Insight* (Minneapolis: University of Minnesota Press, 1986), 187–228.

3. Buck's words are a parody of a passage from Wilde's preface to *The Picture of Dorian Gray*. See Oscar Wilde, *The Picture of Dorian Gray* (New York: Norton, 1988), 4.

4. Also Stephen's aphorism is a parody from Wilde. See the passage from Wilde's *The Decay of Lying* cited in Gifford, *Ulysses Annotated,* 16.

5. Incidentally, the Wildean character of this tug of war between Stephen and Buck reinforces the impression that the line, "[Buck's] arm: Cranly's arm," whose second (inverted) occurrence at line 451 of "Proteus" is preceded, significantly enough, by an allusion to the love between Oscar Wilde and Lord Alfred Douglas, participates in the pattern of alternation discussed above, which indicates the emergence of feelings of resentment toward an estranged friend.

6. Gifford, *Ulysses Annotated,* 33.

7. See Matthew, 22:15–21, in The New Oxford Annotated Bible (New York: Oxford University Press, 1977), 1171–212.

8. Joyce does not capitalize the word "professor" before the name of MacHugh.

9. Aristotle, *Poetics,* trans. I. Bywater, 1451 a36–b5, in *The Rhetoric and the Poetics of Aristotle* (New York: Modern Library, 1954), 221–66.

10. It is worthwhile remarking that this aspect of Stephen's artistic temperament also contributes to highlight the contiguity of characterization in *Ulysses* and in *A Portrait of the Artist* that I have touched upon earlier several times. Proof to it is that Stephen learned to appreciate the Aristotelian contrast between the historian's interest in factuality and the poet's interest in potentiality and fantasy already from his first Latin manual at Belvedere College, where he received his high school education; this was "a ragged book written by a Portuguese priest" and adopted by his Latin teacher, the rector of Belvedere, in whose pages he read the prescription, of evident Aristotelian derivation: "*Contrahit orator, variant in carmina vates*" (*Portrait* 179).

11. See chapter 3, note 43.

12. The conventional diction, "*mentre che 'l vento, come fa, ci tace,*" is translated variously as, "while the wind, for our discourse, is still" (Pinsky), "while the wind is silent, in this place" (Mandelbaum), "as long as the wind will let us pause" (Ciardi). Dante has entered the Second Circle, and Paolo and Francesca, having "turned on the torn sky from the band where Dido *whirls across the air*" (Ciardi, my emphasis), address the Poet from a spot where the perennial *whirlwind* of Hell's hurricane gives them a moment of pause. As I suggested in chapter 3, note 43, translations such as "is silent" or "is still" are much too bland, given the specific context of Stephen's evocation of Dantesque verses in "Aeolus." See Dante Alighieri, *Inferno,* in the translations by Robert Pinsky (New York: Farrar, Straus and Giroux, 1996); Allen Mandelbaum (New York: Bantam, 1982); and John Ciardi (New York: New American Library, 1982).

13. Joyce does not put a period after "F" and "Mr" in "John F Taylor" and "Mr Justice Fitzgibbon."

CHAPTER 6: AENGUS OF THE BIRDS

1. See Karen Lawrence, "Paternity as Legal Fiction in *Ulysses,*" in Bernard Benstock, *James Joyce: The Augmented Ninth* (Ithaca: Syracuse University Press, 1988), 233–43, and Ellen Carol Jones, "'Writing the Mystery of Himself': Paternity in *Ulysses,*" in Benstock, *James Joyce: The Augmented Ninth,* 226–32.

2. Margaret Church, "*A Portrait* and Vico: A Source Study," in Thomas F. Staley and Bernard Benstock, ed. *Approaches to Joyce's Portrait* (Pittsburgh: Pittsburgh University Press, 1976): 79.

3. A. Walton Litz, "Vico and Joyce," in G. Tagliacozzo and H. White, eds., *Giambattista Vico: An International Symposium* (Baltimore: John Hopkins University Press, 1969): 245.

4. Ibid.

5. Jean-Michel Rabaté, *James Joyce, Authorized Reader* (Baltimore: Johns Hopkins University Press, 1991), 68, my emphasis.

6. See Ellmann, *James Joyce,* 340.

7. Domenico Pietropaolo, "Vico and Literary History in the Early Joyce," in Donald Phillip Verene, ed. *Vico and Joyce* (New York: State University of New York Press, 1987), 120–3. Richard Ellmann and Ellsworth Mason share an analogous opinion in their commentary to Joyce's critical writings. See

James Joyce, *The Critical Writings.* Richard Ellmann and Ellsworth Mason, eds. (Ithaca: Cornell University Press, 1989), 83.

8. Emanuel Swedenborg, *Marriage Love* (New York: Houghton, 1907), 233, 270, 432, 477, my emphasis.

9. The specific subject of this discussion must not be confused with the proliferation of references to theosophical writers others than Emanuel Swedenborg, such as Madame Blavatsky, Yeats, and AE (George Russell) in the "Telemachiad" and in "Scylla and Charybdis."

10. Swedenborg, *Marriage Love,* 270.

11. Ibid., 233, 280.

12. Occurrences of the bat motif in relation to women characters are frequent in *Ulysses* even when Stephen Dedalus is not involved in the episode. In the "Nausicaa" episode, for instance, the apparition of the "little bat," twittering here and there, becomes an insistent figural trope of Leopold Bloom's erotic encounter with Gerty MacDowell. See *U* 13.750–53, 1117, 1176, 1277–78, 1286.

13. Joyce, *Selected Letters,* ed. Ellmann, 314.

14. Donald Phillip Verene, *Vico's Science of Imagination* (Ithaca: Cornell University Press, 1981), 83–84, 89, 123.

15. Ibid., 122–23. An analogous observation is found in Norman O. Brown, *Closing Time* (New York: Vintage Books, 1976), 10.

16. See *U* 9.844, and James Joyce, *Letters* II, ed. Ellmann, 106.

17. Among such activities, one may recall Stephen's storing up for the souls in purgatory, the pressing of the keys of his soul's cash register, and the inauguration of a domestic bank and commonwealth with active interests for his family (*Portrait* 98, 147–48).

18. See Alberto Moreiras, "Pharmaconomy: Stephen and the Daedalids," in Susan Stanford Friedman, ed., *Joyce: The Return of the Repressed,* 67–68.

19. When his body must assume a leaning stance (a far from infrequent occurrence), Stephen, the worshiper of Hauptmann's pale sorrowful girls, of Cavalcanti's sweet angelical women, of Yeats's rosy woman, of D'Annunzio's Madonna, of Ben Johnson's forever weary Aurora, always makes sure that this leaning is *weary,* as weary as when his mind wanders among the spectral words of Aristotle and Aquinas. See *Portrait,* 176.

20. May Goulding Dedalus delivered fifteen children according to Leopold Bloom (*U* 8.31).

21. G. W. F. Hegel, *Philosophy of Right,* trans. T. M. Knox (Oxford: Oxford University Press, 1967), sec. 3.18–20 (remark).

22. I have borrowed the term "Daedalid" from the title of Alberto Moreiras, "Pharmaconomy: Stephen and the Daedalids."

23. The neologism "seabedabbled" is coined by Joyce as a variation of Shakespeare's diction "dewbedabbled," a term that appears in *Venus and Adonis,* the work cited in "Scylla and Charybdis" (*U* 9.247–50). See Gifford, *Ulysses Annotated,* 208, 246.

24. See my analysis of Stephen Dedalus's vampire poem in chapter 3.

25. Gifford, *Ulysses Annotated,* 252. Furthermore, In "Oxen of the Sun," another of Stephen's friends, Lynch, will deal the final blow to any delusion of poetic grandeur still nurtured by Stephen with the words: "Those (vine-) leaves . . . will adorn you more fitly when some things more, and greatly more, than a capful of light odes can call your genius father" (*U* 14.1117–23). Also, Buck Mulligan anticipates Lynch's diagnosis in "The Wandering Rocks," when

he says to Haines: "He (Stephen) will never capture the Attic note. The note of Swinburne, of all poets, the white death and ruddy birth. That is his tragedy. He can never be a poet" (*U* 10.1072–75).

26. The thematic of *amor matris* is anticipated by Stephen's brief pedagogical exchange with Cyril Sargent in the "Nestor" episode. See *U* 2.139–67, especially lines 143 and 165.

27. William Shakespeare, *Hamlet* (New York: Norton, 1963), 3.1.571.

28. In truth, Buck Mulligan is very insightful at this juncture. It is a fact that, in the course of his analysis of Shakespeare's creative drives, Stephen evokes rather openly his own flesh and blood: twice he calls Richard Shakespeare, one of Shakespeare's two brothers, with the epithet "nuncle Richie," which epithet refers, in the Dedalus family's lingo, to Richard Goulding, Stephen's maternal uncle. The reference is reinforced by the epithet "lump of love," which in "Scylla and Charybdis" refers to "Lizzie" (Elizabeth Hall, William Shakespeare's first grandchild) and in "Proteus" refers to "Crissie," Richard Goulding's daughter (*U* 9.973, 9.1039, 3.87–88).

29. To my knowledge, Robert Scholes and Richard Kain were the first to notice Stephen's resemblance to "that too-clever nephew of Daedalus who was pushed off a tower by his uncle and turned into a lapwing." See Robert Scholes and Richard M. Kain, eds. *The Workshop of Daedalus: James Joyce and the Raw Materials for A Portrait of the Artist as a Young Man* (Evanston: Northwestern University Press, 1965), 264. The translation of *perdix* with "lapwing" raises complex philological problems, relating to the correct diction of verse 237 from Ovid's manuscript of book 8 of the *Metamorphoses*. In "Pharmaconomy: Stephen and the Daedalids," Alberto Moreiras reports that "verse 237 is nowadays generally taken to read: '*Garrula limosa prospexit ab elice perdix*,'" while the verse from the manuscript "apparently" reads, "'*Garrula ramosa prospexit ab ilice perdix*'" (75). According to Moreiras, both dictions suggest the image of a lapwing rather than that, preferred by several translators, of a partridge.

30. See Ovid, *Metamorphoses* (*Metamorphoseon*), ed. B. A.Van Proosdij (Leiden: Brill, 1975), bk. 8. In "Pharmaconomy: Stephen and the Daedalids," Alberto Moreiras has established that Book 8 of Ovid's *Metamorphoses,* where the story of Perdix is narrated, was clearly important to Joyce during the composition of *A Portrait of the Artist as a Young Man*. Moreiras also contends that Joyce is likely to have been aware of the philological complications relating to the translation of *perdix* into lapwing (75, 84). Several commentators on this episode, including Alberto Moreiras, Robert Scholes, and Richard Kain, refer to the version of the Daedalus story that attributes the name Perdix to the mother of Daedalus's nephew, and the name Talos to the boy.

31. See Blake's *Poems and Fragments from the Note-Book,* no. 15, in Blake, *Complete Writings,* ed. Geoffrey Keynes (London: Oxford University Press, 1967) 168.

32. See Weldon Thornton, *Allusions in Ulysses* (Chapel Hill: University of North Carolina Press, 1987), 208.

33. In "Pharmaconomy: Stephen and the Daedalids," Alberto Moreiras offers a brilliant comment on Stephen's contradictory "displacement of dwelling place" (70).

34. In *Modernism's Body,* Christine Froula argues that the apposition of the feminine adjective, *garrula,* to the name of common gender, *perdix,* indicates Ovid's deliberate transformation of the boy Perdix into a female bird.

Indeed, the ludicrous diction *garrulus perdix* was certainly not among Ovid's options. See Christine Froula, *Modernism's Body: Sex, Culture, and Joyce* (New York: Columbia University Press, 1996), 57. Cf. also Gian Balsamo, *Legitimate Filiation and Gender Segregation: Law and Fiction in Texts by Derrida, Hegel, Joyce, Pirandello, and Vico,* Ph.D. diss. Vanderbilt University, 1994, Ann Arbor: UMI, 1994, 89.

35. See Nehama Aschkenasy, "Biblical Females in a Joycean Episode," *Modern Language Studies* 15, no. 4 (fall 1985):29. The "womanhood of his country" is represented also, in *Ulysses,* by the old milk-woman of "Telemachos," whose simplemindedness evokes another biblical figuration of the lures of womanhood, namely, the "foolish woman" of *Proverbs* 9:13–18 (*U* 1.418–19). (In "Biblical Females in a Joycean Episode," Nehama Aschkenasy draws a parallel, instead, between the "foolish woman" of *Proverbs* and Stephen's feminine dean of studies [36–37]).

36. See Danna N. Fewell and David M. Gunn, "Controlling Perspectives: Women, Men, and the Authority of Violence in Judges 4–5," *Journal of the American Academy of Religion,* 5 (fall 1990): 389–411.

37. Cf. Peggy L. Day, *Gender and Difference in Ancient Israel* (Minneapolis: Fortress Press, 1989), 49.

38. See also *U* 3.46.

39. See Vicky Mahaffey, *Reauthorizing Joyce* (Cambridge: Cambridge University Press, 1988), 81.

40. Joyce, U 9.954; *Critical Writings,* 222; *Portrait* 169.

41. See Dante, *Purgatorio,* 1.9.

42. The French *jarret* and the Italian *garretto* correspond to the English "hock," or the ankle of the hind leg of a quadruped.

43. Carlo Grabher, ed. *Paradiso di Dante,* (Bari: Laterza, 1964), 33.133–38. For the English translation, Singleton, *Paradiso,* 379.

44. Thomas J. J. Altizer, *History as Apocalypse,* 63–78.

CHAPTER 7: THE LAW OF THE OUTLAW

1. Jacques Derrida, *Glas,* 10, 57–63, left column. Subsequent parenthetical and endnote references to the left column are indicated by *Glas* and a page number followed by *a.* My translations.

2. Pardes, *Countertraditions in the Bible,* note 20 to page 95.

3. G. W. F. Hegel, *Philosophy of Right,* 166:115. Parenthetical and endnote references to Hegel's *Philosophy of Right* are indicated by *PhilR,* followed by section and page number, and qualified either with "remark" or "addition" in those cases when reference is made, respectively, to Hegel's explanatory notes or to the notes from Hegel's lectures intercalated into the text by Gans, the editor of the first and third edition of *Hegels Werke,* vol. 8, 1833, 1854.

4. G. W. F. Hegel, *Aesthetics: Lectures on Fine Art,* trans. T. M. Knox, 2 vols. (Oxford: Clarendon, 1975), vol. 2, part 3, 1213.

5. This conflict is also variously defined by Hegel as the conflict between the "law of inward life" and "public law," between the law "of the household gods," or of the "gods of the underworld," and the "law of the land" (*PhilR* 166:115). See also G. W. F. Hegel, *Phenomenology of Spirit,* trans. A. V. Miller (Oxford: Oxford University Press 1977), 456–59.

6. Hegel, *Phenomenology of Spirit,* 457.

7. G. W. F. Hegel, *Science of Logic,* trans. A. V. Miller (Atlantic Highlands: Humanities Press International, 1989), 88.

8. See Exodus, 3.15, 25–30, 36–39 (in TANAKH: 85–152).

9. As to the biblical legislation of the Jubilee, which makes the property of the land provisional, negotiable, and dependent upon a principle external to the Jewish family that owns and/or trades it, see Leviticus, 25.8–55 (in TANAKH: 153–202), and particularly verset 25.23: "But the land must not be sold beyond reclaim, for the land is Mine," [said the Lord]. "You are but strangers resident with Me."

10. Genesis 31:14.

11. See E. A. Speiser, ed. and trans., *Genesis: The Anchor Bible,* (New York: Doubleday, 1964), 31: 15 (note). Subsequent parenthetic and endnote references are indicated by *Speiser/Genesis* followed by the chapter and versets glossed and/or commented upon.

12. Pardes, *Countertraditions in the Bible,* 71.

13. A problem that arises in a discussion of Genesis 31 regards the name by which to address the Lord of Israel. Given that the major sources of the episode are the authors that the "documentary tradition" identifies as J and E, there is a choice between the names YHWH and Elohim. With the exception of two cases where it seemed important to be as faithful as possible to the author's intentions, I have opted for the usage of J's favorite name, YHWH.

14. With regard to the relationship between idols, religious cult, and phallic fertility, see Derrida's analysis of Benveniste's study of the meaning of the words "religious," "holy," and "sacred," in *"Foi et Savoir,"* § 32, 34, 39, in J. Derrida et G. Vattimo, *La religion* (Paris: Seuil, 1996).

15. As Nahum Sarna points out in his Commentary to Genesis, the teraphim "have been widely understood as corresponding to . . . the Roman *penates,"* the household gods from whose possession the Roman *paterfamilias,* turned augur and oracle, derived immense religious and legal privileges over the members of his family. See Nahum M. Sarna, *The JPS Torah Commentary: Genesis* (Philadelphia: Jewish Publication Society, 1989), note to verset 31:19. Subsequent parenthetical and endnote references are indicated by *Sarna/Genesis,* followed by the chapter and verset number. With regard to the role of the Roman *paterfamilias* as augur and oracle, see Vico, *SNS2* § 937–41, 1036, and *UIPF* § 220.

16. According to Genesis 31:22–23, it takes just seven days for Laban, who has a disadvantage of three days, to overtake the fugitives' caravan. This implies that Jacob's caravan would have covered the distance of approximately 400 miles that separates Haran from Gilead in less than ten days. Nahum Sarna suggests that, at the more realistic speed "of about 6 miles" a day, the fugitives' caravan could have covered that distance in a time at least six times as long (*Sarna/Genesis* 31:22–23; see also *Speiser/Genesis* 31:22–23). But it is well known that biblical temporality diverges from the conventional temporality of Aristotelian diegesis; as we will see, Rachel's story serves as a confirmation to the rule. In the second place, it is worthwhile pointing out that the immediate success of Laban's hunt of Jacob's caravan contradicts the opinion, shared by Nahum Sarna and Thomas Mann, that Rachel may have stolen the teraphim so as to deprive her father of their divinatory power (*Sarna/Genesis* 31:19; Thomas Mann, *Joseph and His Brothers,* vol. 1, trans. H. T. Lowe-Porter [New York: Knopf, 1934], 398).

17. Esther Fuchs, "'For I Have the Way of Women': Deception, Gender, and Ideology in Biblical Narrative," *Semeia* 42 (1988): 75–87.

18. This argument finds a frequent obstacle in the credence, posterior to the corpus of writings that constitute the Pentateuch, hence irrelevant to my discussion, that Jewish lineage is transmitted through the mother.

19. Incidentally, Abraham is the first patriarch in Genesis (the second and last, significantly enough, will be Jacob) whose containment of the matrilineal infiltration within his future genealogy is symbolized by the divine imposition of a new name, from Abram to Abraham. (In the case of Jacob, the new name is Israel, of course [Genesis, 17:5, 31:29]).

20. Here it must be noted that the criteria of family succession from Deuteronomy 21:15–16 exclude the option, given to the testator by Mesopotamian customs, of removing the right of inheritance from the elder son.

21. The somewhat derogatory Hebrew *t*erāpîm designates "figurines, sometimes at least in human shape" (*Speiser/Genesis* 31:19). It is significant that the Hebrew name for these pagan gods, protectors of the tribe's fertility, is in the masculine plural.

22. Hegel, *Phenomenology of Spirit,* 475.

23. A limestone relief, uncovered at Tell Halaf in northern Syria, dating from about 900 B.C., depicts a man "seated on a boxlike saddle tied to (a) one-humped camel with crosswise girths." See J. B. Pritchard, ed., *Ancient Near East in Pictures Relating to the Old Testament* (Princeton: Princeton University Press, 1969), picture 188, pp. 59, 271. Sarna remarks that the "box-like object . . . simultaneously serves as a riding saddle and a pack saddle" (*Sarna/Genesis* 31:34–35).

24. See *Sarna/Genesis* 31:34–35.

25. After the reconciliation between Jacob and Laban, nineteen versets relate the sending of messengers and gifts from Mahanaim to Esau in the land of Seir, followed by the separation of Jacob's tribe in the separate camps (Genesis 32:4–22). Eleven versets relate the voluntary separation of Jacob from his family beyond the ford of the Jabbok, and Jacob's struggle with Elohim at Penuel (32:23–33). One single verset suffices to relate the eventless sojourn at Succoth, whose two outstanding peculiarities consist of, first, the absence of any significant plot development and, second, the presence of a diction and a syntax partially divergent from the compact ones of the preceding episodes, which mainly alternate contributions from the authors that the "documentary hypothesis" identifies as J and E (*Speiser/Genesis* 33:17). Thirty-four versets are needed to relate the bloody episode of the negotiation and brutal slaughter of the Shechemites, perpetrated in the course of only three days (33:17–34:31). Finally, twenty versets relate the rapid escape from Shechem, the journey toward Bethel, where YHWH appears to Jacob, and the departure toward Ephrath, in whose vicinities Rachel dies in her labor (35:1–20).

26. Fuchs, "'For I Have the Way of Women,'" 80.

27. Hegel, *Phenomenology of Spirit,* 475, my emphasis.

28. Sophocles, *Antigone,* trans. E. Wyckoff, in *Greek Tragedies,* ed. D. Grene and R. Lattimore, 3 vols. (Chicago: Chicago University Press, 1968), 1:177–228, lines 905–12.

29. Hegel, *Phenomenology of Spirit,* 437.

30. Mieke Bal reads in Rachel's theft an exemplary stage in the transition from the "patrilocal" dominion, which ratifies the supremacy of the father or the father-in-law, to the "virilocal" dominion, which ratifies the supremacy of

the husband. See Mieke Bal, *Death and Dissimetry: The Politics of Coherence on Sisera's Death* (Bloomington: Indiana University Press, 1988), 86–87. See also Bal's illustration of the implications of the transition from patrilocal to virilocal marriage in Judges 19, in her article "Dealing/With/Women: Daughters in the Book of Judges," in *The Book and the Text: The Bible and Literary Theory,* ed. Regina Schwartz (Cambridge: Basil Blackwell, 1990), 16–39.

31. Jacques Lacan, "*Les articulations de la pièce,*" 301, and "*Antigone dans l'entre-deux-morts,*" 324, both in *Le Séminaire* VII (Paris: Éditions du Seuil, 1960), 299–313, 315–33. See also Sophocles, *Antigone,* line 451.

32. Sophocles, *Antigone,* lines 891–928.

33. See Fewell and Gunn, "Controlling Perspectives." This article elaborates the thesis that a man's visit to a woman's tent is equivalent to an intrusion within the cave symbol of her body, with regard to the hospitality offered by Jael to Sisera.

34. In *Countertraditions in the Bible,* Pardes points out that Laban's "feeling" of Rachel's belongings is expressed by the same verb, *mishesh,* used to express the analogous feeling of Jacob's hairy camouflage by which old Isaac mistook the younger son for the older (70; see Genesis 27:18–23).

35. Nancy Jay, *Throughout Your Generations Forever,* 107.

36. See Foucault, *La volonté de savoir,* 183, 193–95.

Chapter 8: Right of *Paterfamilias*

1. See chap. 7, n. 3.

2. G. W. F. Hegel, *Encyclopaedia Logic* (with the *Zusätze*), trans. T. F. Geraets, W. A. Suchting, H. S. Harris (Indianapolis: Hackett, 1991), secs. 220–21, p. 293.

3. The first edition of Von Hugo's *Lehrbuch der Geschichte des Römischen Rechts* [Textbook of the History of Roman Law] was published in 1790, the fifth edition in 1815. Many subsequent editions followed. See T. M. Knox, "Translator's Notes" to Hegel's *Philosophy of Right,* note 19, pp. 307–08.

4. See Montesquieu, C. L. de S. *De l'esprit des lois,* 2 vols. (Paris: Garnier Frères, 1973), vol. 1., bk. 11, p. 484.

5. See Hegel, *PhilR,* 3.18–20 (remark).

6. See Maine, *Ancient Law,* 25.

7. Knox, "Translator's Notes" to Hegel's *Philosophy of Right,* notes 25–26, p. 309.

8. The complete title of J. G. Heineccius's *Syntagma* reads: *Antiquitatum Romanarum jurisprudentiam illustrantium Syntagma.* The version consulted by Hegel was published in Basel, Switzerland in 1752. See Hegel, *PhilR* 3.20 (footnote to remark).

9. Knox, "Translator's Notes" to Hegel's *Philosophy of Right,* note 26, p. 309.

10. As we will see later on, Vico's analysis of the interpretation that the Roman jurisconsults of the *collegium pontificum* gave of the laws of inheritance of the Twelve Tables suggests, instead, that the absence of gender differentiation maintained by Montesquieu was just the result of a misconception dating from the second century C.E., rather than a faithful reflection of the intentions of the ancient Roman legislators. See *SNS2* § 988–90.

11. See, for instance, G. W. F. Hegel, *Encyclopaedia of the Philosophical Sciences in Outline,* trans. Steven A. Taubeneck, ed. Ernst Behler (New York: Continuum, 1990), sec. 415, p. 245, and Hegel, *PhilR,* 135.89 (remark).

12. The above considerations are derived for the most part from John Sallis's treatment of the "place of imagination" in Hegel's philosophy of Spirit. See John Sallis, *Spacings of Reason and Imagination: In Texts of Kant, Fichte, Hegel* (Chicago: University of Chicago Press, 1987), 144–50.

13. See Hegel, *Encyclopaedia Logic,* sec. 15, p. 39.

14. See Sallis, *Spacings of Reason and Imagination,* 143–44, 155.

15. See Hegel, *Encyclopaedia of the Philosophical Sciences,* sec. 457 (remark), and Sallis, *Spacings of Reason and Imagination,* 145, 150.

16. Hegel, *Encyclopaedia of the Philosophical Sciences,* sec. 458 (remark).

17. See Sallis, *Spacings of Reason and Imagination,* 150, and Jacques Derrida, "The Pit and the Pyramid: Introduction to Hegel's Semiology," in Derrida, *Margins of Philosophy,* trans. Alan Bass (Chicago: University of Chicago Press, 1986), 94–95.

18. In the *Science of Logic,* Hegel argues that a diachronic correspondence occurs between the procession of the logical order of intelligent thought and its historical manifestations. See G. W. F. Hegel, *Science of Logic,* vol. 1, bk. 1, p. 88: "What is the first in the *science* had of necessity to show itself *historically* as the first." (My emphasis.)

19. See Vico, *De constantia iurisprudentis. Pars prior: De constantia philosophiae,* Italian trans. Sandro Barbera, § 20, in Vico, *Opere giuridiche,* ed. Paolo Cristofolini (Firenze: Sansoni, 1974), pp. 353–86; *UIPF* § 209–12; *SNS2* § 442–46.

20. The "last jurisprudence" corresponds to the jurisprudence of Vico's "third age."

21. The "heroic jurisprudence" corresponds to the jurisprudence of Vico's "second age."

22. An analogous problem as to the figurative meaning of legal discourse is found in modern romance languages. When the formulation of the legal code is unconcerned with the issue of gender-discriminating expressions, it becomes a matter of delicate interpretation to establish whether or not the usage of a masculine possessive adjective or a masculine pronoun is intended to apply to both genders. In the absence of explicit instructions on the part of the legislator, only a close scrutiny of the linguistic conventions prevalent at the time of legislation can solve the dilemma.

23. See Derrida, *Glas,* 167–71a. See also David Farrell Krell, "Lucinde's Shame: Hegel, Sensuous Woman, and the Law," in Drucilla Cornell, Michael Rosenfeld, David Gray Carlson, eds., *Hegel and Legal Theory* (New York: Routledge, 1991).

24. Montesquieu, *De l'esprit des lois,* vol. 1, bk. 11, p. 17.

25. See Pierre J. J. Olivier, *Legal Fictions in Practice and Legal Science* (Rotterdam: Rotterdam University Press, 1975), 6.

26. Ibid.

27. Maine, *Ancient Law,* 24.

28. See Mark Lilla, *G. B. Vico: The Making of an Anti-Modern* (Cambridge: Harvard University Press, 1993), chapter 4, particularly p. 132; Donald Phillip Verene, *Vico's Science of Imagination,* chapter 4, particularly p. 122, and chapter 6.

Chapter 9: Etiology and Genealogy

1. Jacques Derrida, "Before the Law," trans. Antal Ronell (with Christine Roulston), in Derrida, *Acts of Literature,* ed. Derek Attridge, 198–99 (my emphasis).

2. Hegel, *Aesthetics: Lectures on Fine Art,* vol. 2, part 3, sec. 1, chap. 1.2a.

3. The Book of Esther, 5.1–2 (in TANAKH: 1457–68).

4. Robert Alter, *The World of Biblical Literature* (New York: Basic Books, 1991), 32.

5. Alter describes this methodology in reference to his interpretation of the exchange of lentil stew between Jacob and Esau. See Alter, *The World of Biblical Literature,* 96.

6. See Roland Barthes, "L'effet du réel," in *Communications* 11 (1968): 84–89.

7. See Immanuel Kant, *Critique of Practical Reason,* trans. L. W. Beck (New York: Macmillan, 1956), 70.72. In this and subsequent references, the two arabic numerals indicate the pagination of the Prussian Academy edition and the pagination of Beck's English translation.

8. Ibid., 31.30.

9. Ibid., 30.29, 66.68.

10. See Sallis, *Spacings of Reason and Imagination,* 90.

11. See Hegel, *Encyclopaedia Logic,* sec. 42, pp. 83–84.

12. Martin Heidegger, *Being and Time,* trans. John Macquarrie and Edward Robinson (San Francisco: Harper, 1962), 1.1:23.

13. See Derrida, *Introduction,* in Husserl, *L'origine de la géometrie,* 96–105.

14. Immanuel Kant, *Critique of Judgment,* trans. Werner S. Pluhar (Indianapolis: Hackett, 1986), 353.229. In this and subsequent references, the two arabic numerals indicate, respectively, the pagination of the Prussian Academy edition and the pagination of Pluhar's English translation.

15. Ibid., 354.230.

16. Ibid., 353.228.

17. Ibid.

18. As noted above, Kant does stress the exemplary ideality of pure geometry in his *Critique of Practical Reason,* 31.30.

19. This quotation from a letter by Freud to Wilhelm Fliess, 14 November 1897, comes from *The Complete Letters of Sigmund Freud to Wilhelm Fliess, 1881–1904,* trans. and ed. J. M. Masson (Cambridge: Harvard University Press, 1985), 280.

20. As noted in chapter 8, Hegel's opposition of Kant's method of concept development to the *fictiones* of the Roman jurists of the imperial age presupposes the radical separation of reason and imagination in Kant. See *PhilR,* 3.18–20 (remark), 180.121 (remark).

Chapter 10: Son, Knight, and Lover

1. Anthony Wilden, "Lacan and the Discourse of the Other," in Jacques Lacan, *Speech and Language in Psychoanalysis,* trans. Anthony Wilden (Baltimore: Johns Hopkins University Press, 1989), 246–47.

2. Jacques Lacan, "Subversion du sujet et dialectique du désir dans l'in-conscient freudien," in Lacan, *Écrits 2* (Paris: Seuil, 1971), 160, 167–69. In this chapter, my translations from Lacan are adapted from Alan Sheridan's translations, in Lacan, *Écrits* (New York: Norton, 1977).

3. Roger Dragonetti, *La vie de la lettre au moyen age* (Paris: Seuil, 1980), 9–10.

4. Chrétien de Troyes, *Le roman de Perceval ou Le conte du graal,* ed. William Roach (Geneva: Droz, 1959), lines 1941–42. Subsequent citations will refer to this edition by line numbers. My English translations are based, with adaptations, on those of Nigel Bryant, *Perceval: The Story of the Grail* (Cambridge: D. S. Brewer, 1982) and of William W. Kibler, *The Story of the Grail, or Perceval* (New York: Garland, 1990).

5. Cf. Lacan, "Le séminaire sur 'La lettre volée'," in Lacan, *Écrits 1* (Paris: Seuil, 1966), 61.

6. Cf. Lacan, "La signification du phallus," in *Écrits 2,* 110.

7. Cf. Lacan, "Fonction et champ de la parole et du langage in psychana-lyse," in *Écrits 1,* 157–58.

8. See Lacan, "Subversion du sujet et dialectique du désir dans l'incons-cient freudien," 163, 165, 169.

9. Ibid., 158.

10. The Freudian problematics regarding woman's lack of penis is imbued with gender segregation. Although a critique of the Freudian theory of penis envy goes beyond the limitations of this chapter, it is worth pointing out that Jacques Derrida's critical engagement of the speculative connotations inherent in the concept of the "lack" provides an excellent element for the deconstruc-tion of the psychoanalytic bias. The absence of the penis in the anatomy of the vulva ought not to be taken as the "lack of a negative which may be posited . . . [as] a substantial emptiness, [as the] . . . absence" of a potential presence; on the contrary, the absence of the penis ought to be taken as ". . . . the impossi-bility of *arresting différance* in its contour, . . . [as the impossibility] of localiz-ing . . . what metaphysics calls . . . *lack.*" See Jacques Derrida, *The Truth in Painting,* trans. Geoff Bennington and Ian McLeod (Chicago: University of Chi-cago Press, 1987), 80.

11. A. J. Greimas, *Dictionnaire de l'ancien français* (Paris: Larousse, 1968), s.v. *cor.*

12. I purposefully elect to use the expression "it figures" rather than "it translates," because the latter expression would bring about an equivocation between the hermeneutics of the passage and the related problems of its En-glish rendering.

CHAPTER 11: THE COVENANT OF DYNASTY IN THE OLD TESTAMENT

1. Homer, *The Odyssey,* 1.213–16.

2. Plato, *Timaeus,* 19d.

3. See Lilla, *G. B. Vico: The Making of an Anti-Modern,* chap. 4 (particu-larly p. 132), and Verene, *Vico's Science of Imagination,* chap. 4 (particularly p. 122), and chap. 6.

4. The relationship linking nationalism to the spheres of dynasty and reli-gion has been addressed by Benedict Anderson in *Imagined Communities:*

Reflections on the Origins and Spread of Nationalism (New York: Verso, 1983), 17–28.

5. Vico, *CI2*, § 20.

6. Vico, *SNS2*, § 814.

7. Vico, *SNS1*, § 137.

8. Nicola Badaloni, *Introduzione a Vico* (Roma: Laterza, 1988), 49, 37, 42. My translations. This 1988 book by Badaloni is not to be confused with Badaloni's book of the same title published by Feltrinelli in 1961.

9. Frederick R. Marcus, "Vico and the Hebrews," *New Vico Studies* 13, (1995): 23.

10. See Badaloni, *Introduzione*, 38.

11. Ibid., 37.

12. Robert Alter, *The World of Biblical Literature*, 205.

13. Schwartz, *The Curse of Cain*, 26, 25, 31.

14. Regina M. Schwartz, "Monotheism and the Violence of Identities," *Raritan*, 14, no. 3 (winter 1995): 139.

15. Plato, *Republic*, trans. Paul Shorey, Loeb Classical Library, 5–6 (Cambridge: Harvard University Press 1980), 470b: " . . . the term employed for the hostility of the friendly is στάσις, and the one employed for the hostility of the alien is πόλεμός."

16. Regina M. Schwartz, "Nations and Nationalism: Adultery in the House of David," *Critical Inquiry* 19, no. 1 (autumn 1992): 135. A revised version of this article appears in chapter 4, "Dividing Identities: 'Nations,'" of Schwartz's *The Curse of Cain*, 120–42.

17. The position that polytheistic and monotheistic sacrificial rituals share an analogously covenantal character and function may be derived from theorists as diverse as Thomas J. J. Altizer and René Girard. In *History as Apocalypse*, Altizer writes that "sacrifice, and an original and primordial sacrifice, is the primary center and ground of all full or fully enacted ritual, and most particularly so in the Western or Latin rite [of the Church]. Just as a fundamental difference between Eastern and Western Christianity is the dominant role of atonement and reconciliation in the latter, so, likewise the Western liturgy is distinctive in its centering upon the institution of the Eucharist as itself a sacrificial act, indeed, as the ultimate sacrificial act, an act unreal apart from the death and blood of the Crucifixion" (215–16). In *La Violence et le Sacré* (Paris: Grasset, 1972), Girard argues that the entirety of our history is inscribed within two fundamental covenantal events: the founding lynching of the scapegoat, whose sacrifice purges the community of its impurities in the eyes of the god(s), and the sacrifice of Jesus Christ, which brings to an end the original founding violence (473). For the scapegoat rituals in ancient Greece, see J. Bremmer, "Scapegoat Rituals in Ancient Greece," HSCP 87 (1983): 299–320; W. Burkert, *Greek Religion* (Cambridge: Harvard University Press, 1985), and *Structure and History in Greek Mythology and Ritual* (Berkeley: University of California Press, 1979), 59–77, 168–76; J.–P. Vernant, *Mythe et Societé en Grèce ancienne* (Paris: Maspero, 1974), 121–40.

18. An analogous position as to the contribution given by sacrificial rituals to the power structure of archaic polytheistic communities may be found in Marcel Detienne, "*Pratiques culinaires et esprit de sacrifice*," in M. Detienne et Jean-Pierre Vernant, *La cuisine du sacrifice en pays grecs* (Paris: Gallimard, 1979): 23–24; J.–P. Vernant, "*Le mythe promethéen chez Hesiode*," in *Mythe et Societé en Grèce ancienne*, 177–94.

19. Walter Burkert, *Homo Necans: The Anthropology of Ancient Greek Sacrificial Ritual and Myth,* trans. Peter Bing (Berkeley: University of California Press, 1983): 35–37.

20. Schwartz, *The Curse of Cain,* 30; "Monotheism and the Violence of Identities," 138.

21. Foucault, *La volonté de savoir,* 193–95, my emphasis.

22. Schwartz, *The Curse of Cain,* 36.

23. Schwartz, "Monotheism and the Violence of Identities," 138.

24. Schwartz, *The Curse of Cain,* 135.

25. John Sallis, *Being and Logos* (Atlantic Highlands: Humanities Press International, 1986), 375.

26. See, for instance, Pier Paolo Pasolini's cinematic rendition of the play.

27. See also *Republic* 465b.

28. I have modified Shorey's translation of Plato's *Republic.*

29. Homer, *The Iliad,* trans. Fitzgerald, bk. 14, p. 331.

30. Altizer, *History as Apocalypse,* 215–16.

31. A fundamentally historical difference, however, is that a continuity may be established between the Roman (as well as the Hellenistic) ritual sacrifice and its renewal in the Christian/Latin rite of the Eucharist, while sacrifice "ceased to be cultically practiced in Judaism . . . after the destruction of the Second Temple." See Altizer, *History as Apocalypse,* 217.

32. More specifically, the Twelve Tables give the plebeians the right to marry legally, with the disposition *per conventionem in manum,* i.e., the extension to the plebs of the right of sale, which entitles the future husband to the acquisition *brevi manu* of his future wife's dowry; this disposition makes legal for the first time the plebeian marriage. However, this plebeian marriage is not a *iusta nuptia,* a "just marriage," since the husband is not an interpreter of divine auspices (*SNS2* § 938, 986; *CI2,* § 37).

33. Genesis 32:23–33.

34. Exodus 4:25.

35. Pardes, *Countertraditions in the Bible,* 79.

36. See Harold Fish, *Poetry with a Purpose: Biblical Poetics and Interpretation* (Bloomington: Indiana University Press, 1988), 149.

37. Ibid., 89.

38. Howard Eilberg-Schwarts, *The Savage in Judaism: An Anthropology of Israelite Religion and Ancient Judaism* (Bloomington: Indiana University Press, 1990), 141–76.

39. See Pardes, *Countertraditions in the Bible,* 15.

CHAPTER 12: PROCREATION AND DEGENERATION

1. Plato, *Republic,* trans. Paul Shorey, 26e. Translations adapted.

2. Even though, it should be observed, Socrates does not shy away from degrading the cities built in *lógos* to "constitutions (told) as a myth in speech" (501e).

3. Plato, *Timaeus,* 26c.

4. Eva Brann, "The Music of the *Republic,*" in *ATON* 1, no. 1 (April 1967): 21. For this chronological aspect Brann refers her reader to F. M. Cornford, *Plato's Cosmology* (London: Routledge & K. Paul, 1937), 4–5. For the opposite

point of view, she mentions A. E. Taylor, *A Commentary on Plato's Timaeus* (Oxford: Clarendon Press, 1928), 15–16, 45.

5. *Eikóta mŷthon* is that "discourse of genealogy" spoken by those who relate their own family matters. Since family genealogy, as a discursive subject, lacks both "probable and necessary demonstration," Timaeus points out, ironically, that the outsider is left with no choice but to "follow custom" and simply believe it as it is related to him (40e).

6. See also *Republic* 465b. *Stásis* is the endogenous reversal of the love for ερις and πόλεμοί of which Agamémnon accuses Achilles in the *Iliad*. See Homer, *Iliad,* ed. Willcock, 1.176–78.

7. See also Plato, *Laws,* trans. R. G. Bury, Loeb Classical Library, 10–11 (Cambridge: Harvard University Press 1984), 683e. Translations adapted.

8. Plato, *Sophist,* trans. Harold North Fowler, Loeb Classical Library, 7 (Cambridge: Harvard University Press 1977). Translations adapted.

9. See the attribution of "poetic madness" to the Muses in *Phaedrus.* Plato, *Phaedrus,* trans. Harold North Fowler, Loeb Classical Library 1 (Cambridge: Harvard University Press, 1982), 265b. Translations adapted. The "true Muse, the companion of argument and philosophy," is unfriendly to indigenous discord (*Republic* 548b–c).

10. A precursor of the contraction and exclusion of diversity in the "luxurious" city, to which this discussion is devoted, is already found, of course, in the simple city of artisans, the self-sufficient community that feeds upon its own excrements, and that Glaucon in the *Republic* calls "a city of sows" (372d).

11. It must not be forgotten that the city of Athens is, according to the myth related by the Egyptian priest in *Timaeus,* the *partum* of Athena *parthēnos,* the lover-of-war (*philopólemos*). As a relevant part of the *Republic* is devoted to the degeneration of the city at peace with its neighbors, so a relevant part of the *Timaeus* will be devoted to the city at war with its neighbors. See *Timaeus,* 23e, 24d.

12. It is well known that the luxurious city assigns the procreation of the ruling class to the class of the guardians, who share with each other the community of women and their offspring. In the abolition of privacy entailed by their mating practices, the guardians succumb to the order of a "geometric" necessity—subject to an incestous logic of social planning—rather than, as Glaucon objects to Socrates, to the order of an "erotic" necessity. See *Republic,* 458d.

13. See also Brann, "Music of the *Republic,*" 28.

14. Already within Glaucon's "city of sows" dissension occurs when it turns out that, whereas it is the very principle of this city that each individual practice only one τέχνη, each will have to practice also that of money-making, hence two τέχναι.

15. Brann, "Music of the *Republic,*" 42–43, 45.

16. Brann refers her reader to Aristotle, *Nicomachean Ethics* 1102b(30).

17. Plato, *Symposium,* trans. W. R. M. Lamb, Loeb Classical Library 3 (Cambridge: Harvard University Press, 1983), 209a–b. Translations adapted.

18. See the definition of "generic dominant," and that of the "system of expectations" imposed upon the audience by such a dominant, found in Jauss, *Toward an Aesthetic of Reception,* 81.

19. Cf. Plato, *Republic,* 399e–401b; *Symposium,* 209a–e.

20. Cf. Plato, *Sophist,* 236c.

21. Cf. Plato, *Phaedrus,* 250b.

22. Cf. Plato, *Republic,* 347d.
23. Cf. Plato, *Laws,* 757c.
24. Cf. Plato, *Symposium,* 197a–b; *Phaedrus,* 265b.
25. John Sallis, *Crossings: Nietzsche and the Space of Tragedy* (Chicago: University of Chicago Press, 1991), 33.
26. Friedrich Nietzsche, *The Birth of Tragedy,* in Nietzsche, *The Birth of Tragedy and The Case and Wagner,* trans. Walter Kaufmann (New York: Vintage, 1967), 36.
27. Ibid.
28. As agencies of prophecy, Socrates mentions the prophetess at Delphi, as well as the prophetess at Dodona, in *Phaedrus,* 244a–b.
29. Virgil, *Aeneis,* 6.100. My translation.
30. Virgil, *Aeneid,* trans. Robert Fitzgerald (New York: Vintage, 1990), 6.151–53.
31. Cf. Nietzsche, *The Birth of Tragedy,* 141.
32. Euripides, *Bacchae,* lines 737–68, trans. W. Arrowsmith, eds. D. Grene and R. Lattimore, in *Greek Tragedies,* vol. 3 (Chicago: University of Chicago Press, 1968): 189–260.
33. Ibid., line 1146.
34. See W. Arrowsmith's reconstruction of the *lacuna* between lines 1329 and 1330 in his translation of Euripides' *Bacchae* (page 253), executed on the basis, mainly, of the *Christus Patiens.*
35. Cf. Sallis, *Crossings,* 9–41.
36. Ibid., 42–75.
37. It must be kept in mind, however, that it was Apollo at Delphi who set Socrates on his ascent to truth. See John Sallis, *Being and Logos,* 46–54, and Plato, *Apology,* trans. H. N. Fowler, Loeb Classical Library 1 (Cambridge: Harvard University Press, 1982), 21a–24b.
38. Cf. Plato, *Republic,* 476b–d.
39. Ibid., 477a–78d.
40. The truth of the Socratic philosopher is also of a higher nature, of course, than the truth accessible to the poet who loves beauty and to the political ruler who loves justice.
41. Cf. Plato, *Timaeus,* 47e–49d.
42. Cf. Plato, *Symposium,* 197a.
43. Cf. Plato, *Republic,* 329c.
44. Incidentally, this attempt is conducted by Socrates with the simultaneous aid of thought *and* sensation.
45. Cf. Plato, *Symposium* 202e–3a.
46. Cf. Plato, *Timaeus,* 37c–38c.
47. Cf. Plato, *Republic,* 475b.
48. Cf. Plato, *Republic,* 477b–e, 511d, 518c, 527d; *Phaedrus* 247c–d, 248d; Brann, "Music of the *Republic,*" 44.
49. Cf. Plato, *Phaedrus,* 249b–c. One ought to remark, at this juncture, the instance of degeneration at play in the *interdependence* of collection, recollection, and learning. The *logismô* that collects sensuous perceptions—images of the *eidē*—into speech enables the recollection of the soul by which a prelapsarian *vision of the eidē* takes place *again* in speech. At play within the movement by which *pathēmata* enable learning is a dissolution of the boundaries separating the sensible from the eidetic, the opinable from the noetic. Let me briefly reconstruct the discursive progression by which the *Phaedrus* illus-

trates this dissolution of boundaries (246a–49d). What is said in speech is, by being said in speech, gathered into (the unity of) an *eidos* and according to an *eidos*. This gathering into unity is not just a form of nominalism, correlative, for instance, to the property of a name to name several distinct things. It is, rather, a matter of learning. What is said in speech is implicitly learned according to *eidos*. Derived from the verb εἴδω, to see, *eidos* signifies, in the first instance, the unity of something that is manifest to sight. But one learns from the myth of the chariot in the *Phaedrus* that the *eidē* can only be seen indirectly by man; they can only be recollected. Taking place in man's soul, recollection, *anamnesis,* is the indirect seeing of an *eidos,* provoked by the perception of a sensuous image. Therefore, learning what is said in speech according to *eidos* is a matter of gathering into an *eidos* and according to an *eidos* a thing that manifests itself in the realm of the visible. The *eidos* into which and according to which this gathering is effected is, in turn, recollected as a result of the provocation induced by the sight of the visible thing. However, the progression described above is incomplete as long as one does not draw a distinction between the different degrees by which images of different kinds may be collected in speech and recollected in accordance with *eidos*. In the dialectics of recollection in *lógos,* this is the moment when the erotic comes into play. Of all the *eidē,* the beautiful is the one that shines most brightly, both in the region of the visible and in the vision of the divine banquet described in the myth of the chariot. The special shining of the beautiful is such that it makes manifest the separation of image from *eidos*. Hence, the collection in speech that entails a recollection in accordance with the *eidos* finds an eminent instance of substantiation in the recollection of the beautiful. This distinct recollection entails, in turn, an erotic begetting, a begetting of learning "upon the beautiful"—a musico-erotic *poíesis*.

50. Cf. Plato, *Phaedrus* 246c, 247c–d, 248d.

51. See Hans-Georg Gadamer, *Truth and Method,* trans. (revised) J. Weinsheimer and D. G. Marshall (New York: Crossroads, 1990), 405, 407.

52. Plato, *Theaetetus,* trans. Harold North Fowler, Loeb Classical Library 7 (Cambridge: Harvard University Press, 1977), 176b. Translations adapted. See also Plato, *Republic,* 500c, and Brann, "Music of the *Republic,*" 68.

53. Cf. Plato, *Symposium,* 210a.

54. See Plato, *Republic,* 511b, 534c–d; *Phaedrus* 276e.

55. The above remarks are based upon the assumption that the eternity of the Platonic *eidē* translates, "perhaps," as Derrida suggests in his *Introduction* to Husserl's "The Origin of Geometry," into "another name for a non-empirical historicity"—the scene of a temporality, that is, unhinged from the *logistikòn* of exactitude uttered by the sciences of "reckoning," such as mathematics and geometry (see Plato, *Republic* 522c, 533b–c), and grafted, instead, upon the hospitable cognition of the *lógos* of dialectical inquiry. Rather than as the unmoving and unmovable source of eternal types for a contingent world of *mimesis,* the eternity of the *eidē* might be taken, in sum, as the scene of the Socratic evasion from the hallucination of a temporality (and of the historicity pertinent to it) dominated by the empirical paradigms of "scientific" objectivity. See Derrida, *Introduction,* in Husserl, *L'origine de la géometrie,* 110. These intuitions of the young Derrida blossomed, as is well known, in his enquiry into the Platonic myth of the Chora. See Jacques Derrida, "Chôra," in *Poikilia* (Paris: EHESS, 1987): 265–96; "How to Avoid Speaking: Denials," in Sanford Budick and Wolfgang Iser, eds. *Languages of the Unsayable: The Play of Nega-*

tivity in Literature and Literary Theory (New York: Columbia University Press, 1989): 31–38; *"Foi et savoir,"* in Jacques Derrida and Gianni Vattimo, *La religion* (Paris: Seuil, 1996) § 23–25.

56. See Brann, "Music of the *Republic,*" 69.

57. Cf. John Sallis, *Stone* (Bloomington: Indiana University Press, 1994), 27–29, where one finds a brilliant treatment of the logic of political actuality.

58. Hegel, *Aesthetics: Lectures on Fine Art,* part 3, sec. 1, chap. 1.2a.

59. The Song of Songs (in TANAKH: 1405–17).

60. I owe to Ilana Pardes the insight about the lack of sexual consummation that distinguishes the Song of Songs from its pagan counterparts of erotic love. See *Countertraditions in the Bible,* 125, 132, 138, 142.

61. In this passage I adopt Harold Fish's approach to the Song of Songs in *Poetry with a Purpose,* where he recognizes in the poem "the shifting kaleidoscope of a dream" (89).

62. See Altizer, *History as Apocalypse,* 134.

63. Homer, *Iliad,* trans. Fitzgerald, bk. 16, pp. 382–83.

Bibliography

Alezraki, Jaime. *Borges and the Kabbalah*. Cambridge: Cambridge University Press, 1988.

Alter, Robert. *The World of Biblical Literature*. New York: Basic Books, 1991.

Altizer, Thomas J. J. *Genesis and Apocalypse: A Theological Voyage Toward Authentic Christianity*. Louisville: Westminster/John Knox Press, 1990.

———. *History as Apocalypse*. Albany: State University of New York Press, 1985.

Anderson, Benedict. *Imagined Communities: Reflections of the Origins and Spread of Nationalism*. New York: Verso, 1983.

Aristotle. *Poétique*. Translated by J. Hardy. Paris: Belles Lettres, 1977.

———. *Poetics*. Translated by I. Bywater. In *The Rhetoric and the Poetics of Aristotle*. New York: Modern Library, 1954.

———. *Poetics*. Translated by J. Hutton. New York: Norton, 1982.

Aschkenasy, Nehama."Biblical Females in a Joycean Episode." *Modern Language Studies* 15, no. 4 (fall 1985).

Auerbach, Eric. *Mimesis: The Representation of Reality in Western Literature*. Translated by Willard R. Trask. Princeton: Princeton University Press, 1991.

Augustine. *Confessions*. Translated by R. S. Pine-Coffin. London: Penguin, 1961.

Badaloni, Nicola. *Introduzione a Vico*. Roma: Laterza, 1988.

Bal, Mieke. "Dealing/With/Women: Daughters in the Book of Judges." In *The Book and the Text: The Bible and Literary Theory*. Edited by Regina Schwartz. Cambridge: Basil Blackwell, 1990.

———. *Death and Dissimetry: The Politics of Coherence on Sisera's Death*. Bloomington: Indiana University Press, 1988.

———. *Lethal Love: Feminist Literary Interpretations of Biblical Love Stories*. Bloomington: Indiana University Press, 1987.

Balsamo, Gian. *Rachele accucciata sugli dèi: Il Fallo e la Legge*. Roma: Vascello, 1993.

———. *Legitimate Filiation and Gender Segregation: Law and Fiction in Texts by Derrida, Hegel, Joyce, Pirandello, and Vico*, Ph. D. diss., Vanderbilt University, 1994, Ann Arbor: University Microfilms International, 1994.

Beja, Morris. *James Joyce: A Literary Life*. Columbus: Ohio State University Press, 1992.

La Bibbia Concordata. Milano: Mondadori, 1982.

Blake, William. *Complete Writings*. Edited by Geoffrey Keynes. London: Oxford University Press, 1967.

Borges, Jorge Luis. "Borges and I." Translated by J. E. Irby. *Labyrinths*. New York: New Directions, 1964.

———. "The Circular Ruins." Translated by James E. Irby. *Labyrinths*. New York: New Directions, 1964.

———. "The Garden of Forking Paths." Translated by Donald A. Yates. *Labyrinths*. New York: New Directions, 1964.

———. "The Kabbalah." Translated by Eliot Weinberger. *Seven Nights*. New York: New Directions, 1984.

———. "Kafka and His Precursors." Translated by J. E. Irby. *Labyrinths*. New York: New Directions, 1964.

Brann, Eva. "The Music of the *Republic*." *ATON*, 1, no. 1 (April 1967): I–117.

Bremmer, J. "Scapegoat Rituals in Ancient Greece." *HSCP* 87 (1983).

Brown, Norman Oliver. *Closing Time*. New York: Vintage Books, 1974.

Burkert, Walter. *Homo Necans: The Anthropology of Ancient Greek Sacrificial Ritual and Myth*. Translated by Peter Bing. Berkeley: University of California Press, 1983.

———. *Greek Religion*. Cambridge: Harvard University Press, 1985.

———. *Structure and History in Greek Mythology and Ritual*. Berkeley: University of California Press, 1979.

Cheng, Vincent J. "Stephen Dedalus and the Black Panther Vampire." *JJQ* 24, no. 2 (winter 1987): 161–76.

Chrétien de Troyes. *Le roman de Perceval ou Le conte du graal*. Edited by William Roach. Geneva: Droz, 1959.

———. *Perceval: The Story of the Grail*. Edited by Nigel Bryant. Cambridge: D. S. Brewer, 1982.

———. *The Story of the Grail, or Perceval*. Edited by William W. Kibler. New York: Garland, 1990.

Church, Margaret. "*A Portrait* and Vico: A Source Study." In Thomas F. Staley and Bernard Benstock, eds. *Approaches to Joyce's Portrait*. Pittsburgh: Pittsburgh University Press, 1976: 77–89.

Corea, Gena. *The Mother Machine*. London: The Women Press, 1988.

Cornell, Drucilla. *The Philosophy of the Limit*. New York: Routledge, 1992.

Cormford, F. M. *Plato's Cosmology: The Timaeus of Plato*. London: Routledge and K. Paul, 1937.

Damrosch, David. *The Narrative Covenant: Transformations of Genre in the Growth of Biblical Literature*. Ithaca: Cornell University Press, 1987.

Dante Alighieri. *Vita Nuova*. Milano: EDIS, 1995.

———. *Inferno*. Translated by Robert Pinsky. New York: Farrar, Straus and Giroux, 1996.

———. *Inferno*. Translated by Allen Mandelbaum. New York: Bantam, 1982.

———. *Inferno*. Translated by John Ciardi. New York: New American Library, 1982.

Day, Robert Adams. "How Stephen Wrote His Vampire Poem." *JJQ* 17, no. 2 (winter 1980): 183–98.

Day, Peggy L. *Gender and Difference in Ancient Israel*. Minneapolis: Fortress Press, 1989.

De Man, Paul. *Blindness and Insight.* Minneapolis: University of Minnesota Press, 1986.

Derrida, Jacques. "Before the Law." Translated by Antal Ronell (with Christine Roulston). In Jacques Derrida, *Acts of Literature.* Edited by Derek Attridge. New York: Routledge, 1992: 181–220.

———. "Chôra." *Poikilia.* Études offertes à Jean-Pierre Vernant. Paris: EHESS, 1987: 265–296.

———. *Circonfession.* Geoffrey Bennington et Jacques Derrida, *Jacques Derrida.* Paris: Seuil, 1991.

———. *Circumfession.* Geoffrey Bennington and Jacques Derrida, *Jacques Derrida.* Translated by G. Bennington. Chicago: University of Chicago Press, 1993.

———. *Disseminations.* Translated by Barbara Johnson. Chicago: University of Chicago Press, 1981.

———. "Foi et savoir." In Jacques Derrida and Gianni Vattimo, *La religion.* Paris: Seuil, 1996.

———. "Force de loi: Le fondement mystique de l'autorité." Cardozo Law Review 11, no. 5–6: 919–1046.

———. *The Gift of Death.* Translated by David Wills. Chicago: University of Chicago Press, 1995.

———. *Given Time: I. Counterfeit Money.* Translated by Peggy Kamuf. Chicago: The University of Chicago Press, 1992.

———. *Glas.* Paris: Galilée, 1974.

———. "How to Avoid Speaking: Denials." Sanford Budick and Wolfgang Iser, eds., *Languages of the Unsayable: The Play of Negativity in Literature and Literary Theory.* New York: Columbia University Press, 1989: 3–70.

———. *Introduction.* In Edmund Husserl, *L'origine de la géometrie.* Translated by J. Derrida. Paris: Presses Universitaires de France, 1962.

———. "La loi du genre." Parages. Paris: Galilée, 1986, 250–87.

———. *Margins of Philosophy.* Translated by Alan Bass. Chicago: University of Chicago Press, 1986.

———. *Mémoires d'aveugle: L'autoportrait et autres ruines.* Paris: Ministère de la Culture.

———. *Memoirs of the Blind.* Translated by Pascale-Anne Brault and Michael Naas. Chicago: University of Chicago Press, 1993.

———. "The Pit and the Pyramid: Introduction to Hegel's Semiology." *Margins of Philosophy.* Translated by Alan Bass. Chicago: University of Chicago Press, 1986: 69–108.

———. *Positions.* Translated by Alan Bass. Chicago: University of Chicago Press, 1981.

——— et Gianni Vattimo. *Le religion.* Paris; Seuil, 1996.

———. *The Truth in Painting.* Translated by Geoffrey Bennington and Ian McLeod. Chicago: University of Chicago Press, 1987.

———. "Two Words for Joyce." Translated by Geoffrey Bennington. Derek Attridge and Daniel Ferrer, eds., *Post-structuralist Joyce.* Cambridge: Cambridge University Press 1984: 145–59.

———. *Ulysse gramophone: Deux mots pour Joyce.* Paris: Galilée, 1987.

———. "Ulysses Gramophone: Hear Say Yes in Joyce." Translated by Tina Kendall (with Shari Benstock). Derek Attridge, ed. *Acts of Literature.* New York: Routledge, 1992: 253–309

———. *La voix et le phénomène: Introduction au problème du signe dans la phénomènologie de Husserl.* Paris: Presses Universitaires de France, 1967.

Detienne, Marcel. "*Pratiques culinaires et esprit de sacrifice.*" In M. Detienne et J.-P. Vernant, *La cuisine du sacrifice en pays grecs.* Paris: Gallimard, 1979: 7–35

Dragonetti, Roger. *La vie de la lettre au moyen age.* Paris: Seuil, 1980.

Eilberg-Schwarts, Howard. *The Savage in Judaism: An Anthropology of Israelite Religion and Ancient Judaism.* Bloomington: Indiana University Press, 1990.

Elledge, S., ed. *Milton's* "Lycidas." New York: Harper & Row, 1966.

Ellmann, Richard. *James Joyce.* Oxford: Oxford University Press, 1983.

Euripides, *Bacchae.* Translated by W. Arrowsmith. In D. Grene and R. Lattimore, eds. *Greek Tragedies.* Vol. 3, Chicago: University of Chicago Press, 1968.

Fagles, Robert, ed. *The Odyssey* by Homer. New York: Viking, 1996.

Fauré, Gabriel. *Mallarmé à Tournon.* Paris: Horizon de France, 1946.

Fewell, Danna N. and Gunn, David M. "Controlling Perspectives: Women, Men, and the Authority of Violence in Judges 4–5." *Journal of the American Academy of Religion* 5 (fall 1990) 389–411.

Fish, Harold. *Poetry with a Purpose: Biblical Poetics and Interpretation.* Bloomington: Indiana University Press, 1988.

Foucault, Michel. *La volonté de savoir.* Paris: Gallimard, 1976.

———. *Les mots et les choses.* Paris: Gallimard, 1966.

Freud, Sigmund. *Moses and Monotheism.* New York: Vintage, 1967.

———. *An Outline of Psychoanalysis.* New York: Norton, 1989.

———. *Totem and Taboo.* New York: Norton, 1989.

———. *The Complete Letters of Sigmund Freud to Wilhelm Fliess, 1881–1904.* Translated and edited by J. M. Massou. Cambridge: Harvard University Press, 1985.

Froula, Christine. "Mothers of Invention/Doaters of Inversion: Narcissan Scenes in *Finnegans Wake.*" In Susan Stanford Friedman, *Joyce: The Return of the Repressed.* Ithaca: Cornell University Press, 1993: 283–303.

———. *Modernism's Body: Sex, Culture, and Joyce.* New York: Columbia University Press, 1996.

Fuchs, Esther. "'For I Have the Way of Women': Deception, Gender, and Ideology in Biblical Narrative." *Semeia* 42 (1988).

Fuller, Lon L. *Legal Fictions.* Stanford: Stanford University Press, 1967.

Gadamer, Hans-Georg. *Truth and Method.* Translated by J. Weinsheimer and D. G. Marshall. New York: Crossroads, 1990.

Gasché, Rodolphe. *Inventions of Difference: On Jacques Derrida.* Cambridge: Harvard University Press, 1994.

Gifford, Don. *Ulysses Annotated.* Berkeley: University of California Press, 1988.

Gilbert, Stuart. *James Joyce's Ulysses.* New York: Vintage, 1955.

Girard, René. *La Violence et le sacré*. Paris: Grasset, 1972.

Gordon, John. "Notes in Response to Michael Seidel's '*Ulysses*' Black Panther Vampire.'" *JJQ* 15, no. 3 (spring 1978): 229–35

Grabher, Carlo, ed.. *Inferno* di Dante. Bari: Laterza, 1964.

———. *Paradiso* di Dante. Bari: Laterza, 1964.

———. *Purgatorio* di Dante. Bari: Laterza, 1964.

Greimas, A. J. *Dictionnaire de l'ancien français*. Paris: Larousse, 1968.

Hampshire, Stuart, "Joyce and Vico: La via intermedia." Translated by P. Massimi. G. Tagliacozzo, ed., *Giambattista Vico: Galiani, Joyce, Levi-Strauss, Piaget*. Roma: Armando, 1975, 151–72.

Harper's Dictionary of Classical Literature and Antiquities. Edited by Harry T. Peck. New York: Harper, 1898.

Hart, H. L. A. *The Concept of Love*. Oxford: Clarendon Press, 1962.

Hayman, David. *Joyce et Mallarmé*. 2 vols. Paris: Lettres Modernes, 1956.

Hegel G. W. F. *Aesthetics: Lectures on Fine Art*. Translated by T. M. Knox. 2 vols. Oxford: Clarendon, 1975.

———. *Encyclopaedia Logic* (with the *Zusätze*). Translated by T. F. Geraets, W. A. Suchting, H. S. Harris. Indianapolis: Hackett, 1991.

———. *Encyclopaedia of the Philosophical Sciences in Outline*. Translated by Steven A. Taubeneck and edited by Ernst Behler. New York: Continuum, 1990.

———. *Phenomenology of Spirit*. Translated by A. V. Miller. Oxford: Oxford University Press 1977.

———. *Philosophy of Right*. Translated by T. M. Knox. Oxford: Oxford University Press, 1967.

———. *Science of Logic*. Translated by A. V. Miller. Atlantic Highlands: Humanities Press International, 1989.

Heidegger, Martin. *Being and Time*. Translated by John Macquarrie and Edward Robinson. San Francisco: Harper, 1962.

———. "Language." *Poetry, Language, Thought*. Edited and translated by Albert Hofstadter. New York: Harper and Row, 1975.

———. "The Origin of the Work of Art." *Poetry, Language, Thought*. Edited and translated by Albert Hofstadter. New York: Harper & Row, 1975.

Herr, Cheryl T. "Theosophy, Guilt, and 'That Word Known to All Men' in Joyce's *Ulysses*." *JJQ* 18. no. 1 (Fall 1980): 45–54.

Hesiod. *Theogony. The Poems of Hesiod*. Translated by R. M. Frazer. Norman: Oklahoma University Press, 1986.

Homer. *The Iliad*. Translated by Robert Fitzgerald. New York: Anchor, 1975.

———. *The Iliad of Homer*. Edited by M. M. Willcock. New York: St. Martin's Press, 1984.

———. *The Odyssey*. Translated by A. T. Murray and revised by G. E. Dimock. Loeb Classical Library. 2 vols. Cambridge: Harvard University Press, 1995.

Hyde, Douglas, ed. and trans. *The Love Songs of Connacht*. Irish University Press, 1971.

Iser, Wolfgang. *The Implied Reader*. Baltimore: Johns Hopkins University Press, 1974.

Jauss, Hans Robert. *Toward an Aesthetic of Reception*. Translated by Timothy Bahti. Minneapolis: University of Minnesota Press, 1982.

Jay, Nancy. *Throughout Your Generations Forever: Sacrifice, Religion, and Paternity*. Chicago: University of Chicago Press, 1992.

Jenkins, Ralph. "Theosophy in 'Scylla and Charybdis.'" *MFS* 15, no. 1 (spring 1969): 35–48.

Jones, Ellen Carol. "'Writing the Mystery of Himself': Paternity in *Ulysses*." In Bernard Benstock, ed., *James Joyce: The Augmented Ninth*. Syracuse University Press, 1988: 226–32.

Josipovici, Gabriel. *The Book of God: A Response to the Bible*. New Haven: Yale University Press, 1988.

Joyce, James. *The Critical Writings*. Edited by Richard Ellmann and Ellsworth Mason. Ithaca: Cornell University Press, 1989.

———. "Epilogue to Ibsen's 'Ghosts.'" *The Critical Writings*, Edited by Ellsworth Mason and Richard Ellmann. Ithaca: Cornell University Press, 1989.

———. *Finnegans Wake*. New York: Penguin, 1976.

———. *James Joyce Archive*. Edited by Michael Groden et al. 63 vols. New York: Garland, 1978.

———. *Letters of James Joyce*. edited by Richard Ellmann. 2 vols. New York: Viking Press, 1966.

———. *A Portrait of the Artist as a Young Man*. New York: Penguin, 1976.

———. *Selected Letters*. Edited by Richard Ellmann. New York: Viking, 1975.

———. "The Sisters." *Dubliners*. New York: Penguin, 1976.

———. *Ulysses*. Edited by Hans Walter Gabler. New York: Vintage, 1986.

———. *Ulysses: A Critical and Synoptic edition*. Edited by Gabler et al. 3 vols. New York: Garland, 1984.

———. *Ulysses: A Facsimile of the Manuscript*. Edited by Clive Driver and Harry Levin. 3 vols. New York: Farrar, Straus and Giroux, 1975.

Kant, Immanuel. *Critique of Judgment*. Translated by Werner S. Pluhar. Indianapolis: Hackett, 1986.

———. *Critique of Practical Reason*. Translated by L. W. Beck. New York: Macmillan, 1956.

Knox, T. M. "Translator's Notes" to Hegel's *Philosophy of Right*. Hegel, *Philosophy of Right*. Translated by T. M. Knox. Oxford: Oxford University Press, 1967:298–376.

Krell, David Farrell. "Lucinde's Shame: Hegel, Sensuous Woman, and the Law." In Drucilla Cornell, Michael Rosenfeld, and David Gray Carlson, eds. *Hegel and Legal Theory*. New York: Routledge, 1991.

Lacan, Jacques. "Les articulations de la pièce." *Le Séminaire* 7. Paris: Éditions du Seuil, 1960.

———. "L'éclat d'Antigone." In *Le Séminaire* 7. Paris: Éditions du Seuil, 1960:285–298.

———. "Subversion du sujet et dialectique du désir dans l'inconscient freudien." In *Écrits 2*. Paris: Seuil, 1971: 151–191.

———. "The Subversion of the Subject and the Dialectic of Desire in the Freudian Unconscious." In *Écrits: A Selection*. Translated by Alan Sheridan. New York: Norton, 1977.

————."Fonction et champ de la parole et du langage in psychanalyse." *Écrits 1.* Paris: Seuil, 1966: 111–207.

————. "Le séminaire sur 'La lettre volée.'" *Écrits 1.* Paris: Seuil, 1966. 19–75.

————. "La signification du phallus." *Écrits 2.* Paris: Seuil, 1971. 103–115.

Laurent, Jenny. "The Strategy of Form." T. Todorov, ed. *French Literary Theory Today.* Cambridge: Cambridge University Press, 1982.

Lawrence, Karen. "Paternity as Legal Fiction in *Ulysses.*" In Bernard Benstock, ed., *James Joyce: The Augmented Ninth.* Syracuse University Press, 1988: 233–43.

Levinas, Emmanuel. *Le temps et l'autre.* Paris: Quadrige, 1983.

Lilla, Mark. *G. B. Vico: The Making of an Anti-Modern.* Cambridge: Harvard University Press, 1993.

Litz, A. Walton. "Vico and Joyce." In G. Tagliacozzo and H. White, eds., *Giambattista Vico: An International Symposium.* Baltimore: Johns Hopkins University Press, 1969: 245–258.

McHugh, Roland. *Annotations to Finnegans Wake.* Baltimore: Johns Hopkins University Press, 1991.

Madsen, Deborah L. *Rereading Allegory: A Narrative Approach to Genre.* New York: St. Martin's Press, 1994.

Mahaffey, Vicky. *Reauthorizing Joyce.* Cambridge: Cambridge University Press, 1988.

Maine, Henry S. *Ancient Law: Its Connections with the Early History of Society, and Its Relation to Modern Ideas.* New York: Scribner, 1864.

Mallarmé, Stéphane. *Oeuvres Complètes.* Edited by Carl Paul Barbier and Charles Gordon Millan. Paris: Flammarion, 1983.

————. *Collected Poems.* Translated by Henry Weinfield. Berkeley: University of California Press, 1994.

Man, Paul de. *Blindness and Insight.* Minneapolis: University of Minnesota Press, 1986.

Mann, Thomas. *Joseph and His Brothers.* Translated by H. T. Lowe-Porter. Vol. 1. New York: Knopf, 1934.

Marcus, Frederick R. "Vico and the Hebrews." *New Vico Studies,* 13 (1995): 14–32.

Marion, Jean-Luc. *God Without Being.* Chicago: University of Chicago Press, 1991.

Montaigne, Michel de. *"De l'experience."* In *Les essais de Michel de Montaigne.* Edited by Pierre Villeby. 3 vols. Paris: Alcan, 1922–23.

————. *"Apologie de Raimond Sebond."* In *Les essais de Michel de Montaigne.* Edited by Pierre Villeby.

Montesquieu, C. L. de S. *De l'esprit des lois.* 2 vols. Paris: Garnier Frères, 1973.

Moreiras, Alberto. "Pharmaconomy: Stephen and the Daedalids." Susan Stanford Friedman, ed. *Joyce: The Return of the Repressed.* Ithaca: Cornell University Press, 1993:58–88.

Nietzsche, Friedrich. *Philosophy in the Tragic Age of the Greeks.* Translated by Marianne Cowan. Washington: Gateway, 1987.

————. *The Birth of Tragedy and The Case of Wagner.* Translated by Walter Kaufmann. New York: Vintage, 1967.

——. *Werke: Kritische Gesamtausgabe*. Edited by G. Colli and M. Montinari. Berlin: Gruyter, 1967–.

Olivier, Pierre J. J. *Legal Fictions in Practice and Legal Science*. Rotterdam: Rotterdam University Press, 1975.

Ovid. *Metamorphoses* (*Metamorphoseon*). Edited by B. A. Van Proosdij. Leiden: Brill, 1975.

——. *The Metamorphoses of Ovid*. Translated by A. E. Watts. Los Angeles: Los Angeles University Press, 1954.

——. *Metamorphosen*. Dublin: Weidmann, 1969.

Pardes, Ilana. *Countertraditions in the Bible: A Feminist Approach*. Cambridge: Harvard University Press, 1992.

Pater, Walter. *The Renaissance: Studies in Art and Poetry* (London: Macmillan, 1877).

Paul. Letter to the Galatians. *The New Oxford Annotated Bible with the Apocrypha*. New York: Oxford University Press, 1977: 1410–16

——. Letter to the Romans. *The New Oxford Annotated Bible with the Apocrypha*. New York: Oxford University Press, 1977: 1361–79.

Petrocchi, Giorgio, ed. *La Commedia secondo l'antica vulgata* di Dante Alighieri. *Inferno* Vol. 2. Milano: Mondadori, 1966.

Pietropaolo, Domenico. "Vico and Literary History in the Early Joyce." In Donald Phillip Verene, ed. *Vico and Joyce*. New York: State University of New York Press, 1987.

Pinsky, Robert, trans. *The Inferno by Dante*. New York: Noonday, 1996.

Plato. *Apology*. Translated by H. N. Fowler. Loeb Classical Library 1. Cambridge: Harvard University Press, 1982.

——. *Laws*. Translated by R. G. Bury. Loeb Classical Library 10–11. Cambridge: Harvard University Press, 1984.

——. *Phaedo*. Translated by Harold North Fowler. Loeb Classical Library 1. Cambridge: Harvard University Press, 1982.

——. *Phaedrus*. Translated by Harold North Fowler. Loeb Classical Library 1. Cambridge: Harvard University Press, 1982.

——. *Republic*. Translated by Paul Shorey. Loeb Classical Library 5–6. Cambridge: Harvard University Press, 1980.

——. *Sophist*. Translated by Harold North Fowler. Loeb Classical Library 7. Cambridge: Harvard University Press, 1977.

——. *Symposium*. Translated by W. R. M. Lamb. Loeb Classical Library 3. Cambridge: Harvard University Press, 1983.

——. *Theaetetus*. Translated by Harold North Fowler. Loeb Classical Library 7. Cambridge: Harvard University Press, 1977.

——. *Timaeus*. Translated by R. G. Bury. Loeb Classical Library 9. Cambridge: Harvard University Press, 1989.

Posner, Richard A. *Law and Literature: A Misunderstood Relation*. Cambridge: Harvard University Press, 1988.

Pritchard, J. B., ed. *Ancient Near East in Pictures Relating to the Old Testament*. Princeton: Princeton University Press, 1969.

Rabaté, Jean-Michel. *James Joyce, Authorized Reader*. Baltimore: Johns Hopkins University Press, 1991.

Raleigh, John Henry. *The Chronicle of Leopold and Molly Bloom.* Berkeley: University of California Press, 1977.

Reynolds, Mary. T. "Joyce's Editions of Dante." *JJQ* 15, no. 4 (summer 1978): 380–82.

Rose, Margaret A. *Parody: Ancient, Modern, and Post-Modern.* Cambridge: Cambridge University Press, 1993.

Sallis, John. *Being and Logos.* Atlantic Highlands: Humanities Press International, 1986.

———. *Crossings: Nietzsche and the Space of Tragedy.* Chicago: University of Chicago Press, 1991.

———. *Delimitations: Phenomenology and the End of Metaphysics.* Bloomington: Indiana University Press, 1986.

———. *Double Truth.* New York: State University of New York Press, 1995.

———. *Echoes: After Heidegger.* Bloomington: Indiana University Press, 1990.

———. *Spacings of Reason and Imagination: In Texts of Kant, Fichte, Hegel.* Chicago: University of Chicago Press, 1987.

———. *Stone.* Bloomington: Indiana University Press, 1994.

Sarna, Nahum M. *The JPS Torah Commentary: Genesis.* Philadelphia: Jewish Publication Society, 1989.

Scholes Robert and Richard M. Kain, eds. *The Workshop of Daedalus: James Joyce and the Raw Materials for A Portrait of the Artist as a Young Man.* Evanston: Northwestern University Press, 1965.

Schwartz, Regina M. "Monotheism and the Violence of the Identities." *Raritan* 14, no. 3 (winter 1995): 119–40.

———. "Nations and Nationalism: Adultery in the House of David." *Critical Inquiry* 19, no. 1 (autumn 1992): 131–50.

———. *The Curse of Cain: The Violent Legacy of Mountheism.* Chicago: University of Chicago Press, 1997.

Shakespeare, William. *Hamlet.* New York: Norton, 1963.

Singleton, Charles S., ed. and trans. *Dante's Paradiso.* Princeton: Princeton University Press, 1991.

———. *Dante's Inferno, Commentary.* Princeton: Princeton University Press, 1991.

———. *Dante's Purgatorio. Commentary.* Princeton: Princeton University Press, 1973.

Shlonsky, Tuvia. "Literary Parody. Remarks on its Method and Function." *Proceedings of the 4th Congress of the International Comparative Association* 1964, ed. François Jost, vol. 2 (The Hague, 1966); 797–801.

Sophocles. *Antigone.* Translated by E. Wyckoff. In *Greek Tragedies.* Edited by D. Grene and R. Lattimore, 3 vols. Chicago: University of Chicago Press, 1968, 1:177–228.

Speiser, E. A., ed. and trans. *Genesis. The Anchor Bible.* New York: Doubleday, 1964.

Swedenborg, Emanuel. *Marriage Love.* New York: Houghton, 1907.

Talmud. *Tractate Sanhedrin.* Translated by J. Shachter and H. Freedman. London: Soncino Press, 1994.

TANAKH. Philadelphia: Jewish Publication Society, 1985.

Taylor, A. E. *A Commentary on Plato's Timaeus*. London: Clarendon Press, 1928.

Thornton, Weldon. *Allusions in Ulysses*. Chapel Hill: University of North Carolina Press, 1987.

Verene, Donald Phillip. *Vico's Science of Imagination*. Ithaca: Cornell University Press, 1981.

Vernant, J.-P. *"Le mythe prométhéen chez Hesiode." Mythe et Societé en Grèce ancienne*. Paris: Maspero, 1974. 177–94.

Vico, Giambattista. *De constantia iurisprudentis. Pars prior: De constantia philosophiae*. Italian translation by Sandro Barbera. In Vico, *Opere giuridiche*. Edited by Paolo Cristofolini. Firenze: Sansoni, 1974: 353–86.

———. *De constantia iurisprudentis. Pars posterior: De constantia philologiae*. Italian translation by Sandro Barbera. *Opere giuridiche*: 387–732.

———. *La scienza nuova seconda* (1744). 2 vols. Bari: Laterza, 1942.

———. *De universi iuris uno principio et fine uno. Liber unus*. Italian translation by Carlo Sarchi. *Opere giuridiche*: 17–346.

Virgil. *Aeneid*. Translated by Robert Fitzgerald. New York: Vintage, 1990.

———. *Aeneis*. Torino: Einaudi, 1989.

Wilde, Oscar. *The Picture of Dorian Gray*. New York: Norton, 1988.

Wilden, Anthony. "Lacan and the Discourse of the Other." In Jacques Lacan, *Speech and Language in Psychoanalysis*. Translated by Anthony Wilden. Baltimore: Johns Hopkins University Press, 1989: 157–313.

Wlassics, Tibor. "Nota su Dante nell'*Ulisse*." *Rivista di letterature moderne e comparate* 24, f. 2 (Giugno 1971): 151–154.

Index

Abraham, 283 n. 19; genealogy of, as an example of a gender-exclusive historiography, 39–40, 46–47, 87; norm of circumcision established by, 40, 43, 83, 87, 152, 234; —, dealt with as an apotropaic simulacrum, 234; —, and the theme of genealogical legitimacy, 43, 87, 152; —, and filial incest, 83–84; —, as a warrantee of patrilineal consanguinity, 40, 43, 87, 152; his sacrifice of Isaac and the issue of dynastic supremacy, 230

Adams Day, Robert, 53, 54, 63, 66, 69

Aeschylus, 25, 37, 77, 90, 182

aesthetics: on the crossroad of and ethics, 28, 186–96; —, treated as complementary to the crossroad of genealogy and etiology, 186–92; —, treated as a locus of convergence for the totemic meal and the moral law, 186–87, 192, 195–96; on the of the literary archetype versus the ethics of moral typology, 194–96; of Mallarmé, intended as the self-sufficient realm of artistic creation, and contrasted with female pro-creation, 58–62; on the of primitive phallic architectures, 184; of reception, 76; of Romanticism, 99–100; on the of Stephen Dedalus, in relation to artistic transfiguration, 133; —, and its derivation from Thomas Aquinas, 65, 69–70, 76. *See also* ethics, genealogical chronicle, etiological tale, totemic meal

Agamemnon: and the curse of the House of Atreus, 182; diatribe of with Achilles, 224; —, and the issue of political degeneration, 241, 260; —, as a source of civil war, 229–30, 260; murder of by Clytaemnestra, 182; sacrifice of Iphigenia by and the issue of dynastic primacy, 230

Alezraki, Jaime, 43–44

Alighieri, Dante, 11, 25, 53–57, 65–72, 89, 92–93, 110, 135–37, 274 nn. 41 and 43, 275 nn. 56 and 58, 277 n. 28, 278 n. 12; Beatrice and, 67–73, 92–93, 138; his identification of Christ with Beatrice, 70–71; —, and with Mary, 71, 89; influence of on Stephen Dedalus's vampire poem, 57, 66–71; symbols of Christ's hypostasis in, 69

allegory: affinity of with Hegel's symbolic phantasy, 167–68; treatead as a modality of discourse in Joyce, 100, 102; the of procreation from the Gospel, seen as implicit in Stephen Dedalus's riddle of genealogy, 26, 95, 98–99, 102, 104, 107–13

Alter, Robert, 185, 222

Altizer, Thomas J. J., 10–11, 65–66, 70–71, 138, 230; his treatment of Blake's influence on Joyce, 65–66; Dante's gravest heresy according to, 70–71; his views on the Eucharist, 230–31, 272 n. 29, 288 n. 17, 289 n. 31

amor matris: Cranly's initiation of Stephen Dedalus to, 97, 128; Stephen Dedalus's concerns with, and the contrast of with God's paternity of Jesus, 97; —, and the contrast of with androlineal genealogy, 121; —, and contrast of with the legal fiction of paternity, 127–29; in *Ulysses*, 71 86, 97, 121, 127–29

androlineality: agencies of, 24, 27–8, 40, 115, 266; on kinship and, with

Onan: contrast of Matthew's parable of the "good sower" with the biblical story of, 103–4, 112–13

Orestes: consanguinity and, 182; on the right of blood of, 82; Stephen Dedalus and, 25, 77, 79, 82–83, 90

Ovid, 73, 131–32

parable: the genre of the and the treatment of lineage in *Ulysses*, 95–113; the of the Plums, as told by Stephen Dedalus, 26, 68, 111–12; —, biblical analogies in, 111–12; Stephen Dedalus's contrast of Matthew's of the "good sower" with the biblical story of Onan, 103–4, 112–13

Pardes, Ilana, 37, 142, 147–49, 233–34, 262

parody: distinction between the literary and extraliterary agendas pertinent to satire and in *Ulysses*, 77–79, 89–91; genealogy and in James Joyce, 18, 21, 25–26, 75–79, 89–91; of Genesis and the theme of genealogical legitimacy in Borges, 36–40; on the of patriotic speech in *Ulysses*, 111–12; presence of in Stephen Dedalus's vampire poem, 66. *See also* satire

parthenogenesis: filiation and in Borges's "The Circular Ruins," 36, 39, 42; on the constitution of the identity of the artist as a matter of, according to Stephen Dedalus, 77, 86, 90–91, 128–30; in Mallarmé's *Don du poème*, 58–9; patrilineal genealogy and in *Ulysses*, 82–83; Stephen Dedalus' vampire poem and the of the artist, 58–60, 77, 85–86

Pater, Walter, 54, 70

paterfamilias: *amor matris* and the right of, 84–86; divine auspices and the social primacy of the in ancient Roman culture, 84–5, 116–18, 124–26, 159, 176–79, 231–32; Hegel's views on the origins of modern civil right and the juridical concept of, 142–45, 159–60, 179–80. *See also* family estate, family suc-

cession, *filius*, gender, gender discrimination, legitimate succession

paternity: artistic emancipation and in Vico and in Joyce, 119–22; contrast of maternity and in James Joyce, 90–91, 96; —, dealt with as reflected in the reciprocal contamination of language and religion, 33–34; intended as a legal fiction in *Ulysses*, 18, 32, 34, 114–38; Mallarmé's concerns regarding the reciprocal influence of artistic creativity, maternity, and, 59–60; Stephen Dedalus's attempt at an artistic emancipation from, 127–30; Stephen Dedalus's concerns with *amor matris*, and their contrast with the legal fiction of, 127–29, 84–86, 127–29; Stephen Dedalus's pronouncement as to being a legal fiction, 18, 32, 34. *See also* maternity

patria potestas: in ancient Roman customs and law, 126, 163–64, 173–76

patriarch: comparison of the Roman *paterfamilias* with the Hebrew, 142–46; metaphorical equivalence between the blood of the and the sap of the genealogical tree, 46–47, 87, 235–36; pact linking the Hebrew to his family idols, 147–48; —, in the case of Laban, 151–53; Rachel's contribution to the constitution of the archetype of the Semitic, 154–58; Rachel's symbolic castration of the, 156–57; views of Gena Corea on the urge to self-generate of the, 36–37; traditional connection between the name and the genealogy of the, 37–38, 233

patricide: civil war and in ancient mythology, 182, 184; equivalence established by the Valerian law between all offenses against the private code of law and the crime of, 143, 174; Rachel's theft of Laban's idols, intended as a symbolic, 27, 158

patrilineality: Abraham's name, and the question of, 37, 39–40, 46; con-

174–76, 231–32; *iura imaginaria* and legal fictions in, 84–85, 175–78; *teologia mistica* and *iura imaginaria* in, 125–26. *See also* law
Rose, Margaret, 75
Russell, George William, 131

Sabellius, 86, 100, 107
sacred auspices: birds of, according to Swedenborg and to Vico, 116, 119; role played by in the determination of the primacy of the *paterfamilias* in the Roman family, 84–85, 116–18, 124–26, 159, 176–79, 231–32
sacrifice: blood and, 43, 46–47, 157, 225; genealogical legitimacy and in Borges, 42–49; of Iphigenia, 182; —, related to the issue of dynastic primacy, 230; of Isaac and the issue of dynastic primacy, 230
Sallis, John, 10, 254, 261–62, 264
Sarna, Nahum M., 150, 282 n. 16
Sargent, Cyril, 85, 101–2
Satan, 55, 65–6, 72–73, 136–38
satire: distinction between the literary and extraliterary agendas pertinent to parody and in *Ulysses*, 77–79, 89–91; Joyce's of the Attic tragedies of consanguinity, 76–77, 82–84, 90; role played by the genre of in Joyce's treatment of consanguinity and lineage, 89–91. *See also* parody
Schwartz, Regina M., 11; theory developed by on the affinity between the monotheistic covenant and nationalistic intolerance, 29–30, 220–28
Scripture (Holy): incest and lineage in, 79–82; intended as a literary artifact, 222, 227; sacrality of and scientific enquiry in Vico, 221–22, 237
Shakespeare, William, 77–79, 87, 117–18, 123, 128–32
Singleton, Charles S., 93
Shlonsky, Tuvia, 75
Socrates: consequences of the genopolitics of on the bloodline, 228; inquiry by into the optimal procedures of begetting, 242–44, 251–56; on the anti-Homeric un-

derstanding of civil war by, 229–30, 260–64. *See also* Plato
Sophocles, 77, 155, 173, 181, 194–95, 221, 228
Speiser, E. A., 147–51, 154
stásis: the of body's mortality versus the immortality of procreation according to Plato, 253–57; civil war as in Plato, opposed to *pólemos* (external war), 224, 229–30, 241–44, 247–52, 260–63; the of erotic fortification in the Song of Songs, 265. *See also* civil war, fratricide
Stoker, Bram, 53–55, 58
structuralism: Lacanian psychoanalysis and, 199–201
Swedenborg, Emanuel, 117–19

Tabernacle: structure of the and structure of the Hebrew family, 145–46, 152; symbology of the in Rachel's theft of the idols, 157–58
taboo: totemic meal and moral, 28, 184–86; —, Freud's view of, 160, 183, 195; —, in Derrida and Kant, 183–85, 186–87, 191–96. *See also* totem, totemic meal
Telemachus, 25, 32; expresses uncertainty with regard to his paternal origin, 19, 124, 219–20; Homer's dramatization of Telemachus's genealogical legitimacy, 88, 123–24; Stephen Dedalus and, 25, 77–79, 82–84, 88, 124, 126
teologia mistica: iura imaginaria, divine auspices, and in ancient Roman law, according to Vico, 84–5, 125–26, 175–78, 232
teraphim: family succession, family secession, and Rachel's theft of the in Genesis (ch. 31), 141–47, 158; the pact linking the Hebrew patriarch to his, 147–48; —, and the case of Laban, 151–53; Rachel's theft of Laban's, intended as a symbolic patricide, 27, 158; symbology of the Tabernacle in Rachel's theft of the, 157–58. *See also* Laban, Rachel
Thales, 44, 47
theology, 9–10; Blake's, 65, 73; seen as intrinsic to ancient Roman law, 84,